Mock Classicism

Mock Classicism

Latin American Film Comedy, 1930–1960

Nilo Couret

UNIVERSITY OF CALIFORNIA PRESS

University of California Press, one of the most
distinguished university presses in the United States,
enriches lives around the world by advancing scholarship
in the humanities, social sciences, and natural sciences. Its
activities are supported by the UC Press Foundation and
by philanthropic contributions from individuals and
institutions. For more information, visit www.ucpress.edu.

University of California Press
Oakland, California

© 2018 by Nilo Couret

Library of Congress Cataloging-in-Publication Data

Names: Couret, Nilo, 1984– author.
Title: Mock classicism : Latin American film comedy,
    1930–1960 / Nilo Couret.
Description: Oakland, California : University of
    California Press, [2018] | Includes bibliographical
    references and index. |
Identifiers: LCCN 2017048380 (print) | LCCN 2017050356
    (ebook) | ISBN 9780520969162 (ebook) |
    ISBN 9780520296848 (cloth : alk. paper) |
    ISBN 9780520296855 (pbk. : alk. paper)
Subjects: LCSH: Comedy films—Latin America—History
    and criticism—20th century. | Motion pictures—Latin
    America—History—20th century. | Motion picture
    actors and actresses—Latin America—20th century. |
    Motion pictures—Production and direction—Latin
    America—20th century.
Classification: LCC PN1995.9.C55 (ebook) |
    LCC PN1995.9.C55 C687 2018 (print) |
    DDC 791.43/617—dc23
LC record available at https://lccn.loc.gov/2017048380

Manufactured in the United States of America

27 26 25 24 23 22 21 20 19 18
10 9 8 7 6 5 4 3 2 1

*To my father, who taught me my first joke,
and to my mother, who asked why it was funny*

Contents

List of Illustrations ix
Acknowledgments xi

    Introduction 1
1. *Cantinflismo* and *Relajo*'s Peripheral Vision 22
2. The Call of the Screen: Niní Marshall and the Radiophonic Stardom of Argentine Cinema 68
3. Timing Is Everything: Sandrini's Stutter and the Representability of Time 111
4. Fictions of the Real: The Currency of the Brazilian *Chanchada* 153
5. Comedy Circulates Circuitously: Toward an Odographic Film History of Latin America 192

Notes 235
Selected Bibliography 263
Index 273

Illustrations

1. "The greatest actor in Mexico?" Mario "Cantinflas" Moreno on *What's My Line?* / 2
2. Cantinflas (Mario Moreno) seduces Paz (Dolores Camarillo) for more chicken in *Ahí está el detalle* (1941) / 30
3. Cantinflas (Mario Moreno) is not Manolete (Mario Moreno) in *Ni sangre ni arena* (1941) / 47
4. Cantinflas (Mario Moreno) watches himself on screen in *¡A volar joven!* (1947) / 53
5. Niní Marshall's contract dispute makes headlines in *La nación* / 79
6. Niní Reboredo (Niní Marshall) eavesdrops as a schoolgirl in *Hay que educar a Niní* (1940) / 86
7. Niní Marshall orchestrates high jinks with her all-female band, Lysistrata, in *Orquesta de señoritas* (1941) / 95
8. Casimiro (Luis Sandrini) pines for Sol (Alicia Vignoli) in *La casa de Quirós* (1937) / 118
9. Eusebio (Luis Sandrini) composes his tango at the hardware store in *Los tres berretines* (1933) / 125
10. Berretín (Luis Sandrini) needs help to defend the young ladies in *Riachuelo* (1934) / 146
11. *Hollywood Party* (1934) as Hollywood "chanchada" in *O cruzeiro* / 157

12. The making of *O jovem tataravô* (1936) / *162*
13. Eliana and Grande Otelo perform "No tabuleiro da baiana" in *Carnaval Atlântida* (1952) / *170*
14. Grande Otelo mugs for the cameras of photomagazine *O cruzeiro* in 1957 / *177*
15. Oscarito as Helen of Troy mocks classicism in *Carnaval Atlântida* (1952) / *187*
16. Monsieur Gasse (Charles Boyer) sells Passepartout (Mario Moreno) an itinerary in *Around the World in 80 Days* (1956) / *194*
17. *Ni sangre ni arena* (1941) premieres in Brazil as *Nem sangue nem areia* in 1947, as advertised in *A folha de São Paulo* / *203*
18. Cinesul advertises its Argentina Sono Film pictures in *A scena muda* / *208*
19. "Incomprehensible hostilities toward Argentine cinema": The failure of *Mujeres que trabajan* in Rio de Janeiro in the pages of *A scena muda* / *209*
20. Catita (Niní Marshall) the globetrotter in *Divorcio en Montevideo* (1939) / *214*
21. Luis Sandrini and Niní Marshall commemorative stamps issued in 2002 / *218*
22. Luis Sandrini becomes a contract player for Filmex in postwar Mexico, as seen in the pages of *Cinema Reporter* / *223*

Acknowledgments

This book began as a PhD dissertation completed in the Department of Cinema and Comparative Literature at the University of Iowa. I never wrote the acknowledgments to that dissertation. These acknowledgments therefore are also a confession, an expression of my deepest gratitude and a plea for absolution.

There would be no book without the guidance and support of my dissertation chair, Kathleen Newman. Whether consulting an eighth draft of a chapter or scribbling a diagram of the stakes of the book, her generosity, advice, and feedback made this monograph possible. I am also very grateful to each member of my dissertation committee: Rick Altman, for teaching me how to listen; Steve Choe, for encouraging my speculation; Paula Amad, for grounding my speculative flights with an archival sensibility; Corey Creekmur, for first pointing out my monolithic treatment of classicism; and Brian Gollnick, for telling me to stop translating Latin America. I had the great fortune of learning from many great mentors during my time at the University of Iowa: Steve Ungar, Garrett Stewart, John Durham Peters, Rosemarie Scullion, Michèle Lagny, Michele Pierson, Aimee Carrillo Rowe, and Mark Andrejevic. I wish to thank the Department of Cinema and Comparative Literature for giving me the opportunity as a graduate student to teach a Proseminar in Cinema and Culture on the topic that would eventually become this book. The selection and location of films, the collaboration with speakers and translators, and the comments from students were instrumental to laying out the stakes of this book.

In addition, my time at the University of Iowa was shaped by my peers and colleagues. Iowa City was a vibrant intellectual community because of the likes of Alison Wielgus, David Oscar Harvey, Andrew Ritchey, Richard Wiebe, Ryan Watson, Dana Gravesen, Leslie Delassus, Kyle Stine, Michael Slowik, Michael Hetra, Allison McGuffie, Jennifer Fleeger, Kevin McDonald, Annie Sullivan, Kathy Morrow, Jonathan Crylen, Hannah Frank, Ofer Eliaz, and Andrea Rosenberg. I also wish to acknowledge the support of David DeGeest, who patiently humored my many personal theories, introduced me to a circle of nonacademic friends, and taught me the value of a work-life balance. A special thanks to Sushmita Banerji for her almost-daily support during my final year in Iowa, recommending books that broadened my understanding of the studio period, being a willing spectator to an early job talk, and making sure I claimed my protagonism. I am especially grateful to Erica Stein, whose friendship has meant more than I can put into words. Her commitment to teaching and scholarly inquiry quickly became a model for this rookie graduate student. From helping me through a writing impasse during a writing date at the coffee shop on Linn Street to belting show tunes on a road trip to an academic conference or attending my proseminar despite having finished her coursework, her friendship has sustained me during the past decade.

My time in the Department of Romance Languages and Literatures at the University of Michigan transformed the dissertation into the current book. From the very first interview question forcing me to reckon with the "dated" aspects of my research, my colleagues in Ann Arbor have challenged me to become a better Latin Americanist. Moreover, the interdisciplinary exchanges that have characterized my time at Michigan have made this a book that seeks to complicate the methodological givens of film studies, especially the longstanding relation of cinema to modernity. To that end, I wish to thank Juli Highfill, David Caron, Kate Jenckes, Giorgio Bertellini, Ana Sabau Fernandez, Gavin Arnall, Daniel Nemser, Cristina Moreiras Menor, Garreth Williams, Alejandro Herrero-Olaizola, Enrique García Santo-Tomás, Fernando Arenas, Victoria Langland, Ana María León, Javier Sanjinés, Larry La Fountain-Stokes, Gustavo Verdesio, Jaime Rodríguez Matos, and Mayte Green-Mercado for their encouragement and suggestions. I wish to thank the students who participated in my graduate seminar on spectatorship, especially Emily Thomas, Catalina Esguerra, and Silvina Yi.

I am also very grateful to my colleagues in the Department of Screen Arts and Cultures, including Yeidy Rivero, Caryl Flinn, Dan Herbert, Johannes Von Moltke, Colin Gunckel, and Markus Nornes. Thanks are also due to the staff of the Interlibrary Loan Department at the University of Michigan libraries, as well as Barbara Alvarez and Philip Hallman. I am also very lucky to have begun my tenure at the University of Michigan with excellent colleagues who enriched my life in Ann Arbor, especially Martha Sprigge, Damon Young, Tyler Whitney, and Jennifer Nelson. A special thanks to Aliyah Khan, my Caribbean sister. From reluctant selfies in Brazil and Caribbean nostalgia at a local *arepera* to writing through the night at a twenty-four-hour coffee shop, her adventurous spirit has made me a stronger (more Google-able) scholar, a bolder thinker, and a more confident person.

I am grateful to a wider community of scholars and friends who have supported this project at every stage, providing important rejoinders to the theoretical digressions, suggesting valuable archival resources and films to consult, and granting opportunities to share the work in progress in different forums. This book has developed over the course of many a conference session (and postsession libation) with Nicolas Poppe, Luisela Alvaray, Laura Isabel Serna, Marvin D'Lugo, Leslie Marsh, Rielle Navitski, Jeff Middents, Dona Kercher, Victoria Ruétalo, Sarah Ann Wells, Maricruz Castro Ricalde, Lila Caimari, Matthew Karush, Kathleen Vernon, Arturo Márquez-Gómez, Ignacio Sánchez Prado, Juana Suarez, Jerónimo Arellano, Guilherme Maia, Gilberto Blasini, EJ Basa, Julián Etienne, Olivia Cosentino, Scott Richmond, and Marc Francis. Laura Podalsky was the first person in the field to recognize the merits of the project while I was still in graduate school, twice including me on a conference panel of heavyweights and later inviting me to speak at the Ohio State University. Her willingness to consider scholarship outside her field, read against the grain, and be generous toward junior scholars has shaped my own approach to academia. I am particularly grateful to Ana M. López and Neepa Majumdar for agreeing to read the manuscript in progress during a workshop made possible with the support of the College of Literature, Science, and Arts at the University of Michigan. Additionally, I wish to thank Cynthia Tompkins, Paul Schroeder-Rodríguez, and Juan Poblete, for their thoughtful, detailed, and incisive comments to the completed manuscript under review.

The research and writing of this book were made possible by the Dean's Graduate Research Fellowship and the T. Anne Cleary International

Dissertation Research Fellowship at the University of Iowa and the Fulbright Postdoctoral Research Award in Humanities to Brazil. The latter was made possible by the Departamento de Cinema e Vídeo at the Universidade Federal Fluminense in Niterói, RJ. I wish to thank my colleagues at the UFF, providing excellent recommendations and sharing their own rigorous historical work. I especially want to thank João Luiz Vieira, Rafael de Luna Freire, Mari Baltar, Flávia Cesarino Costa, and Luciana Corrêa de Araújo. These research trips abroad would have been fruitless without the tireless work of archival staff and investigators. I am especially grateful to Celeste Castillo and Fabián Sanchez at the Museo del Cine Pablo C. Ducrós Hicken and Adrián Muoyo of the Escuela Nacional de Realización y Experimentación Cinematográfica in Buenos Aires, Daniel and Caio Brito at the Cinemateca Brasileira in São Paulo, Alice Gonzaga at Cinédia, and Fábio Vellozo and Hernani Heffner at the Cinemateca do Museo de Arte Moderna do Rio de Janeiro.

I am very fortunate to be working with the University of California Press and with Raina Polivka, as well as Zuha Kahn and Kim Robinson. Raina's enthusiasm and faith in the project has made this manuscript stronger than I could have imagined, and Zuha's patience and guidance through the many logistical and intellectual challenges have made it a reality.

Finally, my friends and family have made my intellectual pursuits possible. Abby Rubenstein and Todd Berzon, my oldest friends, made academia imaginable to a son of immigrants who had mostly aspired to be just another professional in the family. Whether waiting in line for "art," watching Brecht in a rainstorm, or traveling to an outer borough for unpronounceable food, your friendships have been transformative. The Selvatici family opened the doors to their home during my long research trip abroad. After six months on the road, that final month in Rio de Janeiro was reenergizing and productive because they made me feel a part of their family. I am particularly grateful to Vera Selvatici for her patience with my Portuguese and for her willingness to be a sounding board during many a lunch *por quilo*. Fernando and Colleen Martinez provided some needed familiarity and comfort during my first year in Ann Arbor. Marta Martinez has been a constant and unwavering fount of love during trying times. I would not be me without my siblings, Alberto Couret and Elvira Couret de Padrón. The recto to my verso, Elvira is a model in empathy, a consummate teacher whose selflessness has been an inspiration. Alberto has always been the gregarious one, and being his brother has meant learning patience, responsibility, and kindness. Sadly, I will be unable to give a personal copy to four relatives who passed away during the completion of the manuscript: my grandfather Nilo Couret, who inspires my baroque disposition and often contrarian positions; my grandmother Yeya Couret, whose anecdotes about watching *Ramona* as a weekly serial in Pinar del Rio sparked my own interest in spectatorship; my grandmother Berta Martinez, a bookworm who made certain I was never complacent; and my aunt Betty Martinez, who is responsible for my cinephilia, emboldening me to take risks and discover new passions but not to forget to cultivate what brings me joy. Finally, my parents are the most important people in my life. An attentive listener and a strategic mind, my father, Nilo Couret, gives the best advice. His resoluteness informs my own determination. Whether carefully preparing a *níspero* for my breakfast or helping me move to Iowa, his is an affection, a self-confidence, and a regard for others that I can only hope to emulate. My mother, Angela Martínez de Couret, is a force of nature. She has taught me to develop success from failures through her refusal to give in to doubt, fear, and inaction. Not only bequeathing me her sweet tooth, her Asturian nose, and her gifted tongue, she made every day a metacognitive exercise, a storytelling opportunity, and a teachable moment. Ultimately, I can find each person mentioned in these acknowledgments at different moments in the book but none more than her, *un alma gemela*.

Introduction

On September 18, 1960, the Mexican comedian Mario "Cantinflas" Moreno appeared on the American television game show *What's My Line?* as the mystery celebrity to promote his upcoming holiday film *Pepe* (George Sidney, 1960). The film would prove to be a critical and commercial failure for Columbia Pictures in the United States and marked a turning point in critical estimations and industrial support of the comedian in his native country.[1] During the show, a panel of celebrity judges asks Cantinflas a series of yes or no questions to discover his identity. After he signs his name on a chalkboard, the blindfolded judges begin with broad questions in an effort to situate the guest (e.g., "Are you well-known in motion pictures?" or "Have you ever appeared on the legitimate stage in New York?"). The comedian answers the questions honestly but must attempt to dissimulate his identity and obfuscate his recognizable traits in order to prolong the enigma. Because his accent is difficult to mask, Cantinflas answers yes and no in different languages (sí, nyet, oui.) Eventually, the panelists discern his accent and ask, "Are you an American?" After discovering that he was not born in the United States, a panelist asks one final question: "Are you a gentleman who is considered the greatest actor in Mexico?" Other than his monosyllabic answers, the comedian had said nothing else during this segment. He is identified, the blindfolds come off, and the mystery is solved.

This appearance by Cantinflas on American television opens onto many of this book's larger concerns. The segment speaks to the material

FIGURE 1. "The greatest actor in Mexico?" Mario "Cantinflas" Moreno on *What's My Line?*

exchanges and discursive relations between Hollywood and Latin America. These are relations of both dependency and exchange that have a long-standing history in the continent: from the importation of European and American film technologies at the turn of the twentieth century to the market dominance of Hollywood cinema through the present day. Further, the segment hinges on conceiving of the comedian as representative of Mexico, a logic that underscores how the discursive legibility of non-Anglo-European culture within the Anglo-European sphere privileges, if not necessitates, representative figures that metonymically stand in for their origin. Finally, the resolution of the mystery turns less on the gradual process of situating him within discursive categories than on his body: his accented voice provides the key to identifying the man. What he does and even who he is seem less important than where he is from. The accessibility of Cantinflas's body and the unintelligibility of his speech suggest that a discussion of a non-Anglo-European practice, particularly one as linguistically situated and contextually specific as comedy, must contend with the linguistic and cognitive as well as the embodied and affective registers of the cinema experience. In other words, this book not only discusses where the comedy is from but also what it says and what it does.

The growing availability and cultural presence of popular cinemas has affected world cinema scholarship in the past two decades. Popular cinemas complicate the production of a national cinema, often conceived as part of an art cinema tradition, in that they underscore the discursive divide between art/popular as well as national/Hollywood categories. If regional cinemas often get constructed along political, auteurist, or movement-based axes, then popular genre cinema has forced a reconsideration of how international film history is written. The inclusion of commercial cinemas in world cinema contexts for metropolitan Western audiences has resulted in a newfound dilemma for scholars of international film. As Walter Armbrust discusses in his attempts to program a retrospective screening series of Egyptian cinema, international film scholars are caught between "the desire to solve the problem of foreignness by overcoming difference" and "to communicate foreignness by revealing difference."[2] Because the goal is neither to make everything the same nor to keep everything radically incompatible, *Mock Classicism* explores and preserves the tension between these two tendencies in global media studies: more particularly, how do specific comedic practices circumscribed to local and regional spheres complicate a shared continental Latin American project or a global transnational cinema?

Rather than map Latin American cinema according to radical politics, film directors, or film movements as do conventional film histories, I trace the continued popularity and cultural significance of film comedies. Why do comedies always seem lost in translation? Why must key examples of national and regional cinemas always focus on serious and dramatic art cinema? This project analyzes how these enormously popular films negotiate local and global cultural influences, even though comedies are alleged not to travel well, and argues that these comedies function as peripheral responses to modernization. The construction of Latin American cinema as a continental project is predominantly mapped along Western frameworks that structure and inform the production and reception of these texts, privileging certain films by certain directors at certain historical moments. The films that tend to be privileged are exalted as representative of a particular nation or region and, particularly after the 1960s, as art cinema. In the context of film studies, comedies have been either relegated to the margins of regional film histories in the shadow of the New Latin American Cinema or articulated to the broader socializing and nationalistic function of earlier commercial traditions. *Mock Classicism* shifts the historical periodization of Latin American cinema in light of the increasing contemporary interest in early cinema and modernity in order to demonstrate how comedian comedies functioned as peripheral responses to modernization and prefigured the more explicitly political New Latin American Cinema of the 1960s.

This project, however, is not merely a history of film comedy; instead, it draws on diverse critical traditions to demonstrate how these comedies represent ambivalent and divergent responses to modernity that are produced, circulated, and understood in redrawn peripheral spaces. *Mock Classicism* addresses the impasse in film studies regarding how to speak about local cultural practice in nonessentialist terms and avoids producing world cinema either as defensive authentic cultural expression or as derivative of foreign (i.e., Hollywood) models. The humor is contingent on thinking within a particular historical context and "in the language," suggesting that these comedies represent a response to modernity that is noncirculatory. *Mock Classicism* capitalizes on both the verb and adjectival form of the word *mock*. The Latin American comedies in the study both poke fun at classical Hollywood and produce a mock-classical cinema that is particular to the Latin American context. To that end, each chapter presents one way that classical Hollywood was constructed within Anglo-European film studies and demonstrates how the ways cinema became classical in Hollywood did not occur identically in Latin America. This means that Latin American cinema from the period cannot be readily aligned with classical Hollywood but that its peculiar classicism, this difference from Hollywood, should not be read as a sign of resistance

In broad strokes, classical (Hollywood) cinema is a concept with film studies roots, derived from rigorous formalist analysis to designate a film style with historical determinants and a narrative modality determined by an industrial mode of production.[3] The empirical turn has taught us that classical Hollywood is more than mere narrative pattern or industrial style, figuring film less as text than as commodity. Such knowledge, Thomas Elsaesser reminds us, is insufficient for approaching the social and historical role of the cinema. If new film history encourages us to view classical cinema as a process of making film a better commodity, I want to ask what makes for a better commodity in Latin America. For Hollywood studios, making the film a better commodity meant standardizing the film as product, text, and experience in order to wrest control from exhibitors. Hollywood cinema became classical by making the screen less dependent on the theater, and developments such as continuity editing, the feature-length film, and the sonic vraisemblable can be partly explained by this impulse to remove contingencies at the site of exhibition. Simply put, Hollywood became classical by building a discrete diegesis and cultivating a fictional sensibility in its spectators. Does the same logic hold in the case of Latin American cinema? To answer this question requires understanding how conditions of exchange are determined by politics, articulating industrial histories and technological analyses to reception histories and theories of spectatorship and consumption, redefining the relation between film and other media, *and* returning to the film text, "but not to its material existence [but as] evidence of a cultural imaginary."[4] Each chapter braids empirical research, close reading, film theory, and Latin American studies to argue that Latin American cinema from the studio period became classical in "phenomenally distinct but structurally kin" ways from Hollywood.[5]

MODERNISM OUT OF PLACE

The use of the term *modernism* is fraught in the Latin American context because the term does not translate between English, Spanish, and Portuguese. In Spanish America, the *vanguardia* (avant-garde) designates the experimental artistic movements associated with the European modernism of Anglo-European visual studies; in fact, Spanish *modernismo* refers to aesthete poetry movements from the late nineteenth century against which the *vanguardia* rebelled. Meanwhile, the parallel contemporaneous movement to the *vanguardia* in Brazil is called *modernismo*. As Esther Gabara notes, the appearance, iterations, and circulations of these terms within and without the continent have made the terms "errant."[6] The rearticulation of *modernismo* to include the *vanguardias* has been due in large part to discursive constraints, comparative analyses as well as the widespread use of the *postmodernismo* in both Spanish and Portuguese. The period of modernist experimentation in Latin America has been consigned mostly to what Daryle Williams in the Brazilian context has termed the period of "culture wars" at the turn of the twentieth century through the mid-1930s, the period preceding the consolidation of political power and the officialization of the cultural sphere.[7] The turn from the culture wars to the period of officialism during the Second World War and the postwar period is characterized by statist plans for modernization and the articulation of modernism to nationalism, a turn Gabara characterizes as one from critical nationalism born in the regional expressions of artistic practice to cultural nationalism born from administrative intervention in the capital cities.[8] Miriam Hansen's rearticulation of modernism allows us to redraw the boundaries of cultural practice to include expressions of mass culture often aligned unproblematically with state cultural apparatuses. Hansen offers a rejoinder to this alignment precisely by interrogating and then provincializing classical Hollywood cinema, which she argues is the first "industrially produced, mass-based" universalized aesthetic form of modernity because it produced and globalized a new sensorium.[9] Hansen's modernism returns to mainstream cinema to distinguish the classical Hollywood norm from the nonclassical traces that endure, foregrounding how these films mediated modernity and were received in heterogeneous ways in local and translocal contexts.

In her inflection of modernism, Hansen rearticulates the term to encompass a broader range of practices that respond to modernization and reflect upon the experience of modernity, discovering in modes of mass and popular culture moments of "vernacular" modernism. Modernist reflexivity does not necessitate a distanced and cognitive aesthetic experience; it also consists of the production of a sensorium, a process in which these commercial films served an integral function "asymmetrically related to modernist practices in the traditional arts."[10] The success of classical Hollywood had less to do with narrative organization than with the ability of its films to provide to mass audiences with an affective-sensory dimension that allowed spectators to confront the ambivalence of modernity. For Hansen, departing from Siegfried Kracauer, slapstick comedy is a key example of the affective-aesthetic experience provided by generic cultural practice, commercially successful particularly during the silent period not because of critical reason "but the films' propulsion of their viewer's body into laughter."[11] For Kracauer, slapstick films highlighted the failures of Fordist mass culture and suggested the latent anarchic excess potentially produced by the same rationalizing industrial impulse, what Americanist literary scholar William Solomon refers to as slapstick modernism.[12]

Hansen's later work focuses on the term *vernacular* as an alternative to the overdetermined *popular,* insisting on the former as articulating questions of everyday life to questions of idiom and dialect as well as circulation and translatability. Vernacular becomes a theoretical metaphor that offers a dynamic model of cultural circulation. The vernacular is not merely on the side of a particular local or an ahistoric traditional but part of the interactions that produce local and global. Hansen emphasizes the circulatory aspect of the vernacular, highlighting "the fluctuating, open-ended, and relational character of vernacular practices in different cultural contexts."[13] Despite her acknowledgment that film objects can function differently in different film traditions and can have different affective charges in different reception contexts, Hansen stresses the way these common concerns gesture toward a modernist aesthetics of contingency—material everyday objects are mobilized to make our responses to modernity sensually graspable. Furthermore, despite the possible multivalence of filmic representation, their circulation can provide comparative sites between diverse contexts responding to local and global forms of modernity. Hansen privileges circulation and translation through star systems and generic homology (e.g., in the context of 1930s Shanghai cinema, she considers Ruan Ling-Yu and the progressive melodrama of the New Woman).

Hansen's approach has provided a useful framework for studies of non-Western cinemas, although uptake of her work has been mostly isolated to recent attempts at reassessing the early cinemas of Asia, particularly those in the Chinese (Zhang Zhen's *An Amorous History of the Silver Screen*), Japanese (Aaron Gerow's *Visions of Japanese Modernity*), and Indian (Neepa Majumdar's *Wanted Cultured Ladies Only!*) contexts. Through Hansen, these histories figure how local debates on cinema were shaped by the encounter with Hollywood as well as pre- and paracinematic performance contexts. More particularly, as Majumdar notes, vernacular modernism proves particularly helpful in shifting discussion of early cinema from a focus on national identity toward a flexible understanding of the experience of local film culture: "a project of radically restoring historical and local specificity to multiple 'vernacular' cinemas, relativizing and thus expanding the variable and sometimes anachronistic local meanings of the 'early' in 'early cinema.'"[14] If Majumdar finds the case of Indian stardom from the 1930s to the 1950s as a rejoinder to vernacular modernism in the differentiated articulation of stardom, modernity, nationhood, and gender, then I argue that the inability of comedy to travel well complicates the circulatory dynamics of the *vernacular* in vernacular modernism and problematizes its transnational and comparative frame.[15] The transition to sound and the emergence of Latin American film comedy make the genre a more ambivalent site. As Franco Moretti notes, comedy relies on "short circuits between signifier and signified [that] are weakened by translation."[16] The declining international box office returns of Hollywood comedies, Moretti argues, are due in part to the way humor arises out of tacit assumptions with particular cultural associations. Taking comedy seriously puts pressure on the vernacular in Hansen's project. Hansen's approach may provincialize Hollywood cinema and may historicize classical narrative and continuity editing, but when used in a transnational and comparative spirit, it threatens to occlude culturally specific film practices that prove less circulatory and less translatable.

Vernacular modernism allows us to think beyond frameworks defined by "high" cosmopolitan modernism (i.e., experimental film practices that emerged within avant-garde movements in the fine arts or modernist international art cinema) in opposition to a local authentic popular culture. *Mock Classicism* studies the commercial cinema from the 1930s to the 1950s without relying on an essentialist popular identity and beyond what Ana López dubs the "nationness" of the film texts—both categories often a retroactive historico-aesthetic telos.[17] Despite the usefulness of getting away from the nationness of early cinema in the periphery through the concept of vernacular modernism, these early cinema histories have also found that the reformulation of local cinematic practices as vernacular has come with a tendency to flatten distinctions between and within local cinematic discourses and their effects. Rielle Navitski makes a similar point in her analysis of the intermedial horizons of reception of the early cinemas of Brazil and Mexico when she faults vernacular modernism for reducing processes of cultural exchange and centering Hollywood.[18] I share these histories' concerns but disagree with their characterization of vernacular modernism, one that struggles to reconcile agreement with Hansen's more expansive understanding of modernism and the sensory experience of the cinema with disagreement about the role of classical Hollywood. These histories respond by either pluralizing vernacular modernism or dismissing the term because of the ostensible centrality of Hollywood. They forget that vernacular modernism meant to rethink the classicism of Hollywood cinema, or "provincialize Hollywood."[19] The use of vernacular modernism in other contexts has not quite worked in the same way, reducing vernacular modernism to difference from Hollywood rather than difference from or in classicism. Its use out of place has supposed an alignment of non-Hollywood commercial cinema with classical Hollywood in order to argue for nonclassical moments as modernist gestures. I want to suggest reassessing the alignment of non-Hollywood commercial cinema with classical Hollywood, particularly in terms of the cinema experience and the spectator. We need to provincialize *classicism* rather than identify difference-from-Hollywood as a criterion for cultural distinction or modernist expression. Rather than ask what exhibits the aesthetics of high modernism outside the West, I want to suggest that a vernacular modernist framework must first mock classicism, not only celebrating cosmopolitan film cultures but also tracing how film culture became classical elsewhere. In other words, what Hansen's vernacular modernism encourages is not simply the recovery of marginalized figures or cultural spaces but a reexamination of fundamental disciplinary questions such as the relation of film history and theory, the status of classical Hollywood as normative popular cinema and the models of film spectatorship it presupposes, the nature of historical documentation, and the heuristic limitations of the discursive categories often overused in regional film studies.

THE IDEA OF LATIN AMERICA IN FILM HISTORY

Rewriting Latin American film history means interrogating the problematic periodization that presumes discontinuity, that is, fundamental incompatibilities with both golden age film (1930s–1950s) and politically engaged cinemas of resistance (1960s onward). *Mock Classicism* attributes this ostensible discontinuity and the marginalization of comedy to the discursive construction of this continental project along Western frameworks: New Latin American Cinema becomes unproblematically aligned with European countercinemas, and golden age film with classical Hollywood cinema. This narrative supposes political modernism as a filmmaking standard that is both aspirational and a historical fulcrum. Earlier films are disparaged as symptoms of a culturally nationalist alignment of mass culture with state cultural apparatuses, redeemable only in progressive moments of heightened realism (see, for example, Matthew Karush's *Culture of Class* or Charles Ramírez Berg's *The Classical Mexican Cinema*[20]), and later films are celebrated for their anti-illusionistic devices and explicit political content. *Mock Classicism* underscores how both positions presume a spectator politicized only through explicit content (and an image that is transparent) and/or critical distance from the text. Moving away from this figuration of political modernism, I take up Latin Americanist debates on transculturation and posthegemony in order to argue for a politics of spectatorship that makes the experience of modernity sensuously graspable but avoids a reconciliation with all social forms of organization tied to modernization.

Articulating these theories to ongoing debates in film studies allows me to consider not only how to write comparatively but also how to write theoretically from a historical and geopolitical location. Posthegemony challenges film studies on several counts. First, it compels film studies to be more than "a mere expansion of the textual corpus within aesthetic-historicist postulates for the sake of the construction and strengthening of the national-popular state and against monopoly capital"—that is, more than simply adding films to the texts we can read in order to understand pregiven forms of social organization.[21] Equating a given social formation with a hermeneutic circle makes the latter a "circle of hegemony," and, too often, the project of Latin American film studies quickly reduces the question of a hermeneutic circle to pregiven forms of social power or social organization (e.g., the nation-state, the market, the local).[22] This type of locational thinking that alters the reach of the hermeneutic circle without questioning the (im)possibility of the hermeneutic or the very conditions of sense making comes under fire in posthegemony. In this way, processes such as transculturation and hybridity must be challenged because, Alberto Moreiras claims, they redraw the hermeneutic circle without questioning the conditions of meaning. Moreiras locates a telos in the *trans-*: "it ultimately implies the acceptance of modernization as ideological truth and world destiny."[23] Transculturation, for Moreiras, is an overdetermined process, always already incorporating a certain goal complicit with modernity. Transculturation reads the Latin American text, characterized by temporal heterogeneity and noncontemporaneity of material, as a symptom of an as yet unfinished modernity. For Moreiras, this "modernity" overdetermines and undermines claims of political resistance.

To that end, posthegemony compels us to revisit the modernity thesis, where modernity threatens to become the new paradigm over and above national identity.[24] Modernity threatens to become "a teleological tool or set of tools for the instrumental rationalization of the world."[25] Posthegemony, however, does not merely recover the specificity of the (Latin American) alternative modernity because that would rely on the "outdated concepts of identity and difference"—that is, cultural difference as constitutive of Latin America's identity.[26] Posthegemony does not want to think alternative modernity so much as to think modernity alternatively, to identify the impact of capitalism without reproducing historiographic categories that would preserve forms of social organization.[27] Film studies offers the possibility of razing aesthetic-historicist paradigms by complicating the equation of a given social formation with a hermeneutic circle. If we can explore the nature of the hermeneutic circle as epistemological limit rather than as closed circle yoked to territorialized forms of social power, then we might undo "the inside-outside polarity on which all aesthetic historicisms and all culturalist theories of modernity rest."[28] If the hermeneutic circle draws boundaries, reterritorializes, and telescopes culture and social power, then Moreiras suggests focusing on irruptive possibilities and deterritorializing flows. By thinking reception studies in light of posthegemony, *Mock Classicism* avoids casting media as either a cultural apparatus of hegemony (and pregiven social formations) or a counterhegemonic practice of resistance. Comedy provides an excellent topos for Latin Americanist study in this vein. Comedy not only designates a genre where a differentiated hermeneutic can yield varied social forms disarticulated from pregiven territorial formations, but it also compels us to reflect on the conditions of possibility of signification within the semiotic and social field. The untranslatability of comedy points to a hermeneutic circle that can never be foreclosed, where forces intrinsic and extrinsic to this circle are continually shaping the horizon of reception. By thinking about the ways comedies succeed *and* fail on multiple fronts—as eliciting audience laughter, as generic text, as commodity, as enduring comic remanence, and as representative of the nation-state—*Mock Classicism* finds in comedy the possibility of a less conciliatory and more disjunctive semiotic and social field. In fact, the challenging conditions for the academic study of Latin American film comedy—with few contemporaneous accounts of reception, little exhibition statistical data, and only limited publicity and paracinematic material—further complicates how this circle can be drawn. The deterritorializing pulse of film comedy *form* works in lockstep with the deterritorializing experience of film comedy *spectatorship* and the deterritorializing conditions of film comedy *study*. Using an approach that encompasses both textual analysis as well as a range of practices from the film experience such as stardom, trade and popular publications, and broadcast media, *Mock Classicism* explores how synchronous sound may have accentuated the nonsynchronicity of the global horizon of film culture.

In lieu of positioning Latin American specificity merely in its difference from Hollywood, this book uses classicism to assess the impact of capitalism on social formations. *Mock Classicism* identifies a critical potentiality in forms of cultural production conventionally figured monolithically, foregrounding how temporal play, spatial practice, and antisubjectivism necessarily complicate both the classical Hollywood cinema as well as the cultural nationalism of interwar and postwar Latin American literary and visual culture, respectively. In this vein, my argument about classical cinema shares much in spirit with Mariano Siskind's account of the globalization of the novel form. Siskind rereads turn-of-the-century Latin American literature through the lens of contemporary world literature debates. Instead of opposing regionalism to modernismo, Siskind argues that Latin American literature articulates the possibility of a cosmopolitan modernity, where cosmopolitanism does not refer to an elite literary practice but a world-making discourse, and modernity is "a global relation and set of aesthetic procedures that mediate a broadened transcultural network of uneven cultural exchanges."[29] This cosmopolitan discourse was an escape from nationalist cultural formations and opened a horizon for the realization of new forms of subjectivity. Siskind argues against simply aligning cosmopolitanism with abstract universality or European hegemony because this cosmopolitanism was a "radical universalism," founded on the contradiction between universality and the marginal conditions of enunciation.[30] Siskind reminds us that cosmopolitanism does not aspire to be or become center but rather to assert a lateral geocultural positionality.[31] I want to conceive a classicism that operates in a similar way, a product of neither the homogenizing tendencies of globalization nor the nativist insistence on difference. In other words, classicism need not be figured within a field of relations governed by a juridic-discursive model of power with a negative relation; to mock classicism is to assert that the margin *also* matters.[32]

Siskind recounts the globalization of the novel form, arriving in Latin America and offering "the opportunity to grasp an experience of modernity that was not available to the reading Creole class in its everyday life."[33] The novel was the first universalized aesthetic form of modernity, not because of a universal impulse to narrate as cognitivist narratology might suppose but because "the novel form was the historical outcome of the formation (through colonialism, trade, and promises of emancipation) of a world."[34] This recalls similar debates about classical Hollywood cinema as universal pattern or deep narrative structure. If Hollywood classical style is indebted to the nineteenth-century bourgeois novel, then perhaps classicism in film studies can be reread in light of world literary discourse. Eric Hayot compels us to think this debt not in terms of realism but in terms of a shared idea of the world manifest as a (diegetic) self-contained unity.[35] World literary discourse, then, would highlight that both narrative-cognitive and aesthetic-affective approaches to classical Hollywood found Hollywood's success on the production of a world as a global cultural totality at the material, aesthetic, and discursive levels. Put simply, more than mere narrative patterning or sensory training, classical Hollywood provided a way to apprehend, categorize, and represent the world as totality. The discrete diegesis of the classical Hollywood style produced an image of the world as a reconciled and available modern world, and studying the aesthetic formation of the diegesis—and the marginal forms of the diegesis—might render the process of globalization visible. Furthermore, Siskind reminds us that the idea of the world is different in a region occupying a marginal position. The world is figured differently in Latin America vis-à-vis the worlds produced in metropolitan locations, and studying how the world is rendered in Latin America allows us "to work through the tension between the desire to join the global order of modernism and the anxiety provoked by the experience of exclusion and the anticipation of the exclusion to come."[36] The diegetic totality cannot be a self-contained unity in a region figuring the world within a network of uneven cultural exchanges. I want to suggest that using classicism in Latin America should neither graft Hollywood industrial structures and aesthetic style onto the region nor delimit cultural production in existing institutions of national sovereignty. Instead, I propose thinking classicism as a discourse that mediates and renders the world, looking at the construction of the aesthetic world as diegetic totality and the circulation of the texts and objects in global circuits of economic exchange.

MAKING LATIN AMERICA GENERIC

An investment in the bodily effects of the film experience articulated to the heterogeneity of Latin American cultural production can be found in the tradition of genre studies and the more recent uptake of affect in Latin American film studies. In her recent book *The Politics of Affect and Emotion in Contemporary Latin American Cinema,* Laura Podalsky discusses the aesthetics of sensation in contemporary Latin American cinema and advocates a similar move away from approaches that symptomatically diagnose film narrative in an allegorical mode or semantically decode the image, turning away from certain semiotic and psychoanalytic approaches and toward an approach that examines the affective dimension of the cinema experience: "Instead of examining how films organize or fix the spectator's visual apprehension of the profilmic space or how they deploy moral distinctions to align us with particular characters rather than others, we need to acknowledge and account for the myriad touch-points through which films and situated audiences encounter each other."[37] Drawing on the affective turn identified by Michael Hardt, Podalsky locates the body as a potential site for "alternative" epistemologies. Articulating the work of Hardt to the work of Gilles Deleuze, Podalsky sees socially inscribed and codified emotions and the deterritorializing flows and punctuating intensities of affect working together to produce alternative subjectivities and alternative ways of knowing.[38] Following Laura Marks,[39] she historically situates the cognitive potential of affect in the late twentieth century at a moment of epistemological crisis wherein the visual record is rendered unreliable if not insufficient. While I agree with Podalsky on the importance of considering affect in the field of Latin American cinema, I diverge from her project on a number of points. First, my study is situated in a different historical period. The epistemological crisis she identifies with the declining currency of the photographic record is not exclusive to the contemporary moment. I trace this epistemological crisis and the concomitant ontological restlessness to the early and transition cinema of the region as well as the theoretical discourses that coincided and at times preceded these film practices both in Latin America and abroad. Second, I oppose her characterization of Deleuze's film theory as one that finds in the film experience the potential for an alternative epistemology. Deleuze does not treat cinema as an art representing an external reality but as an ontological practice that creates different ways of organizing movement and time.[40] What cinema affords is not alternative ways of knowing but alternative ways of becoming and acting in the world. Ultimately, I move away from cognition and critical reason (as critical distance) that affirms what Alberto Moreiras calls an "identitarian space-in-resistance."[41] As such, this book models how to think critical reason beyond the reification of alternative forms or the identification of counterhegemonic resistance by exploring the slippages and disjunctures between the history of capital and the history of social power. If film and media technologies suggest the further interlocking of capital and power in lockstep, then comedies' parodic textuality, intermedial production, variable circulation in space, and specific reception in and across time offer possible sites of disjunction within an apparatus considered paradigmatically to articulate the nation-state.

Most studies of comedy in film studies have focused on the slapstick comedies of the silent era and classical Hollywood comedy types, particularly the musical comedy, screwball comedy, and comedian comedy. These early semiotic studies of comedy showcase how comedic narrative operations and performance styles disrupt the structure of the classical illusionistic fiction film. In his article on Ealing studio comedies, John Ellis identifies two major types of comedy: the screwball or social comedy, which uses natural language and deals with social disruption and its restoration, and the crazy comedy, which displays an awareness of language and convention and works through deconstruction and recombination.[42] This typology is founded on the adherence of the comedic film to the principles of classical dramatic film.[43] Rather than a classical definition of comedy founded on the restoration of order and the avowal of hierarchies, these studies designate comedy in the excesses that temporarily suspend the narrative and locate generic pleasure in the movement between disruption and reordering. The linguistic play and generic deconstruction of the crazy comedy finds its paradigmatic example in what Steve Seidman has termed the "comedian comedy." These films are organized around a particular type of star, a comedian with an extradiegetic and often paracinematic presence. The comedian usually occupies a privileged status relative to the other characters, less fictionally integrated and therefore disruptive of the diegesis. The eventual fictional incorporation of the comedian often characterizes the narrative operations of these films: the disorder externalized in the social comedy becomes internalized in the comedian's body and figured in the comedian's problematic location within the diegesis.[44]

These semiotic analyses provide valuable insight, particularly in their demand that we interrogate the "tautology of genre recognition"—"it's a comedy because it makes me laugh!"—and acknowledge how classical Hollywood narrative presupposes dramatic structures.[45] However, these early studies often fail to examine how comedy functions as a body genre that registers its effects on the bodies of spectators. In order to move away from a semantic decoding of the representational field and the models of identification articulated to this approach, I will refer to Henri Bergson's essay on laughter and *la mécanisation de la vie*.[46] Although they are usually understood in terms of the incommensurability of the mechanic and the natural, I articulate these categories to his discussion of time and duration as well as perception and memory in *Matter and Memory* and *Creative Evolution*.[47] The mechanic designates habitual behavior and a relationship to an absent past; the natural refers to the perceived present that interrupts this force of habit. His understanding of time and duration informs his contradefinitional approach: Bergson avoids making his a nominative endeavor, preferring to imagine the comic as dynamic and infinitely variable, processual, and relational. What happens to thought when its object is not treated as an abstract concept to be grasped but as a living thing affected by and constituted through our engagement? To delimit its mechanics would be to treat it as a thing incapable of becoming. Laughter relies on the recognition of habit and habit out of place, being and becoming, articulating a new relation to the world that forces an awareness of the possibilities existing in the world. The comic spirit is a way of being-in-the-world that privileges "practical, intimate acquaintance" as opposed to instrumentalizing abstraction, a relation to the world that affords fleeting moments of lucidity—throwing light on the workings of the inhabited world. Furthermore, Bergson claims that laughter requires a disinterested spectator, a spectator beside himself, not absorbed but not removed.[48] Laughter produces a sensory incoherence or stepping aside that I argue positions the spectator differently. Rather than locating the spectator as either proximate to or distant from the image, comedy's bodily effects are, as Frank Krutnik observes, a function of "the play between engagement and distantiation."[49] He claims that the pleasure from the comedian comedy derives from the movement between diegetic absorption and filmic recognition.[50] Much like Miriam Hansen's later discussion of female spectatorship and the star text of Rudolph Valentino, the presence of the comedian dissociates the narrative (identification with a character) and the scopic (the recognition of a particular object), forcing any study of the comedian comedy to consider how identification and subjectivity are organized differently.[51] In the spirit of Linda Williams's revision of melodrama, this project offers less a semantic decoding than an exploration of this metaleptic playfulness and its effects on the spatial and temporal relations between screen, theater, and narrative space.[52] Further, Williams characterizes melodrama less as a discrete genre than a mode, a notion that Agustín Zarzosa supports because the mode is less a category within a particular medium than "a set of affinities unencumbered by medium."[53] Latin American film studies has drawn on this language in its own analyses of melodrama in the region. From Silvia Oroz's landmark comparative study to Elena Lahr-Vivaz's recent monograph on Mexican melodrama, melodrama has long been considered a "metagenre" that hybridizes with other generic categories.[54] Unfortunately, melodrama in Latin American film studies often indexes the nation. For instance, despite her continental scope and comparative approach, Oroz argues that melodrama fashions a particular rhetoric based on narratives that are allegorical of the nation and images that depict the nation.[55] I return to the language of mode because it refers less to a taxonomic project than a formal project, "a strategy to solve practically problems of experience."[56] Following Thomas Elsaesser on melodrama, comedy is a mode of social expression and a mode of aesthetic expression;[57] however, if the melodrama attempts to make the moral good legible in an increasingly secular world, I argue that comedy attempts to make the world significant under a regime of economic symbolization.[58] In his canonic discussion of melodrama, Peter Brooks speculates that different kinds of drama have corresponding sense deprivations: blindness for tragedy, muteness for melodrama, and deafness for comedy.[59] The melodramatic narrative is a text of muteness, driven by the desire for expression; comedy, on the other hand, is driven by a desire to exchange. If Williams argues that the melodrama is the predominant mode of popular American cinema,[60] *Mock Classicism* argues that comedy is the predominant mode of Latin American cinema.

UNDERWRITING THE NATION

Though this project attempts to think within and beyond the geographic frameworks of conventional regional film histories, it is delimited by the archival and material limitations of study in the region. Ana López has pointed out the challenges of scholarship on early and transition cinema in Latin America, noting that the more prolific output and more sustained infrastructure of Argentina, Brazil, and Mexico have allowed for a larger scholarly field, adding that film texts and paratexts produce a necessary matrix through which to conceive the cinema experience in these contexts. López laments, however, that these material constraints have bounded the material by "nationness" with few attempts at comparative studies across national contexts.[61] The arrival of sound, in particular, meant a seismic shift in the mediascape, resulting in the American penetration of sound recording and projection technology as well as classical Hollywood film distribution and exhibition alongside a limited space for national producers oftentimes buttressed by interventionist statist policies: "Mexico, Argentina, and Brazil . . . invented, adapted, and experimented, producing a different yet resonant version of early cinema."[62]

The successes and failures of comedy are never punctual textual instants but ongoing processes of reading and rereading within synchronic pregnant moments and along diachronic experiences of remanence. *Mock Classicism* avoids using genre in the taxonomic tradition or the later empirical turn in film studies. The latter tends to reproduce industrial categories, and the former supposes a fixed identity (at worst) or an ontogenetic approach (at best). Instead, I draw on the genre-based paradigms of comparative literature, figured in opposition to older nation-based models. As Wai Chee Dimock argues, genre allows us to speculate what political community or hermeneutic circle comes into being when "measured in duration rather than extension."[63] This kind of map would force us to write a different kind of film history, one that does not appeal to the clock and calendar of national chronology as its time frame *and* also forces us to reckon with film as time-based medium. "The importance of genres comes not from their fixed identity but from the impossibility of such a thing," and comedy is particularly suited to this approach because of the ways its narratives foil designation and determination.[64] To that end, *Mock Classicism* avoids chronology, examining the formal and narrative operations of these transition-cinema comedies and their delimited and particularized circulation within and between diverse national contexts in order to telescope local, regional, national, and continental geographic frameworks.

In lieu of studying figures such as Tin Tan or Pepe Arias, championed for the ways they oppose or subvert the nation either in liberal frameworks that want a more representative national imaginary or in (neoliberal) frameworks that dismiss the national as anachronistic category, this book follows comedic figures and tropes conventionally aligned with the nation. I use these national comedic icons in a deconstructive spirit, following Homi Bhabha, who doubles down on the nation because of its interrupted address. The nation tells itself but cannot help that somewhere else it is told. "This narrative inversion or circulation makes untenable any supremacist or nationalist claims to cultural mastery [and] the position of narrative control."[65] The very finitude of the nation is productive for Bhabha because it emphasizes the failures, if not impossibility, of history: it "demands a time of narrative disavowed in the discourse of historicism."[66] In a historical period overdetermined by cultural nationalism, Bhabha's challenge bears on how we think film histories underwritten by a prefigurative self-generating nation.

First, Mexican comedies of the 1940s and 1950s are often discussed as paradigmatically conservative: the restoration of order during the film's resolution dovetails with the socializing function of a cinema implicated in a resurgent nationalistic project after the ambiguous legacy of the Mexican Revolution. Chapter 1, "*Cantinflismo* and *Relajo*'s Peripheral Vision," revisits the popular comedies of Mario "Cantinflas" Moreno from the golden age of Mexican cinema and argues that these films are not simply escapist and ideologically suspect but represent peripheral spaces of subversive difference that in their cultural and historical specificity cannot be easily co-opted by a cultural-imperialist center. Cantinflas's humor is characterized by his linguistic contortionism, or *cantinflismo*, in which he says plenty without saying anything, a verbal nonsense that sidesteps narrative registers and affords a bodily engagement through laughter that relies on particular cultural codes and learned structures of feeling. I provincialize classical Hollywood cinema by arguing for a *peripheral* vision modeled on the comedic practice of the *relajo*, which plays with the classical spatial arrangement of screen and theater space. Starting with Cantinflas's first successful film, *Ahí está el detalle* (Juan Bustillo Oro, 1941), my analysis examines the comedian's quick verbal play in addition to formal devices, editing techniques, and doubled narrative structures that "sidestep" on multiple levels.

In the Argentine context, the golden age period of the late 1930s and 1940s is often discussed in relation to the forces contributing to the rise of Peronism in the 1940s. Cinema and mass culture are implicated in the intertwined emergence of an integrative nationalist rhetoric and polarizing class stratification that was conducive to the rise of Juan Perón. Film comedies are again described as reactionary, providing through their farcical narratives of upward mobility an imagined (if temporary) solution to the ambivalent tendencies underpinning populist rhetoric. The second chapter, "The Call of the Screen: Niní Marshall and the Radiophonic Stardom of Argentine Cinema," broadens our understanding of the mediascape during the golden age period by examining the film and radio stardom of Marina Esther Traverso, "Niní Marshall," as a case of aural stardom that challenges image-based star studies and provides a framework to consider the particularities of popular Argentine cinema, where radio furnished the framework for the development of its industry and star system. Star-contract disputes from studio archives and evolving sound conventions in film texts are ventriloquial gambits that rearticulate the relationship between voice and body in a shifting organization of the senses.

Remaining in the Argentine context, the modernization of an increasingly urban and industrial Argentina and the effect of modernity on the experience of time provide a backdrop for my discussion of the films of Luis Sandrini in the third chapter, "Timing Is Everything: Sandrini's Stutter and the Representability of Time." More specifically, Sandrini's films rely on the comedian's stutter that literally disrupts the temporal continuum that film records. This chapter uses the stutter heuristically, figuring it within film texts, material film practice, spectatorial experience, and historiography. Radio sound aesthetics and sound technologies played an important role during the transition to sound, not only determining technological developments that affected film production but also providing the material base for the nation's nascent studios. Additionally, by focusing on Sandrini's physical slapstick, I discuss his films as staging a confrontation with standardized time both in terms of the reification of time in modernity and the standardization of film through the registration gate.

The Brazilian *chanchada,* or musical comedy, is a popular genre from the golden age of Brazilian cinema with a substantial Portuguese-language academic literature. These comedies date from the early sound period and persist through the 1940s at the height of the Atlântida studio system and into the 1970s and the emergence of the cheaply and quickly made *pornochanchada.* The literature on the chanchada understands these films as hybrid cultural objects, borrowing liberally from classical Hollywood musicals, Portuguese *fado,* Afro-Brazilian music, and Brazilian popular theater. Instead of retreading these ontogenetic arguments, the fourth chapter, "Fictions of the Real: The Currency of the Brazilian *Chanchada,*" argues the transition from *musicarnavalesco* to chanchada in light of the Estado Novo implementation of centralized monetary policy and the currency conversion to the cruzeiro. As money changes, there is less agreement on evaluative criteria, auguring a crisis of valuation that subtends debates around the value of the genre. Making film a better commodity in a *desmedida* (unmeasured or excessive) economy undergoing a crisis of value presents challenges at levels both material (currency restrictions shaped the development of the industry) and aesthetic (money as a form of economic symbolization coincides with the rise of fictionality). Classicism is mocked once more, now discussed in relation to the rise of fictionality rather than the codification of the classical realist text. Hollywood classical cinema attempted to separate the past-present-future regime of temporal chronology (i.e., screen time) from the pregnant moment of scenic display and the present tense of the spectator (i.e., theater time). The chanchada designates a certain intensification of fictionality where we actively feel the tension between the narrativized diegesis, the singularity of the comedic effect, and the present tense of the spectator.

The final chapter, "Comedy Circulates Circuitously: Toward an Odographic Film History of Latin America," examines the international production and distribution networks in Latin America in order to argue for the cinemas of the golden age period beyond national frameworks. More particularly, I consider the circulation both of and in Mexican, Argentine, and Brazilian comedies in order to engage with the concept of circulation in multiple ways, relating film as narrative, film as commodity, and film as spatial practice or architectonics. Circulation by definition entails traversing, (re)organizing, and (re)coordinating space and time, and this chapter takes advantage of the delimited and particularized circulation of comedy within and between diverse national contexts to telescope local, regional, national, and continental geographic frameworks. The identification of networks of film and media exchange prior to the 1960s challenges the diffusionist and center/periphery models that overdetermine understandings of cinema in the period. Circulation invites us to ask why do certain things travel? How quickly? How far? How long? This would mean writing a film history that considers how the circulation of cultural forms and the forms of circulation produce the region in what I call an *odographic* turn. The unevenness and variability of intracontinental distribution mock classicism, not in necessarily a resistant practice in the mold of European modernism but through a different form of territorialization dictated by the horizon of reception. This (de)territorialization occurs courtesy of techniques that control or reconfigure time and space—that is, techniques of circulation.

Taken together, these parallel examples of comedic practice demonstrate how Latin American film comedies produce a classical mode of spectatorship different from classicism figured in Hollywood. I engage the classical as a framework for the practice of power, but one that is never fully successful in being everywhere the same. Classicism is a category worth recovering (and mocking) in Latin American film studies because of the ways it indexes diverse forms of territorialization, from global Hollywood to cultural nationalism. The transition to sound and the emergence of film comedy provides an *endogenous* and *nonsynchronous* rejoinder to the cosmopolitanism of the former and the nationalism of the latter. Rather than simply relocating culture within ever more particular sites of reception or ever broader flows of transnationalism, mock classicism capitalizes on the limits of different forms of territorialization, figured through industrial practices, narrative spatiotemporal configuration, and aesthetic symbolization.

CHAPTER 1

Cantinflismo and *Relajo*'s Peripheral Vision

In 1967, Jacobo Zabludovsky interviewed the Mexican comedian Mario "Cantinflas" Moreno, then approaching the end of his career, in the television news program *Efemérides*. Pioneers in their fields—television journalism and film, respectively—the two men discuss the origins of the comedic persona *el pelado*. A foreign cousin to Chaplin's tramp, Cantinflas's beloved pelado—his haggard hat, his strip of gabardine draped over his shoulder, his awkwardly groomed mustache, and his pants below the waist—dominated Mexican box office receipts for several decades and became a leading export of this national cinema. Zabludovsky asks the older Cantinflas about the inspiration for the pelado. The interview yields a much-referenced reflection on the provenance of the archetypical character:

> Entonces, todo lo que yo he hecho ha sido observación y ha sido extraído del pueblo. Porque yo, Jacobo, en cualquier condición que esté, soy pueblo. Y lo seré toda mi vida porque, porque muchos años y hasta la fecha, convivo con el pueblo y sé lo que es el pueblo, porque yo, si usted sabe algo de mí, mi extracción, en el aspecto social, fue muy humilde. . . . Entonces sé las necesidades del pueblo, conozco el pueblo y soy pueblo.
>
> So, everything I have done has been through observation and has been drawn from the people. Because I, Jacobo, in whatever condition I may be in, am [of] the people. And I will be my entire life because, because for many years and to date, I live with the people and know what the people are, because I, if you know something about me, my upbringing, in the social aspect, was

very humble. . . . So I know the needs of the people, I understand the people and I am [of] the people.¹

Cantinflas credits his persona to observation, a creative fashioning of real life drawn from the everyday. The conflation of Cantinflas and the people (and arguably the Mexican film industry) means that writing about Cantinflas has meant also writing the history of the golden age of Mexican cinema and even the broader cultural history of statist postrevolutionary Mexico. Being attendant to this star text allows us to trace the construction and reconstructions of this so-called classical period of Mexican national cinema. The progressive liberalism of *cardenismo* is yoked to Cantinflas's restive early film appearances, and the nationalist designs of President Ávila Camacho and the centralization of political power and economic developmentalism of *alemanismo* are articulated both to Cantinflas's involvement in labor and syndicate disputes as well as his new production company and its distribution deal with Columbia Pictures. His becoming establishment augured the escalating authoritarianism of single party rule in the following decades.

The pelado has a specificity unlike that of Chaplin's tramp, less an everyman than an urban peasant from a particular neighborhood in the growing capital city.² The term *pelado,* originally invented in the 1920s, described a certain class of dispossessed urban lumpen: he "belongs to a most vile category of social fauna; he is a form of human rubbish from the great city. He is less than a proletarian in the economic hierarchy, and less than a primitive man in the intellectual one. . . . He is an explosive being with whom relationship is dangerous. . . . His explosions are verbal and reiterate his theme of self-affirmation in crude and suggestive language . . . so crudely realistic that it is not possible to transcribe many of his most characteristic phrases."³ How did a dangerous social outcast become beloved national icon? Although Cantinflas was the pelado par excellence, the earlier success of the popular comic strip *Las aventuras de Chupamirto* by Jesús Acosta led to pelado characters featured in comedic skits at many *carpa* shows—a form of popular theatrical entertainment that combined elements of vaudeville and circus, taking place in tents, or *carpas*.⁴ These forms of popular culture were responsible for the transvaluation of the pelado to the *peladito,* from a sign of urban poverty to a stock picturesque and picaresque type: "Thanks to a comedian, he is rebaptized with the diminutive, the *peladito,* the smiling suburban [*arrabal*] rogue."⁵ Cantinflas and his film success would decisively tame the explosive lumpen figure and make him an irreverent rogue and profitable commodity in the hands of an ascendant culture industry.

Understanding the making of the peladito in relation to the centralization of political power and the expansion of capitalism makes the above transformation a marker for shifting relations between state, people, and mass culture. Both the pelado and the peladito represent the tendency of capital to create surplus labor in the context of a growing capitalist regime in the 1930s.[6] For Gareth Williams, this transformation functions less as a defusion or co-optation of explicit political content than as a marker of "an emerging nexus between politics and mass culture industries."[7] The pelado is a social anomaly whereas the peladito designates a representative subject of and from the people (*pueblo*). The production of the peladito becomes a narrative about the production of cultural apparatuses. Cantinflas's senescent reflection calls attention to the formation of the "people" and how the people come to be intelligible. The comedian's central conceit is "Yo soy pueblo," which translates loosely both as he is *of* the people as well as he is the people. The statement functions both as synecdoche and metonymy: he is literally part *and* parcel of the classed (and loosely nationalized) people. Although this narrative of transvaluation helps us understand the specificity of the Cantinflas character, it reinforces Moreno's own notion of himself as (of) the people. Because Cantinflas was establishment, most read his films to locate his becoming establishment (often nostalgic for the moments of critical potential before this came to pass). We know the end point and so our reading plots the star text along a predetermined narrative. We risk ignoring how a people become represented and representable through cinema, how a viewing subject was fashioned, and how a metonym came to be.

In articulating state, people, *and* cinema, these Latin Americanists often leave the last term unexamined. And yet a study of the shifting conceptions of subjectification and publicness that pivot on a screen image should bear in mind how cinema renegotiates the horizon of public experience—this "people" (become mass) is first and foremost a *viewing public*. Parsing out how cinema shapes this viewing public means returning to the film text but not with a view to assessing the explicit political content of the comedian's quips. Moreno's interview already suggests some lines of inquiry. He insists that his character is drawn from direct observation, a claim to a type of realism that might surprise given the stylization of the archetype. Further, the long-winded response performs the type of baroque verbal spiels that would makes

Moreno's character so popular. All the devices used by the pelado to mock officious speech—the chain of subordinate clauses, the asides addressed to an interlocutor, the redundancies, and the dangling modifiers—are here deployed, perhaps an earnest response that functions as ironic rebuke of the status quo Moreno had become or perhaps a slippage of persona and performer. More likely both. Y ahí está el detalle (And there's the rub).

Starting with Cantinflas's first successful film, *Ahí está el detalle (You're Missing the Point)* (Juan Bustillo Oro, 1940), this chapter examines the comedian's quick verbal play in addition to formal devices, editing techniques, and doubled narrative structures that "sidestep" on multiple levels. A close analysis of this foundational film examines the operations of cantinflismo in multiple registers, from linguistic play to textual instability and from denotative equivocation to spatial practice. Rather than periodize Cantinflas in relation to production histories, sociocultural context, or the evolution of his pelado character, I consider Cantinflas's films in relation to their use of formal and narrative devices that capitalize on his play with referentiality, particularly the (ab)use of proper names that no longer denote, and that foreground the maximal specularity of a star famous for dodging (denotative) representation. Although this sidestepping wanes over time, I understand this erosion as a function of spectatorship becoming classical in a mode I contend is different than classicism figured in Hollywood. In the Hollywood context, the transition from early cinema to classical cinema was not simply a function of narrative devices becoming convention but rather the codification of the proper relations among viewer, projector, and screen.[8] Becoming classical meant changing the spatial arrangement of the cinema experience. Cantinflas's antics, considered at the level of narrative strategies, aesthetic or affective devices, and material practices, gesture toward a different model of spectatorship where the segregation of film and theater space and the normative pleasures implied are different. Cantinflas's films present a mock classicism particular to Latin America that harnessed these "other" pleasures, where the spectator derived pleasure from (mimetic) recognition and from the proximate (or at the very least related) spatial arrangement of theater space and screen space.

CANTINFLISMO *EN DETALLE*

The success of *Ahí está el detalle* marks a turning point for a Mexican cinema that tripled its production of comedies with the arrival of sound in the late 1930s. García Riera credits *Ahí está el detalle* as legitimating the market position of comedies and the growing star discourse around comedic actors that had previously been relegated to supporting parts.⁹ *Ahí está el detalle* presents an intricate comedy of errors where our unnamed protagonist becomes embroiled in a series of escalating misadventures and misunderstandings. By way of synopsis, Cantinflas courts the maid, Paz (Dolores Camarillo), from an upper-class couple's residence. The couple's relationship is tumultuous because the husband, Cayetano (Joaquín Pardavé), suspects his younger wife, Dolores "Lola" (Sofía Álvarez), is having an affair. Lola's former lover, Bobby "The Fox Terrier" Lechuga (Antonio Bravo), threatens to blackmail her with undated love letters meant to incense her jealous husband. At the same time, Cayetano wants to preserve his marriage because of an inheritance his wife is expecting but cannot collect because of the disappearance of her biological brother, Leonardo del Paso. In a complicated play of upstairs-downstairs high jinks, Cantinflas is mistaken for Leonardo. Cantinflas takes advantage of this case of misrecognition until the real Leonardo's partner, Clotilde, arrives with a gaggle of illegitimate children. Cantinflas's subsequent attempts to extricate himself are frustrated when the real Leonardo commits murder, and Cantinflas must use his natural gift—"la facilidad de palabra" (a way with words), as he explains in the film—to keep himself out of jail. The film ends with the real Leonardo arriving at the courtroom in the nick of time to confess his crime and recognize his partner and children.

The film provides one of the earliest examples of Cantinflas as a leading man who cannot be followed. Cantinflas's periphrastic comedic riffs are a function of the circumscribed intelligibility afforded by contingent linguistic markers and the sociocultural specificity of his language. The film's title offers an idiomatic expression that suggests how the film's literal and figurative registers are necessarily inflected by strategic unintelligibility and audience location: *Ahí está el detalle* literally translates to "There is the detail," but its variable meanings are a function of the contingent shifter (i.e., *ahí* [there]) and the idiomatic use of *detalle*. Throughout the film, *detalle* refers to a significant detail, an overarching point, and a casual romantic partner. The comedian's linguistic contortionism—cantinflismo—relies on the circumlocution afforded by a steady chain of shifters indicating a space that never materializes, a circumlocution that produces always-contingent positions to an ostensibly stable referential relationship. Regarded in this light, the English-language title packs an additional sardonic element: *You're Missing the*

Point gestures toward some significance that is always already missing. Drawing on the film's spoken dialogue, narrative structure, and form and style, I demonstrate how the comedian's appeal relies on the evasion of intelligibility and argue that this film comedy more broadly complicates the denotative nature of classical film language and frustrates narrative-cognitive approaches to spectatorship.

Cantinflas's most amusing verbal encounters in the film often position his pelado character opposite the Romantic and polished language of Paradavé's Cayetano. Cantinflas's verbal dexterity undermines Paradavé's attempts to appear grandiloquent, revealing the latter's criollo hypocrisy. In their first encounter on screen, Cayetano searches for his wife's presumed lover and finds Cantinflas raiding his pantry of luxury goods. Cayetano confronts Cantinflas at gunpoint, interrogating the comic and threatening his life. Despite his innocence, Cantinflas eludes questioning not by physically avoiding detection or by denying his complicity; instead, he relies on the vacuity of polite convention to disarm the cuckold:

Cayetano: ¡Sálgase de ahí!

Cantinflas: No, aquí estoy bien muchas gracias. ¿Por qué no entra usted? Aquí hay galleticas, cognatico y puritos.

Cayetano: Gracias, gracias. Acabo de cenar.

Cantinflas: Pues si yo también acababa, pero pues—

Cayetano: Sí, sí—¡sálgase usted de ahí le digo!

Cantinflas: Bueno, así de buen modo, sí salgo. Y me va usted perdonar que me retire pero ya se me hizo tarde. A ver en qué día vuelvo. Con permiso.

Cayetano: Sí, sí. Pase usted . . . ¡Alto allí!

Cantinflas: ¿A dónde?

Cayetano: ¡Allí!

Cantinflas ¿Allí?

Cayetano: ¡Aquí!

Cantinflas: ¿Por fin?

Cayetano: ¿Qué?

Cantinflas: ¿Allí o aquí?

Cayetano: Aquí y conteste pronto.

Cantinflas: No puedo.

Cayetano: ¿Por qué?

Cantinflas: Pues, todavía usted no me pregunta nada.

Cayetano: De veras. ¿Qué hace usted aquí?

Cantinflas: No, pues usted me dijo que me parara aquí.

Cayetano: ¡Le pregunto usted qué hace usted aquí en mi casa!

Cantinflas: Pues si es lo que yo digo. ¿Yo qué hago aquí en su casa? De manera que aclarado el punto con permiso me retiro.

Cayetano: ¡Párese allí!

Cantinflas: Otra vez. ¿Está usted jugando?

Cayetano: No se burle. No se burle y conteste antes de que le pegue un balazo.

Cantinflas: Será mejor antes.

Cayetano: ¿Qué hace usted aquí?

Cantinflas: ¿Y usted?

Cayetano: Eso a usted no le importa.

Cantinflas: Con usted no puede uno entenderse, señor. Si a mí no me importa, ¿por qué a usted le importa lo que a mí no me importa?

Cayetano: ¿Qué no se ha dado cuenta que yo soy el marido?

Cantinflas: ¿Cuál marido?

Cayetano: ¡Su marido!

Cantinflas: ¿Mi marido? ... No diga usted esas cosas que a lo mejor lo están oyendo y mi reputación ...

Cayetano: No disimules. Soy el marido de mi mujer.

Cantinflas: ¿También?

Cayetano: Sí.

Cantinflas: Bueno, y ¿eso qué? ¿A mí qué me importa? Yo nunca me meto en cosas privadas.

Cayetano: ¿Qué no? Yo le voy a decir a usted lo que usted está haciendo aquí en mi casa.

Cantinflas: Pues si me hace el favor y es tan amable.

Cayetano: Come out of there!

Cantinflas: No, thanks. I'm fine in here. Won't you come in? There's cookies, brandy and cigars.

Cayetano: Thanks. I just ate.

Cantinflas: I just did too, but you know—

Cayetano: Sure, I know.—Come out right now!

Cantinflas: Now that you put it so nicely. Sure, I'll come out. Now, if you'll excuse me, I really have to go. I'll come back soon. Excuse me.

Cayetano: Sure. Go ahead.—Stop right there!

Cantinflas: Where?
Cayetano: There!
Cantinflas: There?
Cayetano: Here!
Cantinflas: Make up your mind.
Cayetano: What?
Cantinflas Here or there?
Cayetano: Here, and answer me quickly.
Cantinflas: I can't.
Cayetano: Why not?
Cantinflas: You haven't asked me a question.
Cayetano: You're right. What are you doing here?
Cantinflas: You told me to stand here.
Cayetano: I mean what are you doing here in my house!
Cantinflas: I've been asking the same question. What am I doing here? So I guess I'll leave now.
Cayetano: Stop there!
Cantinflas: Not again. Are you joking?
Cayetano: Don't mock me. Answer me before I shoot!
Cantinflas: You better ask before [you shoot].
Cayetano: What are you doing here?
Cantinflas: What about you?
Cayetano: None of your business!
Cantinflas: I don't understand. Why is it my business if it isn't your business?
Cayetano: Because I am the husband.
Cantinflas: What husband?
Cayetano: The husband!
Cantinflas: My husband? Don't say that. People might hear you, and my reputation—
Cayetano: I am my wife's husband.
Cantinflas: Hers too?
Cayetano: Yes.
Cantinflas: So? Why should I care? I never meddle in private affairs.
Cayetano: You don't? I'll tell you what you're doing in my house.
Cantinflas: If you'd be so kind.

FIGURE 2. Cantinflas (Mario Moreno) seduces Paz (Dolores Camarillo) for more chicken in *Ahí está el detalle* (1941).

This exchange between the pelado and a straight man was a typical carpa skit for two, "a collision of social classes in the collision of languages."[10] The exchange here is characterized by the use of pronouns (*su marido*) missing antecedents and shifters (here/there) missing referents. The confusion of second- and third-person address—Cayetano is *su* (your/her) husband—results in an amusing misunderstanding. Cantinflas semiotically rewires Cayetano's florid language, misrecognizing referential relationships for strategic effect. Moreover, in occupying the position of the antecedent, Cantinflas not only derails the husband's questioning but also reveals that he considers himself to be a social equal.[11] Cantinflas's pelado is an *igualado,* or a person who (mis)behaves as a social equal. The humor in this sequence is not simply a matter of misunderstanding but of class permeability and the arbitrariness of social hierarchy.

Beyond this discussion of speech content and the classed origins of the genre, this humor derives from a structure of analogous signification that unmoors referentiality. For Carmelo Esterrich and Angel Santiago-

Reyes, this scene illustrates how Cantinflas disarms through an imitative process. This imitation, however, is not intelligible to the interlocutor and therefore makes the "man of the house lose hegemony over his discourse."[12] Much like a child's game of parroting back what is being said, this iterative game or a manufactured echo discloses something unintended in the original to a spectator who knowingly laughs at what the Cayetano character does not understand. Their analysis has two implications that merit further exploration: How to describe a process of mimicry that does not reflect or rather that reflects more than what is originally there? And how can speech be selectively incommunicable? In other words, Cantinflas's antics gesture toward a realism that functions otherwise—a mimetic or analogous representation different because it requires positing (if not producing) an interlocutor incapable of understanding. Through the use of shifters with imprecise referents in the above exchange, Cantinflas upends simple one-to-one signifying relationships. If the pronoun use above provides an example of misdirection reliant on culturally specific (classed) convention, the shifter use provides an example of misdirection that relies on the spatial and temporal organization afforded by the film form of early Cantinflas comedies. The exchange occurs in three spaces in three separate medium long shots. Early in the sequence when Cantinflas excuses himself to leave, he moves from one space to another space. Cayetano, still in the first space, demands Cantinflas stop "there," in a space off screen. When Cantinflas asks for clarification in the second shot, Cayetano joins Cantinflas in the second space while repeating his command; however, "there" is no longer off screen. Cayetano's second use of *there* refers to the "here." The film avoids cutting away to "there," which heightens the comedic effect but also allows referential relationships to remain in suspension. The spatial relationship between these three shots may be continuous, but the humor resides in equivocation: "there" could be here or there, on or off screen. Throughout this comedy of mistaken identity, the film withholds cutaways that would denote objects of narrative significance or clarify allusions. Cantinflas is seldom edited in shot-reverse-shot patterns, and his position to other objects, people, and spaces is seldom articulated by the patterns of continuity editing. The film, like the comedian, is free to toy with referential relationships for comedic effect. The humor comes from "over there," from the ability to establish unexpected referential relationships. The minimal editing coupled with the play of shifters results in a film form that communicates differently. The humor arises both from the on-screen exchange as well as the virtuality of the off screen, the possibility that the off-screen "there" will become actualized otherwise.

Throughout the film, unmoored referentiality is not merely a function of missing antecedents in verbal exchanges but also unclear indices. Both proper name and photographic image are types of indexical signs, and the rigamarole of this comedy of errors, at the level of both carpa-derived narrative tropes as well as film form, complicates how these signs function. A proper name conventionally functions as a "rhematic indexical legisign."[13] It refers only and exclusively—and through arbitrary legal convention—to the object to which it points. The narrative in this film, however, relies on doppelgänger misconstrued because the proper name no longer denotes. The context-dependent indexical relation of the proper name becomes untenable. Leonardo del Paso kills Bobby the Fox Terrier twice: Cantinflas as Leonardo kills Bobby, the fox terrier dog, and Leonardo kills Bobby the Fox Terrier, the extortionist. Remarkably, Cantinflas is never referred to by his own proper name. Throughout the film, Cantinflas is never himself; he is always construed as someone else. Nearly every character in the narrative would prefer Cantinflas be Leonardo: the husband needs Leonardo to claim the inheritance; Lola needs Leonardo to conceal the blackmail; and Clotilde needs Leonardo to recognize and support her children. Would that the proper name functioned correctly as an index, but the humor arises from its failure of designate. The narrative is driven by multiple attempts to ontologize the connection between the name and the designated person, but Cantinflas avoids being positioned.

Cantinflismo refers then not simply to the comedian's linguistic dexterity but more importantly to his textual instability. He is mistaken for someone else and refuses to designate himself. He slips in and out of positions that intra- and extratextual others have produced. Cantinflas is everyone but Cantinflas: he simulates others and dissimulates himself. His refusal to be wedded to his proper name allows Cantinflas to occupy multiple positions, and this unwillingness to become legible and referential sign is perhaps paradigmatically shown in his coerced marriage to Clotilde Regalado, the real Leonardo del Paso's partner. Cantinflas looks for a way out: a way out of the marriage, a way out of the frame, a way out of the guise. The sequence features Cantinflas anxious to escape—"Yo preferiría que fuera por allá" (I'd rather go that way)—but physically restrained by his bride—"No es por allí, es por acá" (It's not that way; it's this way). The bride clutches his arm and refuses to let him out of her grasp, and the camera frames his body and refuses to let him out of its sight. The ceremony begins with Cantinflas confined in a crowded medium long shot, surrounded by all the players in this farce: Clotilde, Cayetano, Dolores, Paz, and the gaggle of illegitimate children. A restrained Cantinflas takes to his trademark evasive verbal maneuvers. When asked explicitly by the judge whether he is del Paso, Cantinflas responds that he is "de Tepito" (from Tepito). The proper name becomes prepositional phrase, no longer indicating someone but somewhere. A string of similar jokes relying on homonyms and misunderstandings is of little use. Cantinflas then claims that he cannot marry because he cannot sign his name. His illiteracy is of little consequence, the judge assures, because Cantinflas can agree to the marriage by using his fingerprints:

> Si no sabe firmar, mejor. Muchos han burlado la ley contrayendo matrimonio con nombres opuestos pero ninguno firmando con sus huellas digitales. Este señor firmará con sus huellas.
>
> If he can't sign, even better. Many have mocked the law by marrying under false names but none by signing with their fingerprints. This man will sign with his fingerprints.

Cantinflas risks being yoked to his (im)proper name through the fingerprint. Using the Peircean account of signification, we have a change in sign-vehicle (from signature to fingerprint) and an escalation of the interpretant sign.[14] This shift from signature to fingerprint represents an escalation in singularity, in definitively locating Cantinflas within a signifying economy. Cantinflas understandably hesitates, but Clotilde and Cayetano grab Cantinflas's hands to record his fingerprints in the wedding registry. Cantinflas's fingers deftly avoid the page, and the comedian attempts to explain that he is not del Paso. The renunciation of the proper name goes unheeded, but before Cantinflas can be bound by his fingerprints, the police interrupt to apprehend Leonardo del Paso, suspected murderer. Cantinflas's fingerprints are never registered, and his unstable referential position remains intact.

A return to narrative order is always one stable referential relation away, and the promise of referential certainty drives the narrative to its conclusion. The film concludes with a prolonged courtroom sequence, yet another setting where language is performative. As in a wedding, what we say is what we do: we do not simply report facts; we testify and swear under oath.[15] Cantinflas is eventually acquitted after the ostensible restitution of referentiality. The film's conclusion delivers on this promise but only after bringing the semiosphere to the brink of collapse.

Cantinflas confesses to killing Bobby, the rabid dog, but the court thinks he is Leonardo confessing to the murder of Bobby, the extorter. We are in a signifying hall of mirrors where every proper name has multiple referents. By the end of the sequence, the participants mimic and reproduce Cantinflas's speech acts and effectively participate in *cantinfleo*. Without direct one-to-one analogy, testimony and legal discourse lose performative conviction, becoming nothing but legalese with arbitrary effects.

The sequence has rightfully received significant critical attention, but scholars remain divided about its subversive effect. On the one hand, the narrative presents Cantinflas triumphing over a baroque legal system. The social control maintained by the legal system operates through language that is as impenetrable as Cantinflas's speech.[16] Cantinflismo's *relajo*—a defensive tactic with a characteristic lack of seriousness—parodies and disarms the rhetorical stranglehold of officialism, a strategy that was particularly effective in the context of the reigning illiteracy of 1930s Mexico, with nearly 70 percent of the population unable to read.[17] On the other hand, the subversive effect is only momentary. Relief arrives soon enough, while the injustice of societal rules stays intact.[18] The latter position represents a common refrain directed against comedy: that it is politically ineffectual because of its often restorative conclusion. For critics, the resolution of the film ignores larger questions about the legitimacy of the trial and the wrongful accusation and near conviction of an innocent man. As Gareth Williams elaborates, "In the final scene of the film, everything has returned to where it was at the beginning. Chaos has been averted and social order has been restored."[19] Williams offers a structural complement to Daniel Chávez's symptomatic argument, arguing that the peladito, as "a zero point of all reason," makes capitalism and bourgeois ideology common sense by default; his necessary exclusion affirms the social order.[20] Both authors argue that Cantinflas's language becomes captive to the mechanisms of power through the all-or-nothing logic of melodrama. Ana López has demonstrated, however, the logic of the melodrama is seldom that Manichaean: "even when [melodramatic] narrative work suggests utter complicity with the work of the law, the emotional excesses set loose and the multiple desires detonated are not easily recuperated."[21] The narrative containment of comedic excesses—the capture of cantinflismo—must be similarly interrogated, as it risks reducing the question of political representation to one of narrative content and the explicit and direct critique of order. Why must the space opened through the misdirection of relajo be always already foreclosed? What this reveals is a misunderstanding of the kind of space relajo affords and its relation to the cinema experience. The audience is not a function of signification that is accessible to some but rather is shaped by the absence of meaning as an affective horizon of experience driven less by the desire for meaning than the pleasure in the inability to mean.

CANTINFLAS IS OURS

After his initial successes, Moreno continued working with the director Miguel M. Delgado and the screenwriter Jaime Salvador, who became his partners in crime for the duration of his film career. The trio capitalized on and eventually ossified the formula of the pelado confronting the powerful: Cantinflas, a man of the people, courts a young and humble girl while, behind his back, some villains mock his naïveté only to be stymied by his unexpected cleverness. This codification of the Cantinflas film has been discussed mostly in biographical and contextual terms.

As briefly sketched above, Cantinflas's rise and fall can be traced alongside the diverse histories of the so-called golden age of Mexican cinema. Cantinflas's generic codification and becoming establishment were yoked to the institutionalization of the Partido Revolucionario Institucional (PRI) with the presidencies of Manuel Ávila Camacho (1940–1946) and Miguel Alemán (1946–1952). Similarly, although the foundations for a legitimate film industry were laid in the 1930s, it was in the following decade that Mexican cinema blossomed. During Ávila Camacho's presidency, the film industry was put on commercial footing through state support to private producers, particularly with the creation of the Banco Cinematográfico in 1942. It began as a private institution with indirect federal support from the Banco de México and the Nacional Financiera and functioned as a credit institution that centralized the sporadic film activities of undercapitalized producers.[22] Eventually, the bank was nationalized in 1947, becoming the Banco Nacional Cinematográfico, with state and private initiatives collaborating to offer funding. The Second World War also saw waning competition in film production from Europe and the United States. Additionally, the United States supported an allied Mexican industry during the war years, offering financial and material assistance through the U.S. Office of the Coordinator for Inter-American Affairs under the direction of Nelson Rockefeller. The period became retrospectively evoked as a golden age, although critical opinion varies considerably on its duration: Carl Mora argues that the golden age coincided with the economic miracle of alemanismo; Monsiváis argues for a generous period spanning the years 1935–1955; and Emilio García Riera narrows the period to the years of the Second World War.[23]

Although the esteem and duration of Cantinflas's creative peak are similarly contested, the height of his cultural influence arguably spans the period from 1940 to 1960—from the beginnings of Ávila Camacho's organization of the film industry to Cantinflas's full-scale Hollywoodization with his roles in *Around the World in 80 Days* (1956) and *Pepe* (1960).[24] The decline of the comedian's films—and arguably the golden age *tout court*—was a function of declining Hollywood investment following the Second World War and the cronyism of state financing and syndicate entrenchment, as well as the broadening and formula-driven narratives of the films. Some critics, however, dismiss the comedian's entire oeuvre: Jorge Ayala Blanco notes that Cantinflas avoided departing from his always and already anachronistic peladito from 1936, stuck performing the same debasing character in Delgado's immobile frame, a relic of a national and bourgeois institution that attempted to make an apolitical and ahistorical Mexico a reality.[25] Similarly, Rafael Medina de la Serna privileges the comedian's biography, his decline a function of the unprecedented success of *Detalle*. Cantinflas's success caused him to mollify the class character of his comedy while preserving the trappings of the peladito. For Medina de la Serna, the comedian's films post-*Detalle* – nearly his entire filmography—feature the pelado in a variety of professions that would blunt the satiric edge of his humor.[26] These criticisms turn on the cultural function of his pelado character. Even his staunchest defenders cite *Si yo fuera diputado* (1951) as a turning point in Cantinflas's filmography because his persona ceases to be a lumpen representative. The film finds Cantinflas becoming a congressman, breaking with the pelado's marginality.[27] Monsiváis adds that the film marks the end of Cantinflas's popular restive phase because of the moralizing and cautionary nature of the later Cantinflas films.[28] In a less sociohistorical vein, Ilan Stavans problematically identifies Cantinflas's apex between 1942 and 1950, extolling his collaboration with cinematographer Gabriel Figueroa; however, Figueroa works with the comedian mostly outside this period, only sporadically in a handful of films from the early 1940s and then again in his later films *El bolero de Raquel* (1957), *Su excelencia* (1967), and *El profesor* (1971).[29] Privileging this collaboration simply reinforces auteurist attempts to redeem golden age genre and popular filmmaking: Figueroa's landscapes and Arcady

Boytler's direction are both often indebted to Eisenstein's sojourn in Mexico.[30]

These periodizing debates about Cantinflas's (and arguably the golden age's) impact hinge on what Mexican cultural critic Carlos Monsiváis might call the socializing function of cinema. Monsiváis argues that cinema was a significant socializing force in the Mexican context after 1910 because it emerged in a postrevolutionary historical moment of nation-state rebuilding and created a set of identifiable types that gradually became codified as Mexican.[31] This historical narrative underscores the alignment of film and media with a postrevolutionary developmentalist ideology; however, it risks a too-neat linear narrative that presupposes a nationalist telos.

Complicating the nationness of industrial filmmaking from the golden age period has meant turning from production to reception, a disciplinary shift from more interpretive analyses that read the film as text to empirical reception studies that use the film as pretext and document. Maricruz Castro Ricalde and Robert McKee Irwin's excellent historical study is paradigmatic of this shift, arguing that cinema from the period has a complex transnational dimension when considered through the lens of distribution and reception.[32] Through detailed historical and statistical research, they demonstrate how the Mexican films from the period had major success abroad and penetrated domestic markets in other Hispanic countries. For these authors, the box office success of these films abroad is evidence of a newfound position for Mexico as cultural imperialist center and synecdoche for Latin America.[33] They paint the picture of Mexican golden age cinema as a more benevolent form of cultural imperialism that managed to interpellate its linguistic neighbors.[34] When seen through market presence and distribution, Mexico has more in common with Hollywood.

The widespread popularity of Cantinflas is evidence of the reach of Mexico's film industry beyond its borders. Castro Ricalde and McKee Irwin skillfully trace the comedian's success across the continent, from his Peruvian and Chilean successes in 1941 and 1942, respectively, to his box office record-breaking films in Venezuela, Colombia, and Argentina in 1943, when Cantinflas was undoubtedly the most popular star in the Hispanic world. Their study adds texture to the conventional Cantinflas narrative that foregrounds his collaboration with Boytler and his first Mexican success, *Ahí está el detalle*. As watershed as those films are for the development of his star text within Mexico, his circulation within Latin America is staggered and occurs mostly courtesy of later films, especially *Los tres mosqueteros* (Miguel M. Delgado, 1942) and *Romeo y Julieta* (Miguel M. Delgado, 1943). And yet Cantinflas also points to the limits of the assumptions these authors made in their empirical approach. They do not mention that the circulation of his films in the period happens courtesy of RKO and later Columbia Pictures and the material exhibition circuits of classical Hollywood. Further, without textual analysis, their analysis of his films is limited to comments on his street smarts and his ability to manipulate language, and they marvel at his success "pese a su humor y su vocabulario tan emblemáticamente mexicanos" (despite his humor and vocabulary so emblematically Mexican).[35] Cantinflas's Mexicanness is taken as a given, despite the fact that those first successes outside of Mexico are in fact adaptations of non-Mexican (and non-Hispanic) source material circulating through American distributors.

When Castro Ricalde and McKee Irwin explain, "donde quiera que residan los mexicanos . . . la demanda cultural genera mercados que se definen de acuerdo con la demografía y no la cartografía" (wherever Mexicans reside . . . the cultural demand generated by markets is defined according to demography and not cartography), they gesture toward the problem of national film histories.[36] This statement may very well sum up empirical reception studies in a nutshell: making the question of the location of culture a matter of demographics rather than cartography. And yet they cannot rid themselves of the nation-state as frame of reference. The popularity of these films to Mexicans residing outside the geographic territory and their popularity to non-Mexicans abroad both avow the Mexicanness of these films rather than unmoor or complicate the nation-state as a frame of reference. The success of Mexican cinema overdetermines their reading of the causes. That is, any case is immediately read in light of (if not a testament to) the success of Mexico as a film industry looking to monopolize the Hispanic market. Using the language of hegemony, these authors argue that this subordination was successful because the films garnered consensus, and audience identification with the films meant accepting Mexican interpellation.[37] Castro Ricalde and McKee Irwin ultimately suppose that Mexican cinema invited identification—"al recurrir a tradiciones y géneros no anglos sino hispanos, invitaba a una identificación por parte de las audiencias locales y foráneas" (by resorting to traditions and genres that were not Anglo but Hispanic, [Mexican cinema] invited identification by local and foreign audiences)—but the nature of this identification remains underexplored. Box office receipts become evidence of audience identification.[38]

The problem with the model of identification supposed and unexamined in the text crystallizes with a passage on a different star text, Jorge Negrete, written by a Colombian film critic. The critic extols the star's charro persona and claims that the everyday Colombian would like to have the same love interest, the same guitar, the same voice as the charro. Castro Ricalde and McKee Irwin claim that this is an example of how "los latinoamericanos de todas partes aspiraban volverse mexicanos" (Latin Americans from everywhere aspired to be Mexican).[39] This logic is problematic, as the film critic is aspiring to be the character, perhaps Negrete, but not necessarily Mexican. The authors conclude: "El proceso inevitable de identificación con Negrete, entonces, implicaba para los no mexicanos una subordinación de su identidad nacional a una identidad latinoamericana siempre mexicanizada" (The process of inevitable identification with Negrete implied for non-Mexicans a subordination of their national identity to a Latin American identity always already Mexicanized).[40] This makes three dramatic assumptions: that Negrete is conflated with Mexico, that identification with a star is identification with a nation, and that identity works in an either-or logic of subordination. The question of identification then is crucial to this study that seeks to make Mexico analogous to classical Hollywood. The authors borrow from Monsiváis their understanding of identification: "El sentimiento de formar parte de una nación se fortaleció con esta industria que logró homogeneizar la manera en que un amplio sector ciudadano se veía a sí mismo" (The feeling of belonging to a nation was strengthened by this industry that homogenized the way a broad public sector saw itself).[41] These authors assume this model of identification devised to describe a national process must also describe what occurs outside the nation. If we accept that material transnational reception must broaden our understanding of the Mexican golden age, then should we not also entertain the possibility of broadening how we conceive identification as a function of textual processes and star texts? Put another way, this study too quickly reduces the question of reception, what Alberto Moreiras might call the hermeneutic circle, to pregiven forms of social power or social organization (e.g., the nation-state or the market).[42] Perhaps we can revisit reception with an eye toward complicating the reterritorializing logics of these empirical studies by focusing on deterritorializing possibilities. In other words, *complicating nationness means complicating identification.*

The question of national cinema is not simply the stuff of contemporary film studies. Examining both film criticism as well as film exhibitor catalogs reminds us that a national cinema is not simply a discursive project of contemporary film historians. These primary sources constellate a debate where the autochthony/derivative binary gets articulated differently, negotiating cinema as cultural *and* industrial practice. Cantinflas again takes center stage as a figure on both sides of the debate. On the one hand, advocates for autochthony located the national in representations of the nation. Edmundo Baez makes a nuanced case for a national Mexican cinema in the popular film magazine *Cinema Reporter*. He acknowledges cinema as an industrial practice but rejects the claim by producers that broad-based appeal and circulation demands less locally marked subject matter: "los productores tienen una gran razón, el cine es una industria . . . pero los productores olvidan, muchas veces, que también es la expresión artística de un país, expresión que es llevada a otras tierras, a otros países, y que tiene la obligación de llevar arte, arte de altura, para hacer saber lo que siente, lo que hace, lo que le gusta a todo un pueblo" (producers are right that film is an industry . . . but they often forget that it is also the artistic expression of a country, the expression taken to other places, other countries, and that that they have an obligation to take art, high art, to transmit what is felt, what is done, what is liked and valued by a people).[43] Worth noting here is how Baez does not erect the nation in contradistinction to Hollywood or European cinema and its dominant market presence; instead, the nation becomes a question of representation deemed (in)authentic but complicated by the industrial logic that cinema had to circulate abroad. Baez notes that Paris had applauded the Tito Guizar *ranchera Allá en el Rancho Grande* (Fernando de Fuentes, 1936), South America had spent buckets of money on Mexican cinema, and New York had laughed at Cantinflas *because* of his nationness. National specificity is less a function of representation than reciprocal receptivity.

The reception of Mexican cinema in Argentina paints a more complicated picture. Exhibitor catalogs underscore how Argentina held Mexico at a remove while also embracing certain elements "as their own." Writing about Mexican cinema in Argentina, one critic notes that Argentine interest in Mexican cinema had waned in the past—"no lograron interesar a nuestro público y, en consecuencia, nuestros empresarios no las exhibían" (they did not manage to interest our public and, therefore, our exhibitors would not show them)—because of its too "local picturesque" subject matter in the attempt to replicate the charro success of *Allá en el Rancho Grande*.[44] The increased market presence of Mexican cinema in the 1940s is credited to a course correction and the production of "subjects of international interest": "Hoy Cantinflas es ya uno de los ídolos de nuestro público" (Today, Cantinflas is now one of our very own idols).[45] When this foreign critic celebrates Cantinflas as a subject of "international interest," I do not take it as a sign of being interpellated by Mexico. "Cantinflas is now ours" is less a sign of non-Mexicans becoming Mexican than perhaps a call to reconsider the nationness of Cantinflas and star studies more generally. Cantinflas bears the tensions within Latin America over the local, the national, and the regional. He is both autochthonous expression *and* a subject of international interest, used in both the demarcation and the blurring of national boundaries (all while being distributed through American distribution networks). I do not mean to suggest that Cantinflas should not be aligned with the nation or with partisan forms of postrevolutionary power; rather, his suspensive antics open onto questions of how the "national" gets built in correspondence with a sign that rejects signification.

Cantinflas's elusiveness from linguistic signification *and* techniques of inscription means complicating (if not questioning) narratives that privilege his capture by a nationalist cultural apparatus. In other words, the circumvention in Cantinflas comedies is related to the circumvention of Cantinflas's reception and circulation in a way that complicates the nationness of his star persona. Consider the case of *El gendarme desconocido* (The unknown/undercover policeman) (Miguel M. Delgado, 1941). Its basic plot parallels W. C. Fields's *The Bank Dick* (Edward Cline, 1940) with elements from Abbott and Costello's *Buck Privates* (Arthur Lubin, 1941). Cantinflas's pelado idles about in a café trying to court the daughter of its hatchet-faced owner. A slapstick confrontation with three bank robbers in the café leads to Cantinflas being credited with their capture. After being appointed Officer 777 at the police precinct, he comically foils the disciplinary attempts of the police academy. After a series of exploits as a bumbling policeman, the police commissioner assigns Cantinflas to go undercover as the "King of Diamonds" to apprehend diamond thieves preparing their big heist. In a later moment in one of the film's most protracted gags, the comedian discovers a bomb in the basement of his sweetheart's café. The bomb is set to go off at noon but could be detonated by any sudden movements. After Officer 777 discovers the bomb, he takes official notes of the proceedings. In a rote and stilted tone, Cantinflas speaks aloud what he scribbles on his pad:

A las 11:35 encontré en el sótano u bodega una bomba de aspecto terrorífico con síntomas de no haber explotádo en el ángulo exterior, externo y paralelo al mismo rectangular por lo que procedí a recogerla y investigar con síntomas sospechosos procedencia, lugar u incumbencia. Post data: cuidado con la bomba.

At 11:35 I found in the basement or storeroom a terrifying-looking bomb with symptoms of having not exploded in the exterior, external and parallel angle to the same rectangle and so I proceeded to retrieve it and determine with suspicious symptoms its provenance, place and purpose. Postscript: be careful with the bomb.

Cantinflas's report attempts to record and communicate the events as transpired; however, his parodic use of official-sounding speech obfuscates. The ostensible purpose of institutional language may be to report events objectively, but his baroque testimony is more than mere communicative act. Cantinflas's actions are ineffectively captured by the official record because his oral and gestural performance exceeds the documentary capabilities of the record. Cantinflas's inability to bear witness is underscored by the conclusion of this bomb sequence. After a race against the clock that includes a series of slapstick pratfalls, a dawdling Cantinflas mesmerized by a street vendor, and the bomb being jostled by unsuspecting bystanders, Cantinflas arrives at the precinct with a car-brake sound effect Mickey-Mousing his body's halting near-stumble. He barges into the commander's office in a panning long shot that includes a clock in the background with mere minutes to our deadline. Cantinflas finally exclaims: "¡Va a estallar!" (It's going to blow!). Cantinflas and his superior engage in a back and forth "who's on first" routine in shot/reverse shot. His superior asks him to explain himself as clearly as possible, and Cantinflas reads his report:

«Según la remisión a las 11:30 am, como quién dice, amaneciendo, encontrándome en susodicho café, me comunicó un infante lo que sigue. Qué "interrogación" "puntos suspensivos" qué cosa. Vamos a ver—asuordens, jefe—que a las 11:35 y precisamente en el lugar de los hechos "coma" sucedió "punto".» Perdón jefe pero como no sé escribir me cuesta trabajo leer lo que me escriben.

"According to the record, at 11:30 am, as they say, at dawn, finding myself in the aforementioned café, an infant communicated to me the following. What 'question mark' 'ellipsis' what. Let's see—yes, sir—that at 11:35 precisely in the site of the events 'comma' it happened 'period.'" Sorry, boss, but since I can't write, it's hard for me to read what they've written for me.

Cantinflas continues to "read" his report, finally displaying the bomb he has brought into the precinct. His alarmed superior glances at the clock on the wall and races toward the door. The clock chimes noon, and the camera cuts to a medium shot of Cantinflas climbing a hat rack. The package does not explode. Officer 777 had misplaced the bomb along the way to the precinct. In this instance of Cantinflas speaking "on the record," the reports do not match: what transpired on screen, what was written, and what was read do not coincide. Although we could consider this through the sociohistorical context of widespread illiteracy in the growing urban centers of the country, what I want to foreground is the ways that Cantinflas eludes being captive to transcription. Cantinflas's indirect reporting demonstrates a paradigmatic form of cantinfleo: "You have been speaking for two minutes and have said nothing," says his boss. The baroque language of officialism is compounded by the interjection of spoken asides and vernacular expressions. Obsequiousness becomes irreverence as "a sus órdenes, jefe" becomes a compound word, with the syllables mangled and the consonants dropped: "asuordens, jefe." Moreover, Cantinflas "reads" the punctuation; the grapheme becomes phoneme, undermining semantic transparency.

Cantinflismo is not nonsense; rather, it presents a collision of linguistic registers: the formal and vulgar, the official and vernacular, the oral and written, the material and discursive. Less important is that language fails to signify than that the failure to communicate "creates a speech *open to everything* but meaning."[46] Cantinflas's performance foregrounds the limits of institutional discourse *and* cinematic documentation. Perhaps a metaphor for his status on the celluloid itself, Cantinflas's verbal and corporeal dexterity cannot be contained by the fact of inscription and representation. His performance must be understood beyond the communicative and documentary competency of the filmstrip. Comedic effect is a function of a selective intelligibility—"laugh or get lost"—which carves out particular spaces of reception.[47] A cultural practice that risks (if not relies on) being unintelligible flies in the face of conventional wisdom on popular culture and commodity form. Cantinflismo begs for a notion of popular culture wedded neither to its site of production nor to the mere purchase of the consumer because intelligibility is the price of admission into a mass constituted by a sensuous mode of address. We need instead a framework that accounts for the "comprehension" of non-sense and a public not founded on transparent communicative acts.

MOCK CLASSICISM

This framework would require moving away from criticism that foregrounds the cultural function of the pelado in recuperative narrative structures, criteria that presuppose the transparency of cinematic representation and presume classical structure and modes of spectatorship. If Hollywood classical cinema was industrial analogue to Mexico in Castro Ricalde and McKee Irwin's reception history, Charles Ramirez Berg's recent neoformalist study of golden age Mexican cinema takes Hollywood classical narrative as its paradigm. Drawing extensively on the foundational work of David Bordwell, Kristen Thompson, and Janet Staiger, Ramirez Berg presents a comprehensive survey of the subjects and themes of the period in order to delineate a national cultural style.[48] The classical for Bordwell designates a group style determined by a mode of production. The classical Hollywood film presents a psychologically defined and goal-oriented protagonist who struggles to attain his goal and so motivates a series of causally related events that lead to a resolution. That a different mode of production or different conditions of reception might yield a different group style as a *mode of address* is conceded in his early work: "Hollywood cinema cannot be identified with classicism *tout court*."[49] Although Bordwell's later work subsumed all film language to the telos of classical Hollywood narrative, his early work speaks instead of *classicisms* and the need for comparative study that pursues analysis of form and style elsewhere.

Ramirez Berg seems to take up this challenge; however, the desire to locate the specificity of Mexican cinema founded almost entirely on semantic content and drawing exclusively from Bordwell leads to a confusing portrait of the period. Using Bordwell's narratological lens yields two arguments at odds with each other in Ramirez Berg. The first is an ontogenetic argument that loosely delineates the emergence of classical narrative in the early cinema period in Mexico. The second is a periodizing argument that uses a neoformalist and neoauteurist approach to erect a canon of "classical" Mexican cinema. Ramirez Berg's golden age has a mainstream Mexican cinema, which was retrograde and conservative and without style or poetics because it was merely derivative of Hollywood, and a classical Mexican cinema, which was founded on film auteurs that made exceptional films representing Mexican themes in a mode with a certain national specificity. His is a classicism built on exceptions, a paradoxical conceit. Comedy again is included (and discarded) within mainstream Mexican cinema for being "formally identical to U.S. movies."[50] I elaborate on the ontogenetic to imagine how a classicism located elsewhere might function and resoundingly reject a neoformalism articulated to questions of national ontology.

Supplementing (if not correcting) these foundational narratological analyses in the American context meant turning away from insular questions of narrative patterning to broader questions about the perceiver/spectator/consumer and the shifting relation between industrial production and local exhibition. Bordwell and Thompson would have us believe continuity editing is about natural narrative configurations.[51] Others like Stephen Heath point to the ideological work behind continuity editing that aligns the spectator with the apparatus.[52] Miriam Hansen grounds Heath's structural critique by turning to the spectator made consumer through the conventions of continuity editing that separated the theater space from the screen space.[53] Bordwell's critics complicate his model, turning from what is on screen to who is addressed. Their approaches inspire my project, which suggests a classicism premised differently and founded on different pleasures. As Miriam Hansen argues, we must resist seeing the rise of the classical system as a "linear evolution of techniques [or] a gradual perfecting of a natural film language."[54] The golden age of Mexican (and Latin American) cinema merits a similar shift in analyses: turning from definitions based on what is represented and where and who is the location of film practice to thinking how and to whom the film is addressed. For Hansen, the transition from early cinema to classical cinema is not simply a function of narrative devices becoming convention. Instead, it is about making the film a better commodity, allowing producers greater control over their product at the expense of local exhibitors, and inventing a spectator as consumer. Underscoring the classical as a mode of address allows Hansen to see classical narration as the codification of the proper relations among viewer, projector, and screen. This transition occurs thanks to certain technologies that standardized exhibition and certain formal devices that afford secondary identification with characters.[55]

Comedy, however, provides a limit case for these accounts of classical Hollywood. For Bordwell, comedy relies on neither an enigma that motivates the accumulation of narrative information nor the organization of time as a function of cause and effect. Instead, time is organized as a function of the punch line, and space according to the necessities of the gag. Hansen struggles to account for comedy in the transition she describes because it offers a less self-contained narrative space. Comedy capitalizes on an intertextual horizon and produces a semblance of continuity between screen and theater. Comedy proves difficult to reconcile with the classical precisely because of its relation to the texture of experience. If comedy functions as a limit case in these classical Hollywood debates, then perhaps Latin American comedy can offer a similar heuristic value in delineating a mode of address particular to Latin American cinema.

Hansen discusses how film spectatorship was a cultural practice to be learned by referencing fish-out-of-water or rube-in-the-city comedies, where errant film spectatorship was depicted on screen. The comic effect hinged on a disparity between the spectator-in-film and the spectator-of-film, the former providing a negative example and marking certain spectatorial pleasures (mimetic, kinesthetic, voyeuristic) as partial or regressive. Similar instances in the Latin American context that showcase spectatorship-of-film and spectatorship-in-film gesture toward a different model of classicism. What happens when the "rube" is *also* on screen, or when the spectating subject is also the object spectated?

The doubling of viewing positions is textualized in Cantinflas's *Ni sangre ni arena* (Neither blood nor sand) (Alejandro Galindo, 1941), when Mario Moreno portrays two different characters: the bullfighter Manolete and the nameless pelado. The title of the film is an allusion to the silent success of Rudolph Valentino's *Blood and Sand* (Fred Niblo, 1922) and a Rouben Mamoulian film of the same name starring Tyrone Power and Rita Hayworth from 1941. An adaptation of an earlier successful Spanish novel, the 1922 film follows the transformation of Valentino from a village boy born into poverty into the greatest matador in Spain. Valentino loves a virtuous girl from his village but embarks on an intense affair with a seductive widow. His romantic troubles result in recklessness in the arena and eventually being killed by a bull. In Cantinflas's parody, the title is categorically negated and the film narrative is inverted. Rather than a straightforward coming-of-age narrative featuring women in the prescribed roles of virgin and vamp, the parody features a doubled male protagonist and undercuts the identification that comes with the masculinist bildungsroman. After a bout of mistaken identity where the peladito arrives in town as a stowaway before Manolete and then the bullfighter is arrested as the law-skirting peladito, a climactic bullfight sees the bum nearly lose his life before order is restored.

We first see the bullfighter Manolete in the arena, the camera framing him in a medium shot from behind, ostensibly the point of view of the spectator Cantinflas. Manolete enters the arena in a high-angle shot from the stands, gesturing toward the crowd and dedicating the fight to

FIGURE 3. Cantinflas (Mario Moreno) is not Manolete (Mario Moreno) in *Ni sangre ni arena* (1941).

his patron, Don Pancho, who happens to be the father of his romantic foil, Anita. The bullfighter tosses his hat into the stands, and Cantinflas thanks Manolete: "Gracias, hermano." An extended sequence of bullfighting in extreme long shot is punctuated with close-ups of an excited Cantinflas cheering on his doppelgänger. The narrative hinges not on disentangling the pelado from an assumed identity (e.g., Leonardo del Paso or *El gendarme desconocido*'s King of Diamonds) but in the confusion derived from having a physical double. In other words, *Ni sangre ni arena* is his first film where the failures of signification are not a function of deliberate cantinflista play that capitalizes on the assumptions (both material and linguistic) of others. Instead, these mistakes are due to the legitimate confusion derived from identical physical aspects. The mise-en-scène, particularly the pelado's wardrobe and characterization, help spectators avoid the same confusion, but the signifying universe begins to solidify around Cantinflas.

The above sequence presents a particularly uncanny experience of spectatorship, where the pelado as absorbed spectator ostensibly watches himself in the arena. If Valentino's *Blood and Sand* functions as a key text in Miriam Hansen's critique of classical Hollywood cinema and Anglo theories of spectatorship, then its parody, *Ni sangre ni arena,* suggests a way to consider the horizon of reception for Cantinflas as well as the specificity of the spectatorial experience in Mexican golden age cinema. Hansen draws on Valentino's star text to suggest that the star phenomenon challenges the paradigm of classical Hollywood. The reconstruction of the horizon of reception for a star requires considering spectatorship inside and outside the film: both the textual configuration of the performer—with tensions between reading positions marked by tensions of narrative and spectacle—as well as the public discourses surrounding Cantinflas. Star texts articulate material paracinematic phenomena and (inter)textual cinematic performance, making them an ideal site for exploring the vicissitudes of identification: "The star's presence in a particular film blurs the boundary between diegesis and discourse, between an address relying on the identification with fictional characters and an activation of the viewer's familiarity with the star on the basis of production and publicity intertexts."[56] If formalist discussion of narrative foregrounds the unity and closure of the textual system of classical Hollywood, then the presence of a star activates a collective and centrifugal process of spectatorship and identification. The star dissociates the narrative (identification with a character) and the scopic (the recognition of a particular object) and undermines claims of "primary" identification with the look of the camera because there is necessarily a collective dimension to the star system. We gawk at the star aware that (and perhaps because) others also marvel at him or her.[57]

The specificity of both the material conditions of reception and the mode of address of film comedies suggests that identification was routed differently in the case of Latin America. If Valentino functions as a site to reconsider the question of female spectatorship, his gaze one of reciprocity and ambivalence rather than mastery and objectification, then Cantinflas becomes a site to discuss the possibility of a spectatorship located elsewhere and in relation to a (mass) public sphere shaped by a different scopic economy. Monsiváis articulates the star system to the national and modernizing impulses in Mexico in order to imagine a cultural and historically specific mode of spectatorship. His foundational essay "All the People Came but Did Not Fit onto the Screen" argues that cinema plays a role in the cultural processes of modernization and Mexicanization, mitigating the effects of the rural exodus to growing urban centers, the illiteracy and the transformation of the public sphere, and the declining tradition of "democratic" popular theatrical entertainment.[58] The star system and the pilfering of a repertory of popular types represent a diminution in collective experience. Cinema mediates "between the shock of industrialization and the rural and popular urban experience which has not been prepared in any way for this giant change."[59] His Adorno-inspired musings imagine both a culture industry imitating Hollywood and contemptuous of its spectator as well as a spectator reassured by the turns of the familiar.[60] And yet his bleak picture of popular cinema from the period actually supposes a spatial arrangement and a model of identification with a collective dimension that are rather different from Hollywood's routed secondary identification.

We must avoid taking for granted a linear process of identification with the image premised on the separation of diegetic and theatrical space and the routing of identification through a goal-oriented protagonist. The doubling of Cantinflas affords both centripetal *identification* with Manolete the character and a centrifugal *recognition* of Cantinflas the star. A protagonist with no goal always ensnared in a plot hinging on mistaken identification, the nameless pelado is only loosely inscribed in the film narrative. We are not captured through a linear process of identification with a character but instead marvel at a star persona animated through shared intertextual and paratextual knowledge.

During the bullfighting sequence, the pelado is figured as cinematic spectator, observing the torero as a member of a public while projecting himself into the figure of Manolete. Like the spectator who "does not fit on screen," the pelado does not fit in the arena, experiencing the spectacle by proxy of his double while the performance allows him to imagine (and eventually realize) his place in the arena. The eventual climax of the film features the pelado in the ring, successfully, if unexpectedly, defeating a bull in lieu of Manolete. If the assumed identity was ill-fitting in Cantinflas's previous films and collapsed in a farcical resolution, the narrative in *Ni sangre* affords a moment of narcissistic doubling whereby the subject of the look constitutes itself as object, undone with Manolete's eventual return to the arena. The narrative depends on our recognition of Cantinflas and the other characters' inability to differentiate Manolete from the pelado.

If the separation of the screen space from the theater space and the production of a hermetic diegesis gave producers greater control over their product and made the commodity less open to intervention and interpretation at the site of exhibition, then we could ask whether Latin American producers made their films better commodities in similar ways. Conventional film histories already underscore how the narrative content in Latin American films borrowed from local subject matter as a form of product differentiation within a crowded marketplace. Monsiváis adds the thrill of (possibly) seeing oneself on screen. If the transition to classical cinema supposes secondary identification, then Monsiváis read through Hansen might suggest how this process of secondary identification is fundamentally one that also contains a mimetic-narcissistic strain. This other pleasure is a function of the different spatial arrangement in golden age Mexican cinema: "At its best, these were films distinguished by their sincerity, which I would define in this context as the inability to keep themselves at a distance, physically or culturally, from their audience."[61] Crucial here is not the production of a diegesis separate from the theatrical space but a continuity between screen and theater. Latin American cinema emplots space and publicness differently, and the spatial arrangement of the cinema implies different normative pleasure. This is a proximity that harnessed other pleasures, where the pleasure derived from (mimetic) recognition and from the proximate (or at the very least related) spatial arrangement of theater space and screen space matter. With a different public horizon, an uneven implementation of sound technologies, different preceding media histories and industries, different relationships between production and exhibition, and different precedents for representation and narrative structure (beyond the nineteenth-century short story), the structural conditions for the articulation of experience in the Latin American contexts are very different. *Ni sangre ni arena* plays with these other (mimetic, kinesthetic, voyeuristic) pleasures: in a veritable *mise en abyme,* the pelado watches Manolete; we spectators watch Cantinflas; and Moreno watches Valentino. We bear witness to and consent to being incorporated into a series of overlapping collective bodies, belonging at once to publics local, national, and global.

The reflexive scenes of spectatorship-of-film and spectatorship-in-film in Latin American comedies illustrate this drama of telescoped identification. As spectatorship becomes classical, the trouble of placing Cantinflas in language and on screen erodes and the nature of this differently routed identification becomes clearer. To understand how the cantinflista slippage finds firm footing through narrative and aesthetic devices and a more deliberate arrangement of space, I turn to the film *¡A volar joven!* (Miguel M. Delgado, 1947). Based on the Fernandel and Noël-Noël film *Adémaï aviateur* (Jean Tarride, 1933), the film features our comic hero as a conscripted soldier and former farmhand shirking his military responsibilities while courting a lovely maid from his former workplace. The owners of the hacienda have a sickly and plain-looking daughter, María, whom they coerce Cantinflas into marrying. To avoid the marriage, Cantinflas attempts to secure a spot in a rigorous and secluded aviation school, but his wealthy father-in-law foils his plans, orchestrating the ceremony before Cantinflas's departure. Cantinflas marries the plain María against his will before being shipped off to aviation school. The film culminates with an extended sequence where Cantinflas and another first-time pilot meet in their instructor's office for their first lesson; however, each novice believes that the other is the instructor. The two board a plane and successfully take off before realizing that neither knows how to land the plane. The inexperienced pilots remain airborne, breaking the record for the longest sustained flight and becoming national heroes.

After nearly a dozen films in over a decade that featured Cantinflas in a variety of guises entangled in farcical scenarios of mistaken identity, *¡A volar joven!* was his first film since *Ahí está el detalle* to refer to the pelado by his own proper name. In a brief scene nearly halfway through the film, a commanding officer refers to the protagonist as Cantinflas. Although the narrative still relies on misrecognition, the naming of Cantinflas changes the effects of cantinflismo. Earlier films relied on doubling, on producing multiple versions that dislodge an original. These comedies of errors had either shoehorned the pelado into the guise of another (Cantinflas as long-lost brother Leonardo del Paso) or relied on the actor playing dual roles (Cantinflas as Manolete). The pelado used his linguistic doublespeak to avoid self-identity; his inability to communicate was a tactic deployed to avoid being captive to the narrative, the semiosphere, and the apparatus. In *¡A volar joven!*, Cantinflas's inability to communicate becomes a hindrance. The valence of cantinflismo has changed: transparency becomes desirable and his doublespeak, a shortcoming. Cantinflas constantly attempts to clarify, but his surroundings obscure and his interlocutors ignore. For example, after going missing for an extended period of time, Cantinflas attempts to explain to a commanding officer that he does not wish to marry María. His explanation is interrupted by the sound of an airplane engine that overwhelms the soundtrack and is disregarded by a general influenced by the status of Cantinflas's future father-in-law. He falls into comedic situations because of who he is rather than who he is not.

During the wedding ceremony in the film, we observe an inversion of the marriage to Clotilde Regalado from his early success, *Ahí está el detalle*. If the early film features explicit performative speech acts that become indirect speech and a cunning Cantinflas that avoids becoming inextricably linked to indices, then this film finds Cantinflas ineffectually resisting the yokes of matrimony and referentiality. A medium long shot finds Cantinflas in a similar predicament, overwhelmed in a crowded frame and struggling to breathe in a necktie knotted too tightly. The justice of the peace races inarticulately through the formalities, barely audible over the wedding march. He pauses to ask the groom whether he accepts María as his wife. Cantinflas says that he does not accept María while simultaneously nodding his head as he struggles with his necktie. The judge takes Cantinflas's nod as a sign of acceptance over his explicit utterance. The indirect speech act takes on greater force than the explicit illocutionary vow. The ritual takes effect despite the misfire that should have voided the act.[62] Cantinflas is interpellated by an institutional framework despite his equivocation. The pelado still relies on his evasive tactics—the majority of the film finds the soldier going missing or requesting a transfer to avoid marriage, literally attempting to flee from the diegesis—but the coded world constantly ensnares him in its referential matrix.

¡A volar joven! marks a significant moment in the comedian's career because it literalizes the ossification of the pelado. By ossification, I do not mean to suggest that the character is metaphorically ineffectual because he functions as therapeutic stereotype; rather, nominative operations and formal conventions gradually solidify the semiosphere and put the pelado in his place. The centrifugal process of spectatorship enacted by the presence of the star folds onto the centripetal hermeneutics of the narrative. The intradiegetic recognition of Cantinflas qua Cantinflas telescopes these modes of identification and organizes subjectivity more forcefully. This signifying calcification is nowhere more evident than in the film's final moments. The first-time pilots successfully land the plane and are hoisted on the shoulders of their peers. The camera pushes back into a long shot of the moving image now framed on a movie screen, a self-reflexive newsreel film within the film. The camera cuts to a close-up of a couple in the audience, Cantinflas and a transformed María. Cantinflas swallows some popcorn and points to the screen, exclaiming: "¡Ese soy yo!" (That's me!). The literalized narcissistic doubling discussed in *Ni sangre ni arena* is figured more categorically in the conclusion of ¡A volar joven!

The classical Hollywood film aspired to a neutral spectator position by producing a diegesis or self-contained narrative world; that is, the classical Hollywood cinema wants us to forget we are present in the theater.

Cantinflismo and *Relajo* | 53

FIGURE 4. Cantinflas (Mario Moreno) watches himself on screen in ¡*A volar joven!* (1947).

The Latin American spectator occupies this position only precariously. Jason Borge's history of film criticism suggests a similar dilemma for the film critic. Even the most rigid formalists or aesthetes who aspired to the neutrality of this "international" medium had to confront their material relation to Hollywood and Europe.[63] This is a spectatorship only partly routing identification to the apparatus because there is necessarily a sideways glance. Watching a Latin American film means watching for the flash of recognition ("I know what that is!") with a gaze that measures comparatively what is experienced ("That is (un)like what I know!"). This is a pleasure derived not from linear processes of identification but from a peripheral vision—a vision outside the center of our gaze—that looks around and opens onto a larger field of vision.

Watching the cinema with peripheral vision—with an immersive reflexivity—is less about cataloguing references from multiple origins than it is about thinking how spatial arrangement shifts depending on the film text and the horizon of reception. Unlike classical Hollywood cinema, where the frame or screen space becomes narrative (metaphoric) space rather than scenographic (metonymic) space courtesy of continuity editing and narrative causality, this immersive reflexivity occurs in a comic frame.[64] Does the contiguous relationship between screen and theatrical space (the not-quite classicism of Latin American cinema), afforded by narrative strategies, aesthetic form, and exhibition practices, yield the conditions for a different type of critical (reason) practice? This is not to say that any spatial arrangement that is unlike the continuous narrative space of classical Hollywood (separate from a particular theater space) works identically. Examples of discontinuity in cinema have readily been aligned with a modernist reflexivity. And yet, although the screen space in a European modernist film avoids being merely narrative space, it remains legible as pictorial space. The critical distance celebrated by modernism in fact imagines a spectator evicted from the narrative space but not necessarily returning to a theatrical space. Both classicism and modernism thus conceived are premised on separations and distances: the former "sutures" in order to produce a diegesis *separate* from the theatrical space; the latter *distantiates* in order to evict the spectator from the narrative space. Classicism and modernism conceived as separations and distance depend on abstracting space (and ourselves from space) in order to make space and image legible. Cantinflismo and more broadly Latin American film comedy make space legible in a different mode, through an immersive reflexivity that privileges perceived and lived space above abstract or coded space.

AN ENDOGENOUS VERNACULAR MODERNISM

Popular genre cinema in Latin America would seem to be far removed from any discussion of modernism conventionally understood as critical nationalist in Latin American studies or aligned with studies of "international art cinemas of both interwar and new wave periods" in film studies.[65] And yet the sensuous registers of communication that these popular comedies indulge gesture toward "new modes of organizing vision and sensory perception, a new relationship with 'things,' different forms of mimetic experience, of affectivity, temporality and reflexivity, a changing fabric of everyday life, sociability, and leisure."[66] Opening up modernism beyond the scope of art cinema and critical nationalism, Miriam Hansen capitalizes on the confluence of mass culture, mainstream cinema, and high modernism during the interwar period in order to redraw modernism to encompass a broader range of practices that respond to modernization. Hansen broadens modernism in a Benjaminian spirit to include practices that articulate and mediate the sensory experience of modernity, discovering in modes of mass and popular culture moments of *vernacular modernism*. As she argues, the success of mass cultural production had less to do with "what these films showed ... [than with] the way they opened up hitherto unperceived modes of sensory perception ... [and with] their ability to suggest a different organization of the daily world."[67] Articulating modernism to popular genre cinema means shifting our attention toward the sensory and material conditions under which mass culture was received.

In the context of Mexican golden age cinema and arguably most industrial Latin American cinemas from the period, this means reconstructing the reflexive horizon they afforded, a reflexivity anchored in both sensory experience and affect as well as processes of partial or excessive identification.[68] Excessive or partial identification—particularly evident in popular genres such as melodrama, comedy, horror, and pornography—involves the viewer's body in ways that defy conventional notions of modernist reflexivity as a cognitive-aesthetic experience of ironic removal or distance. For instance, Cantinflas's *Los tres mosqueteros* (Miguel M. Delgado, 1942) has a self-reflexive framing narrative that explains his incongruous insertion into a period film; however, this device functions differently than the self-reflexivity often associated with high modernism. In a parody of Dumas's classic *The Three Musketeers*, Cantinflas stumbles onto a job as an extra on the set of a straight adaptation of the French novel. His antics cause the production to falter, and to get the meddlesome extra out of the way, the director has a script girl read the screenplay of the film within the film to Cantinflas. The pelado dreams the period film, casting himself as D'Artagnan, becoming a musketeer and defeating the cardinal.

The dialogue of this oneiric adaptation is perhaps one its most particular features, as all the players speak with an antiquated affectation. Every verb in the second person is conjugated in the formal second person *vosotros*, and Cantinflas's orthographic and grammar mistakes (e.g., *traiba* instead of *traía* as the imperfect conjugation of the verb *traer*) as well as his inclusion of contemporary vernacular best highlight the tension and interplay between official and vulgar speech that characterize vernacular speech as well as the conflict between peninsular and continental Spanish. In his rush to join the musketeers, Cantinflas runs into some obstacles that he attempts to explain to the leader of the legion:

> *Leader:* Supongo que traeréis alguna carta de introducción.
>
> *Cantinflas:* Suponéis mal porque no traigo nada. Bueno, la traía, verdad? Pero resulta de que cuando ya la traiba en una de esas cosas, pues, me la robaron.

Leader: ¿Os la robaron? ¿Quién?

Cantinflas: El hombre maloso. Sabe usted, cuando al llegar yo, ya está yo todo . . . comenzó el choteo . . . yo correctamente porque uno correcto, verdad. Y luego me bajo yo del caballo y al bajarme luego luego comenzó a reírse el hombre porque era amarillo.

Leader: ¿Un hombre amarillo? ¿Sería chino?

Cantinflas: Mi caballo, el que traiba era amarillo.

Leader: ¿Cuál caballo?

Cantinflas: El que me regaló mi papi.

Leader: Un caballo amarillo, me gustaría verlo.

Cantinflas: A mí también, pero ya lo vendí.

Leader: I suppose you have a letter of introduction.

Cantinflas: You suppose incorrectly because I bring nothing. Well, I was bringing, right? But it so happens that when I bringed in one of those things that, well, they stole it.

Leader: They stole it? Who?

Cantinflas: The villain. You know, when I arrived I, I was all . . . and the mocking . . . and I uprightly because one upright, right? And then I get off the horse and when getting off real fast he began the man began to laugh because he was yellow.

Leader: A yellow man? Was he Chinese?

Cantinflas: My horse, which I bringed was yellow.

Leader: Which horse?

Cantinflas: The one my daddy gave me.

Leader: A yellow horse, I'd like to see that.

Cantinflas: Me too, but I already sold him.

Cantinflas inserted into a period piece relies on many of the diverting tactics from his earlier films: chains of clauses that never become sentences, grammar mistakes, and pronouns with unclear antecedents. Noting particularly the confusion of the yellow horse and man, this example highlights the logic of referentiality Cantinflas unsettles. Cantinflas's interlocutor presumes the antecedent is the most recent noun in the sentence; however, Cantinflas is both redundant and vague in the same breath, linking the man to his laugh but not the horse to its color. Referentiality submits neither to proximity nor recency. If earlier films contrasted cantinflismo to class-based civility or institutional code, this film relies on an archaic and peninsular language as foil.

The film's self-reflexivity, however, complicates how Cantinflas affects referentiality. The film within a film is produced at the CLASA film studios, the actual shooting location for most of Cantinflas's films from the period. Cantinflas as film extra causes problems on the set: from inserting anachronisms in his costume to misunderstanding hierarchy on the set and from improvising his dialogue to mistaking the designed set as an actual space. Cantinflas is banished from the set by the director not merely because he is *igualado*—demanding the lead role despite being an extra—but because his performance draws attention to the artifice presupposed by representation. If cantinflismo, as we have demonstrated, relies on unclear referentiality and a slippage between terms and referents, the humor in this self-reflexive sequence demonstrates a failure in signification founded on a different logic. *Ahí está el detalle* relied on the uncertain relationship between signifier and signified and a penchant for always simulating others (i.e., "Leonardo del Paso"). In this self-reflexive example, Cantinflas's inability to distinguish the real from the simulated—leaning against a styrofoam column and collapsing the set—and his inability to represent someone other than himself reveal an understanding of signification that yokes signifier and signified. Cantinflas ascribes to a logic of presentation, unwilling to absent in order to represent. The conventional cantinflista play that unmoors referentiality in the narrative world becomes inverted.

Understanding this self-reflexive play as an extension of cantinflismo allows us to regard self-reflexivity in a new light. This is a sensory affect that yields a broader understanding of modernism, expanded to include a range of practices with a "distinct reflexivity beyond the Marxist realist (reflection) and modernist formalist (self-reflexivity)."[69] Conventionally, self-reflexivity designates a practice that comments on the circumstances of its own making. When aligned with high modernism, it becomes a device of critical distantiation, foregrounding the gap between signifier and signified in order to produce an awareness of how meaning is made: "Don't be fooled by representation!" Perhaps this alignment capitalizes too quickly on this gap in signification because it ignores how this device relies on also imagining the gap foreclosed. In other words, if self-reflexivity comments on the circumstances of its making, then it necessarily means supposing something made and an imagined person taken in by this something. "I didn't fall for it" means imagining someone who has fallen or entertaining the possibility that someone could, perhaps even disavowing that for a moment we might have, too. Our being ironically distanced means supposing a proximity occurring elsewhere; self-reflexivity has a necessarily public dimension that the hermetic introspection of high modernism disavows.[70] In the context of popular cinema, self-reflexivity relies less on producing a self-conscious awareness in the individual spectator than on opening onto an act of public reception *through the star text*.[71] Self-reflexivity does not function simply as inward commentary on textual production but also as the outward projection of a sense-making public—a conventional modernist device made vernacular. The legibility of space (and the image) is less a function of its objectification and parcelization through reference to an external code than a function of sensory extension and orientation.

The vernacular for Hansen is exogenous and outward looking, and circulation yields an always cosmopolitan cinema. Hansen's approach may provincialize Hollywood cinema and may historicize classical narrative and continuity editing, but when used in a transnational and comparative spirit, it threatens to occlude culturally specific film practices that prove less circulatory and less translatable. How to account for the uneven experience of modernization and the asymmetric relations of exchange across these contexts? The experience of modernity that vernacular modernism claims to reflect must not simply be situated in space but also in time. Studying the transition to sound and the emergence of film comedy provides both an *endogenous* and a *nonsynchronous* rejoinder to the cosmopolitanism of Hansen's vernacular modernism.

The inability of comedy to travel well complicates the circulatory dynamics of the "vernacular" in vernacular modernism and problematizes its transnational and comparative frame. Comedy relies on "short circuits between signifier and signified [that] are weakened by translation."[72] Taking comedy seriously puts pressure on the cosmopolitan dimensions of the vernacular in Hansen's project. Film comedy makes the experience of modernity sensually graspable but as an *inward-looking* reflective experience of a modernity situated in the periphery. In addition to this endogenous turn in geopolitical orientation, we must also consider the historical specificity of vernacular modernism when using the concept to articulate global and local interrelations. The production of a global sensorium—classical Hollywood cinema as global vernacular—occurs under the aegis of a dominant American silent cinema and the emergence of classical Hollywood narrative and style. Sound technologies that particularize the cinema experience underscore how the "vernacular" of this theoretical metaphor paradoxically supposes silent cinema. Using vernacular modernism out of sync means comparison is founded less on common periodization, which overwhelmingly privileges the impact of and the differentiated relations to classical Hollywood, than in identifying competing visions of modernity within film culture. In mobilizing vernacular modernism in her discussion of early Chinese film culture, Zhen also studies early (silent) cinema but finds the category less a rigidly defined period or aesthetic than an emblem of "the 'nonsynchronous synchronous' global horizon of film culture."[73] This time lag in periodization compels us to understand how synchronous sound may in fact accentuate the nonsynchronicity of the global horizon of film culture.[74]

Vernacular modernism has proven useful as a film historical framework in contemporary film studies, helping us rearticulate the question of national cinema, particularly as conceived along an autochthonous/derivate binary, in order to rewrite film histories within the broader project of modernity and the category of experience. Cantinflismo, through the vernacular modernist lens, blurs (periodizing) boundaries between silent and sound cinema and telescopes Hollywood, Hispanic, and local references through an inversion of a prototypical narrative structure of the modern subject. This shift in geopolitical orientation and historical periodization presents a way to further complicate the cosmopolitan/national spatial coordinates and the early/classical-industrial temporal coordinates that have determined analysis of this period. These commercial film comedies inscribe endogenous and nonsynchronous responses to modernity. And yet the deterritorializing potential of vernacular modernism—thinking film as a generative matrix—often leads to a hasty reterritorialization within a rapacious modernity relatively monolithically conceived. Thinking vernacular modernism in film historical terms must avoid making modernity mere context and symptomatic fact.

If cinema reflects on the experience of modernity, then Latin Americanism asks what is being presupposed in the concepts of both "experience" and "modernity." The answer: a rational critical subject. For a critic like Alberto Moreiras, the use of modernity as frame of reference (in lieu of the nation-state) risks an aesthetic-historicist paradigm that fails to deconstruct historicist assumptions (which also become pregiven conclusions): "the aesthetic was therefore a means toward historicism" and a sign of the modern because modern.[75] Taking a particular cultural product as a sign of the modern assumes an almost-deterministic relation between culture and social power rooted in capitalism and does little but reaffirm the modern. The rational critical subject endures but is recast: contemplation, distance, and the engagement of rational faculties occurs through a realignment of perception. Hansen's project recovers the modern liberal subject within the context of a mass culture often figured as anathema to critical reason. Hers is a modern subject constituted within a sensory reflexive horizon, arrived at through innervation as encounter and extension. Similarly, Hansen's redemptive reading of the category of experience in the Frankfurt School supposes a certain distribution of the sensible as determined by technology and publicness that occurs differently (and unevenly) in Latin America. Latin Americanism asks us to examine the (im)possibility of critical reason. Being critical in Hansen means being a modern liberal subject, having a certain distance, having a certain awareness; Latin Americanism asks whether there is another mode of being critical that does not imagine reason as simple reterritorialization or categorization of the critical subject and/or critical object. Put differently, who is the self being reflected in these conventional forms of self-reflexivity, and could we think a form of reflexivity that does not hinge on a discrete self?

A SELF-REFLEXIVITY WITHOUT A SELF

This is a self-reflexivity that is less directed toward (and reterritorializing of) the subject, less an innervating reflexivity than a *denervating* or "loosening" reflexivity characterized by the dynamic interplay between the pro-filmic, the filmic, and the extrafilmic. This reflexivity may not always be critical, but it emerges as a mode of (dis)organizing sensory perception, a relationship with things made non-sense, a form of temporality in suspension, and a fabric of sociability founded on the relajo.

Although literally meaning "relaxation," *relajo* designates a broader collective behavior, a reiterated and at times uproarious collective mode of joking that emerges sporadically in everyday life.[76] Cantinflas is often aligned with the comic practice of relajo, which is often ascribed to Mexico although the term has significant currency in other Caribbean contexts. Contra innervation, the word provocatively suggests a loosening of this collective, a body in fact constituted through this loosening. Mexican philosopher Jorge Portilla provides the definitive account of relajo, less to yoke this behavior to some form of national essence than to tease out a mode of collective experience shaped by history and location that manifests as a form of a lateral intentionality.[77] More broadly, *relajo* refers to the suspension of seriousness, with seriousness designating an attachment to the world or a commitment to value and duty: "La seriedad es el compromiso intimo y profundo que pacto conmigo mismo para sostener un valor en la existencia" (Seriousness is the intimate and profound commitment I make with myself to sustain a value in its existence).[78] Relajo does not reject a serious object but our serious attachment to the object. It does not modify an object; rather, relajo is an action in the world whereby sensuous extension modifies relations between objects.[79] This extension or distance is conceived phenomenologically and not cognitively; that is, *relajo* posits a self-reflexivity without a subject. The fact of being attached—and not the lost object itself—provides the continuity of the subject and the activity of living.[80] This means the object is the effect of my towardness or orientation rather than pregiven and awaiting my intention.[81] This is not a reflexive distance but a reflective distance; that is, this is not a critical distance of contemplative attention but a distance of constitutive apperception.

The cantinflista play with proper names takes on new meaning in this light. After being mistaken for someone else in his first commercial success, Cantinflas is never referred to by his own proper name in his first dozen films. Proper names are always inappropriate in both senses of *inappropriate,* improper because not discrete and not well-suited. Cantinflas's textual instability begins to affect the signifying order of his surroundings: not only does Cantinflas occupy multiple registers, but so do other people. *Gran Hotel* (Miguel M. Delgado, 1944) represents a veritable compendium of the gambits used in the comedian's early films to avoid using his proper name. Loosely based on the MGM classic *Grand Hotel* (Edmund Goulding, 1932), the film follows the pelado taking odd jobs after being evicted from his home, eventually securing a position as a bellboy at a prestigious hotel courtesy of his chambermaid girlfriend. Cantinflas gets mistaken for the Duke of Alfanje by a seductive heiress who is the victim of a plot by jewel thieves masquerading as royalty. The bellboy foils the jewelry heist but succumbs to amnesia and to his given role as duke. The conclusion of the narrative hinges on Cantinflas remembering the location of the jewels and arriving at his own identity. From juggling multiple monikers to unmooring the referential currency of the proper name, Cantinflas floats along the surface of the text, and the narrative restoration of equilibrium demands that he be put in his place. When introduced to the jewel thieves who are posing as aristocracy, Cantinflas forgoes not merely decorum but also the indexical singularity of the aristocrat's proper name: The so-called Italian Count Zapatini becomes misnamed by the bellboy as Count Pantfulini and Alparagatini. This play on words here is a function of symbolic equivalence: *zapato* is Spanish for "shoe," and Cantinflas substitutes other shoe types (*pantufla* [slipper] and *alpargata* [espadrille]) in the con artist's alias. Of course, the proper name is doubly unreliable. The proper name is already inappropriate as the criminal's false identity within the narrative, and it becomes in-appropriated as the subject of cantinflista play.

Cantinflas is always ersatz and never original, and the narrative tries to produce him as original, as self-identical. This drive toward self-identity is perhaps most manifest in the later sequences in the film when our hero suffers from amnesia after receiving a blow to the head, a typical conceit in physical comedy. When Cantinflas wakes up after being knocked unconscious, a doctor asks him who he is, and Cantinflas responds:

Cantinflas: ¿Y a usted qué le importa?

Doctor: ¿Cuál es su nombre, joven?

Cantinflas: ¿Y usted no lo sabe?

Doctor: No, yo no.

Cantinflas: Y entonces, ¿para qué me pregunta a mí? Yo tampoco sé.

Cantinflas: What's it to you?

Doctor: What is your name, young man?

Cantinflas: You don't know?

Doctor: No, I don't.

Cantinflas: Then, why are you asking me? I also don't know.

Eventually, he is misidentified and begins to play the part of another man. The remaining players get desperate, assaulting Cantinflas in order to jog his memory so he can remember his identity. The stakes of the initial interview are echoed in an absurdist way with three different characters breaking into his room and bonking him on the head. Cantinflas's memory may be back but he remains elusive in a police interrogation:

Police: ¿Quiere decirme quién es usted?

Cantinflas: ¿Usted quién cree que sea yo?

Police: El Duque de Alfanje.

Cantinflas: Pues se equivoca usted. No ande creyendo eso.

Police: Entonces, ¿quién pretende ser?

Cantinflas: Yo no pretendo nada. Yo soy quien soy y no me parezco a nadie. Soy el bellboy número 13.

Police: Would you care to tell me who you are?

Cantinflas: Who do you think I am?

Police: The Duke of Alfanje.

Cantinflas: Well, you are mistaken. Don't go around believing that.

Police: Then, who are you supposed to be?

Cantinflas: I don't suppose [pretend] anything. I am who I am and I don't resemble anyone else. I am the bellboy number 13.

Cantinflas reveals his true self: he does not pretend to be anything at all. A succinct distillation of the logic undergirding the cantinflista play with proper names—"Yo soy quien soy y no me parezco a nadie" (I am who I am and I don't resemble anyone else)—his self-identity is a constant movement between undifferentiated and differentiated states. There is no pretense or claim to specificity ("no pretendo nada") and yet he resembles no one else. Cantinflas does not express but rather transmits the sensations of language; his bouts of relajo become hypnotic sessions with the body struggling against the unknown.[82] With signification in suspension, the plasticity of language provides the ground for sensory experience.

Portilla identifies three component movements to Cantinflas's relajo: a displacement of attention, a movement of de-solidarity with the proposed value, and an invitation to others to participate in de-solidarity.[83] This displacement of attention does not entail being attentive to something else but being attentive differently: "con una mirada distraída miro las cosas en torno a mí sin 'poner atención' en ninguna en particular; la conciencia se desliza de una a otra sin que medie para nada el propósito voluntario de explorar atentamente" (with a distracted gaze [I] look at things around me without "paying attention" to any in particular; consciousness glides from one to the next without the mediation of the purposeful will to explore attentively).[84] Portilla clarifies this process through an instructive aural metaphor: meaning functions as sound, and relajo as background noise, a noise that risks dissipating as a single emission but becomes sustained interference through echoes and subsequent emissions.[85] How do we make noise the object of attention without making it meaningful sound? We listen distractedly, less shifting focus or intention onto a new object than changing our apperception or extension. Relajo's distracted glance does not call for refocusing central vision but moving from central vision to peripheral vision (without making it become central). In other words, turning to the peripheral not to disclose its objects but to give "an account of the conditions of emergence for something."[86] This is a mode of apperception that ranges and does not scope: what is the shape of the field of vision (or signification) rather than what is *in* the field of vision (or what is significant). This model yields a subject enmeshed in a world that is always unfinished rather than removed (or located discretely) from the world that is always meaningful. The subject is not constituted before encountering the world but is constituted in the encounter with the world, and this means that publicness is more a generative matrix than a group of individual subjects. These reflective (not reflexive) responses figure the publicness here not as a sphere of exchanges (and rational communicative acts from individuals with interiority) but as a cacophony of resonation, hence *de*-solidarity. For Lauren Berlant, solidarity is sentimentally affective and effective for politically motivated agents because it requires minimal affective likeness and only the shared recognition of a problem.[87] Berlant calls for cultivating new kinds of "affective collective ground" by embracing the *form* of solidarity, and the de-solidarity of relajo's peripheral vision represents exactly this type of new collective ground. With the relajo, we are not bound to the "problem that *has brought us together* [italics in the original]" but are unbound to avoid being brought together at all.[88] The relajo produces "la comunidad de los no comunicantes,"[89] loosely translated as "the community of both noncommunicators and non*communicants*." A public without communication and without communion does not rely on cognitively reflexive acts but on sensuous extension and orientation.

Articulating vernacular modernism to relajo as peripheral vision means thinking self-reflexivity as a movement of de-solidarity, less indicative of a "shrinking subject" than a de-solidary (extensive and projective) action.[90] Peripheral vision reorients bodies and space *and* invites others to sustain and propagate this makeshift space.

Concluding with the bullfighting spectacle in *Ni sangre ni arena*—a sequence that finds Cantinflas both inside and outside the bullring—means understanding how Cantinflas toggles between textual archetypical (and parodic) persona, paratextual star comedian, and extratextual amateur bullfighter. Examining how these different registers shape the public horizon of reception returns us to the Zabludovsky interview from the beginning of the chapter. During the interview, where the actor Mario Moreno reflects on his national legacy and recalls his origin story, the journalist asks Cantinflas about his interest in bullfighting. Cantinflas responds:

Comencé a torear y me gustó. Lo curioso es que cuando yo toreo, pienso hacerlo en serio. Lo siento. Y no me salen las cosas muy en serio, que digamos. Y el toro, yo creo que también me entiende así, porque pocas veces me ha agarrado. Y colabora conmigo. Yo no sé si él verá que en realidad yo no soy una gente que quiere hacerle mucho daño. Pero se presta a todo lo que yo le hago.

I began to bullfight and I liked it. The curious thing is that when I fight, I think I'm doing it seriously. I feel that way. And yet things don't turn out very seriously, let's say. And the bull, I think he also understands me that way, because he seldom hurts me. And he collaborates with me. I don't know if he sees that I am someone who doesn't really want to hurt him. But he lends himself to what I do to him.

More than his brief history of popular entertainment types or his discussion of national popular sectors, Cantinflas's musings on bullfighting provide perhaps the most insight into his comedic practice. Both operate within a comic frame founded on a shared lack of seriousness. Both require a collaboration between players that organizes the social field differently via implicit engagement and ritual performance. Both suppose a levity where serious intention yields unserious results, a mutual lending of the self as unserious attachment, where serious feeling does not necessarily yield serious action.

Bullfighting provides a fitting analogue to this comedic film practice. A so-called blood sport, "good bullfighting is about being 'moved,'" about the projection of emotion into the audience through the display of tactical immobility despite (or because of) the physical proximity of the animal.[91] Cantinflismo similarly depends on knowing when to sidestep as a way of orchestrating suspense and affect, knowing how to recoordinate space in unexpected and pleasurable ways. More particularly, Cantinflas's comments suggest that proximity subtends both practices. The outcome of a bullfight is a function of both the bullfighter's proximity to the bull *and* the audience's proximity to the contiguous bullring. The latter plays a fundamental role: its cathectic energies also affect the motions and emotions of the players in the ring. Thinking our comedian as bullfighter and the cinema as a bullring means recasting the conventional scopic economy of cinema. The functional (textually structured) contiguity of screen and theater space is instrumental to the production of the comedic effect just as much as the comedian's (unserious) engagement with the world. No longer a noncorporeal gaze, film comedy spectatorship restores the body and the senses in a space that is lived because proximate and not represented or conceived.

When we speak figuratively of "sidestepping the issue" through linguistic equivocation, we recognize the production of a tangent space, a space encoded differently, a space related to a central question that it endlessly avoids, a mock classical experience we are invited to join. The chase sequence represents a paradigmatic form of coordination of space in classical Hollywood cinema, and a chase sequence in a Cantinflas film recoordinates this space differently. *Ni sangre ni arena* opens with an extended sequence in and around the bullfighting arena. Cantinflas is outside the arena, scheming to get inside to watch his idol in action. Failing to sell enough cigars and embroiled in conflict with other salesmen and eventually the police, Cantinflas decides to approach the guards, claiming that the troublemaker is over yonder and that they should follow in pursuit. The character performs the type of doubling-as-misdirection that the film narrative also enacts: he is the troublemaker in question but produces another self off screen. Cantinflas is both on screen and off screen, here and there (and by extension now and then). In effect, Cantinflas has no place. The sequence is motivated not by a logic of suspense or causality but rather as a matter of space: a winding chase that fails to constitute a path, fragmentary shots unable to produce an abstract trajectory or conceived space. To yearn for plot advancement and narrative resolution would be to set a destination to the path, to foreclose this peripheral space, to avoid becoming immersed in a space not subject to an abstract code (of classical narrative space).

Later in the sequence, Cantinflas is both spectator and spectacle in a way that both complicates the hierarchic coordination of narrative space in the text and models a different horizon of reception. The figurative splitting as evasive tactic (here/there) becomes diegetic splitting in the film narrative (pelado/Manolete) and becomes literal splitting on the screen (Cantinflas/Mario Moreno). Cantinflismo unbinds: Cantinflas emancipates words from phrases and sounds from words and invites us to experience a sensuous relationship to meaningful speech. But how is this unbinding sustained, particularly given the restorative narrative conclusions characteristic of the genre? To suppose that a narrative resolution binds and undoes the work of cantinflismo is to ignore the para- and extratextual dimension of the star text and to bracket the materiality of the experience of cinema. Sustaining this makeshift space depends on thinking cinema not as communicative interface but as a spatial practice determined by the open temporality of reception. In other words, Latin American film comedy offers a mode of experience that couples an open temporality determined by the contingency of future reception (and not the narrative ambiguity of high modernism) with the motor-sensory orientation of an image that is contiguous or proximate. If Hollywood cinema became classical by codifying the proper relations among viewer, projector, and screen—separating the diegetic space from the theater space through methods both technological (e.g., continuity editing or the multiple-reel film) and narrative (identification routed through a goal-oriented protagonist)—then Cantinflas films mock classicism by sidestepping these proper relations. His relajo makes the cinema experience an ersatz bullfight, one that plays with the spatial relations between theater and screen to unserious and denervating effect. The coming of sound added another arena in which to play with these proper relations, and the next chapter considers how sound made the steadfast distinction between narrative space and theatrical space more porous, analyzing Niní Marshall's vocal antics to demonstrate further how these spaces were rearranged in Latin America's mock classicism.

CHAPTER 2

The Call of the Screen

Niní Marshall and the Radiophonic Stardom of Argentine Cinema

In one of her last public interviews, in 1993, the beloved comedian Niní Marshall was asked to reflect on her prolific career and to address whether women could be funny.[1] Marshall began her career as a radio personality portraying dozens of personae before becoming one of the most prolific film stars of the golden age of Argentine cinema. The comedian crafted her own scripts, using orthographic and grammar mistakes as well as an array of accents to produce a repertoire of beloved characters that represented both the Old World inhabitants of turn-of-the-century Buenos Aires as well as the more recent migrants from the interior provinces. Marshall's response speaks to the ways women were evicted in ways both textual and material from sites of production:

> Como actriz no tenía problemas, algunos trataron de entorpecer mi trabajo de libretista. Los citados prejuicios que consideraban poco apta a la mujer para ocupar lugares que eran privativos de los hombres ... más aún en mi caso, porque sostenían que las mujeres no tenían el sentido del humor como los hombres.
>
> As an actress I had no problems, [although] some tried to obstruct my work as a writer. The aforementioned prejudices made it unsuitable for a woman to occupy places that were exclusive to men ... more so in my case, because they believed that women did not have a sense of humor as men did.[2]

This chapter elaborates on Marshall's response, exploring both the material determinants and textual conditions of her stardom. With regard to the former, I chart the emergence of Marshall's stardom through the competing claims to Marshall's screen presence. The actress was embroiled in contract disputes that became newspaper headlines in October 1939. These disputes provide insights into the particular industrial practices of the nascent studios in Buenos Aires that complicate any facile alignment with the Hollywood studio system. Moreover, the fact of *one* actress having *three* "exclusive" personae for *three* studios represents a case of aural stardom that complicates image-based star studies. Accomplishing this meant separating the preestablished radio characters from their star's body and voice behind the scenes while also rearticulating their relation on screen. The textual (and paratextual) construction of this star delineates a cinema less fixated on sync than forms of ventriloquial play that produce an implicated space loosely contiguous with the theatrical space.

A STAR IS BORN: RADIO, CINEMA, AND STARDOM

October 1939 was a busy month for Niní Marshall, one of the most popular film stars of the golden age of Argentine cinema. Her first film for Estudios Filmadores Argentinos (EFA), *Cándida,* premiered on October 4, 1939, in the downtown movie palace Cine Monumental and became an immediate box-office success. Marshall wrapped production in mid-October on her third Catita feature, *Casamiento en Buenos Aires* (Manuel Romero, 1940), for a second studio, Lumiton. The month would climax with a protracted contract dispute featuring a third studio, Argentina Sono Film, played out in the pages of both daily periodicals and weekly film journals. The series of escalating articles appearing in the daily newspaper *La nación* are not simply the few traces of this feud but were quite literally the terrain where the contest played out, launched by a deliberately provocative and misleading press release by one studio hoping to strong-arm and poach the talent of another smaller studio. As a radio personality turned movie star, Marshall provides an excellent site through which to unpack the industrial-historical and aesthetic-narrative relations of radio and early sound cinema.

Let's set the stage for October 1939. Niní Marshall, already an established radio personality, began her film career first with Lumiton as well as later with EFA in the late 1930s, before a much-publicized contract dispute with a third studio, Argentina Sono Film, arguably transformed the foundations of the country's nascent star system. The three studios involved were the largest studios in Argentina, whose film industry had been growing steadily since the transition to sound. Local filmmakers released thirteen films in 1935, twenty-eight in 1937, forty-one in 1938, and an average of fifty films each year between 1939 and 1942.[3] By 1937, Buenos Aires hosted nine film studios and thirty production companies. The dominant narrative of Argentine cinema in the period begins with the arrival of sound in 1933, traces the emergence of genres, directors, and stars in relation to the circulation of popular culture, and charts the growth of the domestic studios in the late 1930s and early 1940s. The growth of national cinema was determined on the one hand by Hollywood classical cinema and on the other hand by parallel forms of local mass culture and the incorporation of Argentine popular culture (i.e., *sainetes* and tangos).[4] With regard to the former, Hollywood cinema provided the material technologies of film production and exhibition, the film product that sustained continued moviegoing, and the models for a burgeoning studio system. With regard to the latter, local subjects provided narrative content that differentiated Argentine films within a crowded marketplace. Both the borrowed industrial structure and the co-optation of popular culture by forms of mass culture usually lead to the cinema being characterized as a cultural apparatus of the state. In fact, the golden age period of the late 1930s and 1940s is often discussed in relation to the rise of Peronism, the military coup of 1943, and the election of Perón in 1945. An industrial structure using popular content (as did Argentine cinema) aligns with the corporative nationalism and populist content of Peronism. Cinema and mass culture were implicated in the intertwined emergence of polarizing class stratification and an integrative nationalist rhetoric that was conducive to the rise of Juan Perón.[5] The restricted political system ushered in by the military coup of 1930, its conservative economic interventionism, and the massive internal migration revived labor militancy in the 1930s and Argentine workers' sense of exploitation, creating a receptive audience for Juan Perón's populist message of the 1940s and 1950s.

Alongside film equipment, film genres, and narrative forms, stardom may be regarded as one of the cultural technologies imported from Hollywood, a technology that included not only Hollywood films but also the material practices of publicity and the ideologies underlying stardom.[6] Paradigmatic (classical Hollywood) star studies rely on film roles, biographical information, and extracinematic discourses in order to constellate the star as a visible social icon. Star studies outside classical Hollywood often forget that the "star as social icon" is an artifact and cultural production. Put simply, they take stardom as a pregiven category rather than assess how stardom as a cultural phenomenon emerges. Often consigned to a series of star-is-born narratives read symptomatically, could star studies outside Hollywood think stardom genealogically rather than ontologically? Neepa Majumdar's discussion of stardom in early Indian cinema reconstructs its stars' cultural orbit but also traces how the emergence of the concept of a star needed to be rearticulated to existing local forms of entertainment. Majumdar argues that film discourse in the Indian context delinked stardom from the ideologies of conspicuous consumption and visibility underpinning Hollywood stardom, which were antithetical to the project of Indian nationalism.[7] Film stardom outside Hollywood, then, borrows from Hollywood mechanisms while receiving local inflections as a function of the material conditions of mass culture and the particular social horizon of experience. Stardom, therefore, provides another arena through which to tease out and complicate the foreign/autochthonous binary undergirding film histories, only less as a function of the content of the star's persona or her biography than as a function of how stardom emerges and operates as cultural technology. The historically situated film practices in early sound film production in Argentina reveal the problems of applying a framework based on Hollywood stars to their Argentine counterparts. These Argentine stars emerged during the transition to sound, decades after the consolidation of film stardom in the classical Hollywood period. The transition in Argentina was characterized by a demographic transformation in the working class that preceded and endured during the Peronist regime, consolidated in part through a mediascape where other forms of mass culture—especially radio—played larger roles.

Although historians often cite the overwhelming presence of radios and movie theaters in neighborhoods as indicative of the conservative impact of mass culture, film studies has attempted a more concerted investigation into both the empirical audiences as well as the narrative content of these early sound films. Tamara Falicov, for instance, credits the cinema as "a special cultural space, an avenue for working people to develop their own views on Argentina."[8] Arguing that working-class people were excluded from political and economic arenas, she credits the progressive themes and socially conscious filmmaking, determined by the class identity of select filmmakers, for affording a cultural arena as counterpublic. In order to characterize mass culture differently, Falicov foregrounds the progressive elements of local content, privileging the social-folkloric and urban realist genres for their progressive realism (at the expense of most melodramas and comedies). Complicating histories that reduce mass culture to tools of hegemonic capture, however, means not only looking at semantic content but also syntactic structures in narrative forms. Further, mass culture gets too readily aligned with Hollywood industrial practices, and many histories avoid exploring how mass culture becomes "mass" outside the Anglo-European context. October 1939 provides a window onto the Argentine film industrial landscape, where the growing screen popularity of a radio personality and the competing interests and strategies of rival studios demonstrate how mock classicism was taking shape through film industrial practices evolving from and determined by radio industrial practices.

Radio has broadened our understanding of the mediascape during the golden age period and has provided an important rejoinder to analyses that too quickly graft the industrial filmmaking in Argentina onto the Hollywood studio system. Radio histories make us acutely aware that Argentina's industrial cinema did not emerge ex nihilo through the importation of Hollywood structures but was built on (and perhaps another iteration of) a well-disputed media landscape. In Argentina, radio in the 1930s was a widespread medium, heavily indebted to the importation of technologies in the 1920s from Europe and the United States. The two most popular radio stations—Radio El Mundo and Radio Belgrano (formerly Radio Nacional)—offered a similar repertoire of classical and popular music, *radionovelas,* and comedic programs. Marshall became a major radio personality for Radio El Mundo before launching her film career. The escalating competition between the two stations came to a head with the eventual officialization of radio diffusion by the state in the late 1930s.[9] Subsequently, radio sound technologies played an important role during the transition to sound in cinema, determining not only technological developments that affected film production but also providing the material base for the nation's nascent studios. Among the early studios, Lumiton and Sociedad Impresora de Discos Electrofónicos (SIDE) were developed by entrepreneurs in sound technologies: radio pioneer Eduardo Susini and discography engineers the Murúa brothers, respectively; and Establecimientos Filmadores Argentinos (EFA) was developed out of national laboratory facilities that expanded to build studios equipped for sound recording.

Despite these industrial-historical relations, the role of radio in the emergence and development of this golden age cinema in recent scholarship in Latin American film studies either foregrounds the social (nationalizing) function of mass media within a cultural studies framework or examines the diegetic uses of radio in film narrative and the borrowed narrative conventions from radionovelas. Within the cultural studies framework, historian Matthew Karush examines how cinema and mass culture promoted the integration of the migrant into a common national culture.[10] Comedies for Karush function pedagogically, endorsing an assimilationist project because they provide types that we deride in a negative identificatory mode. In a less symptomatic vein, Ana López's recent work on the radiophonic imaginary of Latin American cinema astutely examines how radio and mass culture provide both a material and discursive framework for the evolving formal and narrative practices of early sound cinema in the region, from featuring prominently as diegetic setting or plot device to determining serialized narrative structure or syntactic narrative operations.[11] Foregrounding the sociocultural function of the technology (its overdetermined status as cultural apparatus of the state) or its influence on popular cinema narratives (radio as plot device), however, has meant ignoring other significant aspects of the radiophonic underpinnings of Argentine golden age cinema, particularly those pertaining to film industrial practices as well as sound aesthetics and form.

Radio complicates the historical narrative of the golden age of Argentine cinema on multiple fronts, lending cinema its industrial structures and sound technologies, its model of broadcast stardom, and its sound aesthetics and narrative content. The case of Niní Marshall touches on all these fronts. October 1939 provides an opening onto how radio industrial practices shaped and were transformed in cinema. If we follow Jane Gaines's Marxist history of Hollywood stardom as product differentiation and monopoly control and conceive the actor as labor in addition to media image or persona, then Marshall demonstrates how film stardom in Argentina became defined in an evolving relation to "radio personalities" and Hollywood forms of stardom. This means thinking the star system not merely as a semiotic construction or a poststructural iteration but also as an economic strategy used by studios to secure control of exhibition and distribution markets.[12] Gaines's emphasis on the emergence of a star system in the mid-1910s amid studio bids for monopoly control needs to be resituated historically in the case of Argentine golden age cinema. First, if the Hollywood star emerges through the transformation of the picture personality of early cinema and the articulation of a private person in 1909–1914, then Marshall suggests that the Argentine star emerges with the transformation of the radio star in the 1930s, relativizing and thus expanding the variable and sometimes anachronistic local meanings of *early* in early cinema.[13] Second, if product differentiation and market penetration shape the contours of the star system, then we need to consider how the market in Argentina is contested differently, with bids for monopoly control operating distinctly. The market share of national productions is already limited in relation to Hollywood and European productions, and parallel media technologies provide the material basis for the early studio system in the region. Additionally, if radio stardom in the American context during the golden age of radio from 1934 to 1941 borrowed its strategies from cinema, then in an inversion of the American narrative, radio arguably furnished the framework for the development of cinema's star system in the Argentine context.

BROUGHT TO YOU BY . . . RADIO-ERA MARSHALL

Niní Marshall's career began as a polyglot chanteuse on a minor station, Radio Municipal. According to Marshall's biographers, her characters were discovered when Marshall would joke and improvise between songs off the air. Goofing off between live broadcasts, she would perform a bit part as a Galician maid and cook, Cándida.[14] Marshall was persuaded to perform the character in the context of a larger comedic program, *El chalet de Pipita*. The success of her character prompted a sponsor, Llauró Soaps, to hire the performer for her own show in the larger and more prominent Radio El Mundo, an example of the radio industry practice of indirect advertising.[15] Marshall wrote the comedic scripts, often framed as a conversation with the former crooner Juan Carlos Thorry. Eventually, another sponsor for a popular department store, La Piedad, approached her about starting a different radio show. She developed the character of Catita, a second-generation working-class girl, modeled on the young women outside the recording studio who waited to get an autograph from Thorry. As Marshall describes, these women were "gossips, busybodies, and meddlers who dressed with bad taste, almost extravagantly. They represented a social stratum, the product of the tenements that existed in that period."[16] Despite the initial resistance of her sponsor, who feared that auditors would think themselves mocked, the character was a resounding success and eventually prompted studio owners to approach the actress to appear on screen.

Although initially apprehensive to appear on screen, fearing audiences would find her performance dissonant with their imagined characterizations, Marshall was persuaded by director and screenwriter Manuel Romero to appear as her most popular radio character, Catita, for the film studio Lumiton. Modeled after the indirect advertising of radio broadcasts—a particular company (e.g., Llauró Soaps or La Piedad Department Store) sponsors the radio hour of a particular character (e.g., Cándida or Catita, respectively)—Lumiton acquired the exclusive rights to a radio personality. Her success as Catita for Lumiton in her first feature-length films, *Mujeres que trabajan* (Manuel Romero, 1938) and *Divorcio en Montevideo* (Manuel Romero, 1939), resulted in EFA approaching the actress to develop her earlier radio personality in the feature-length film *Cándida* (Luis Bayón Herrera, 1939). Following the precedent of Lumiton and modeled on radio practices, EFA acquired the exclusive rights to this other radio personality. Lumiton and EFA did not contract the actor as labor but acquired the intellectual property rights over fictional characters for a discrete period of time as exclusive "sponsors." When Argentina Sono Film approached the actress in October 1939, Marshall signed a contract that represented an escalation in the monopolistic film industrial practices of the era. Three different studios, then, approached Marshall in the late 1930s. Marshall signed "exclusive" agreements with each studio. How can an "exclusive" film star appear simultaneously in films for three different studios and not be in breach of contract? Unlike the exclusivity of Hollywood stars, cemented by the 1937 decision over the no-competition clause in Bette Davis's contract in *Warner Bros Pictures Inc. v. Nelson,* the specifics of Marshall's contract exclusivity suggest one way that these early studios were as informed by Hollywood structures as they were by already extant media practices.[17] Marshall's contract dispute demonstrates how early industrial film practices recast radio's advertising and programming practices before gradually shifting to the division of labor more characteristic of classical Hollywood studios. Tracing these public debates as they played out in the local press and popular magazines demonstrates how discussing stardom in the Argentine context necessitates reconsidering the relation of body (and voice) and persona to questions of labor and property, respectively.

¿A QUIÉN PERTENECE CATITA? (WHO DOES CATITA BELONG TO?)

October 1939 began with news of the imminent premiere of *Cándida,* extolling the original script by the female comedian and radio personality: "En esta producción de la EFA se ha utilizado un libreto original de la citada intérprete en colaboración con Luis Bayón Herrera" (This production from EFA used an original script by the aforementioned actress written with the collaboration of Luis Bayón Herrera).[18] A few days after the film's premiere, news came out in the weekly column Por los estudios locales (Around the local studios) that the actress was in the process of concluding the film of *Casamiento en Buenos Aires* for Lumiton. The short news item added how the director, Manuel Romero, would conclude the film and move on to another feature he had not scripted: "La [próxima] película será dirigida por Manuel Romero quien por primera vez realizará un asunto que no ha sido escrito por él—actitud loable que señala un necesario cambio de ruta en la política de nuestros estudios—y producida por la Lumiton" (The film will be directed by Manuel Romero who for the first time will direct a script he has not written—a commendable attitude that marks a necessary change in direction in our studios' policy—and produced by Lumiton).[19]

This shift in studio policy is an early index of the broader industrial shift occurring at the time. This item offers a first clue into how film practices (as labor practices) in Argentina were evolving: a shift away from an artisanal mode reliant on content penned and directed by a singular organizing vision toward a more industrial mode with filmmaking broken into its component parts. A similar shift toward increased task differentiation and coordination was announced two days later by rival studio EFA when its head of production, Luis Bayón Herrera, agreed to a new role as in-house film director in a press release touting the company's "planes de reorganización" (reorganization plans).[20] Marshall's star persona was crucial to EFA's plans, as the reorganization was announced in a press release announcing the studio's plans to continue working with Marshall: "La popular actriz Niní Marshall se comprometió ayer con la EFA a animar en 1940 otra película para ese sello con su personaje de Cándida, que con mucho éxito de público acaba de hacer su absorbente presentación cinematográfica en el film de ese título, estrenado el miércoles último en el Monumental" (The popular actress Niní Marshall committed yesterday with EFA to star in 1940 in another film for the studio as her character Cándida, that with much box office success just made her engrossing film debut in the eponymous film, which premiered last Wednesday at the Monumental).[21]

This early contract announcement is the first in a series of exchanges and press releases concerning Marshall's film commitments. Marshall's much-publicized contract disputes crystallize this shift in policy: competing studio interests lobby both for greater task differentiation at the level of production and greater control over Marshall's laboring (star) body. The day after EFA's announcement, Argentina Sono Film released a misleading press release, announcing the hiring of Marshall in her capacity as Catita: Marshall "ha sido contratada ... por la Argentina Sono Film para aparecer en una producción de esta compañía que se comenzará a rodar a mediados del año próximo, y en la cual presentará de nuevo su personaje de Catita" (has been contracted by Argentina Sono Film to appear in a production for this company that will begin shooting in the middle of next year, and in which she will again present her character of Catita).[22] This announcement by the Sono Film mogul Angel Luis Mentasti staked a claim to a character owned in exclusivity by the rival studio, Lumiton. A few days later, Lumiton would respond in the pages of the same newspaper in the weekly column Por los estudios locales: "La Lumiton nos informa que la popular actriz Niní Marshall sólo podrá aparecer en su personaje de Catita durante 1939 y 1940, pese a la comunicación dada a conocer en estos días por otra productora local, en películas de su sello, de conformidad con el contrato entre ambas partes" (Lumiton informs us that the popular actress Niní Marshall can only appear in her character of Catita in 1939 and 1940, despite the announcement made recently by another local studio, in films made under its brand, as per the contract between both parties).[23]

La nación followed the back-and-forth disputes over the course of the next several days, describing the row as "el entredicho implícito planteado entre dos empresas productoras locales, la Argentina Sono Film y la Lumiton, a propósito de la actuación de la actriz Niní Marshall en su personaje de Catita en 1940" (the implicit dispute between two local production companies, Argentina Sono Film and Lumiton, concerning the performance of the actress Niní Marshall in her character of Catita in 1940).[24] This conflict reached a climax with a memorandum from studio owner Angel Luis Mentasti that included a transcript of the star's contract agreement. Mentasti maintained that he had been approached by a representative on behalf of Marshall who had expressed an explicit interest in working with the studio's director Luis César Amadori. The transcribed contract is reproduced here:

Buenos Aires, octubre 10 de 1939.
Sra D. Niní Marshall. Presente.
 De nuestra consideración: A fin de realizar las tareas preparatorias de la película que filmará usted para esta productora cinematográfica y confirmando las conversaciones mantenidas al respecto, rogamos a usted tenga a bien manifestarnos su conformidad con la fecha convenida

para la filmación de la misma: 15 de abril al 15 de junio de 1940, y con el honorario estipulado en la suma de cuarenta y cinco mil pesos m/n. Ha quedado también convenido que fuera de la película que está usted actualmente filmando en la 'Lumiton,' no podrá antes actuar con ninguna otra empresa fuera de la EFA, para la cual podrá realizar una película interpretando el personaje de Cándida y no el de Catita. Por último se ha convenido que dirigirá a usted el Sr. Luis César Amadori.

Saludamos a usted muy atte.

(Firmado) Angel Luis Mentasti, presidente de la Cinematográfica Argentina S.A.

Expreso a ustedes mi conformidad con los términos que anteceden.

(Firmado) Niní Marshall.

Buenos Aires, October 10, 1939.

Mrs. D. Niní Marshall. Present.

Dear Sirs/Madams: In order to complete the preparatory tasks for the picture you will film for our studio and confirming the conversations carried out in this regard, we ask you declare your agreement to the dates convened for its production: 15 April to 15 June 1940, and with the stipulated salary in the sum of forty-five thousand Argentine pesos. It is also agreed that outside of the film you are currently filming with Lumiton, you cannot act for any company other than EFA, for which you may complete one film interpreting the character of Cándida and not Catita. Finally, it is also agreed that Mr. Luis César Amadori will direct.

Yours very sincerely.

(Signed) Angel Luis Mentasti, president of the Cinematográfica Argentina S.A.

I express my agreement with the preceding terms.

(Signed) Niní Marshall.[25]

Mentasti's letter concludes by reiterating that Marshall would appear as Catita in a film for the studio in 1940, despite the fact that the above agreement makes no explicit mention of that arrangement. The unusual transcription of a star contract in a popular daily periodical is unprecedented. Not only does the document provide the actress's salary,[26] but it attempts to bind the actress to the studio in perpetuity. The agreement is ostensibly to appear in one film and to secure her availability during a two-month period, but it becomes pretense for disallowing her continued involvement with other studios. Despite the studio's insistence that the actress would be appearing as Catita, the agreement makes no explicit reference to their joint project being a vehicle for Catita, a fact that Marshall herself made clear the following day in her own statement.

A propósito del contrato de una intérprete

Conocen nuestros lectores, por informaciones insertadas en estas columnas, el entredicho implícito planteado entre dos empresas productoras locales, la Argentina Sono Film y la Lumiton, a propósito de la actuación de la actriz Niní Marshall en su personaje de Catita en 1940. En nuestra edición del miércoles último se anticipó que la primera de las compañías nombradas había contratado a la intérprete para que apareciese —en la caracterización de su personaje de Catita— en un film de su sello, que se rodaría a mediados del año próximo. Publicada esta noticia, la Lumiton hizo llegar a nuestro poder un comunicado — reproducido, en lo substancial, en "Por los estudios locales" en nuestra edición del domingo último— en el que se afirmaba que "la actriz Niní Marshall seguirá actuando como Catita exclusivamente con Lumiton durante este y todo el año próximo, conforme al contrato que tiene subscripto en ese sentido". Así las cosas, el director general de la Argentina Sono Film, D. Angel Luis Mentasti, nos remitió ayer una nueva comunicación, firmada, en que ratifica y apoya la información original de su empresa en la siguiente forma:

"A la Argentina Sono Film (C. A. S. A. C. I.) le fué ofrecida el día 8 del actual, por medio de un representante, la labor de la intérprete Niní Marshall (Catita), quien, según lo afirmó dicho representante, deseaba filmar una película bajo la dirección de Luis César Amadori. Accedimos a tratar el asunto y luego de conversar con la Sra. Marshall y su esposo, se llegó a celebrar el contrato que transcribimos textualmente:

"Buenos Aires, octubre 10 de 1939. Sra. D. Niní Marshall. Presente.

"De nuestra consideración: A fin de realizar las tareas preparatorias de la película que filmará usted para esta productora cinematográfica y confirmando las conversaciones mantenidas al respecto, rogamos a usted tenga a bien manifestarnos su conformidad con la fecha convenida para la filmación de la misma: 15 de abril al 15 de junio de 1940, y con el honorario estipulado en la suma de cuarenta y cinco mil pesos m|n.

"Ha quedado también convenido que fuera de la película que está usted actualmente filmando en la "Lumiton", no podrá antes actuar con ninguna otra empresa fuera de la E. F. A., para la cual podrá realizar una película interpretando el personaje de Cándida y no el de Catita.

"Por último se ha convenido que dirigirá a usted el Sr. Luis César Amadori.

"Saludamos a usted muy atte. (Firmado) Angel Luis Mentasti, presidente de la Cinematográfica Argentina, S. A.".

"Expreso a ustedes mi conformidad con los términos que anteceden. (Firmado) Niní Marshall".

La Argentina Sono Film, según se nos manifestó anoche, se propone hacer efectivo el compromiso transcripto y presentar en consecuencia en su programa para la temporada próxima una película animada por la actriz Niní Marshall en su personaje de Catita.

FIGURE 5. Niní Marshall's contract dispute makes headlines in *La nación*.

Marshall weighed in on this controversy with her own correspondence to Lumiton, which the studio made available to *La nación* the following day. Marshall assured the general manager of Lumiton, Julio Lofiego, that she had neither appointed someone to speak on her behalf nor had she expressed a particular desire to work with Luis César Amadori. She instead recounts the events that transpired:

> A raíz de habérseme propuesto la realización de una película para la Argentina Sono Film, tuvimos en mi casa particular una conferencia con los dirigentes de esa productora en la que se consideró la posibilidad de esa realización, firmándose por mi parte la carta transcripta en el comunicado prealudido; pero debo significarle que en ese documento no se establece mi obligación de interpretar el personaje de Catita, cuya exclusividad corresponde a la Lumiton, como así lo manifesté verbalmente a la Argentina Sono Film.
>
> Because I had been offered the chance to make a film for Argentina Sono Film, we had a meeting in my home with the studio's executives, in which we considered the possibility of this project and I signed the letter transcribed in the earlier press release; but I must clarify that this document does not establish my obligation to portray the character of Catita, whose exclusivity belongs to Lumiton, as I verbally expressed to Argentina Soon Film.[27]

Marshall correctly points out that the rights to her radio personality remain with Lumiton and are not claimed in the Sono Film contract. Sono Film had only secured the performer's availability for a two-month period. If the Lumiton and EFA contracts were modeled after radio sponsorship agreements for particular characters, then Sono Film's agreement contracted for the actress's labor. The concluding sentences of the Sono Film contract point to this shift, insisting that beyond one further Cándida film for EFA and the already-completed film for Lumiton, the actress would be unable to appear in other studios' films, but fail to clarify that this would be due to her schedule and not the lapse of rights to the characters.

The controversy concludes the following day with a final press statement from Argentina Sono Film:

> Con el deseo de dar término a la discusión pública suscitada por la contratación de una de sus artistas, la Argentina Sono Film manifiesta que, de acuerdo con el contrato que ha hecho conocer textualmente, filmará una película con la Sra. Niní Marshall, entre los días 15 de abril y 15 de junio de 1940. En dicha película la Sra. Marshall desempeñará el papel que la empresa le asigne, de acuerdo con el director y autores. La exclusión de la posibilidad de que dicha intérprete encarne el personaje de Catita no surge en forma alguna del contrato, que, por lo contrario, veda a la intérprete—a favor de la Argentina Sono Film—utilizar dicha caracterización en futuras filmaciones.

In the hope of concluding the public discussion generated by the contract of one of its artists, Argentina Sono Film expresses that, in accordance with the contract made known in print, it will produce a movie with Mrs. Niní Marshall, between 15 April and 15 June 1940. In this film Mrs. Marshall will play the role the studio assigns her, in accordance with the director and authors. Barring the actress's portrayal of the character of Catita does not appear in any way in the contract, which, on the contrary, prohibits the actress—in favor of Argentina Sono Film—from using said characterization in future productions.[28]

Lumiton would dispute this final claim and actually fast-tracked two additional Catita films in production in 1940 in order to ensure it got its money's worth from its earlier agreement with Marshall. More importantly, however, rather than insisting on the transfer of the rights to the characters, Sono Film secures the actress herself. This was the innovation of Argentina Sono Film. Marshall's contract dispute presents a window onto film industrial practices in transition, a shift toward increased integration coupled with skill specialization and task differentiation. A legal loophole, Argentina Sono Film insists that she will not portray her beloved radio character but rather "the role the studio assigns her"—a role, we shall see, that was a thinly disguised copy of Catita. This industrial change meant separating the preestablished radio character (Catita and Cándida) from its star's body and voice (Mrs. Niní Marshall) behind the scenes while preserving the radio characterizations on screen.

This public controversy around a star contract reveals a shift in industrial practices: from leasing the character as brand to claiming the character as property, a shift from the actress as contractor to the actress as salaried worker. The case of early sound film stardom in Argentina arguably has less in common with classical Hollywood studio stardom than with later American broadcast stardom. The broadcast star operated less as the hermetic textual system or discrete articulation of image and private person of the moving picture star than as a more overt commodity and promotional platform. Classical Hollywood film stardom supposed the star as a limited commodity with a rarity value: each time a star made an appearance, her currency slipped, or her value would be spent. Broadcast stardom and its ties to advertising supposed a different logic, one less tied to rarity ensured through the centralized control of screen persona and private person than to frequency reliant on a loose uniformity between "star and product brand."[29] Marshall's unusual "exclusivity" is a function of indirect advertising practices as well as the different logic of broadcast stardom, an exclusivity driven less by rarity of appearance than by branding rights. Her contract negotiations suggest a shift from a character or radio personality as *brand* to a star as *labor*.

The transition from broadcast stardom to film stardom in early Argentine sound cinema also plays out in the relationship between professional existence and private personality. A key difference between film stardom and broadcast stardom in the American context was how stage names (or performers with an articulated private person) were less significant than characters-as-brands in broadcast media. Much like the picture personality of early cinema, the radio personality in Argentina already seldom articulated the private personality to the professional existence of the locutor and the brand awareness of the character.[30] In the Argentine context, this was motivated in part precisely because of the logic of radio personality as brand.[31] The Argentine case of Marshall demonstrates how her stardom was a matter of slowly articulating a private person to the radio personality, a shift from a characterization incarnated to a role performed by an actress. We went to the movies to see Catita in the flesh, but now we go watch Niní Marshall on screen. This subtle distinction is made evident in the credit sequences of Marshall's Lumiton films after October 1939. Niní Marshall does not appear by name in the credits. Instead, the credits simply herald Catita before listing the other players and personnel involved with the film. Argentina Sono Film, on the other hand, foregrounded the actress and her stage name, going so far as to have her role for her debut film for the studio have the same first name (i.e., Niní Reboredo) and bear the star's name in the film title, *Hay que educar a Niní (Educating Niní)* (Luis César Amadori, 1940).

Despite these comparisons, the historical emergence and consolidation of film and radio occur differently in the United States and Argentina. American broadcast consolidation occurs in the 1930s and through the postwar period so that radio and television stardom borrowed star management strategies from extant film studio paradigms. On the other hand, film industrial production in Argentina reaches its heights with radio already relatively consolidated by the late 1930s so that film stardom emerges from extant radio practices (as well as Hollywood studio practices). American radio stardom meant transforming the persona of the sound-film comedy star to "fit" radio: "the star of the talkie is seen and is heard, and in a close-up can almost be tasted. But the radio star is present only to the ear."[32] In the case of a radio star such as Marshall becoming an eventual sound-film comedy star, the opposite holds true. The industrial and economic structures that supported radio carried over to Argentine golden age cinema, determining how stars were used and what types of stars would succeed.

THE SIREN CALL OF THE SCREEN

Marshall as broadcast star allows us to complicate the narrative of transition cinema in Argentina on two fronts: comedy as a film genre (genre) and the female body on screen (gender) have proven historical sites for unpacking "the industry's own social and aesthetic contradictions between debased early 'attractions' and bourgeois ideals of narrative integration."[33] If the classical mode of address meant multireel features constructing narrative diegeses that absorbed spectators, then how to account for the spectacular attractions and episodic structures that characterized the enduring slapstick genre? As Maggie Hennefeld claims, "the comic series provided an important bridge for the industry between one-reel shorts and the rise of the feature film, the standard commodity form of classical cinema."[34] Furthermore, using the case of the slapstick genre in American silent cinema, Hennefeld also argues for the plastic bodies of female comediennes in the transition from early cinema to classical cinema. She charts "the emergence of film syntax through the visual metamorphosis of women's bodies."[35] In other words, the experimentation and play with female comedians' bodies provided a testing ground for teasing the limits of narrative space and the development of continuity editing conventions. Hennefeld insists that unruly women's bodies "functioned as screens for negotiating the medium's own transformations during a period defined by formal messiness and class instability."[36] This invites a similar question in the case of Niní Marshall and Argentine cinema: how do her shape-shifting characterizations and malleable voice negotiate transformations in film form during the historical transition to sound cinema? Marshall's "unruly" voice provides a testing ground for sound film practice.

Answering this question means turning to sound studies and its characterization of the transition to sound. The intelligibility of classical cinema was thrown for a loop with the emergence of sound, opening up a new process of transition characterized by formal experimentation. Standardizing film production and removing the contingency of exhibition secured through continuity editing needed to be updated given sound technologies. If continuity editing secured a narrative space or diegesis distinct from the theatrical space, then sound made this steadfast distinction porous once again. Comedy and female voices once again prove a useful site through which to trace the rearrangement of these spaces. The reconstruction of the diegesis in the sound era relied on gradually learned sound conventions that differentiated diegetic and nondiegetic sound and produced a sonic vraisemblable. In his study of early sound Hollywood cinema, Michael Slowik thoroughly documents early film music and sound experiments and coins the term *diegetic withdrawal* to discuss how the diegetic/nondiegetic distinction is erected gradually through the course of a film, as music that initially features an explicit source slowly drifts toward increased ambiguity in later sections of the same film. Slowik demonstrates that the drift from diegetic to nondiegetic occurs through the presentation of "other worlds," defined as "any situation that differs markedly from familiar, material reality . . . [which] tended to be white Christian Americans living in a large American city."[37] These sites of exoticism and heightened emotion are ostensibly all racialized and feminine bodies. Instances of music and sound effects with ambiguous diegetic sound sources coincide with these "other" bodies on screen, loosely justified in narrative terms so as to naturalize the apparatus—for example, "The film's discontinuity and foreboding music cues can thus be read as an expression of [a female character's] mental condition"—papering over discontinuity and securing the separation of narrative space from theater space.[38] Slowik casts this 1930s interest in exoticism and fantasy as simply a testament to "the creation of escapist cinema"; however, I would argue that the historical process of transition to sound Slowik describes is a reconfiguration of classicism, a rearrangement of narrative space and theater space secured through racialized and feminized bodies.[39] Slowik provides the tools through which to think about this historical transition differently.

If women's bodies were the ground for instantiating the distinction between diegetic and nondiegetic sound in the early sound period, delineating the play with Marshall's voice means not simply cataloguing her characterizations but tracing how the diegesis as such was erected in Argentine cinema. Recall that constructing the diegesis means carving out a narrative space in relation (in opposition) to theatrical space. The arrival of sound upset the assumed classical separation between screen and theater space, and sound film practices in studio-era Hollywood worked to reinstantiate this separation. Latin American sound film comedies demonstrate how outside Hollywood this relation was renegotiated differently, less a discrete narrative space than a proximate screen or social horizon of experience. Put another way, if early sound cinema was a ventriloquist act learning to dissimulate, sound film comedy and particularly Marshall's many characterizations suggest a mock classical variation on this ventriloquist effect.

Much like her labor becoming more securely contracted off screen, we can tease out a similar narrative on screen, from a voice occupying multiple characters for different studios to a stricter yoking of voice and body in later films. On film, we bore witness to Cándida and Catita's misadventures, but what happens with her first film "role" proper? If Catita and Cándida films for Lumiton and EFA, respectively, featured Marshall in the guise of her radio characterization to a fault, her "roles" for Argentina Sono Film played with her ability to take on multiple characters. The comparison between *Hay que educar a Niní* and her final Catita film for Lumiton, *Yo quiero ser bataclana (I Want to Be a Chorus Girl)* (Manuel Romero, 1941), is telling. In the latter, Catita is a chorus girl in a theatrical revue, whereas in the former, Marshall is a struggling actress and film extra. Although both scenarios suggest a self-reflexivity that should allow Marshall the opportunity to perform other roles diegetically, her Catita film turns on Catita's inability to fashion herself as someone else. Catita stubbornly remains Catita: her dancing is off rhythm, her singing is off pitch, and her acting is left off stage.[40] This chapter examines Marshall's Argentina Sono Film projects, which showcase the many voices the actress invokes; that is, it considers the turn from already established radio characterizations to "roles" assigned by a studio within the context of larger narrative and aesthetic negotiations during the transition to sound.

Billed as Niní Marshall by Argentina Sono Film, her film roles provided the opportunities to represent other characters, either through self-reflexive narratives such as her studio debut *Hay que educar a Niní* where she plays the part of a screen double, or through a framing narrative, such as her portrayal of Carmen in an extended dream sequence in the later *Carmen* (Luis César Amadori, 1943). Her first film "role" that was not a direct incarnation of a radio characterization occurs in *Hay que educar a Niní*. Marshall plays an out-of-work actress hired to pretend to be a wealthy man's daughter, but the blackmail conspiracy requires that she portray the daughter full-time. The film opens with Niní as an extra in the fictional Cachi Mayo Films studios. Desperate for money in order to afford her wedding, Niní manages to secure an audition in a morality propaganda film with the help of her fiancé, Arturito. Unfortunately, Niní's only previous on-camera experience

FIGURE 6. Niní Reboredo (Niní Marshall) eavesdrops as a schoolgirl in *Hay que educar a Niní* (1940). Image courtesy of Museo del Cine Pablo Ducrós Hicken.

was as a prostitute in another film within the diegesis, *El ángel del puerto*. She loses the job because of her ostensible immorality and decides to sue the studio for sullying her reputation and jeopardizing her career. She unsuccessfully lobbies two small-time lawyers to her defense, but these men have higher hopes. They persuade the actress to play the part of a wealthy businessman's long-lost, teenaged daughter. They attempt to extort the businessman, but he agrees to support the girl in a boarding school because he has no children of his own. Niní must remain in school in order to secure payment, playing the part of a mischievous young schoolgirl. Marshall eventually reveals herself to her fake father and upends the grifters' scheme, so all's well that ends well. In one feature-length film, Marshall is a movie extra, film double, screen siren, and young schoolgirl. Marshall the actress (and Niní Reboredo, her film role) puts on a variety of hats, or rather gives voice to a menagerie of people. We witness not so much the transformation of her body through trick cinematography and editing that we do with silent comedienne bodies but rather we listen for the *ductilidad* of her voice synced time and again to the same body.

The tension between what you hear and what you see accounts for the initial appeal of Marshall's foray into the cinema. As the studio press releases and the newspaper reviews from the period demonstrate, Marshall's appeal as preestablished talent lay in seeing what until then had only been heard. Argentina Sono Film had ingeniously secured the actress but not the radio characterization. Marshall's first film with the studio, therefore, had another element of suspense, which was not a function of narrative structure but rather extratextual information: what would we see if we had not yet heard?

The film opens with an establishing shot of the Cachi Mayo Films studio and follows a young girl with a delivery for the actress Miss Rubi through a series of dissolves that takes us from the exterior to the dressing room and finally to the closed set. The young girl arrives on the set and asks whether Miss Rubi is on set. The camera turns to a medium close-up of a woman wrapped in a white fur, facing a camera within the frame and lit with three-point lighting, the backlight visible behind her. Our pro-filmic star, Niní Marshall, turns to the camera and waves, recognizing the young girl who has just arrived. We recognize the star and wait: what voice will come from this screen body?

An off-screen voice commands her to remain still, adding, "Es un primer plano y si se mueve no la puedo iluminar" (It is a close-up and if you move I cannot light you). This self-reflexive direction, referring at once to both the diegetic close-up as well as the filmic close-up of our comedic star, initiates a complex series of doublings. The young girl approaches the actress, and Niní addresses her while keeping her face motionless, ventriloquizing so as to not disturb the production of the image. Her first appearance on screen for Sono Film finds her voice and her image split. The production of the image may demand her silence, but the actress throws her voice, generating an unusual effect where the sound source is visible yet the sound cannot be matched. The boom microphone bobs into frame and nearly falls on the actress. She lets out a scream as the sound technician further reprimands: "¡Silencio! Si usted habla antes del tiempo, no puedo controlar el sonido" (Silence! If you speak before you're supposed to, I can't control the sound). Marshall replies: "Y para eso tiene que meterme el micrófono en la boca usted?" (And for that you have to shove the microphone in my mouth?). The actress's thrown voice appears to have no visible source, and the intrusion of the microphone figures as the apparatus's response to the uncanny effect of ventriloquism—an overly literal attempt to locate the source of the sound in the actress's body. The sound can be located in relation to the image *or* the extratextual star text. Again, the narrative space is less contained as a sound envelope than related tangentially to the theatrical space. We attribute the ventriloquized voice to the extratextual radio star and the material sound apparatus.

More is at stake in synchronization in order to avoid dissociating the narrative (location of a sound source) and acoustic (recognition of a sound) processes of audition. If we earlier noted how the star image could dissociate the narrative and scopic registers of spectatorship, then the case of Marshall performs a similar feat on the soundtrack. Sound cinema had promised to present a radio star—to see sound, to represent the materiality of the voice, to demonstrate the site of production. In fact, the star's throat appears as the site of fascination for Argentine critics, regularly mentioned in the paratexts surrounding her star persona. In the magazine *Sintonía,* critic Gerardo Bra discusses the arrival of Marshall in 1937: "Niní Marshall ingresa al mundo de la farándula radiofónica con toda la gracia de su simpatía y la expresividad de una garganta diez puntos. Actúa con libretos propios interpretando personajes tornados de la vida real, enriquecidos por su ductilidad" (Niní Marshall enters the world of radiophonic show business with all the grace of her charm and the expressiveness of her A+ throat. She acts with her own scripts, interpreting characters taken from real life and enriched by her versatility).[41] Later on, in the prologue to Marshall's autobiography, Claudio España notes that "La imitación, la creación en fin, de un personaje con su privilegiada garganta fue su mejor modo de comunicación" (The impersonation, the creation in fact, of a character with her exceptional throat was her best method of communication).[42]

Marshall's throat functions as a nonrepresentable site of production that cannot yield to the apparatus, making the sound hermeneutic a game of (gendered) anatomic display. Kaja Silverman has written extensively on how this sound hermeneutic is gendered in classical Hollywood cinema, aligning synchronization with specularization so that the display of the woman's body and the diegetic containment of the woman's voice—"the double diegeticization" of the female character—are symptoms of the same phallocentric signifying economy.[43] The location of sync points in the image as a game of "vocal striptease" seems at first glance an apt characterization of Marshall's comedic films. *Hay que educar a Niní* repeatedly restages this moment of display, ostensibly organizing the film as a series of attempts to present the throat as site of production. This opening sequence seems to confirm our expectations: here is the voice we came to see. The film, however, playfully evicts our star from the film within the film. The director enters the frame, consulting with his crew on the particulars of the shot. After agreeing that they can begin shooting, he yells: "¡Fuera la doble!" (Get rid of the double!). This is not a female character doubly diegeticized and consigned to diegetic interiority. The film playfully dissociates the narrative and the scopic, comically capitalizing on our misrecognition—that is our star but she is not the star.

The influence of radio sound aesthetics and the experimentation with film sound convention come to a head in a later scene in the film, which presents the first instance on film where the comedian uses her voice to impersonate multiple characters in a reflexive staging of her radio program. The actress seeks legal counsel to file a lawsuit against the movie studio for tarnishing her reputation by casting her as the vamp in an urban melodrama. With the waiting room full and growing impatient, the actress harasses the staff in order to get a brief moment with the lawyers. After being dismissed multiple times, the actress decides to impersonate their priority clients. One of the lawyers calls for a Sra. Mitoski to enter the office, and sensing an opportunity, the actress knocks on the door. The two lawyers are framed in a medium shot inside as the camera whip pans to the door and the source of the knock. Marshall peers in, introducing herself with an Eastern European accent as Sra. Mitoski. The camera pans with her as she approaches the confused men, who do not recognize her. Marshall, now framed between the men in a medium close-up, engages them. She claims to be Sra. Mitoski's sister who has come to refer them to the case of her actress self, Niní Reboredo. The men ask the question organizing the film narrative, if not the extrafilmic star discourse: "Who is Niní Reboredo?" Marshall responds in the voice of the actress: "That's me." The men interrupt the actress, dragging her away from the camera and out of the office. The outraged actress begins yelling once again with her affected accent.

Moments later, the actress finds a note on the receptionist's desk instructing the receptionist to call on a theater actress, Trinidad Madrid. The camera frames the lawyers in a medium shot, their conversation interrupted by a voice-off speaking in heavily accented peninsular Spanish. The person is asked to step inside the office to reveal the source of the voice. The camera cuts to a medium close-up of the door as Marshall steps inside and speaks to camera in character as Madrid, smoking a cigarette while making excuses for her tardiness. The sequence capitalizes on what Rick Altman calls the sound hermeneutic for comedic effect. The listening mode or process fundamental to the sound cinema experience "whereby the sound asks where? and the image responds here!" is literally performed in this sequence. And yet the image is not quite "here!"[44] The actress interrupts as voice-off, her guise working only as long as she remains unseen. Marshall's strategic use of her voice is betrayed by her visage. Altman insists that this sound hermeneutic is an ideological ploy, a "rerouting of the sound from the apparatus to the diegesis."[45] Separating the narrative space from theater space means yoking the sound from the loudspeaker to the lips on screen, but what happens when these lips emit more than one sound or when the rerouting is reflexively staged? The camera cuts to the irate men who stare at each other before approaching the woman. The camera pulls back as the men frame the woman and reprimand her: "See here." The actress interrupts the men, "I won't see anything because my case is very urgent!" The men explain that now she will be seen only after everyone in the waiting room has had their turn. From seeing to not seeing to not being seen, this brief exchange runs the gamut of possible alternative workings of the sound hermeneutic.

Of course, Marshall need not be seen, only heard. Marshall takes off her hat, tousles her hair, and grabs a pen and notebook. She enters the waiting room in long shot and speaking in a less nasal voice with fewer idiomatic expressions—in the manner of someone from a professional class—announces that the lawyers are retiring for the day and instructs all the clients to leave the offices. The waiting room empties, and the actress secures her meeting with the lawyers, remarking: "Se fueron todos, doctor" (They're all gone, doctor). The irate lawyer invites the actress into his office, but corrects the woman, "Yo no soy doctor, señora" (I'm not a doctor, Mrs.). Marshall responds, "Yo tampoco soy señora" (I'm also not a Mrs.). This exchange, like so many in the film, hinges on misrecognition even in the instance of ocular proof. The man is not a lawyer, he is a charlatan who cons wealthy men by extorting them with claims of parentage or manufacturing a long-lost sibling in order to seize an inheritance. If the early exchanges indicate that what you hear is not what you get, then the film suggests that what you see offers little epistemological comfort.

The throat proves an unstable fetish site, and the diegesis as discrete narrative space never quite comes together. Each mischievous episode relies on the *ductilidad,* to borrow Gerardo Bra's suggestive term,[46] of Marshall's voice, whether she remains off screen and then reveals her body as sound source or she is on screen as an unexpected or unstable sound source. The plasticity of silent comediennes that Hennefeld celebrates becomes refigured in the sound era as the ductilidad of the female voice. Rather than a discrete narrative space reliant on "diegeticized" female characters, we a have a different relation between narrative space and theater space courtesy of the ductilidad of Marshall's voice that blurs distinctions between diegetic and nondiegetic sound, cannot be located reliably in a definitive screen body, and relies on extra- and paratexts. This is not a self-reflexive play of high modernist subversion— "look at the apparatus and see how it works!"—but a process that results in a less stable and more ductile diegesis that opens onto a social horizon of experience.

The self-reflexive moments in Marshall's films are often staged as visual and aural punch lines. After getting fired by the film's director, Niní speaks to her friend about her plans while sitting in a theater box and listening to what appears to be diegetic music. Ostensibly in a concert hall or cinema, the two women speak in hushed tones until the younger girl spots Niní's fiancé. The women get up from their seats as if exiting the box but instead of leaving through the curtain behind them, they step through the wall and into the neighboring box revealing that they have been sitting in a movie set. They continue traversing the movie set until they meet Arturito, when her fiancé helps them climb off with a makeshift ladder. What is the status of the music to which they have been listening? The music accompanying this sequence is diegetic but we spectators have misattributed its location. Watching the gag unfold, we are forced to redraw the boundaries of the diegetic space with this reframing. The music is not only diegetic in relation to the filmic space (Marshall and her friend) but also nondiegetic accompaniment to the scene being filmed in the movie studio. Recalling Slowik, if the woman's body provides a diegetic guarantor for film music—a ground for the gradual separation of screen space and theater space—then Marshall provides a false guarantee.

THE DUCTILIDAD OF THE DIEGESIS

The (female) voice conventionally articulates three spaces through the classical cinematic apparatus: the space of the diegesis, the visible space of the screen, and the acoustical space of theater work in lockstep to envelop the spectator.[47] Both the institutionalization of viewing practices and the signifying practices of film bind these spaces together, and film sound—particularly the voice—occupies a privileged place in this process of unification. The use of level sound, room tone, reverberation, and sound perspective spatialize sound and contribute to the impression of reality in the space of the diegesis; in other words, the operations of film sound rely not upon actual sounds but upon a sonic vraisemblable, an acoustic organization that affords an impression of reality.[48] More importantly, when we hear the voice of a character who is not visible in the frame—a voice-off—the space of the diegesis exceeds the space of the screen, denying the frame as limit and affirming the unity of diegetic space.[49] In the above sequence, the film music (as singular acoustical space) belongs to two film diegeses: the one on the virtual screen (the film within the film) and the other on the actual screen. Instead of a coherent "substitute fictional field" that reinforces the boundaries of the diegesis and occludes the material heterogeneity of the cinema, the comedic organization of vision and audition means that any particular moment can occupy either register, and the boundaries of the filmic and diegetic are constantly blurred.[50] The female body may be the linchpin of the diegetic soundscape and narrative space in classical Hollywood cinema, but Marshall's ventriloquism does not so much expose the coordination of space by the apparatus as it recoordinates these spaces for comedic effect.

Ventriloquism has a long-standing history in sound studies as a model for understanding sound-image relationships in the cinema. The dummy/image disguises the source of the sound (the ventriloquist/sound track) in a relationship of mutual redundancy that convinces the viewer that the image/sound relationship exists independently of the technology.[51] This model assumes a discrete one-to-one relationship between sound and image (the trick works!), but Marshall's star text redraws diegetic boundaries differently through the use of her voice. Her films do not so much detach sound from source in an antirealist modernist modality as they provide multiple and incompatible synchronization effects articulated to the same star image. Let's switch gears from textual production to reception and from thinking Marshall as ventriloquist to thinking sound film (comedy) spectators as witnesses to ventriloquism. The ventriloquial structure relies on the separation of voice from sound source and the compensatory ascription of source, so that characterizing any mode of ventriloquism, including sound cinema, means a readjustment in sound and sight. Steve Connor suggests that the eye is the organ of space, an instrument that organizes through the extension of awareness into space through measurement and sequence. The ear can also extend our awareness into space but through the return of the self by the world (in the echo). Space is explicated (unfolded) by the eye but implicated (enfolded) by the ear.[52] Sound points to a different quality or government of space.

The transition to sound threatens this arrangement of discrete spaces because sound implies and relatively distributes space. If we take Connor's lesson with a view to the larger project of sound studies, we can see how a classical cinema modeled on the separation of screen space and theater space takes for granted the visual and the way it places bodies in a fixed field. The transition to sound staged a large-scale ventriloquial gambit, hoping to fix a dissociated voice to an object, a synchronicity that conspired to preserve the separation of screen space from theatrical space. The question of cinema as (mass) cultural sensorium takes on a different dimension in the transition to sound cinema, less a matter of its mass appeal as universal language than a testing ground for the changing hierarchy of the senses. The gradually defined conventions of sound cinema, much like successful ventriloquism, recoordinate space and fix the power of the voice in a compensatory mode. What Marshall's performance suggests is a ventriloquial structure that plays out differently. Her radio stardom produced voices in implicated space—that is, a space implied by the propagation and reverberation of sound and the imagined vocalic body.[53] Unlike the transition to sound in classical Hollywood where the integrity of a narrative (explicated) space was threatened by implicated space, here we have an implicated space threatened by explication. This is not a case of an image getting a voice—Garbo talks!—but of a voice getting an image. Marshall's is a cinema less fixated on the synchronicity of lips and voice that would preserve the integrity of the narrative space. This means characterizing the contiguity of screen and theater space as the production of implicated space in a mock classical mode.

Can we think distance and proximity in the case of implicated space? The question of distance and proximity that undergirds questions of aesthetic judgment necessarily becomes figured differently when considering the voice. The voice "hold[s] me apart from the world" because of the extension of the self into the world, and yet hearing the voice necessarily occurs through some contiguity of sound object and ear.[54] A space relatively distributed rather than coordinated means that distance and proximity are less fixed points than scalar gradations. What would it mean to think space not coordinated but gradated, where being in one site versus another is a matter of a difference in degree and not a difference in kind? In other words, what would it mean to think of location less as "I'm here and not there" and more as "I'm less here and more there." This subtle shift implies changing how we conceive subjectivity, not grounded in identification-as-differentiation but as a dynamic movement of continuous de- and reterritorialization. This is not a process of yoking sound to image in order to avow sensory hierarchy and identification with the image but a game of seeing what sounds are capable of coming from the same image. The more general diffusion of voice(s) across the screen and performer's body as well as the reliance on extratextual radio cues meant a different spatial arrangement for early sound cinema, not only in the case of Marshall but arguably in the broader Latin American context.

The arrangement, or rather the orchestration, of sound space for comedic effect occurs explicitly in Marshall's second film for Argentina Sono Film, *Orquesta de señoritas (Girls' Orchestra)* (Luis César Amadori, 1941), which finds the actress billed as Niní Marshall, portraying the conductor of a classically trained, all-female band. Although the film seems to provide a less self-reflexive frame for the actress, her role as conductor suggests that her body will quite literally determine the rhythm and tempo of sound in the film. The film opens on a close-up of the band's name, Lysistrata, before panning to Marshall, her body swaying in time. After a series of cutaways introduces some of the key players (e.g., her brother, the surly Italian bar owner, and a young mandolin player dressed in a wedding gown for an impending marriage arranged by Marshall) and a deft sound mix plays with the relative intensity of the music to the spoken dialogue, a reverse long shot of the bar shows a young man, Rodolfo, entering and approaching the orchestra. Quickly recognizing the groom, Marshall gesticulates wildly, a bodily shift that accelerates the tempo of the music. Marshall wonders why the groom has shown up and so "fast-forwards" the musical performance, an acceleration achieved mechanically but made to appear diegetic. Ostensibly conducting the on-screen band, her body also orchestrates the relation of soundtrack to image track with a variable rate of sound synced to a standard frame rate in the image.

FIGURE 7. Niní Marshall orchestrates hijinks with her all-female band, Lysistrata, in *Orquesta de señoritas* (1941). Image courtesy of Museo del Cine Pablo Ducrós Hicken.

In order to orchestrate narrative action, Marshall relies on sound technologies that help throw her voice in ways both literal and metaphoric. The film's plot centers on the turbulent first days of this marriage. The groom's past comes back to haunt him in the form of a former flame who threatens to reveal his past affairs to the new wife, Blanca. This not only threatens to upset Blanca but also puts in jeopardy the generous wedding gift from his morally righteous uncle who has come to Buenos Aires to keep tabs on his reformed nephew. Marshall intervenes to help the young man, exclaiming, "Yo te lo arreglo todo" (I'll take care of everything), which also happens to be the name of the signature tango from the film. In order to extricate the man from his responsibility to his former lover and maintain the appearance of moral uprightness for Rodolfo's uncle, Marshall concocts a relatively simple stratagem—she will confront the ex-lover as the wife who accepts her husband's past indiscretions because of her own long list of former paramours—that farcically snowballs into an intricate comedy of errors. Marshall's first interaction with the other woman occurs over the phone when Marshall pretends to be the household *mucama,* or maid. The simple exchange occurs in a conventional shot pattern with the characters in different spaces edited in a shot/reverse-shot structure: discontinuous distant spaces made ostensibly proximate in this linchpin of continuity editing. More importantly, Marshall's "Fermina" has a deeper voice with a hint of a rural accent that likely references her Galician maid radio character, Cándida. Her subsequent meeting with the other woman finds Marshall pretending to be Rodolfo's wife. Marshall boasts about her indiscretions, even taking a phone call in her guise and cooing into the receiver in French. These first incidents of ventriloquial play, of conjuring a vocalic body other than the screen body, sets up a narrative where the appearance of the star elicits a peculiar form of suspense: in any given scene, what voice will come from this body?

During Marshall's meeting with the ex-lover, Rodolfo's uncle arrives so that Marshall is forced to remain Rodolfo's wife indefinitely. Marshall's ruse also forces Rodolfo's real young bride into the part of the household maid. Unlike Cantinflas as a stand-in for Leonardo del Paso, Marshall devises a panoply of additional characters each with their own voice; we have less the sidestepping of Cantinflas than the splitting of the self or the production of other selves. The film's narrative proceeds episodically, each episode a complication that Marshall must *arreglar*—appropriately meaning both "to fix" and "to (musically) arrange"—usually by fabricating another story, another character, or another version of herself. For instance, in the second half of the film, Marshall must pretend to be an Italian diva for Rodolfo's suspicious uncle. When the uncle wanders into the cabaret-bar where the all-woman band plays and he spots Marshall at the helm, she must somehow persuade him that she is not the same woman he supposes is married to Rodolfo. Marshall quickly changes the set list and sings an Italian aria, later introducing herself in spoken Italian as a twin sister. The close-up of Marshall when she spots the suspicious uncle ratchets the farce: how will she avoid detection when she is very much on display? Marshall grabs some fabric on the nearby piano and dons a shawl. Will she change her appearance? The camera pushes out as Marshall begins singing in a different voice and language. The transformation occurs in one take: she cannot change her appearance, so she changes her voice.

The song concludes and the uncle approaches Marshall, who carries on a humorous conversation with him in spoken (if broken) Italian: "Io sono la sorella di la sposa de Rodolfo. La sorella ... la hermana. Oggi lei ha sposato e sono venuto ... siamo come si dice gemellas [/dʒe'melas/] ... Ecco! Gemelas [/xe'melas/]!" (I am Rodolfo's wife's sister. The sister ...

the sister. Today she married and I came. We are, how do you say it, twins. That's it! Twins!). The Italian and Spanish words for *twin,* barely separated phonemically, are an apt metaphor of the actress's transformation: the same word sounds different because of a single consonant. The "g" is written identically but spoken differently (i.e., /dʒeˈmela/ in Italian becomes /xeˈmela/ in Spanish). Marshall appears identical on screen, but the screen body is spoken differently. Later, Marshall explains that their father was a tenor and punctuates the exchange with a play on words: "Somos las dos del mismo tenor." Marshall says that they both share a father who is a tenor, but she is also saying that they are cut from the same cloth or have similar dispositions. The turn of phrase that capitalizes on the several meanings of the word *tenor*—both the adult male vocal range and the meaning sustained through something written or spoken—also suggestively characterizes Marshall, articulating a vocalic register with an ontological condition (that is replicable). Marshall flirts with the uncle, and her seduction eventually yields the dirt used to extort his approval and support for the married couple.

The farcical conceit of pretending to be someone else is nothing new. For instance, other characters in *Orquesta* play along: Marshall's brother *(el nene)* is at times her son; Rodolfo's wife is at times his maid; Marshall's music professor is at times a public official. But none of these players don a different voice or are quite as adept at throwing their voices. When the uncle wakes up from a long night of heavy drinking having forgotten his marriage proposal to the Italian diva, he goes to the hotel lobby with Rodolfo and his fake wife. Marshall steps out of frame and a concierge shortly thereafter interrupts the two men with a phone call from the *signorina*. Marshall performs a mediated voice-off, stepping out of the frame to throw her voice (into frame) telephonically. The uncle goes toward the phone booth bank in the lobby. After stepping inside one of the booths and picking up the receiver, Marshall pops up from below the window in the adjoining booth and begins a conversation with the uncle. As Marshall gushes about the impending wedding, the uncle alleges he is at the train station about to leave the city. He begins voicing the various sound effects associated with the station: a train whistle, a hiss of steam, and the metallic rumble of wheels. He lays the receiver down and attempts to create some sound perspective by playing with the distance from mouth to receiver in order to simulate a departing train. The traffic of voices in this sequence astonishes: a single shot contains Marshall as conspiring orchestra conductor, fake wife, and Italian twin sister. Each voice implies a different space, whether the actual space of the hotel lobby or the false tele-technological space separating the Italian diva in her hotel room from the uncle at the train station.

If Marshall can be anyone at any time, then her ensemble proves less adept at putting on other guises. At play is a structure of misrecognition comically devised—less "I'm afraid you've mistaken me for someone else" than "I'm afraid you've mistaken me for who I am." The film's climax at the cabaret-bar where the uncle thinks he has finally figured out Marshall's duplicity features yet another playful misrecognition. The uncle enters the space and sees a woman on stage in Marshall's costume with her back to the audience. The uncle confronts the woman who turns around. In a punctuating close-up, we see *el nene* in drag, Returning to a long shot, the dumbfounded uncle grows impatient, and the camera pans to the door as Marshall darts into the scene. Who will she be? Marshall produces other selves. Her method of orchestration is quite literally to produce voices or aural signs that remain out of scene but will intervene on the scene or threaten to appear in the scene. From her brother's whistle to the Italian diva's phone call, a scene without Marshall on screen can be interrupted by her voice-off, and a scene with Marshall on screen is subject to the suspense of which persona she will invoke. Watching her film is to laugh at the tension between screen sound space and diegetic narrative space. We watch a scene unfold in a long take, on edge with the possibilities of interrupting off-screen sound events and on-screen invocations.

Much like Marshall's body becomes the site of multiple synchronizations, the visible space of the screen becomes the site of multiple synchronizations, thereby complicating our ability to wed the space of the screen to the space of the diegesis. Miriam Hansen insists that classical cinema wants us to forget we are present in the theater.[55] Kaja Silverman puts this problematic slightly differently when she argues that classical cinema wants us to forget that what is on screen is absent. More generally, both align classicism with diegeticization, a narrative space secured through dramatically motivated, cause-and-effect relations in the image (continuity editing) and on the soundtrack (sound hermeneutic and synchronization). The previous chapter argued through Hansen that mock classicism arranges space differently, capitalizing on our presence in the theater for comedic effect. Mustn't Latin American film comedy similarly complicate Silverman's account of Hollywood classicism? For Silverman, sound proves an excellent technology of disavowal of the foreclosure of the real: We forget the diegesis's absence because of the fact of the synchronization. Marshall's films' ventriloquial play with synchronization therefore affects this process of diegeticization, mining this absence for comedic effect (i.e., "Made you look!").

NOBODY'S DUMMY: VENTRILOQUISM
IN IMPLICATED SPACE

The confusion of diegetic boundaries is arguably most evident in her third film for Argentina Sono Film, aptly titled *La mentirosa (The Little Liar)* (Luis César Amadori, 1942). Marshall portrays Niní Martínez, a working-class woman working as an assistant in a lawyer's office who concocts elaborate lies that get her into intractable if amusing situations. By way of synopsis, Marshall and her fiancé hope to earn enough money to get married and set up their home. Meanwhile, her boss represents the estate of a man who has left his fortune to a child raised by his sister. Marshall plots to pretend to be the heir (only briefly, she promises) in order to secure a guarantor for her loan. Of course, she becomes entangled in a conspiracy to defraud the estate and steal the inheritance. The film's final act occurs in a country estate with ominous sounds and mysterious near-accidents devolving into a parody of Gothic romance. Marshall's Niní is the titular liar. Although most later synopses of the film claim this character is Catita, she does not—in fact, cannot—portray her radio persona but rather a film "role." Whereas Catita remained resolutely Catita in her early films for Lumiton, this film title more accurately suggests she is less a proper name than a structuring duplicity—a liar paradox become film narrative. Marshall is more commedia dell'arte's Brighella than Colombina in her films for Argentina Sono Film.[56]

The film's opening sequence introduces the lawyer's office, with an unhappy customer leaving the firm because he was told the lawyer had left his practice. A confused paralegal glances toward Niní who defends the lie: Niní explains that she had thought the man was a bill collector. She explains that her boss has more bill collectors than clients and that she is charged with keeping them at bay by creating increasingly elaborate excuses for being unable to pay. In a later exchange with a representative from the power company, Marshall figuratively amputates her boss's legs in a horrific automobile accident to explain his failure to pay. During a subsequent encounter with the same man who wants a signed letter from the lawyer, Marshall severs her boss's arms: "He will not be able to sign anything." The boss stays in business because she lies to his creditors. She occupies this necessary (if disavowed) position that allows the law to "keeps the light on"—giving lie to the truth, so to speak.

The film proceeds somewhat predictably, with Marshall's lies belied by the film events. Of interest to us is how these lies rely on Marshall's play with vocalic space. In other words, Marshall orchestrates how sound travels and determines who and what can listen. An early scene of the reading of the will usefully illustrates how Marshall plays with the registry of sound. Flanked by the executor on one side and a relative on the other, the lawyer discusses the inconvenience of not knowing the whereabouts of a relative. He instructs Marshall, off to the side in her own medium shot, to take notes. Marshall looks up and exaggeratedly scribbles across her steno pad. The lawyer narrates each action and reads the contents of the testament in a crowded medium long shot without Marshall: "Procedo entonces a romper los sellos y dar lectura al continido del documento" (I proceed to open the seal and read the contents of the document). Marshall yells off-screen in a reverberant voice: "¡Un momento!" The camera sets its sight on Marshall, now close-miked in sound design that scale matches, as she tries to transcribe her boss's words: "do-cu-men-to." Marshall stalls the proceedings, serving as a less-than-mechanical mode of voice transcription. Her boss rebukes, "Escriba sin hablar" (Write without speaking). The boss speaks (as Law), and Marshall records. The scene aligns power and voice along the gendered axis Silverman identifies as constitutive of subjectivity in psychoanalysis. Woman is excluded from symbolic power by making her passive in relation to sight and sound.[57] The male subject identifies with enunciative agency after a disarticulation of speech and voice: the male voice can be disembodied and aligned with speech (enunciation/*énontiation*), and the female voice is resolutely embodied as voice (spoken */énoncé*). For Silverman, this occurs in classical Hollywood cinema by diegetically containing the female body and female voice. In the sequence, Marshall is ostensibly reduced to body and medium of transcription so that her boss can speak as law. To speak "on the record" is to speak through the woman's body.

The legal proceedings continue for several minutes, a discussion among men on screen, with Marshall remaining off-screen throughout. The proceedings conclude when the lawyer asks the men to leave their details with Marshall. The camera finally returns to Marshall: the steno pad at arm's length and the pen brushing the pad's surface only on occasion but never in sync with the conversation. If Marshall were transcribing, her boss's off-screen command should register, and yet Marshall remains distractedly scribbling. She responds only when he changes his intensity and embodies his voice (rather than the content of his speech). Marshall rises and the camera pans with her as she approaches the men. The lawyer asks her to take note of the gentlemen's information *taquigráficamente* (in shorthand). Marshall asks him to clarify, and he rebukes, "¿No sabe taquigrafía?" (Don't you know shorthand?). Marshall assures him she knows shorthand and as the man speaks at length, the long take features Marshall at his side dotting the page in what might very well be Morse code. The exchange concludes with the man winding down and asking his secretary if she's finished. Marshall hands him the pad: "Ahí está escrito todo lo que used me dictó" (Everything you dictated is written there). The lawyer asks her to read it back, but Marshall explains that she does not know what it says: "Escribir como las taquígrafas sí sé, pero a leer lo que escribo todavía no aprendí" (I know how to write like a stenographer, but I haven't learned how to read what I write). Marshall proves less than reliable ground. The displacements that locate the male voice at the site of enunciation at the expense of the diegeticized or excluded female voice cannot occur here. In the scene, Marshall is less figurative microphone and recorder than sounding board.

That Marshall uses sound technologies less as a matter of record becomes again figured in her uses of the telephone. Capitalizing on a conversation where the interlocutor remains at a spatial remove, the phone becomes an important weapon in her arsenal. In the film, instead of shoring up the diegesis by ensuring us that both sides of the conversation are part of the same narrative world, the constant misuses of the phone destabilize the interlocking of the space of the diegesis and the visible space on the screen. Later in the film, Marshall's character pretends to be the missing heir by intercepting phone calls. After receiving a phone call from the private investigators to inform the lawyer that they will be unable to find the missing heir, Marshall intercepts the lawyer's phone call to the investigators and speaks with a different voice to inform the lawyer that the heir is none other than Niní Martínez. The lawyer eventually reconciles with Marshall, who feigns having a vague memory of a woman whom she called Mother. So far, it would seem we can manage to keep straight what belongs in the narrative world and what has been fabricated by our protagonist.

Under questioning by the lawyer, Marshall doubles down on her lies. She continues to add details to the story, claiming her aunt promised some kind gestures, including a chauffeured car, a bouquet of flowers, and a check in her name. The lawyer decides to call the investigators, who explain they were never able to find the heir. Confronting Niní in his office, the lawyer paces in a medium long shot in a mock cross-examination. Marshall worries she has been caught, when suddenly her boss stops and does a double take out the window. Music creeps onto the soundtrack with a cut to a high-angle, extreme long shot of an approaching chauffeured car that masterfully pushes into a medium shot of the executor carrying flowers into the building's lobby. Has Marshall been telling the truth the entire time? The lawyer is dumbfounded: "¿De manera que era verdad? Le pido mil perdones y le juro que no entiendo nada" (So it was all true? My sincerest apologies, and I swear I don't understand a thing!). The lawyer, Niní, and we spectators have lost track of what is true and what is not true. Suddenly, Niní's voice seems to conjure things out of thin air. The ventriloquial structure is at its limits: if she speaks it, it materializes.

Diegeticization gives truth to the lie through operations that coordinate sight and sound, and this is a film where we lose track of what is truth and what is lie. As the film turns into a genre-fluid comedy with elements of Gothic horror during the final act, the inability to keep track of the truth (and the inability to shore up the diegesis) occurs in part through sound events with unreliable origins and gags capitalizing on the incongruity of sound and source. Marshall is whisked off to her aunt's estate in Pilar, on the outskirts of the city. She remains astonished at her newfound powers. En route, in a medium shot inside the car, Marshall wonders what else could possibly happen: "A ver si se nos pincha una goma!" (All we need is to get a flat!). Of course, that stray comment is punctuated with a sound effect suggesting some off-screen explosion. Is Niní's voice affecting the events within the narrative space? Hers seems an invocatory power that upends the causality fundamental to the hermeticism of a classical narrative space. The car slows down in a long shot with the driver stepping outside to check the tires that remain suspiciously intact. A subsequent medium shot inside the car returns to Marshall and the executor, a bullet hole in the rear windshield now visible to us spectators and eventually to the characters. We begin to sense that Marshall's voice is less in control of narrative events than we might have imagined: a shot was fired at the car. And yet the sound effect anticipates the change in mise-en-scène that only the misdirecting editing can allow. This is a gunshot construed after a delay. Although we could explain this as a discontinuity in the mise-en-scène, Marshall's (and our) doubts about the origin of the sound event—the playful equivocation of gunshot and flat tire—would be deflated without this misdirecting editing. The gag works because of this delay in the sound hermeneutic, because of the delay between sound event and its on-screen manifestation. This is not a continuity editing that coordinates space according to dramatic cues and narrative causality but a misdirecting editing that orchestrates a gag by playing with the boundaries of the fictional world.

Marshall arrives at the estate and meets a live-in doctor who cares for her older aunt and a sickly housekeeper. Eventually, Marshall learns that the "housekeeper" is the real heir being held against her will by the executor, the doctor, and the older "aunt," who are simply attempting to swindle the woman. They want to capitalize on Marshall's lie: if Marshall could pretend to be the heir, then they could coerce Marshall to give them the inheritance. Marshall had no invocatory power, but this is a complicated restoration of order that forces us to reread the narrative. Each interested party is caught in a mirroring improvisation exercise: Marshall unsure why (or whether) her lies are true, and the grifters mirroring these lies in order to make them seem true. After Marshall arrives, the older woman immediately recognizes Marshall. They reminisce (or improvise?) as the aunt asks Marshall whether she remembers details about her childhood. The aunt asks whether she recalls the song she sang to her as a child. Marshall hesitates before humming a few bars. The older woman immediately recognizes (or feigns to recognize?) the song, and the camera pushes into the two women singing in near unison. Marshall gains confidence: perhaps this is all true! The singing is interrupted by a piercing off-screen scream. The camera pans and tilts toward the presumed sound source. The doctor later explains the scream was from a radio: "Todo está bien, era la radio. La habían dejado abierta en una transmisión de esas novelescas" (Everything's all right; it was the radio. They left it turned onto one of those soaps). As she is encouraged to go to bed, a nervous Marshall hears another scream. The butler explains there is no radio in the house. Marshall is suddenly Jane Eyre, hearing voices and sounds with unlocatable origins. She eventually finds the injured "housekeeper" who yells, echoing Marshall's own situation: "No veo nada pero oigo" (I don't see anything, but I hear). She continues, "Oigo tres golpes. Es la muerte" (I hear three knocks. It is death!). The camera tracks with Marshall as she leaves the bedroom, but she hears three knocks off-screen. With high-contrast lighting, canted angles, and overwhelming sound effects, the house becomes the setting of a Gothic horror. The knocks come from the main door where a silhouetted figure appears who claims to be the aunt's son. Eventually, he too vanishes. To hear what isn't there, to speak what will occur, to see what wasn't there: this is the narrative logic of the film's final act.

The comedy began by establishing a hierarchy of information so that we (but not the other characters) know that we cannot trust what Marshall says. The eerie turn of events suggests we (and the characters) might be wrong. The diegesis seems to exceed the boundaries we had drawn, and we watch to realign ourselves in relation to its shifting boundaries, shored up in the restorative final scene, when the police apprehend the grifters. Rather than reinforcing the boundaries of the diegesis and locating us spectators proximate to the absent site of cinematic production, the comedic organization of vision and audition instead yields an implicated space. If the classical spatial arrangement we have been describing is a function of the more general "operations of the signifier and the foreclosure of the real," then these film comedies and their askew spatial arrangement suggest a different logic of representation less predicated on recording and absenting (as the foreclosure of the real).[58] In other words, we cannot easily forget that what is on screen is absent because what is visibly on screen never quite seems to coincide with what is audible in the theater and what we conceive exists in the fiction.

Figuring out what is true and what is false proves so confusing in *La mentirosa* that the character even consults a doctor! Marshall explains: "Cuando uno inventa una cosa muy pero muy grande y después se hace cierta, ¿es que uno está loca . . . [o] se han dado casos?" (When one makes up something that's really big and later it turns out to be true, is that person crazy or have there been cases?). The doctor gives a lengthy explanation that indulges in psychoanalysis: "Un recuerdo verdadero alojado en estado latente en las circunvoluciones centrales puede aparecer de pronto como una aparición de la propia imaginación. En psicología eso está clasificado como reminiscencia" (A true memory kept in a latent state in the central circumvolutions can suddenly manifest as a vision of the imagination. In psychology, that is called a reminiscence). He asks whether this has happened to her, and Marshall claims it happened to a friend: "Un amigo mío que se inventó un tango todito como si fuera de él y después resultó que ya estaba escrito en una ópera del Colón" (A friend of mind made up an entire tango as if it were his and later it turned out that it had already been written for an opera in the Colón [Theater]). This exchange provides a narrative justification for the unusual turn of events. Marshall is not lying but rather reminiscing or remembering some forgotten truth. The doctor prescribes avoiding parsing the true and the false because the fictive may very well be (latent) truth. Marshall's punctuating anecdote takes this one step further by aligning the doctor's explanation with the question of an original and a copy. Although the humor derives from Marshall's misapplication of the term in an anecdote where a plagiarized text was passed off as the original, the doctor's explanation provides the grounds for thinking of a copy as more than just a copy.

In fact, that a copy is never simply a copy proves a valuable rejoinder to detractors of Marshall and, more broadly, film comedy. Early film histories and contemporaneous criticism, more concerned with writing an authentic national cinema, dismissed comedies from their narratives. For instance, Argentina film scholar Pascual Quinziano found comedy's relation to radio narratives and theatrical characterizations an impure origin for his national cinema, preferring instead a canon with aesthetic unity and auteurist vision.[59] For Quinziano, the lack of auteurist style or generic cohesiveness among disparate comedic texts, in addition to the borrowing from precinematic and paracinematic cultural forms, prevents discussion of comedy as an "authentic [i.e., medium-specific] phenomenon within our filmmaking."[60] This quest for the authentic becomes an overriding project for critics and scholars writing a national film history, articulating ontological modernist arguments onto nationalist claims of specificity. The authentically cinematic and the authentically Argentine configure an interpretive matrix that can discuss comedy only as a problematic phenomenon. The medium's adulterated origin makes it a shaky ground for writing the nation-state if what counts is only the opera in the Colón Theater and not the tango it may have inspired.

When the doctor claims that a falsehood might reveal a latent truth, he suggests that the ground for the truth might be somewhere unexpected. What we see may not always be what we get because the manifest may very well be ventriloquized, and what appears false or inauthentic may have an authorizing origin located elsewhere or else-when. When an authorizing source is separated from its expression, we are back in the structure of ventriloquism, a structure that invites us to look at falsehood and truth differently. Much like psychoanalysis broadly conceived, we learn not to take the manifest at its word. In this scene, the doctor's language draws on psychoanalysis to explain how something might be different than it appears, and, when cast through a ventriloquial structure, suggests a slightly different mode of reading. In this figuration, the manifest is not always inauthentic but rather the product of a particular routing of voice and body (and our willful investment or belief in that relation). The narrative space seems real because we route it to a hermetic diegesis rather than a profilmic reality loosely continuous with our own space.

Psychoanalytic feminist film theory teaches that this routing occurs along gendered lines, that the specularity of the female body and the synchronization of the female voice align woman to the appearance at once indecipherable and readable, opaque yet immediate.[61] The gendered binary at the heart of the apparatus leaves few possibilities for locating a female spectating position in classical feminist film theory: the female spectator can either identify masochistically with the feminized image or identify with the masculinized gaze. Unlike the voyeuristic pleasure of the male spectator that assumes a distance relative to the image, the female spectator's pleasure can be described only in terms of a narcissistic closeness and overpresence. Mary Ann Doane bristles against these options because they assume the proximity of the female spectator to the image: "Female specificity is thus theorized in terms of spatial proximity. In opposition to this 'closeness' to the body, a spatial distance in the male's relation to his body rapidly becomes a temporal distance in the service of knowledge."[62] To move beyond this gendered binary, Doane thinks representation and spectatorship through masquerade. Masquerade designates a play of surfaces that complicates how we read the surface (as diegesis). An unstable image or object makes the (phallocentric) subject unstable in turn. For Doane, masquerade appropriates and adapts the processes of identification by simulating distance between oneself and one's image. In other words, masquerade simulates a critical distance and temporal removal, which are the psychoanalytic ground for subjectivity; however, by advocating for distance and temporal removal, masquerade also perpetuates these as criteria for critical subjectivity. We neither identify with the gaze of the camera nor do we identify too closely with the image; instead, we only seem to identify. Pleasure still derives from identification predicated on vision and subjectivity predicated on distance. How might sound complicate this model of identification and subjectivity?

I want to use ventriloquism once more to complicate this binary. Ventriloquism appears as a theoretical metaphor in Latin American feminist criticism precisely to address this deep ambivalence in the Latin American (female) subject.[63] Latin American feminist critics teach us to reread French feminist theory against Anglo-American feminist film theory. A mask and a ventriloquist both play with concealment, but they engage with the senses differently. A mask covers the face; a ventriloquist throws her voice. The former privileges vision and the inability to see beyond surface. The latter puts an emphasis on hearing coordinated with limited vision (i.e., an inability to see beyond surface coupled with a compensatory ascription of source). Anglo-American feminist film theory objects to self-presence and proximity as the conditions of feminine specificity because it locates the female spectator's desire in a kind of narcissism. What the Latin American invocation of ventriloquism reminds us is that narcissism is predicated on vision and a determinate organization of the senses. If the successful ventriloquist recoordinates space into a fixed field, then plays with ventriloquism that comically suspend habitual perception and sensory operation implicate us in a space we constantly draw and redraw. The spectatorial bind of identifying with (proximate) image or (distant) gaze relies on a working ventriloquist act. When we see a ventriloquist's lips moving, however, this scopic regime does not quite hold. This represents a shift from thinking the subject in explicated space versus thinking the subject in implicated space, a shift from a cartographic (cognitive mapping) model to an echographic model. We do not fix and locate the subject but range the subject within a distributed space or "a makeshift dwelling place."[64] If we take seriously the reorganization of the senses that ventriloquism compels, narcissism (and the concomitant positions of distance and proximity that it determines) must be rethought. As a commentary on Marshall's tactics (and arguably the cinematic apparatus), watching Marshall is less about locating the true Marina Esther Traveso than taking pleasure in the different iterations of Marshall, the different fits between voice and body. This is not proximity as overpresence but as implication. In the case of Marshall, her characterizations function as literal invocations, with a body containing multiple selves not quite contained in a screen space itself only loosely discrete. Being critical does not mean being radically removed from the screen space but becoming implicated.

How do we think identification in the case of a body that can never quite be located in explicated space and where pleasure derives from becoming implicated in space? That proximity and distance in sound are measured mostly by reverberation or sound persistence (e.g., echo) provides one avenue for working through this question. Gayatri Spivak takes up the figure of Echo to deconstruct the Narcissus myth as foundational structure for ego-ideal formation—"a tale of the construction of the self as object of knowledge."[65] Echo may appear a passive subject, and yet the incongruence and delay of her echo (which is never quite a copy and never quite coincides) comes from "a space already insufficiently inscribed—an insufficiency that is the name not of the limits of self-knowledge but of the possibility of deconstruction."[66] In this vein, proximity is less a symptom of a regressive primary narcissism than becoming implicated in a (sound) space that persists as it resists visualization. The echo figures as a different and deferred utterance that shares in the ventriloquial structure: "there is nothing but voice [with] the structural possibility of being severed from its referent or signified . . . cut off from its alleged 'production' or origin."[67] With a ventriloquism that does not quite work (that is cut off from its alleged origin) and a copy that is more than mere copy, we return to the sequence from *La mentirosa*. Now the deferral and difference of the doctor's "reminiscences" point to a structural resonance with the echo as deconstructive movement, as a way of speaking otherwise in an implicated space.[68]

Thought methodologically, the ventriloquial structure suggests we should not simply disparage the inauthenticity of the diegesis and celebrate the profilmic as the site of the real (as do certain strains of cinematic high modernism). Contra apparatus theory *and* new film history, which both suppose pitting a reality (ideological or historical, respectively) against a falsehood, what would it mean to read film not to explicate some reality through a necessary detachment (a defamiliarizing avant-garde that disrupts the ideological smoothness of the apparatus or a historical remove that uses the text as document, respectively) but to consider how we are implicated given the contingency of reception?[69]

Throughout Marshall's films for Argentina Sono Film, the tension between what is depicted and what is invoked means making the narrative space necessarily incongruous with the screen space and, in its reliance on paratextual and extratextual iterations and allusions, loosely continuous with the theater space. By way of conclusion, let's return to her first film for the studio, *Hay que educar a Niní,* which self-reflexively stages a scene of film spectatorship that turns on recognition and (or as) misrecognition and on diegetic confusion and the production of implicated space. Midway through the film, we watch as Niní gets a small part in the urban melodrama *El ángel del puerto* (The angel of the docks). Niní arrives on set and discusses her lines with the director. She asks: "¿A quién se lo digo?" (To whom should I say this?). The director instructs her to address him. A confused Niní asks the director, "And who are you?" The outraged director exasperatedly repeats his title within the production hierarchy. Niní's "you," however, refers to a fictional interlocutor within the film's diegesis and not the profilmic director: "Digo, ¿quién figura ser?" (I mean, who are you supposed to be?). The director suggests she imagine a street vendor. This brief exchange expresses a characteristic confusion in Marshall's film between self and fictional role(s). Marshall begins the exchange as Niní the actress only to slip into the registers of her fictional character. The director occupies one position in the diegesis; Marshall occupies positions in both the diegesis and the film within the film. The comedic misunderstandings arise from her playfully equivocating between these positions, a conflict between a rigid hierarchy and scopic organization of space and her intersubjective fluidity within this space. This equivocation between filmic and diegetic is reinforced in the remainder of the sequence. An assistant director stands next to Marshall in a medium shot filling in the details of the shot in a clapboard. Marshall asks some final questions as the camera pushes into a close-up. The director yells, "Camera! "Action!" A dissolve from the clapboard to the marquee of the film's opening night punctuates the sequence and jumps forward in time. The close-up that ends the sequence on the soundstage is also ostensibly a close-up in the film *El ángel del puerto*—the omniscient camera becomes diegetic camera. This instance of self-reflexivity echoes the opening of the film: the close-up in the film within the film is also a diegetic close-up of the fictional actress on a soundstage as well as a filmic close-up of Marshall, our comedic star.

The subsequent sequence finds Marshall in attendance at the movie's premiere with the producer of the morality propaganda looking to cast the actress in his next project. The extreme interior long shot of the screen of the movie theater displays the film within the film. The shots of the docks give way to a congregation of men around a detective who complain about the misdeeds of a woman just off screen. While Marshall explains to the producer in the theater that the woman in question is the villainess of this melodrama, the men on the screen urge the detective to take a gander at the woman. A low-angle long shot and point of view of the detective of *El ángel del puerto* sights a woman looking out onto the street: our actress makes her film debut as a melodramatic villainess. Marshall watches herself on screen propositioning a man on the street. Her brief part, which originally entailed merely glancing out a window, has been edited into a sequence where her look is now charged with sexual desire within a phallic scopic economy. Her glance is inserted into an exchange of looks that positions her as vamp; her desire is manufactured in a stroke of Kuleshov-like mischief. The fate of her character on screen befalls the actress as well when the producer drops the actress from his picture, even threatening to denounce her to the police for lewd conduct. The actress insists, "A mí me dijeron que era un caramelero. A ese marinero yo ni lo conozco" (I was told he was a confectioner. I don't even know that sailor"). The producer appears unable to differentiate the actress seated next to him from the role performed on screen, but perhaps even more noteworthy is the actress's relationship to her on-screen self. The first part of the actress's defense suggests that, unlike the producer, she locates herself in the scene of production, understanding the distinction between self and fictional other. The second sentence however, situates her in the diegesis of *El ángel*. The actress appears to undergo becoming spectator and becoming image. If psychoanalytic feminist film theory claims that classical cinema produces an atemporal subject that disavows difference and the materiality of the apparatus, the actress both affirms and denies difference, inscribing temporality into the viewing position by articulating her relation to the image in both past and present tenses as well as referring to the scene of production while also figuring the unity of the diegesis. In Marshall's film, the actress's first-person "I" is the site of multiple selves that surface differentially in relation to the image. Marshall is never quite in sync, is never quite embodied, is never quite diegeticized. This failure to diegeticize mocks a Hollywood classicism that differentiated diegetic and nondiegetic sound in order to secure a narrative space distinct from the theatrical space. The previous chapter argued that mock classicism arranges space differently by capitalizing on our presence in the theater; Marshall mocks classicism by mining absence for comedic effect. The boundaries of the filmic and diegetic are constantly blurred in her ventriloquial play with synchronization that comedically (dis)organizes vision and audition. The next chapter continues this concern with synchronization to consider less the (in)discreteness of the diegesis as narrative space than the temporality of film as medium and the diegesis as récit.

CHAPTER 3

Timing Is Everything

Sandrini's Stutter and the Representability of Time

Luis Sandrini was an accomplished circus performer and stage actor who became one of the most popular Argentine movie stars of the 1930s after appearing in the first Argentine sound feature-length film, ¡*Tango!* (Luis Moglia Barth, 1933). In a later film, *Bartolo tenía una flauta* (Bartolo had a flute) (Antonio Botta, 1939), Sandrini plays the role of struggling musician Bartolo Carlomagno who performs as flautist in an itinerant band. Produced by the actor's newly formed production company, Corporación Cinematográfica Argentina, the film follows the flautist as a struggling artist who composes songs in order to make ends meet and provide for his ward. When one of his songs is plagiarized, Bartolo earns a large settlement in court. His song becomes distributed successfully as a vinyl record and circulates widely on the radio. His earnings allow for some social mobility and his eventual engagement to his sweetheart, a nurse who helped care for his sick ward.

In an early sequence, after returning to Buenos Aires with his newly orphaned ward and a stray dog, Sandrini composes his song by candlelight in the middle of the night. Sandrini's early films rely on the stutter of his character, and this sequence of music composition comments on the stutter in the text as an effect of technology on the scene of production. The fluid camera frames Sandrini from behind in a medium close-up. As he transcribes the lyrics to his song, the camera pans across the darkened small apartment. His young ward sleeps in Sandrini's bed, and the blinds cast shadows against the wall in the shape of a beatific beam of light. The camera continues to pan and settles on a long shot of a dog's house. A pulsing light from the signs and advertisements on the street intermittently flashes onto the doghouse as Sandrini repeats the chorus of his song: "El amor se acaba" (Love ends). The camera tracks out into a long shot of the shoebox apartment and returns to Sandrini, now in profile and suggestively positioned under the beam of light. An awkward cut to a medium shot finds Sandrini remarking that his candle is down to its nub—"y la vela también [se acaba]" (and the candlelight, too [ends]). The cut appears disjunctive because the earlier shot featured a yawning Sandrini still finishing the lyric and lit by the pulsing light while the subsequent shot has Sandrini quickly beginning the lyric and the pulsing light "turning on" to light Sandrini. Sandrini blows out the candle and laments that he will never be able to finish his song. Suddenly, the pulsing light from advertisements floods into the room, and Sandrini looks up: "Después quién dice que la publicidad no sirve para nada?" (Who says that advertisements are useless?). The pulsing light shines, and Sandrini furiously returns to his composition. He rushes through his lyrics before the light turns off and quips: "se acabó el amor" (love ended). His ward wakes up, and Sandrini assures him that every time the advertisement returns, he composes a verse, adding: "Claro que el valse escrito así a cachito va a parecer tartamudo" (Of course, the waltz written like this in fits and starts is going to seem to stutter). Sandrini scolds the child and reminds him to go to bed. The child apologizes: "No te enojés, Bartolo" (Don't be upset, Bartolo). The child's response has a lot of reverberant qualities that were missing from the earlier dialogue, suggesting a change in microphone setup to match the shot distance. Riddled with discontinuities in sound and image, this brief sequence suggests the formal, technological, and narrative traits that would characterize the early comedian comedies of Luis Sandrini, a Chaplinesque everyman.[1]

From the representation of the stutter as an effect of modern urban experience in the film content to the jump cut that disrupts temporal continuity and the sound scale-matching across different shot distances that disrupts spatial coherence, the figure of the stutter encompasses a wider range of film practices pertaining to comedy in general. The stutter proves a particularly evocative figure in the Latin American context of the transition to sound cinema, its halting rhythms a counterpoint both to concerns about sound synchronization and the industry's standardization of frame rates and apertures as well as the implementation of a uniform public time nationally and regionally. I use the stutter heuristically, figuring it within film texts, material film practice, and spectatorial experience. Seen in this light, the stuttering waltz in this sequence must be understood in relation to the film's title, *Bartolo tenía una flauta*. The title refers to a nursery rhyme and children's single verse song in a march style often performed as a loop, a suggestive repetition of the same that produces a temporal structure suspended between infinite iteration and possible closure.

Sandrini's films stage a confrontation with standardized time, understood both in terms of the standardization of film through the registration gate and the reification of time in modernity. Technological innovations and the theory of relativity in the late nineteenth and early twentieth century "created distinctive new modes of thinking about and experiencing time and space."[2] Stephen Kern demonstrates how the modern invention of a uniform public time attempted to standardize the plurality of local times but also laid the ground for speculative arguments in favor of heterogeneous private times in the European and American context—an example of what Peter Osborne calls "the dialectics of homogenization and differentiation constitutive of the temporality of modernity."[3] These mid- to late-nineteenth century changes in the Anglo-European context occur nonsynchronously in Latin America. The implementation of a public uniform time in Latin America roughly coincides with the debates about film standardization, arguably another manifestation of the same tendency, and film comedy provides a natural site for examining how the process of standardization yielded ambivalent results. A public uniform time was never quite actualized in Latin American modernity in the same way. Argentina was the first South American country to adopt *any* national standard—the official time from the Córdoba Observatory—as late as 1891, and only adopted the Greenwich meridian in 1920.[4] As late as 1927, the very same year of the first feature-length film with synchronized dialogue sequences (i.e., *The Jazz Singer*), Argentina, Brazil, and Perú were the only countries in South America synchronized with the Greenwich meridian as timekeeping standard; in fact, Ecuador still had two national standards, with Quito roughly five minutes ahead of Guayaquil.[5]

Turning to Latin America highlights how modernity is less an already established structure than "a fruitless attempt to achieve structure and coherence."[6] For Henri Lefebvre, Taylorist innovations or scientific progress are exercises in comic failure. The forward march of abstract space or the advances in the social sciences are complicit in modernity's Sisyphean project of totalization, and have the uncanny effect of producing new modes of countering them—namely, differential space and everyday life. The new "modes of experiencing space and time" augured a form of historical consciousness that both high modernism and popular film comedy contend with, but the former often reduces this engagement to "a model of social experience founded on the new" and "a totalizing history from the standpoint of an ever-vanishing atemporal present."[7] Somewhere between the loop and the stutter, Sandrini's films and film comedy provide a locus for rethinking the structure of temporalization of modernity. Looking to film comedy means identifying an anti-instrumental comic spirit *and* tracing the process of genrification. Sandrini's films are particularly productive sites to unpack the temporality of modernity. On the one hand, the development of conventions in growing industrial filmmaking ventures churned out formula-driven comedic films with a repertory of stock characters. On the other hand, the carefully orchestrated gags and propulsive rhythms coupled with the public horizons of these comedic films often belie the very techniques of standardization in a mock classical spirit.

THE COMEDIAN STUTTERS

Bartolo was not the first time Sandrini had trouble composing a song on screen. In his first film performance, in Luis Moglia Barth's *¡Tango!* (1933), Sandrini's Berretín character has a bad case of writer's block as he strums his guitar and searches for the right words to finish his verse. In the film, Sandrini has a supporting role as the childhood friend of the lovestruck protagonist, Alberto, played by real-life performer Alberto Gómez. In the film, Alberto is hopelessly in love with his neighborhood sweetheart Tita (Tita Merello), who falls in with a rough crowd headed by Malandra (Juan Sarcione). Berretín's stutter is the topic of self-derision throughout the film. In a conversation with Tita's friend Mecha, Sandrini playfully mocks her husband: "Eh-Che me-Mecha, te felicito . . . po-por el marido que-que te echaste . . . ¿Có-cómo la [unintelligible] el pobrecito? ¿Te-te lo sacaste con un cupón de-de los cigarrillos?" (Mecha, congratulations . . . on the husband you landed. How did you meet? Did you redeem him with some trading stamps?).

The woman quickly retorts: "Y vos, ¿de dónde sacaste la lengua?" (And where did you get your tongue?).

Sandrini defends himself, "Me-me la compré po-por mensualidad. E-estas minas son así. U-uno le-le da un consejo y le-le contestan con una papa, eh, pa-patada" (I bought it in monthly installments. These girls are all alike. You try to give them some advice and they answer with a kick).

Sandrini's stutter occasions a couple of amusing double meanings: the inversion of syllables of *Mecha* to "Che me" finds a proper name become an invocatory and reflexive pronoun, and *pata[d]a* becomes *papa*, the repetition of syllable produces an entirely different word. The brief exchange comments on the way social relations become reified, with "cigarette coupons," a type of retail loyalty program in variable denominations, used as the currency facilitating the social relation. More significantly, Sandrini figures his own stutter as a function of a hire-purchase or installment plan, a mode of exchange characteristic of finance capitalism and credit systems. The tongue is less organ than a leased good, Sandrini's body not quite his because of also belonging to the owner or the bank.[8] The tongue is figured less as a natural organ than an instrument assembled in parts; its utterances determined less by the expression of some interiority than by the temporality of layaway.

This confrontation of the mechanic and the natural recalls Bergson's canonic views on laughter and *la mécanisation de la vie*.[9] Bergson's treatise is usually understood in terms of the incommensurability of the mechanic and the natural. In film studies, Chaplin's *Modern Times* provides a useful reference point that Garret Stewart calls the "quintessential Bergsonian comedy" because of the artificial mechanization of the human body.[10] The mechanic and the natural, however, refer not only to actual machines and bodies on screen but also to temporal relations: the mechanic indicates habitual behavior and a relationship to the absent past; the natural refers to the perceived present that interrupts this force of habit. Laughter relies on the recognition of habit and habit out of place, articulating a new relation to the world that forces an awareness of the possibilities existing in the world. The comic spirit is a way of being in the world that privileges "practical, intimate acquaintance" as opposed to instrumentalizing abstraction, a relation to the world that affords fleeting moments of lucidity—throwing light on the workings of the inhabited world.

My turn to Bergson is partly in the spirit of film studies' reassessment of his work in light of both Deleuze's Bergsonism as well as historical accounts of Bergson's relationships with key figures in early cinema and European high modernism.[11] Looking at comedy in Latin America during this period, however, demonstrates the currency of Bergson's philosophy outside Europe in the early twentieth century. In Latin American literary journals, popular periodicals, and even daily newspapers, Bergson was a frequent subject of analysis, and his essay on laughter often explicitly articulated to his broader philosophical project. A summative article from 1939 in the Argentine daily *La nación* characterizes Bergson's project in relation to the rationalization of life, tracing this tendency from ancient philosophy through Enlightenment Ratio, and argues that his ideas are particularly relevant in a Latin American context with a history of institutions and "intelligent" planning.[12] Appearing in the same year as Sandrini's *Bartolo,* this article suggests an affinity with Bergson rooted in a common reaction to "el imperio del racionalismo" (the empire of rationalism), figured historically in Latin America as the lettered city and, I would add, the implementation of uniform public time.[13] The conflict between élan vital and instrumental abstraction manifests in the comic mode as a conflict in forms of temporalization.

When Sandrini stutters, we get an embodied manifestation of the conflict between what should be and what is. In *¡Tango!* Berretín defends his stutter in a later exchange with Alberto, reminiscing about the barrio and lamenting the departure of so many from their generation to the big city. Alberto remarks that Berretín had been a true friend, and Sandrini adds, "A-amigo de-de verdad. Yo te-tendré la lengua a la miseria, ¿no?, pero el-el corazón ta-tá en su lugar" (A true friend. My tongue might be a mess, but my heart is in the right place). On screen and off screen, Sandrini explicated the character's disfluency as a problem of actualization, differentiating the message from its medium. As Sandrini explained in a later interview, he developed the stuttering character in the stage play *Los tres berretines:*

> No era un tartamudo, sino un tipo que no sabía explicarse. Lo saqué así: Yo vivía en La Paternal donde estaba la cancha de Argentinos Juniors. Se juntaba la hinchada en la vereda de casa, en la esquina; muchachos que hablaban y hablaban, discutían, y había uno que no sabía expresarse; era un hincha rabioso, quería decirlo pero no le salía. No era el tartamudo común.
>
> He was not a stutterer but a guy who didn't know how to explain himself. I got him like this: I lived on La Paternal where the Argentinos Juniors pitch was. The fans would get together on the sidewalk, on the corner; boys who would talk and talk, discussed, and there was one who couldn't express himself; he was a rabid fan, he wanted to express that but it wouldn't come out. He was not your typical stutterer.[14]

What was at stake was the medium and not the message, with the comic effect deriving less from *what* was said than *how* it was said.

The stutter then foregrounds how meaning is affected (if not determined) by its medium. In order to elaborate on how Sandrini's character was not a "typical stutterer," let's consider a significant exchange from Luis Sandrini's second collaboration with Luis Moglia Barth from 1937, *La casa de Quirós*. Argentine film historian Domingo di Núbila cites the film as a moment of adulteration for Argentine cinema, a first symptom of hybridity given its origins in the Spanish *sainete*. The film was adapted from a theatrical piece by the Spanish playwright Carlos Arnices, who collaborated on the adapted scenario. The original sainete from 1915 tells the story of a condescending Asturian nobleman whose only daughter falls for a decent boy without title.[15] The Argentine film ships the bankrupt nobleman overseas to Argentina, where distant descendants of his family promise immediate accommodation given his lineage. The nobleman, Don Gil (José Olarra), proves to be an abrasive boor who constantly laments his provincial surroundings and emphatically foregrounds his noble distinction. His only daughter, Sol (Alicia Vignoli), falls in love with Casimiro, Luis Sandrini's character, the son of a local merchant, Valeriano (Miguel Gómez Bao), who is rejected by Don Gil despite the fact that the merchant family subsidizes the Quirós estate. The film follows Sandrini's escalating attempts to court Sol.

Don Gil prides himself on his family name; however, *Quirós* abounds in examples of syncopated play with proper names. In a sequence at Valeriano's general store, a distracted Sandrini is unable to listen to his father's directions or the customers' orders. The father confronts the comedian, idly mooning over the store's merchandise: "¿En qué piensas?" (What are you thinking about?). The comedian replies with a stutter: "En la—en mi—en fa." The father asserts, "En Sol." What begins as a stutter, a seeming evasion of the question at hand, becomes a musical scale. "En la" (About the) signals the beginning of a response that uses *la* as a determinate article. Sandrini falters and appears to begin anew: "en mi" (about my) marks a second attempt to respond using *mi* as either a possessive or object pronoun. Sandrini apparently stumbles again, restarting with "en fa." This third moment can be construed as the beginning of yet another response, with *fa* being the first syllable of whatever Sandrini will claim is on his mind; however, it also ostensibly functions as a punch line, forcing us to reread the fits and starts and apparent reticence of our character as musical notes. Sandrini's stutter occasions this moment of signifying equivocation; *fa* is both a discrete word with a concrete meaning as well as a meaningless phoneme that can only gesture toward a closure in signification. The father's response, "En Sol," functions as a tag to the joke. *Sol* is a homonym, designating in this instance both the musical note as well as the

FIGURE 8. Casimiro (Luis Sandrini) pines for Sol (Alicia Vignoli) in *La casa de Quirós* (1937). Image courtesy of Museo del Cine Pablo Ducrós Hicken.

proper name of his love object. In the above joke structure, we can note how multiple temporalities are generated by the stutter, and a circular and linear temporality coexist: what appears to be repetition or a temporal loop proves to be a sequence of musical notes only to culminate with a beat that functions as both the closure of the temporal loop and the continuation of a sequence, marked perhaps by Sandrini's response, "Sí," both the Spanish word for yes and yet another musical note.[16]

The humor in this exchange derives from the familiar play with proper names, (mis)understood as bearing a context-dependent indexical relation to the person. Although the humor registers as a failure of signification whereby the index becomes symbol, Sandrini does not suspend nomination altogether. Instead, Sandrini generates new meaning from inserting a gap into the word. By treating the word as mere sign and obviating its indexicality, Sandrini stutter-steps to unbind the syllables and suggest new latent meanings—at both indexical and symbolic registers. If Cantinflas's film narratives were driven by frustrated attempts to locate, then Sandrini's film narratives are driven by the desire to specify, or *precisar*. In other words, Cantinflas sidesteps to generate a chain of indices always already pointing elsewhere (and ultimately nowhere); Sandrini pauses so that the same sign can point to multiple elsewheres. His sidestepping is less circuitous dance than it is syncopated rhythm.

The temporal elasticity of the stutter is perhaps literally figured in the protagonist's name, Casimiro. The son's name, Casimiro, is abridged to coin a nickname, Casi. *Casi* is also the word for "almost" or "nearly" in Spanish. Sandrini's character becomes suggestively yoked to an adverb and adjective that refers to incompleteness and lack. In a later sequence when Sandrini attempts to open a wooden box containing the Quirós's belongings, Sandrini stubs his thumb with a hammer. A concerned Sol asks: "¿Se lastimó mucho, Casi?" (Did you hurt yourself, Casi?). Sandrini stutters while holding onto his aching hand: "Casi-casi nada" (Almost nothing). *Casi* perhaps self-reflexively refers to the stutter as such. The comedian's words, the joke's punch line, and the sequence's resolution are *casi*, or nearly, at hand.

The stutter suggests a strategy for working within and between competing temporal registers, and meaning is contingent on how the medium temporalizes. This emphasis on medium or the conditions of meaning making helps explain why the stutter has been cast more broadly as a symptom of modernity within literary studies of high modernist experiments with language. The tropes of linguistic impairment and expressive failures in modernist literature are held in opposition to an episteme that figures knowledge as totalizing and language as a system of correspondence.[17] Sandrini's stutter figures the limits of language; however, his stutter also suggests how this tradition must be recast in the case of popular film *and* Latin America. With regard to the latter, the role of language and its correspondence with the social-symbolic order played an important (and still enduring) role in Latin America. This project of totalization occurs unevenly and nonsynchronously in the region, and the stutter as comic technique manifests this disjuncture accordingly. Furthermore, film recasts the question of intelligibility as a question of temporality and the threshold of the sensible rather than the threshold of the significant. The stutter within a time-based medium is more than an interruption of language that demands textuality and interpretation because it occurs in the play between chronologized and differential time.[18] When the comedian stutters, he allows us to apprehend the noninstrumental potentialities laden within everyday language, but Sandrini's films also allow us to apprehend, at the formal and material levels, the conditions of possibility of the time-based medium. His films do not simply propose the discovery of film's structural properties in a conventional modernist model of medium ontology. They force us to reckon with *how* film became time-based—that is, how the forms of expressiveness of film were explored (if not renewed) with the advent of sound.[19]

THE SOUNDTRACK STUTTERS

¡Tango! is a milestone in Argentine film history for being the first feature-length sound film to use optical sound technology.[20] Film histories about the golden age of Argentine cinema often depict an industry built atop Hollywood technologies and industrial structures merely mining local examples of popular culture. *¡Tango!* is invoked as an obvious example of a successful marriage between foreign technology and popular content mobilized toward nationalist ends. If the tango represented "the character of the people," rooted in the capital city's working-class *arrabales,* then this first melodramatic musical, which celebrates the barrio as the font of the singer's inspiration, provides a useful glimpse into the ways popular culture was being mobilized on screen.[21] For historian Matthew Karush, the transvaluation of tango "exemplifies the familiar process whereby commercial culture depoliticizes the popular traditions that provide its raw material."[22] His project ultimately traces the origins of different forms of popular culture and, in a culture industry narrative, traces their cooptation and transformation into depoliticized objects of mass culture. This paints a familiar portrait of popular culture aligned with class identity formation and political resistance in opposition to mass culture as a site of hegemonic capture. I return to *¡Tango!* neither to reiterate these arguments about film and its complicity with nationalist projects nor to redeem the film as a site of counterhegemonic resistance. Both these arguments read the film image in similar ways, highlighting the same narrative content and situating it within preexisting social formations or given theoretical frameworks about mass culture. Instead, I use Sandrini to highlight the challenges posed by the movietone system and later developments in sound recording and reproduction.[23] This means treating the film sound and image differently, less for the valence of its content than for the particularities of its production and reproduction. These films do not simply represent the nation as an imaginary site for identity construction, whether in a consenting hegemonic mode or in a restive counterpublic. These films are themselves material sites of contestation, which do not simply present

the visible world but present our conditions of viewing, opening onto "the possibility of being present to the self."[24]

Looking more closely at the aforementioned sequence where Sandrini tries his hand at tango composition, frustrated composition not only characterizes Sandrini's Berretín but also early sound cinema in Argentina. The sequence is unusual in the melodramatic musical film because it is structured around gags. It follows the first musical performance by Alberto, where he is persuaded by another friend to pursue a career as a singer and composer. A fade to black from Alberto's performance transitions to a close-up of a hand at a guitar, and we anticipate that the hand will belong to Alberto trying to succeed as a performer. A subsequent long shot reveals that the owner of the hand is none other than Sandrini. The scene is premised on misdirection; whether in the editing or the punch line, the film establishes an expectation and delivers a plausible if unexpected outcome that elicits humor. More particularly, Sandrini is made the site for negotiating different durations: a few seconds of screen duration contain a loop and a leap, a repetition in plot and a six-month jump in story duration.

Curled up on his bed, Sandrini begins singing to his poorly tuned guitar: "Te encontré en un colectivo con la banda repintada / me encajaste en una curva el fuego de tu mirada / desde entonces, me tenés esperándote en la esquina" (I saw you on the bus with the repainted strip / your fiery look struck me when we turned / since then, you've left me waiting on the corner). Sandrini briefly pauses and repeats the last lyric. He plucks a string and grimaces, repeating the words: "de-desde ... esperándote en la esquina." His eyes look toward the ceiling as he sits up in the bed and remarks, "Ha-hace diez días que-que estoy amparado en la-la esquina sin poderla hallar" (It's been ten days that I've been stuck on the corner without being able to find her). The joke relies on equivocating the lover's plight and the writer's impasse. Sandrini continues addressing an absent Alberto, asking for inspiration given the composer's rapid success after only six months: "a ver si me ajudás [y] así me salgo de la esquina" (let's see if you can help me so that I can get out of the corner). Sandrini starts singing again, repeating his stumbling refrain—"Desde entonces, me ténes"—three times, each time more frustrated and with a higher volume. His final refrain comes with a cut to the comedian in profile and Alberto appearing at his door. A slight elaboration is audible in the sound track, as the final syllable is repeated and extended until Alberto interrupts with a more reverberant voice.

Listening more intently to the soundtrack yields further insights. The introduction of Alberto occurs over a shot transition that appears continuous because occurring over Sandrini's song. And yet the editing adds an extra note, if not an extra syllable, to Sandrini's verse. Ostensibly a function of "bad" editing, the slippage is barely noticeable, particularly issued from the lips of a stutterer. His stutter is a more forgiving ground for the editor because slippages in continuity editing are more difficult to identify if something is already jerking or discontinuous. Sandrini's stuttering sounds provide an excellent testing ground (if not scapegoat) for developing sound editing practices.

These editing practices pertain not simply to the coherence of dialogue and the avowal of temporal continuity but also to the coherence of the sound space. In the opening of the sequence, the intensity of the guitar changes with the shot distance, louder and fuller in close-up but fainter in the long shot. Matching the intensity of the sound event to the shot distance is a technique of sound recording relatively common in early sound cinema and is now referred to as scale matching. This "commonsense" approach to sound figured the relation of image and sound to the relation between a body's eyes and ears. Our embodied judgment of the direction and distance of sound depends on directional hearing (unavailable with the monaural microphone) and the ratio of reflected sound to direct sound (manipulated through controlling reverberation). Early manuals and standards suggested scale matching in the early 1930s, designing sound to emulate natural hearing:

> [If] the camera is equipped with a lens for making a long shot, the microphone should be placed facing partly toward the actor and partly toward some large, hard surface . . . so that it will receive mostly the reflected voice of the speaker. Then when the sound is reproduced in a theatre, the proper illusion of distance of the speaker . . . will be obtained. But if the camera is set for a close-up, the microphone should be hung in front of the actor and close to him, so that it will receive practically nothing but the direct voice.[25]

This set up, however, failed to account for analytic editing, which begins with an establishing shot and long shot before cutting to different shot distances as demanded by dramatic exigency. The corresponding changes to sound intensity in the same space disrupted the spatial coherence of the scene. Scale matching would decline as a practice; the fidelity of sound recording and reproduction became less significant than the coherence of the sound space in relation to narrative space. The latter would occur over time as sound equipment evolved, as sound libraries grew, and as radio practices were adopted. Sandrini and his stutter paper over some of these early discontinuities in the soundtrack but arguably also figure the negotiations that occur as sound practices *(casi)* become standard operating procedure.

Early sound cinema was haunted by the stutter; its sound engineers worked to ensure fidelity across transcription, storage, and reproduction. The transition to sound may have temporalized the image by controlling sound-film recording speed through recorder motors kept in synchronism and by normalizing film projection speed; however, this temporalization relied on a material delay manifest as metric distance in the composite print.[26] Sound engineers referred to sound recording and reproduction equipment as a "delay circuit," designed to store sound on film (or a wax disc), or "delay material," so as to be reproduced in the future.[27] Further, the equipment in the movie theater had a 14.5-inch distance between "the picture aperture of the projection machine and the small light aperture of the sound apparatus," so that movietone or composite prints had sound printed roughly twenty frames ahead of the action print (i.e., just over a half second) in order to secure synchronization.[28] From the possible flutter during sound transcription to the development of competing storage formats to the material determinants of sound reproduction equipment in exhibition, perhaps it should not be surprising that contemporaneous accounts in Argentina characterized the first years of the 1930s as a "cine 'tartamudo'" [a "stuttering" cinema].[29]

Understanding the development of sound practices in Argentina is tricky business given the varied sound technologies, the limited professional organizations, the few accounts of sound engineers from the period, and later preservation policy. I trace the development of sound practices through an approach that weds media archaeology to radical formalism, articulating historical accounts from American and European professionals working or doing market research in Latin America to close reading of the films from the transition-to-sound period. Despite the complicated status of close reading in reception studies as well as histories of technology, studying film texts proves crucial to delineating sound practices in the period. For instance, if the composite print had a sound track twenty frames ahead of the action print, then editing a sound film meant always accounting for this half-second delay with every cut. Studying editing, then, provides one way to understand evolving sound practices. The aforementioned challenges in sound recording and reproduction must be understood as exercises within a delay circuit, and film texts function as the actualization (as transmission) of this delay and storage system. In addition to sound editing, changes in sound mixing, the standardization of close-miked sound, the evolution of scoring practices and nondiegetic musical cues, and the growth of sound libraries and sound effects engineering are all additional components to be listening for in the soundscape of films from this period. Sandrini is a useful figure for our purposes not only for his comedic performance but also because he was the star in the first sound film of three different film studios and his own production company. Aside from ¡Tango!, Sandrini starred in the film adaptation of *Los tres berretines (The Three Amateurs)* (Enrique Susini, 1933) for Lumiton, *Don Quijote del altillo* (Don Quixote in the loft) (Manuel Romero, 1936) for the Sociedad Impresora de Discos Electrofónicos (SIDE), and *El canillita y la dama* (*The Newsie and the Lady*) (Luis César Amadori, 1938) for his own production company, Corporación Cinematográfica Argentina.[30] The stutter is not simply a metaphor for the development (and not quite standardization) of sound practices because its inscription in film becomes an audible marker of the negotiations occurring at the material level.

Sandrini starred in the original stage version of *Los tres berretines* as Eusebio, yet another frustrated tango composer who can neither read sheet music nor write lyrics. The play was adapted for the screen in 1933 by Enrique Susini (working with cameraman John Alton), becoming the second feature-length, sound-on-film release from Argentina. This story depicts the impact of three *berretines*, or popular passions—soccer, tango and cinema (originally radio in the stage version)—on an immigrant household and its three sons. Often used in histories to thematize the rise of mass culture, the film was a huge success for the new Lumiton studio. Premiering only twenty days after Argentina Sono Film's ¡Tango!, the film cost the studio eighteen thousand pesos but yielded nearly one million pesos at the box office.[31] Eusebio was the role that spawned Sandrini's "Cachuso" type, frustrated not because he does not have something to say but because he does not have the means to say it. Eusebio has a tune in his head, taking inspiration from the percussive rhythms of the everyday; however, he cannot reproduce this tune because he cannot transcribe it. Inspiration strikes during a sequence at the patriarch's hardware store. The sequence begins with close up of a newspaper article and a medium long shot of the father, with a piercing whistle from an unknown source on the soundtrack. We eventually find the sound source in a foreshortened medium close-up of a whistling Sandrini marking beats with a pot. Unlike the sequence in ¡Tango! where different shots had different sound qualities, here the

FIGURE 9. Eusebio (Luis Sandrini) composes his tango at the hardware store in *Los tres berretines* (1933). Image courtesy of Museo del Cine Pablo Ducrós Hicken.

sound from one shot is laid over the earlier shots, inserting a sound hermeneutic that makes the narrative space cohere. The percussive sounds Sandrini elicits from his father's hardware store items inspire the would-be composer, who abandons his post in order to find a transcriber. The film follows his attempts to enlist the help of others to get his melody onto paper, to get his tango onto a delay material in a dilemma not unlike that of silent cinema during the transition to sound.

The search for optimal transcription and an effective "delay circuit" was conducted differently by these two early studios. Unlike Argentina Sono Film, founded by former employees of film distributors who imported their sound equipment and leased studio space until building their own in 1937, Lumiton erected its own studios in 1932 with its own sound recording technologies developed by founders Cesar Guerrico, Enrique Susini, and Luis Carranza, who were sound and electrical engineers from the radio industry.[32] Both early studios used Bell & Howell film cameras, and Lumiton had French DeBrie developing machines; however, they used different sound recording equipment, one imported and the other native.[33] Unlike the musical numbers from *¡Tango!*, which featured songs whose popularity preceded the film's release, the songs in

Los tres berretines were relatively better integrated into the narrative, including an original composition released as an RCA Victor recording and performed by Osvaldo Fresedo and his orchestra in the film's concluding scenes.[34] The role of the musical number in these early films has been the subject of analysis, particularly in delineating the evolving forms of the musical film genre in the region. These analyses, however, avoid discussing the music in relation to film sound practices, often privileging the musical content and its relation to film narrative as the distinguishing feature of the Argentine (or Latin American) musical. When we watch and listen to these two early films, however, we can also identify a difference in sound practices and the construction of a coherent sound space. The different sound practices in these "first" films demonstrate the still-unsystematized sound practices of early soundtracks, characterized by unresolved relations between the sound and image and changing interrelations between the component soundtrack elements (i.e., dialogue, music, sound effects). Looking more carefully at how the sound space is being orchestrated through sound design, sound editing, and sound mixing in transitional cinema allows us to reframe the question of the location of culture away from "what is particular on the soundtrack?" to "how is the soundtrack particular?"

Rather than simply identifying a sound or interpreting soundtrack elements as supplements to the operations of the image, we want to consider the normalization of particular sound practices in a historical and cultural context.[35] Sound studies reminds us that film sound is neither an innocent recording of ostensibly natural sounds nor technologically neutral. It must be understood as a "site of conflict . . . a theater of war" between competing technologies, industrial practices, and aesthetic conventions.[36] As Rick Altman notes, earlier sound practices oftentimes exhibited an all-or-nothing logic for music and effects "wholly dependent on earlier sound practices," suggesting that each of these functioned as an autonomous and uncoordinated track.[37] He suggests a historical view of film sound—a process of soundtrack maturation—through evolving intercomponent and intrasoundtrack relationships. His "mise-en-bande analysis concentrates on the interaction among the various components making up the soundtrack."[38] A mise-en-bande analysis traces how the relationships among soundtrack components changed over time as a function of particular industry practices, aesthetic conventions, and available technologies. In the context of classical Hollywood, moving away from accurate sound reproduction to sound realism (or a sonic vraisemblable) meant the appearance of discursively oriented narrative sounds, such as loud punctuating sound events or the musical reinforcement of narratively significant information, which organized flow and addressed audiences.[39] The discursive manipulation of sound for narratively important material—the orchestration of sound realism—meant scale mismatching, level-volume dialogue, nondiegetic music use, and the reduction of spatial characteristics. Could this process occur differently within a context negotiating local and foreign sound practices and technologies? The maturation of the soundtrack in mock classicism occurs along different axes. In the Argentine (and by extension Latin American) context, we must also consider how this process occurs later in the decade and necessarily includes the negotiations and exchanges between local and foreign sound practices and technologies. The normalization of film practices through both foreign and local as well as intranational and regional competitors becomes inscribed and manifest in the stutter of the film soundtrack. If our discussion of Marshall explored the relation of sound to image in order to argue for an implicated (sound) space in Latin American film comedy, then Sandrini opens onto questions about relations within the soundtrack and the different configuration of (sound) realism. The musical numbers in these early films are not only examples of popular content (with mass-commodity or class-identitarian implications) but are also key "site[s] of conflict" between soundtrack components. A mise-en-bande approach during these privileged moments examines how—or whether—these soundtrack components worked in tandem and what effect their interrelations had on producing a continuous sound space.

The musical numbers in *Los tres berretines* revolve around Eusebio's quest; however, the comedian is never the performer but always an onlooker, an organizing point of view (but seldom a point of audition). His speech or movements usually bookend the musical performance. His jerky movements or his stuttering speech provides a convenient mask or segue. The first extended musical performance occurs after Eusebio gets his melody transcribed by a dishonest pianist who transcribes a generic tarantella rather than the original melody. Sandrini rushes to see a friend who is in the middle of performing "Ventanita florida." The sequence begins with a hard cut from the pianist's home to another interior with an off-screen male singing voice. A piano run serves as a makeshift sound bridge with an unclear sound source: is it diegetic or nondiegetic, and if diegetic, is it issuing from the first space or the second space? The second space is a nondescript stairwell. The camera watches Sandrini arrive and climb the stairs. A subsequent high angle shot from the landing ends on a close-up of Sandrini's feet at a standstill, and all the while the voice-off continues into the following extreme long shot of the interior of a café. The sound source within this final extreme long shot is difficult to parse because the music has few directional cues and there are no changes to the sound quality to establish a point of audition relative to a sound source. Sandrini enters center frame and faces the two musicians frame left. Only the staging can cue us into the sound source, in part because of limitations with monaural sound technology and in part because of an aversion to analytical editing. The music blares as the camera cuts within the scene, from a medium close-up of Sandrini to another of the singers. This sets up a familiar pattern where music accompanies a mobile camera, more shot transitions, and a shorter average shot length. Throughout the film, sequences with multiple shots use synchronized (and usually direct) sound. Shot transitions threaten spatial coherence because of variable microphone placement, scale matching, and actor staging and performance; however, in this sequence music frees the camera within the narrative space. The single music recording simulates a coherent sound space so that editing and camera movement can construct a continuous space without worries. This mobility is again evident at the end of this jam session when another pianist plays what Eusebio believes is his tango composition but will learn is a tarantella. The gag begins with a high-angle medium shot of a pianist playing the sheet music. The music accompanies the subsequent tracking shot featuring the faces of each listener, which culminates with a close-up of Sandrini. As the music plays, confusion gradually dawns on each listener in what is very nearly a time-lapse study of a single listener's face. Sandrini has an appropriately delayed reaction and does not quite understand what has happened for a few additional beats. The time-lapse effect is foiled by a delay in recognition—even Sandrini's reaction is just out of sync.

The return of direct sound and spoken dialogue presents certain challenges, which the technical team deals with in two different ways in both musical moments in this sequence. The later tarantella moment ends with a series of dialogue exchanges with a static camera; each line of dialogue is uttered visibly on screen and each transition occurs only when there is no direct sound on the soundtrack. The difference in sound editing during and after the musical performance is noteworthy because after the remarkable tracking camera movement, we return to synced dialogue and shot/reverse-shot editing without split edits or matching action. The earlier performance of "Ventanita florida" provides a different approach to the return of direct sound. The song concludes with the singing voice's final note and instrumental coda over a medium close-up of Sandrini staring in admiration. The following shot begins with the musician strumming his guitar once as if punctuating the conclusion of the song, its different timbre suggesting an element added simply for the purposes of continuity. This punctuating shot uses remarkable deep-focus photography, with the musicians in the foreground, Sandrini in the midground, and another onlooker in the background. As the singers speak with Sandrini in a long take, the singers' voices and Sandrini's voice have different intensities and reverberant qualities, the microphone placed with the camera as a point of audition. The sound design attempts to produce a "deep-focus sound" to go along with the deep-focus photography in the image, except the difference in sound qualities that accurately suggests depth has a deleterious effect on the production of a coherent narrative space.

After finally finding a trustworthy scribe at the local café's *orquesta típica*, the production circuit concludes in one final sequence where Sandrini collects his composition.[40] Sandrini happily takes his sheet music: "¿Acá están todos los chiflidos que le largué? ¿No me [falta] ninguno?" (All the whistles are here? None are missing?). Sandrini's suspicion is that of the cinema, that of the different legibility of the transcribed or recorded sound, reliant on symbolic and indexical rather than iconic sign systems that require performance or transduction/reproduction, respectively. Sandrini excitedly wants to see his tango performed but now needs lyrics. His friend points out the dive's resident poet, and they approach the starving artist. The poet agrees to write some lyrics for a cup of coffee and a bite to eat. He pores over a piece of paper, pulling at his hair until he finally puts pen to paper. An elliptical fade to black "fast forwards" to a drowsy Sandrini yawning distractedly. The poet reads his composition, a stilted funereal poem. Sandrini coerces the poet to change the lyrics by withholding payment in kind. The poet scribbles some "versos pedestres" (pedestrian verses) and in a matter of seconds in a single long take finishes: "Araca la cana, ya estoy engrillao / un par de ojos negros me han engayolao."[41] From the baroque elegiac poem to the melodic *lunfardo*[42] about a frustrated romance, the scene has been discussed as illustrative of the homogenizing tendency of mass culture forms.[43] In this sequence that culminates with a musical performance, however, we must listen for the particular relation of sound space to the classical arrangement of diegesis/narrative space and theatrical space. Again, the introduction of sound meant the integrity of the visible space of the screen was compromised by the sound space of the diegesis, and the institutionalization of sound-signifying practices quickly bound these spaces together to preserve the integrity of the screen space as separate from the acoustical space of the theater.[44] Mock classicism unbinds these spaces to augur a different spatial arrangement that also bears on the relation between the film as text and the site of film spectatorship.

The characters approach the poet in a panning medium long shot with audible background music that becomes more muted in the following close-up of the poet, whose eyes track the strangers as they sit at his table. When Sandrini and his friends sit in a medium long shot, the sound changes abruptly with an audible fiddle suddenly added to the again audible background noise and the now reverberant dialogue. The poet glances at the sheet music and some music swells on the soundtrack. Is it a nondiegetic transitional cue? Is the café's band gearing up to play? Could it be the sheet music in the poet's head? More likely, the music is a useful way to conceal discontinuities in shot transitions. Where we locate the music in relation to the screen space speaks to how we reconcile the sound space and the narrative space and the spatial arrangement of the cinema to which we are accustomed. The music, however, occupies a certain zone of indiscernibility between the diegetic and the nondiegetic so that the relation between sound space and narrative space is mutable. The music halts during the fade to black. The poet's first declamation is edited unusually. Unlike the editing in rest of the film, which waits for pauses in the conversation or a change in on-screen speaker before a cut, the poet ends his first line and the camera cuts to a close-up. The rhythm of the recital serves as a good cover, and yet the poet's speaking voice and the change in background noise undermine the narrative space being built through continuity editing conventions. A subsequent reverse shot shows Sandrini's very expressive face, a sneer that contorts with each spoken verse. Despite the change in camera placement and the visible background, the sound levels remain the same as in the previous shot. This suggests the direct sound from the previous shot was simply laid over Sandrini's reaction, an assumption confirmed when the same camera setup later features direct sound with a very different sound signature. Once the poet finishes his "pedestrian" composition, Sandrini and company exit toward the stage. The music finally gives the camera license to explore a coherent narrative space at its leisure. More than generic punctuation or local color, these musical interludes are privileged moments when narrative space and sound space work in lockstep. If shoring up narrative space in opposition to theatrical space allowed film to be a better commodity, then this mise-en-bande analysis suggests that sound space intervenes on this classical spatial arrangement. The maturation of the soundtrack and the production of sound realism occur through a reconfiguration of classicism and the removal of contingency. In this sequence, we bear witness to the conclusion of a certain mode of commodity production in the film content (i.e., the tango), but we also begin to see the how Argentine sound film sought to become a better commodity.

Sandrini's next "first" sound film for SIDE was *Don Quijote del altillo* (Manuel Romero, 1936). SIDE was a new studio, also responsible for the early film successes of Libertad Lamarque, spearheaded by sound technicians Alfredo y Fernando Murúa. The Murúa brothers had developed a native sound-on-disc technology used in the earliest sound film experiments of the late 1920s and early 1930s in association with the production company Ariel, notably releasing the first feature-length, sound-on-disc film *La via de oro* (Edmo Cominetti, 1931).[45] After years of working as a sound studio for other production companies and even leasing studio space, the studio produced its first feature using a variable-density optical soundtrack.[46] *Quijote* was filmed with recording equipment developed by the Murúa brothers. By the mid-1930s, Hollywood's soundtrack had quickly matured, with sound-on-disc falling in disuse and early examples of competing sound-on-film technologies consolidating around industry standards.[47] Most notably, the development of a multiple channel recoding (also known as a multiplane sound system) was crucial to addressing many of the difficulties presented by sound editing in earlier soundtracks. The ability to record each soundtrack component separately and rerecord them together onto one soundtrack while manipulating their volume levels meant that film sound needn't be direct sound *and* that intercomponent and intrasoundtrack relationships were no longer simply sequential (e.g. dialogue then music) but also simultaneous (e.g., dialogue in relation to music).[48] The availability of this technology in Argentina was uneven, with some studios importing equipment—Argentina Sono Film and Estudios San Miguel were equipped with RCA studio units by 1941—while others continued to develop their own sound recording equipment—Lumiton, Pampa Film, and SIDE all developed native-built sound recording equipment using or adapting available technologies such as the Eric Berndt galvanometer.[49]

Quijote used this native-built sound recording equipment and provides an interesting document of early attempts to improvise or orchestrate multiplane sound design, particularly evident in the use of foley sound effects in relation to other elements on the soundtrack. In the film, Sandrini continues building his persona of an idle and unattractive if well-intentioned and decent young man living hand to mouth. His character, again Eusebio, is unemployed and three months late on the rent on his *altillo,* an attic studio apartment. By way of synopsis, Eusebio falls for his new neighbor, Urbana (Nuri Montsé), a young receptionist at a local textile factory who begins a romantic affair with her boss, Martínez (Eduardo Sandrini, the comedian's brother). Eusebio discovers that Martínez is married and bribes the boss into providing him a job and staying away from Urbana. Eusebio eventually proves himself worthy of his new position and winds up engaged to Urbana.

Quijote presents discontinuities in the image—ostensible "errors" in relation to the (by then) established conventions of continuity editing. In the opening minutes of the film, Sandrini stands atop the stairs in front of his attic apartment in a medium long shot, frustratingly trying to one-up Urbana's mischievous young brother by convincing the boy to descend the stairs backwards. The boy claims not to understand, and, as Sandrini begins to demonstrate, the boy pushes his sister's suitor down the stairs. Sandrini falls out of frame. The extreme long shot of the steep stairs captures the comedian violently tumbling down in a supposedly continuous shot; however, the body does not fall in continuous motion. The continuous shot is in fact a stuttering trick shot: Sandrini does three separate somersaults in three separate shots edited to appear continuous. Sandrini jerks from one step to the next; his body—like his speech—unable to simulate continuity. The ostensible continuity of the shot is secured only through the film sound. The tumbling body in the image is accompanied by labored sound effects that loop continuously despite the discontinuous trick shot.

Listening more closely to the soundtrack reveals the seams of this aural trick and forces us to consider the stutter in terms of the component elements of the soundtrack and the resultant sound-image relations—that is, between the verbal tics of the comedian, the foley sound effects, and the score by Alberto Soifer.[50] In the aforementioned sequence, the long shot at the top of the stairs features synchronized dialogue that ends with the child screaming in delight as the comedian falls out of frame. The child's cry jarringly stops once the tumbling sound effects begin and the image cuts to the subsequent extreme long shot. Once Sandrini lands at the bottom of the stairs, the image cuts to a medium shot. Despite having finished his tumbling pass, the sound effects continue for a few additional beats and are just as suddenly removed from the soundtrack with the arrival of new dialogue. The dialogue and sound effects function as autonomous sound elements each driven by their own logics. The stutter, then, also refers to a conflict between component parts, a visible and audible manifestation of ongoing negotiations of technological and industrial practices.

Quijote provides additional examples of "early sound-cinema's characteristic jurisdictional conflict" and the relation of sound practices to evolving narrative conventions.[51] In a subsequent scene when Martínez gets his warehouse workers to threaten Sandrini, the comedian uses his well-trained dog to outsmart his foes. Sitting on the sidewalk outside the factory in a silent extreme long shot, Sandrini waits for Urbana to leave work. Three large men approach the comedian, entering into a tighter long shot. The image cut precedes the arrival of ambient sound by several beats. The men stand looming over Sandrini and threaten the comedian, the volume levels of their speaking voices relatively high to ensure intelligibility. Sandrini's dog responds to the threat, barking three times while framed in close-up. The bark unsettles for several reasons. First, the barking is not synchronized to the dog's mouth. Further, as the scene pulls out to a long shot, with the earlier shot's sound setup for capturing dialogue, the dog bark has dropped out of the soundtrack. Finally, there is an audible difference in the space occupied by the dialogue and the dog bark. The former's reverb lends a sense of space missing from the flattened and nonsynchronized dog bark.

Not only does the film display a conflict *between* soundtrack elements but also *within* an ostensibly autonomous component; the dialogue, music, and sound effects are similarly not monolithic. The dog bark again provides a useful reference point, now in conflict not with narratively consequential or humorous dialogue but with other sound effects. Later in the film during their romantic affair, Urbana and her boss exit the factory together in a silent extreme long shot while Sandrini looks on disconsolately. The soundtrack remains silent until the slamming doors of the car are accompanied by shuddering sound effects. A subsequent cut to a final long shot shows the comedian's dog barking and following the accelerating car. The dog barks are more carefully synchronized to the dog's mouth but are awkwardly intercut with the sound effects of the moving car. The sound effects are not layered but alternated on the soundtrack, producing a syncopated and stuttering effect.

Rather than an unsophisticated soundtrack, which would presume an incompetence or technological backwardness with Hollywood sound realism as standard, Sandrini's mock classicism discursively manipulates sound for comedic effect. During a later sequence in *Quijote,* the play with the sound hermeneutic compromises the sequence's spatial and temporal continuity. Sandrini sullenly mopes in the frame, having been rejected by Urbana, until in a flash he rushes into his studio apartment and retrieves his dog and a gun. The melodramatic music swells as he rushes in and out of shots before a hostile exchange of words between the landlady and Sandrini. Sandrini pulls out his gun and threatens the woman, who drops some plates while stumbling to the ground. The sequence cuts to a close-up of the broken plates on the ground without providing any subsequent shots of the woman, the gun, or Sandrini. Has Sandrini harmed the meddlesome landlady? Has she simply fainted upon seeing the gun? The clash of the plates as a sound event operates both as a synchronous effect as well as an ostensible symbolic substitute for the gunshot. If the cinema experience relies on a sound hermeneutic whereby the sound and image mutually reinforce their dissimulation through their apparent redundancy, then this sequence undermines this process by positing a sound with both an indexical (breaking plates) and symbolic (gunshot) relation to the image.[52] The comedic polysemic play of the comedian, capitalizing on animating the semiotic possibilities of the word, finds a counterpart in the soundtrack. Tethering the sound space to narrative space relies on the spectators' rerouting from apparatus to diegesis; however, a sound with two possible sources compromises the integrity of the diegesis. A sound that is both narratively significant and discursive convention, the "gunshot" (mis)perceived at levels both diegetic and extradiegetic blurs the distinctions between narrative space and theater space. This is not a high modernist reflexivity that reveals the medium as such because there is no stable narrative space from which to be distanced.

Immediately following this polysemic sound event, *Quijote* features a sequence with parallel editing where the manipulation of sound space(s) draws and redraws the boundaries of the visible spaces on screen. After his encounter with the landlady, the film shows Sandrini in an extreme long shot in a forest. The relationship of this space to the previous space is unclear, accentuated by the lack of both a sound bridge and natural diegetic sound effects in the green space. Sandrini ambles across the frame before the sequence cuts to another extreme long shot of a broad street and a waiting car. A man—not Sandrini—enters the frame, racing to the car. What is the relation between these spaces? The continued silence on the soundtrack confuses the relation between spaces despite a suggested continuity in screen direction. The camera moves in to a medium long shot of the parked car with two goons peering off frame left as the man approaches the car to announce the arrival of someone else. These two visible spaces remain separate or unrelated without nondiegetic sound cues or diegetic sound relations between them; in other words, without the discursive manipulation of sound to produce diegetic coherence, the simultaneity suggested by the parallel editing becomes compromised.

The film cuts to Sandrini in long shot as he pulls out his gun. Sandrini brings the gun to his head but hesitates, encouraging his pet to leave him to die. The dog stays at the comedian's side. The comedian gesticulates with the gun, its barrel pointing toward and then away from the comedian. The sequence returns to the road in an extreme long shot. Another car approaches to the left of the waiting vehicle; the goons approach the moving car. The camera reveals a young woman behind the steering wheel ambushed by the would-be kidnappers. The woman screams for help, "¡Socorro!" We leave the roadside to return to Sandrini, still standing with his gun pressed to his temple. Sandrini pulls the trigger, but the gun fails to shoot. Sandrini opens the gun chamber before trying several more times—the audible click of the defective gun the only audible sound. On the road once more, the woman still loudly struggles against the might of the two kidnappers. The camera returns to Sandrini, still pulling the trigger ineffectually until the barely audible pleas of the woman are faintly heard in the distance. What were two separate visible spaces with reinforcing discrete soundscapes become connected narrative space through the discursive manipulation of sound. Sandrini, unaware of the screams, throws the gun to the ground in frustration. The gun discharges, and the gunshot motivates a cut to a medium shot of the woman as she is released by her startled kidnappers. We return to Sandrini in long shot, staring at his gun in annoyance. Suddenly, the woman's screams are perfectly audible, and Sandrini turns in their direction. The two spaces are brought together through editing once Sandrini enters another silent extreme long shot of the road. The woman runs toward him and is framed in a medium shot with her erstwhile savior. The resolution of this parallel sequence suggests that Sandrini was a few feet away from the kidnapping, just off the road. The discontinuous spatial relations, reinforced by the absent discursive sound markers, are less significant here than the way the sound resolves these relations for comedic effect. The faint pleas of the woman just before the crucial gunshot suggest that the separation of the spaces is less a function of shoddy sound mixing than the orchestration of a gag. The errant gunshot is doubly misdirected: the bullet misses the comedian's temple, and the kidnappers mistake the bullet's direction. Both plot lines proceed unaware of the other until a loud punctuating event brings the two screen spaces together on the soundtrack before they are finally connected visibly on screen.

The misapprehension of the sound event allows the comedian to rescue the damsel in distress but perhaps also figures the sound film spectator's constitutive misapprehension. The sound cinema uses the illusion of synchronized sound and image to convince us that the sound is coming from the narrative world rather than a loudspeaker.[53] Much like the spectator rerouting the source of the sound from loudspeaker to diegesis, the kidnappers misattribute the source of the gunshot. In an aural riff on Noel Carroll's switch-image gag, these two sequences punctuated by gunshots rely on conflicts in designating aural objects.[54] These sequences display the operations of a discursive sound system in tension with a narrative system, but one less invested in the narrative-oriented conventions and sound realism of Hollywood classical sound treatment. Hollywood sound treatment articulated narrative sound and visible screen space as distinct from theatrical space. The tension between narrative and discursive sounds in the Sandrini film comedy is predicated not on narrative economy but on gag structure. In other words, sound design is less dictated by the transmission of plot information or the construction of a story world than by the production of moments of misapprehension that coordinate spaces differently. In this mock classicism, we hear a sound "realism" where sound is insignificant but never incomprehensible.

OF TYPES AND MEN

Luis Sandrini sustained his commercial success throughout his career, but critical (and later public) esteem did not always follow. The vicissitudes of critical and popular opinion open onto questions of temporality in star studies. Luis Sandrini began a pioneer, became dated, and now is (mis)remembered. The rise-and-fall narrative is only partly about actual success and is more about the relation of the figure to time and memory. In discussing the star as a visible social icon, star studies either inserts the star into a rise (and fall) narrative within a historicist chronology or treats the star as a semiotic construction and iterative or recurrent formation in an analytical space where the temporality immanent to the object of inquiry is repressed. Rather than reconstruct the star or use the star as symptom, could we use the star as a way of understanding the category (and temporality) of experience in the age of mechanical reproducibility?

During the late 1940s and early 1950s, Sandrini was winning accolades for his film work (including two Premios Cóndor de Plata, in 1950 and 1954) and was hobnobbing with international celebrities as ambassador in the Mar del Plata Film Festival. Indeed, an article in the biweekly magazine *El hogar,* a popular lifestyle publication in Argentina throughout the early twentieth century, celebrated Sandrini as "un hombre con una visión cómica extraordinariamente humana" (a man with an extraordinarily human comic vision).[55] The author "Celuliode" celebrates Sandrini's natural and honest approach. Instead of appearing in films that invented "stupid stories" and indulged in caricature or "maquieta," Sandrini appealed directly to the heart of the spectator by remembering that "reality was more powerful than fiction."[56] Two decades later in a more politically restive context, Sandrini was still prolific and already the subject of tributes in the popular press. The star became myth during his lifetime:

> Lejos en el tiempo, pero no en el recuerdo, la imagen de un Sandrini distinto vuelve a moverse, a vivir, a imponernos su gracia y su poesía elemental.... Es un poco el payaso que empieza a desvanecerse y el actor que empieza a nacer.... Son por supuesto imágenes evocadas al azar. Hay muchas otras ... vivas seguramente en la memoria de infinidad de espectadores.
>
> Far back in time, but not in memory, the image of a different Sandrini stirs once again, alive, to impose its grace and elementary poetry.... The clown begins to vanish and the actor begins to be born.... Of course, these are images randomly evoked. There are many others, ... surely alive in the memory of countless spectators.[57]

Others would not have such fond memories:

> Siempre digo que algunas escenas protagonizadas por Sandrini me persiguieron y me persiguen como ejemplos de golpes bajos bien dados.... [Él] ayudó a construir una filosofía de consumo masivo que es toda una actitud frente a la vida: la que intenta que todo quede como está, que nada cambie.... Atravesó 40 años de vida argentina y las más variadas crisis nacionales e internacionales ajeno a todo, lejos de cualquier realidad, vendiendo siempre la misma mercancía. Con el tiempo desfiguró lo auténticamente noble de su talento artístico: el elemento tragicómico de su personalidad ... desde su máscara de anti-héroe conformista complaciente.
>
> I always say that some Sandrini scenes haunted me and still haunt me as examples of well-delivered low blows.... [He] helped construct a philosophy of

mass consumption that is an attitude toward life that tried to keep everything as is, that nothing change. . . . He lived removed from everything through 40 years of Argentine life and the most varied national and international crises, removed from any reality, always selling the same product. Over time, he warped what was authentically noble in his artistic talent: the tragicomic element of his personality . . . from his mask of a conformist, complacent anti-hero.[58]

The author laments feeling cheated by Sandrini, who he claims a false representative of the popular. Sandrini becomes the ultimate figure of a growing culture industry, not only because he was a film and television star and not only because of his biographical politics but also because the generic formula of his films and the repetition of his stock character ostensibly abided by the logic of commodity production.

By the time of Sandrini's death, the star's currency was gone. His films no longer seemed relevant. The laughter did not come as easily. The tragic notes in Sandrini's performance dominate these posthumous tributes:

> Se trataba de un modo especial de jugar damas, en el que ganaba el que lograba perder todas sus piezas (el gana-pierde). . . . Algo de esto tiene el humorista. Es un proceso de integración por disgregación. . . . Y el humorista, que más dispuesto esté a perder, a ceder, a entregar todas sus piezas, es quien gana. . . . Sandrini no fue nunca un payaso sino un ser de carne y hueso transfundido en las naturalezas de sus personajes.

> It speaks to a special way of playing checkers, in which the winner was the person able to lose all his pieces (loser takes all). . . . Something like this characterizes the humorist. It is a process of integration through disaggregation. . . . And the humorist who is most willing to lose, to cede, to give his pieces wins. . . . Sandrini was never a clown but a being of flesh and blood transfused into his characters.[59]

From the comic to the sentimental, from honest naturalness to anachronistic affectation, how do we discuss a star when his reception never quite yields a stable picture? On the one hand, the selection of a synchronic instant seems insufficient precisely because his contemporaneous appraisal was so fraught, and contemporary estimations are seemingly torn between commemoration and disdain. On the other hand, attempting to narrate these changes in reception along a diachronic timeline of Sandrini's biography or the changing cultural sensibilities of Argentine film criticism overdetermines the star text. How to conceive the star without the biographical time of succession or the atemporality of analytical space? Somewhere between the fact of successive film texts and biographical trivia, the cultural remanence of the star, and the shifting horizon of reception of his films, speaking about a star necessarily means speaking about different forms of temporalization articulated to one figure. If the recognition of a star means negotiating succession, recurrence, *and* remanence, then the study of the star must also engage with these forms of temporality. The complaint that Sandrini and his persona never changed over the course of his career—"siempre vendiendo la misma mercancía" (always selling the same product [or commodity])[60]—may in fact perpetuate the very form of historical time characteristic of modernity, which valorizes the new and transfers duration onto a scale of differential development.[61] What kind of structure of temporalization do we privilege when we laud novelty and celebrate development, or when we dismiss repetition or claim that something has dated? Much as Benjamin finds in the commodity form the possibility of a new form of historical experience—an object or "a *constellation*" (emphasis mine) always new and therefore always already obsolete, a paradoxical temporal structure capable of disrupting linear time[62]—the star text affords a similar form of experience as a "fissure in the temporal structure" of historicism.[63] If the commodity is the modern "measure of time,"[64] then figuring Sandrini as commodity underscores how his novelty-become-datedness suggests a possible form of historical experience not grounded on the emplotment of continuous homogeneous time but on the stutter, the interruption, the "simultaneously contracting [of] the present into the stasis of its point-like source and expanding [of] its historical content to infinity."[65] Instead of the serial time of the commodity where repetition of the same is the basis for standardization (of time), the recurrence and remanence of the star makes intelligible a different form of temporalization.

When Sandrini defends himself against these accusations, his comments open onto a series of questions about the forms of narrativity, the assumptions about realism, and the structure of temporality that undergird dismissals of his work and film comedy more broadly:

> Estoy cansado de leer a quienes dicen que me repito. Pero yo creé un personaje, no me repito. Chaplin es Chaplin. Cantinflas hace de Cantinflas. . . . Para hacer un personaje, para crear un prototipo y reiterarlo . . . durante 30 años, hay que serlo, confundirse con él, olvidarse del tiempo y obstinarse en un momento de esa vida ilusoria. En algún momento confieso ser ese personaje.

> I am tired of reading those who say I repeat myself. I created a character, I do not repeat myself. Chaplin is Chaplin. Cantinflas pretends to be

Cantinflas. . . . To make a character, to create a prototype and reiterate it . . . during 30 years, one has to be him, confuse oneself with him, forget time and remain in a moment of that illusory life. At some points, I confess I am the character.[66]

When Sandrini claims, "I created a character, I do not repeat myself," we might stand confused at the oxymoronic construction. Isn't a stock character readily recognized by audiences because of frequent recurrences, common tropes, and cultural types? Isn't he a generic or underdeveloped cliché?

Figuring his performance style within the early twentieth century discourse of the *type* and the context of vaudeville theatrical performance clarifies some of these ostensible contradictions. Consider the language used in American cultural critic Caroline Caffin's 1914 book on vaudeville to describe the character comedian and his process of imitation as translation: "It is the quality of translating by his body, voice and actions, the impressions received, just as the action of the light on the sensitized plate translated the objects before it, which is the medium of expression of the imitator."[67] This suggestive metaphor not only figures the performer as a technology but also pictures the photograph as a medium of translation and not reproduction. Caffin analogizes the performer's character study to the photographer's mise-en-scène because the arrangement and coordination of characteristics is integral to both photographic meaning and theatrical performance. The character comedian was thus called because of his character study: he "presents his types with a few bold strokes that stimulate our imagination. . . . The salient traits of their subject are made larger and more perceptible but never willfully distorted."[68] The results of his character study are compared to novelty photographs that enlarge the sitter's head in proportion to the body but do not alter the likeness. The character comedian is not any mere photograph; he is a trick photograph. The process of absorption and transmission requires not a distortion of the message nor a change in its substance but a manipulation of proportion. Imitation means receiving (sense) impressions of "salient traits." The use of *salient* is suggestive given salience's etymological origins in jumping or leaping, implying that the opposition to depth is not surface but salience.

Here, photography and comedic performance are arts of salience and reiteration rather than depth and progress. The photographic metaphor persists when Caffin describes the difference between the dramatic actor and the character comedian or imitator. The latter presents an instantaneous picture—a "flashlight presentation" of qualities from concentrate—whereas the former sustains gradual development.[69] The character comedian is the performer for the age of the photograph. Within a logic of salience, the face and body do not have forensic value—the face is not a site of unmediated expression of inner life—but rather deictic value. To use Béla Balázs's turn of phrase, the face is not a semaphore for the soul but a surface for collective perception.[70] Further, unlike dramatic action come from some imagined interiority, the character comedian absorbs external traits. As Sandrini explains, he loses himself in the character, not in a Method logic of characterization premised on psychological motivation, but through reiteration that can suspend time and allow Sandrini to remain in a pregnant moment. This is not a character that develops but a performer who remains. Sandrini's "personaje" belongs within a representational regime were salience finds expression in the type. As Luis Sandrini would later reinforce in a late-in-life interview: "Yo he tratado siempre de parecerme a mí mismo, cosa bastante difícil; más fácil resulta imitar, aunque parezca al revés. . . . Para ser natural debe parecerse a sí mismo." (I have always tried to seem like myself, a very difficult thing; it is easier to imitate, although it may seem counterintuitive. . . . To be natural you must seem like yourself).[71] Sandrini's main retort is grounded on a form of authenticity, perhaps even realism, another ostensible contradiction. How do we reconcile realism with typicality and a comedic tradition reliant on stock characters?

Typage seems an antiquated tradition, an anachronism from simpler times, and yet its roots lie in thoroughly modern positivism and its techniques of classification and hierarchization later coupled with behaviorist psychology.[72] Typage is of interest here only partly as a historical tradition of performance. More to the point, typage appears in various forms in realist theories of representation from the same period. What now seems like the height of artifice and inauthenticity was seen in classical film theory as crucial to the redemptive potential of the cinema apparatus, perhaps not surprisingly given the way cinema was very much a political technology of that very same positivist tendency in late nineteenth and early twentieth centuries. Rather than discard typage in these arguments as historical naïveté or write these defenses off as contextual particulars that had their day, I want to suggest that looking at typage and its relation to realism actually complicates if not challenges the very system of reference that subtends our more commonsense ways of approaching realism. We might ask differently, what does the dismissal of typage as inauthentic reveal about what we suppose is authentic and how we believe we acquire knowledge? For starters, the type is opposed to the developed character, an individual with psychological depth and goals that motivate logical action and develop over time. To yearn for a developed character, goal-oriented and acting with a consistent and coherent personality "contributes to a pervasive cultural ideology of the self which serves the established social order."[73] What Leo Bersani finds in nineteenth-century realism (and by extension classical Hollywood narrative) is a cult of personality, a desire for a coherent self as stable center of desire, a self that is intelligible. The type is not inauthentic but a function of different ontological assumptions and different types of social organization.

The relationship of typage to realism also means reexamining the latter term and its relationship to epistemology and aesthetic judgement. If realism in its progressive mode promises to reveal or supposes that to make visible is to make known, then it seems typage only mystifies and occludes because it is not directly observed fact. Realism in this light not only yokes knowledge claims to visibility but also supposes that knowledge is gleaned in either inductive or deductive ways—that is, either from a plurality of objects from which we induce a generality or from an individual then related to a generality or law exterior to it. In addition to the ontological assumptions described above, then, this dismissal of realism comes with epistemological assumptions.

What I wish to suggest is the possibility of thinking typage as auguring a realism founded on different ontological assumptions and following a different epistemological method. With regard to the ontological stakes, the changes in Sandrini's currency might speak to changes in "what a self is" and changes in social organization. Consider an "insolent" interview where Sandrini remarks on the difference between the comedian and the dramatic actor:

> ¿No cree que Cary Grant es Cary Grant? ¿Por qué yo tengo que ser superior? Los galanes cambian de traje; las actrices de vestidos. . . . Yo me entrego a los personajes; en los actores cómicos se pretende descubrir al hombre que los hace; en los serios, no. . . . Yo toco un solo instrumento. Me parece demasiado pretender que sea el hombre-orquesta.
>
> Don't you think Cary Grant is Cary Grant? Why do I have to do more? Leading men change suits; actresses, their dresses. . . . I give myself to my characters; with comic actors, [the audience] intends to discover the man who makes the character; in serious [actors], no. . . . I play one instrument. I think it a bit much to pretend to be an one-man orchestra.[74]

The pleasure derived from watching Luis Sandrini is precisely in the confusion of his character and the performer, an iteration of a paradigm coupled with the possibilities it contains, a pleasure derived not from progress but from actualization. The pleasure in watching Sandrini is akin to the pleasure derived from watching the gags in comedian comedy films: pleasure derived in "the delight of anticipating and recognizing perfection."[75] Sandrini's earlier comparison to Chaplin proves suggestive. As André Bazin notes, Chaplin's tramp was a "mythical figure" determined by external actions in and reactions to the world (and not a depth of interiority), who becomes type because of the possibility of his iteration across films over time.[76] Comedy suggests less a readable personality with continuities in desire or a coherent portrait within a meaningful temporal frame than an unhinged organizing position, a disorganizing replicant with a different relation to time.

With regard to the question of epistemology, types function neither as universal rule nor specific individuals, so that induction and deduction become fruitless operations. The type instead might be understood by a third epistemological method, the *paradigm*. The type is neither a revealing detail in an inductive inquiry nor a universal constant in a deductive process, but an example in a logic of analogy. The example is a particular historical phenomenon that functions as a common model but cannot be reduced to a universal rule exterior to the historical phenomenon.[77] The paradigm then operates by reiteration with a collective dimension—a structure reminiscent of our earlier account of the *relajo*—that reinforces a rule that cannot be made universal, presupposed, or explicitly stated. The paradigm is the typical element of a set that makes the set intelligible.[78] Rather than fault the type for being inaccurate or unrepresentative, the former relating the type to an exterior law and the latter relating the type as one of many objects, thinking the type as paradigm means the type makes something knowable. To think the type this way means to suspend or neutralize its denotative function or its relation to a system of reference. Instead, the type exhibits the particular phenomenon in its medium of knowability. Thinking typage and realism together simply means moving away from thinking representation within a logic of correspondence and a system of reference and toward a technique that makes the self and the world intelligible, away from a difference between original and inauthentic copy and toward successful iteration of a paradigm.

This revised understanding of typicality affects our reading of Sandrini's films, moving away from discussing film comedy merely in terms of narrative content and cultural signifiers. If we take the case of *Riachuelo* (Luis Moglia Barth, 1934), most film historians discuss the film and its use of vernacular, or *cocoliche,* born in the circus of the nineteenth century, perpetuated in tango and popular theater, and circulated en masse in the cinema.[79] The film also features location shooting of the Riachuelo River in the busy port of Buenos Aires, images that are understood as representing the industrial modernity of the port and the thriving national commerce as well as the picturesque flavor of the working-class La Boca neighborhood.[80] Matthew Karush lauds this early commercial success for the documentary representation of the shipyards and its working-class labor, a valorization of film's reflective capacity and the politics of a realism as an expanded representational field. When discussing the film's narrative, however, Karush equivocates on its political valence because its recuperative narrative is not easily reconciled with Sandrini's resistance to discipline and subjection.[81] Karush's historical project struggles to reconcile his understanding of realism with the fact of typicality, arguing instead that this contradiction is symptomatic of growing class polarization in the period. To avoid discussing comedic films as progressive in their "realistic" moments and regressive in their melodramatic episodes, we need to reinsert Sandrini within the discourse of typicality.

Outside this discourse, Sandrini's performance would prove difficult to reconcile with a realism conventionally understood as the accurate portrayal of the state of affairs. And yet the comedian was celebrated as a pioneer in subverting the codified language of emotion inherited from the theater: "Su criatura escénica estaba despojada de exageraciones. Fue uno de los primeros actores argentinos que desarrolló la dificilísima naturalidad" (His stage creation was free from exaggeration. He was one of the first Argentine actors who developed a very challenging naturalness).[82] Sandrini departed from the performance tradition of named emotions where communication outweighed expression and belonged to a newer performance context of typicality. In this performance style, Caffin adds that the performer "must feel like the subject he is portraying and he must be able to impress this feeling on his audience."[83] Feeling what the subject feels is not a function of empathy but of observation and sympathy. The aesthetic type reflects reality in a "sensually unfolded" and concrete way—that is, a subjective reflection that is both constitutive of and constituted by external reality.[84] Suggestively, the audience is also figured as photographic plate being impressed upon by the performer. This sympathetic viewer is not an active or passive spectator as a function of (re)cognition. The spectator as sensitized plate absorbs sense impressions and is affected by and changed through the performance. "True imitation" is not a function of fidelity to a copy but of a traffic in sense impressions. The relationship between performer and spectator is a game of telephone where pleasure derives from transmission, from susurrant sounds coursing through bodies loosely connected, from the delight in shaping and reshaping meaning, from the *comparison* of original and copy. The spectator is constituted by and constitutive of the work of art's expression.[85]

In this light, typicality is public feeling mobilized toward depersonalization and alienation best exemplified in the performance of the mime who absorbs the characteristics of his model. The mime is less mirror than sponge, a mode of "affective identification that precedes the very difference between self and other."[86] Contra a model of linear class-based identification that assumes that audiences identified with the characterization of Sandrini as a lazy *berretín* (i.e., an amiable yet idle member of the Argentine popular classes), Sandrini's stutter is not just his shtick on screen but, borrowing from Bergson on Don Quixote, also "plays on the same chord within ourselves."[87] We follow Don Quixote run after the ideal but stumble over realities—his comic rigidity elicits our palliative laughter. However, we also stumble ourselves, our habitual suspension of disbelief upended by corrective reality. This is spectatorship less as psychological identification than "physiological imitation": less "that's just like me" than "that elicits something in/from me." When imitation is concerned with the successful traffic of impressions, accuracy becomes less important than the capacity to impress. This means reading not for depth but for salience. From representation grounded on the difference between appearance and reality—a duplicity that motivates a hermeneutic—we arrive at representation grounded on the play of salient features.

Returning to *Riachuelo,* typicality requires we move away from considering the accuracy of Sandrini's cachuso type and instead discern what his typicality makes intelligible. Sandrini's character, Berretín, is a pickpocket who lives on a tugboat in the working-class docks. In an early sequence in the film, Berretín is walking two women home when neighborhood gangsters confront him and accost the women he accompanies in the midground of a long shot of a city sidewalk. The following medium shot reframes the confrontation from the side as the gangsters proposition the women. Both shots feature overwhelming, nondiegetic music, barely attenuated to make the synchronous sound and dialogue intelligible in the latter shot. Sandrini defends the women and attempts to intimidate the men. One man easily shoves Sandrini while the leader

FIGURE 10. Berretín (Luis Sandrini) needs help to defend the young ladies in *Riachuelo* (1934). Image courtesy of Museo del Cine Pablo Ducrós Hicken.

grabs the younger woman. The camera cuts to a long shot of a new character entering the frame who lands several punches and singlehandedly defeats the gangster. Sandrini attempts to help the man but struggles with his umbrella in a bit of slapstick humor. The gangsters retreating, the camera shows a close-up of our romantic hero, Remanso (Alfredo Camiña), before pulling back to a medium shot of our group.

In this sequence, the early shots use synchronized sound; however, once the fight begins, the long shot occurs without synchronized sound and with a slower frame rate that seems to accelerate the action. We bear witness to continuous action over discontinuous frame rates, ostensibly due to the sound technologies and practices of the period. The fisticuffs were filmed without synchronized sound and without the standardized frame rates required by sound recording. More remarkably, however, is that Sandrini's movements, due in large part to his slapstick struggle with the umbrella, remain closer to the frame rate of the earlier shots. Sandrini appears slower than his surroundings, still beholden to a standardized frame rate. Sandrini literally stumbles between shots—both at the level of the narrative brawl and the material frame rate. If diegetic and synced sound inscribed the image in a rigid, linearized time, then Sandrini's stumble recovers the elasticity of time.

The stutter stages a confrontation with standardized time not simply in the comedian's linguistic performance but also in the materiality of the film. Despite the vectorization of time on screen (through the collusion of synchronous sound and classical narrative) and off screen (the forward march of technological progress and industrial modernity through the codification of sound practices and the circulation of sound recording and projection technologies), Sandrini's films suggest a modernity experienced nonsynchronously, with both the performer's body and the spectators' bodies caught in material and figurative noncoincidence.

Sandrini's "stutter step" is a sensuous expression of an encounter with technology achieved not through antirealist critical distance but through a particular engagement with standardized time. As Siegfried Kracauer suggests, this is a case of a performer mastering the recording devices on the set through his bodily comportment in order to be successfully expressive.[88] The stutter, following Miriam Hansen, affords a "mode of cognition involving sensuous, somatic, and tactile forms of perception, a non-coercive engagement with the other that opens the self to experience."[89] If the verbal stutter defamiliarizes the word and makes us attendant to the instrumentality of our listening, here we move from an instrumental mode that perceives images as associated with habit to an intuitive receptivity attuned to incidental and aleatory configurations that are necessarily provisional. Sandrini's performance affords moments for sensuous apprehension through the "powers of mimetic production and comprehension."[90] Benjamin's concept of mimesis represents a departure from the traditional Platonic concept of mimesis, positing a relationship with nature that "would dissolve the contours of the subject/object dichotomy into reciprocity and the possibility of reconciliation."[91] Benjamin celebrates our mimetic faculty, the ability to perceive similarity and the concomitant compulsion to become similar. He does not necessarily advocate a return to "primitive" mimesis but rather seeks avenues for the recovery of image-based, sensuous communication in a world dominated by linguistic representations. Lukács's eccentric reading of Benjamin suggests that typage and its play of salient features offers one possible avenue. For Lukács, mimesis is an "anthropomorphizing response to the world which constitutes the foundation of aesthetic reflection."[92] He characterizes mimesis as an imitation of natural processes that represents the salient aspects of the world (through *types*) in a totalizing manner in order to gain knowledge of things as mediators of human relations.[93] Chaplin's type, for instance, affords the possibility of transcending abstraction by disclosing the salient aspects of reality made available paradoxically only through his abstraction. His mimicry of technology's fragmenting effects on the human body gives the encounter with technology an expression in the image (and not linguistic) world.[94] If self-alienation is made perceivable in the mimetic innervation of Chaplin's movements, then Sandrini's stutter affords a similar moment of sensuous experience in mimicking sound technology's fragmenting effects on the human body and voice.[95]

Sandrini's engagement with representation reveals a playfulness that sees in (or perhaps through) linguistic correspondence an opportunity for mimicry. Mimicry as sensuous communication cannot transmit a message in the same way as a rational communicative act, which supposes an exterior law of correspondence. It does not signify within an oppositional signifying economy subtended by the difference between signifier and signified, message and medium, sender and receiver. Instead, mimicry operates within a tensional system of analogy; it signifies not by reference to another sign but by being a typical example of set. Sandrini operates within a logic of (mimetic) representation less concerned with the perceptual likeness between sign and reality (i.e., iconicity).[96] Recall, Sandrini once explained, "I [want] to *seem* like myself," and not "I want to be someone else." This language recalls Agamben's definition of the paradigm as "something which is what it seems so that in it being and seeming are undecidable."[97] The type operates in this paradoxical way, both belonging to its set (seeming) while being excluded from the set (being) at the moment it exhibits what it makes known. It does not represent or depict an (absent) reality or idea but makes something knowable by making seeming and being indiscernible.[98] Perhaps we could recast classical theories of film realism in this light, with cinema as a way of making the world intelligible. Cinema shows the world in a paradigmatic mode not simply by showcasing types in the image content but arguably because of the conditions of its visibility, an iteration with a collective dimension that persists. Sandrini's typicality then is not *stereotype*; the successful iteration of a type is more significant for making the conditions of its actualization (i.e., the historical present) intelligible.

If the developed and consistent character corresponds to an ideology of the coherent self, the type as always already an iteration corresponds to a model of subjectivity where the self is to be actualized and where the activity of living is a function of habit and its possible disruption. This model of subjectivity has epistemological implications. Mimicry articulated to the recurrent temporality of the type foregrounds how sensuous expression does not claim some preideological relation to the world; rather, it involves the sensuous relations and habituated dispositions that allow us to manage the present as potentiality and to use these as a way of apprehending the historical present. The type is an aesthetic practice that is a practice of adjustment and collective mode of sensual activity that registers and produces the historical present.[99]

THE HISTORIAN STUTTERS

Returning briefly to the film that opened this chapter, *Bartolo tenía una flauta,* during the band's trip to the outskirts of Buenos Aires, the director of the band meets several prominent members of the community in a pub. The director is soliciting patronage from established and wealthy families summering out of the city, and the older men give the director a list of the prominent members of the community. One of the men interrupts the conversation, warning against approaching the family in the Estancia El Trébol. The three men agree and warn the director to avoid the El Trébol at all costs. The director asks unconvinced: "¿Qué hay en ese Trébol? ¿Fantasmas?" (What's in that Trébol? Ghosts?). They caution that its owner is a crazy woman who could very well give you a fortune or shoot you on sight. The camera cuts to a close up of a third man who adds: "Vea que la Señorita Toledo es una —" (See here, Miss Toledo is a —). The camera abruptly cuts to a medium close-up panning away from this third character. Despite the continuity in dialogue over the cut, the editing appears disjunctive because the cut appears unmotivated. Moreover, the character never finishes his sentence and an abrupt change in the background noise between this suspended characterization and the subsequent dialogue seems to point to another moment of disjunctive sound editing. Close scrutiny of these fissures in the scene suggests that there is missing recorded material. The changes in background noise suggest that the conclusion of this insulting sentence will remain forever suspended, excised by choice (obscenity) or lost to circumstance (obsolescence). These lacunae might compel a rote dismissal of any close reading of the film text; however, such a position would only contribute to the continued neglect and possible disappearance of these popular films. More importantly, such a position denies the historicity of the text and presumes that any close reading necessitates an ideal original text and reader. Rather than dismiss close reading of the film text, these gaps both inform how the text generates narrative meanings and stages a confrontation with the historicity of the text and, by extension, our own historicity as spectators.

At the level of the narrative, the missing dialogue suggestively characterizes Miss Toledo through its absence, ostensibly functioning as an ellipsis: so objectionable is Miss Toledo that to finish the sentence would be obscene. Arguably, the entire narrative of the film could be construed as operating between and within ellipses: the original running length of *Bartolo* was a feature-length 78 minutes, but the extant material available amounts to just over 52 minutes.[100] If the stuttering comedian embodies nonsynchronous experience that points to unforeseen meanings that can arise from noninstrumentalized perception, then this stuttering text generates unforeseen meanings through elliptical suspension. The disparate temporal relations in this case, however, are not between the rigid body of the comedian and his fluid meaning-making speech but between an extant text and a missing hypotext—a conflict between the historicity of the spectator and the historicity of the text. Rather than dismiss textual reading or historical claims as incomplete, these lacunae compel us to reflect on loss, consider the processes of destruction and discursive sleep, and examine the remanence of these forms of popular culture. This is not simply a film history that aspires to reconstruct the empirical past in the name of accuracy but also a film history where what is deemed salient about the past makes the historical present intelligible.

In this light, the changing reception we schematically reconstructed earlier in the chapter is less a testament to the quality of Sandrini's performance than a demonstration of how the type recurs over time, each iteration making a different historical present intelligible. This means shifting from a historiography of past events in a causal narrative and toward a historiography of evolving sensuous relations and actualizations, a history of evolving modes of relating to the world.[101] Simply put, the type makes the historical present apprehensible to us contemporary spectators. We, too, perceive salient features, perhaps different from those of spectators elsewhere or *elsewhen* (e.g., recall Kracauer's grandmother's photograph and her crinoline jacket). We, too, receive sense impressions. We, too, are constituted by and constitutive of what the type can express. This brief aside to Kracauer reminds us that photography and historiography are corresponding operations that look past in order to gather in the present for future reading.[102] This temporal compositeness, occluded in most official histories that either value the film as document or symptomatically read the film for its context, becomes foregrounded in the type's expression and our stuttering receptivity.

The comedic type may appear to freeze the past but actually functions as a relay through which time can be sensed. As Sandrini would muse, "Es muy importante hacer reir. Usted y yo hemos nacido en un mundo que se nos escapa de las manos" (It is important to make people laugh. You and I are born into a world that slips through our fingers).[103] This is an aesthetic expression of how the present was (and is) affectively (un)available. When we watch with an eye toward salience, we do not look for what the image represents but for what the image elicits. We "take the measure of the impasse of the present to see what is halting, stuttering . . . to produce some better ways of mediating the sense of a historical moment that is affectively felt but undefined in the social world."[104] We sensuously grasp the historical present when we confront the type in its particularity and must resituate our attachment to the historical, cultural, and political context. The comic stages an encounter with the world where we sense the present and adjust accordingly before intelligence reifies and forecloses the present.

Let us take a final moment from *Riachuelo* to understand this stuttering apprehension. After following Sandrini's pickpocketing exploits, the film presents an extreme long shot of the metallic constructions in the port of Buenos Aires. In a transitional sequence, the film features an early example of a trick transition from an exterior to an interior space. The camera tilts down the length of the edifice and pauses at its base. A very subtle jump cut punctuates the pause and the camera begins to track back, the image of the docks now framed on a wall, designating that the camera has gone through a window and into a new space. This trick shot uses a still photograph of the docks to conceal the transition from exterior to interior space. The camera begins to track inside a room, pulling back to reveal the main hall of a cabaret bar, its working-class patrons enjoying the music from the all-female band. Although on-location exteriors, here shot with silent film equipment, were not new to early Argentine sound cinema, the representation of working-class spaces was less common at the time.[105] However, the expanded representational field is perhaps less significant than the discontinuity, the subtle jump cut, which opens onto these questions of temporality. The transition from moving picture to still photograph perhaps best illustrates how the historical present is made intelligible. Not only is there a transition from movement to stasis but the fixed frame within the frame provides a moment of hesitation, of doubling back—the photograph is legible as framed photograph and diegetic window. The comic represents the impingement of presence that undermines habitual perception and frustrates attempts to absent the signified real—"ceci n'est pas une fenêtre." The stutter on screen elicits a "double take," a doubled awareness of the actual and virtual possibilities that inhere in experience, of our shifting attachment to the world. If comedy is "all about timing," then its effect comes from affording an immediate experience through which to resitutate oneself within moving reality. The Sandrini comedy produces us as stutterers, functioning as a form of sensuous communication that makes us aware of multiple meanings that inhere in nonsensuous codified language and provides an experience of noncoincidence that makes reification perceivable. His stutter functions as a visible and audible manifestation of a (mock) classicism characterized by the ongoing negotiations of technological and industrial practices and narrative and formal devices. Sandrini's films provide another example of studio film practices developing in phenomenally kin but structurally distinct ways from classical Hollywood. Classical Hollywood may have aspired to a hermetic diegetic world, but Sandrini mocks classicism with a stutter that makes the world salient precisely because it acknowledges that the world "slips through our fingers."

CHAPTER 4

Fictions of the Real

The Currency of the Brazilian Chanchada

On the weekend of Carnaval 1952, the downtown movie district of São Paulo had theaters on either side of the avenida Ipiranga programming two musical *filmes carnavalescos*: the Ipiranga screened the early sound film *Alô, alô carnaval* (Hello, hello carnival!) (Watson Macedo, 1935) and the Marabá premiered the musical comedy *Tudo azul* (Moacyr Fenelon, 1952). Film critic Carlos Ortiz uses this happy coincidence to reflect on the status of Brazilian cinema, arguing that the former film is the "marco zero" (ground zero) and the latter represents "a mais recente etapa do cinema brasileiro" (the most recent stage of Brazilian cinema).[1] Ortiz's comparison challenges the gripes of most defeatist critics, who complain that national cinema does not progress in narrative or technical sophistication: "Não é preciso ser técnico nem ter conhecimentos eruditos de estética cinematográfica de problemas de roteiro, de montagem, de fotografia e de som, para verificar a diferença profunda entre os dois filmes, o abismo que transpusemos em apenas dezessete anos de experiência do filme sonoro brasileiro" (You do not have to be technical or knowledgeable about the aesthetics of story, editing, photography or sound to note the profound diference between the two films, the abyss we have surmounted in a mere seventeen years of Brazilian sound film experience).[2] In contrast to the "primitive" narration of the Cinédia classic, with its immobile camera, painted sets, and theatrical framing, *Tudo azul* is a testament to the "etapas superadas" (stages overcome) in national cinema and the promise of overcoming any future obstacles to

153

"a definitiva consolidação industrial do cinema brasileiro" (the definitive industrial consolidation of Brazilian cinema).[3]

The following week the Atlântida studios feature *Barnabé tu és meu* (Barnabé, you are mine) (José Carlos Burle, 1952) premiered in Cinelândia. While *Tudo azul* was touted as the carnavalesco fully realized, *Barnabé* was panned for continuing "a invariável linha de carnavalesco da Atlântida, em que uma história de 'gangsters' serve de pretexto para apresentar canções de carnaval" (the unchanging tradition of the Atlântida carnavalesco, where a "gangster" story serves as the pretext for performing carnival songs).[4] The Atlântida film is panned for the repetition of generic elements: "estes enredos tragi-cómicos, repetindo-se de ano para ano sem nenhum senso de procura e de originalidade, acabam tornando-se enfadonhos" (the tragicomic plots, repeated every year with no sense of progress or originality, become tedious).[5] If *Tudo azul* is the future of musical comedy, *Barnabé* is "retardatario e infeliz" (outdated and wretched) *chanchada*.[6]

This snapshot of *cartazes*, or marquees, in the center of São Paulo provides a window onto the debates about national cinema and the controversial role of the Brazilian chanchada, or musical comedy, in its development. The chanchada was *the* popular genre of the golden age of Brazilian cinema, sometimes maligned as a symptom of underdevelopment and other times touted as the model for a commercially viable national cinema.[7] Featuring comedic plots interspersed with musical numbers, these comedies date from the early sound period and persist through the late 1940s at the height of the Atlântida studio system and into the 1970s and the emergence of the cheaply and quickly made pornochanchada. If contemporaneous criticism in Brazil disparaged the genre and its anaesthetic vulgarity, subsequent considerations of the genre have been decidedly mixed. More recent surveys trace the evolving uses of the term, arguing that the genrification of the chanchada is "uma operação discursiva retrospectiva e totalizante efetuada por críticos, cineastas e historiadores" (a retrospective and totalizing discursive operation by critics, filmmakers, and historians).[8] In the spirit of Rick Altman, Rafael de Luna Freire does not seek to define the chanchada but rather to understand how a national genre is made. Although now referring to a national tradition of musical comedy that grew out of the silent era *filmes cantantes* and the early sound period's carnavalescos, the chanchada must be reinserted into its particular historical context.

The chanchada moniker was not an industrial term in the 1930s and 1940s; musical comedy films were referred to as *carnavalescos* because of their use of popular *marchas* and sambas as well as their release schedule during the summer holiday window.⁹ *Chanchada* was used only occasionally by critics to depreciate these popular, low-quality films, seen as antithetical to a representative national cinema. By the late 1950s and 1960s, the term begins to be used as a noun and generic modifier, consolidated in opposition to Cinema Novo: "Chanchada passou a representar os filmes ditos vulgares, desonestos e comerciais que representariam até um perigo para um cinema nacional 'autêntico'" (*Chanchada* came to refer to films considered vulgar, dishonest, and commercial that posed a threat to an "authentic" national cinema).¹⁰ By the 1970s and 1980s, the chanchada was recuperated in film histories, a project of transvaluation Freire likens to the feminist recuperation of women's cinema, during a period of industrial crisis when critics turned to the chanchada as a model for an economically viable national cinema.

Beyond simply claiming that a genre is less an essential category than a discursive formation, Freire's historiography invites us to reflect on how questions of national ontology persist in each estimation of the chanchada. The chanchada adds certain political stakes to conventional genre studies because the debates about its definition, characteristics, and periods are also debates about the nation—every invocation of the chanchada fashions the nation. Further, as I have argued throughout, questions of national ontology here again overlap with questions of medium ontology: from the nation defined by a pure or authentic medium to the nation defined by the medium as social practice. Early dismissals of the popular genre claim the *filmusical* is not representative of the nation because of its theatrical and radio origins. The "authentically national" Cinema Novo abandons these differential medium-specific arguments for an emphasis on film language, so that again the chanchada's borrowed trappings are seen as inauthentic. More recently, the reclamation of the chanchada derives from a cultural turn to medium specificity, where media are defined by the social or cultural context in which they are practiced.¹¹

I want to expand and complicate this historiographic survey, which replaces a genre ontology with a discursive genealogy. If this book seeks to complicate the nationness of industrial cinema, what do we make of a genre figured entirely in relation to the nation? Could we think the chanchada outside the framework of *brasilidade* and the practice of combing for local references that reflect a period of nationalist politics or popular identity?¹² I want to avoid reinscribing the nation as origin and telos. Unlike Freire, who wants to identify how a genre became national, I want to examine how the national became generic.

This chapter returns to the chanchada's early uses not to offer a definitive definition but to unpack the relation between national ontology and medium ontology as they intersect with genre building. This genre history teaches us that the process of genre definition, nation building, and medium specificity is normative. *Chanchada* is a slippery term because it was the excluded term that secured the identity of the nation (and the medium) before film historians used it at cross-purposes. The chanchada was neither national nor cinema before being reappropriated as the paragon of national cinema.

THE HOLLYWOOD CHANCHADA?

Well before the first use of the pejorative in relation to Brazilian popular cinema in a 1940 column on the problems confronting the development of Brazilian cinema,[13] the 1934 MGM revue *Hollywood Party* (1934) was dubbed a chanchada on the eve of its premiere in the Palácio theater.[14] The full-page advertisement in the weekly cultural magazine *O cruzeiro* called the film "uma chanchada em seda e lamé . . . um espectáculo para divertir—uma colecção de disparates loucos como um carnaval" (a chanchada in silk and gold lamé . . . a spectacle that entertains—a collection of absurd craziness like a carnival). Not only does the precode MGM film get aligned with a carnival and the chanchada, but the advertisement's drawings translate the spoofs featured in the film; for example, Jimmy Durante's Schnarzan becomes "Narizan, imitação barata de Tarzan" (Narizan, a cheap imitation of Tarzan).[15] The parodic inversions on the page—whether Jimmy Durante as Marco Polo atop a horse playing polo or an off-brand Mickey Mouse chased by Ping-Pong, "sobrinho de King-Kong" (King Kong's nephew)—represent *avant la lettre* the comedic operations that would come to define the chanchada in later film histories.

To claim the chanchada is the quintessential national genre is to ignore its regular use by exhibitors and journalists to characterize foreign films. These reviews are particularly useful because they make us redefine the chanchada without reference to the nation. The nation has overdetermined the definition of the chanchada, whether in periodizations that claim the chanchada refers to films made in Brazil from 1900 to 1960,[16] the descriptive definitions that identify the *brasilidade* of film content and the cultural mixing of local elements and foreign influences,[17] or the ontogenetic histories that take the nationness of the genre for granted, so that the origin of the genre gets traced to the *filmes cantantes* of the silent era.[18] These reviews of foreign films give us a defini-

FIGURE 11. *Hollywood Party* (1934) as Hollywood "chanchada" in *O cruzeiro*. Image courtesy of D. A. Press.

tion of the chanchada less related to the specificity of content (where is the genre from?) than to the specificity of medium.

The case of Carmen Miranda is particularly enlightening. A 1943 reader review opines that Miranda, the biggest Brazilian star of her time, was better in films made in Brazil than in her pictures made in Hollywood: "Em *Banana da terra,* Carmen agradou mais porque estava no seu elemento, cantava e dansava [sic] 'O que a baiana tem.' ... Soltaram-na em *Aconteceu en Havana* e foi aquele ridiculo ... parecendo desfêcho de comedia chanchada dum teatro popular aqui no Rio" (In *Banana da terra,* Carmen entertained because she was in her element, singing and dancing "O que a baiana tem." ... They put her in *Weekend in Havana* and it was ridiculous ... something like a spoof in a chanchada from a popular theater here in Rio).[19] In an interesting reversal, the chanchada is used to characterize the American film, aligning it with the theatrical revue and its comedic pochade in opposition to the song and dance from the earlier national musical film. And yet the earlier national musical film is regularly included in contemporary film histories as a model chanchada from the Cinédia studios.

Chanchada does not refer to local generic content but to narrative strategies reminiscent of popular theater. The 1941 review of the Hollywood adaptation of *Pride and Prejudice* (Robert Leonard, 1940) lauds the film's period stylings and acerbic dialogue but laments the "conçessões ao sal grosso, quasi fazendo o filme descambar para a 'chanchada'" (concessions to popular taste that make the film almost descend into a chanchada).[20] This descent is a function of the film's overtly theatrical narrative structure, a criticism similarly lobbed against the United Artists picture *Twin Beds* (Tim Whelan, 1942). "Este filme, afinal das contas, nada mais é do que teatro filmado. . . . O celuloide, portanto, não tem o dinamismo que constitúe a característica principal principal do cinema, tornándose muitas vezes monótono. . . . É uma verdadeira 'chanchada,' igualzinha aos espectáculos que estamos acostumados e assistir em nossos teatros" (Ultimately, this film is nothing but filmed theater. . . . The celluloid, therefore, lacks the dynamism that is the main feature of cinema, often becoming monotonous. . . . It is a real chanchada, just like the shows we are used to seeing in our theaters).[21] *Chanchada* is wielded by critics mindful of medium specificity, where "filmed theater" cannot be cinematic. A later review of the MGM Greer Garson–Clark Gable vehicle *Adventure* (Victor Fleming, 1945) is perhaps the most unequivocal on this point. Explicitly categorized in an exhibitor catalog as a chanchada, the review states: "Perfeita lição de

'De como não fazer uma fita,' essa 'Aventura' não possui cinema. Sua cotação artística é zero" (A perfect lesson on "how not to make a film," this "Adventure" does not possess cinema. Its artistic rating is zero).[22]

In addition to these Hollywood comedies, Mexican comedies were panned along similar lines. Cantinflas's first box office success, *Ahí está el detalle,* is dismissed as "uma autêntica chanchada," explicitly declared inferior to the Luiz de Barros films from 1940 also given the generic appellate.[23] In fact, the term *chanchada* is borrowed from Spanish America. Sérgio Augusto traces the term to the Argentine word for pig, *chancho.*[24] In this derivation, the *chanchada* is an alternative form of *cochinada,* as in "pig slop."[25] The porcine metaphor, a close relative of the Portuguese *porcaria* and the Spanish *porquería,* is slang for "filth" but also means "a trick, an ill-disposed action, a grift."[26] *Chanchada,* then, does not simply refer to something worthless but an attempt to pass off the worthless as something valuable, a crisis in valuation I read in light of the economic crisis that coincided with the transition to sound: the steep decline of coffee prices and the abandonment of the gold standard in 1930, the subsequent currency conversion in 1942, and the fixed (overvalued) exchange rate established in 1945.

THE WORTHLESS CHANCHADA

Before the conversion to the cruzeiro in 1942, there was no centralized monetary policy in Brazil. The *real* had been the colonial currency and was retained after Brazilian independence. By the late nineteenth century, the currency had been so affected by inflation that the practical currency unit shifted to one thousand *réis* and then to the *conto de réis* (one million réis). The réis were issued unevenly by the Caixa de Conversão, the Banco do Brasil, and the National Treasury, making it difficult to coordinate minting and standardize the currency, especially because only some of the issued paper money was convertible into gold. The cruzeiro, whose name derives from the Southern Cross constellation, meant to stem the speculative dealings, or agiotage, due to having paper money with identical nominal values and different actual values. Although conceived in the final years of the Republica Velha, the conversion took place only under the Vargas regime, with one cruzeiro equal to one thousand réis. The new currency was a cornerstone of the nationalist Estado Novo regime, not simply at the symbolic level of currency as a site for national identity but more concretely in redressing the problem of the lack of a national mint.

The implementation of centralized monetary policy and its coincidence with the establishment of Atlântida studios might seem a quirk of fate, and yet I want to suggest that the emergence of the chanchada (as mock classicism) and the peak of Brazilian industrial cinema relatively later than in Argentina and Mexico are inextricably related to the shift from réis to the cruzeiro. The money economy interposed an objective quality or monetary value between person and object or property. Money functions as a universal equivalent, making possible "the connection of the remotest things under equal conditions" by making these items equivalent in a system for distributing signifiers with no referent.[27] Georg Simmel identifies the historic emergence of paper money in varied denominations as a function of the need for greater forms of mediation for external relationships, of finding equivalents in a colorless means of exchange beyond any specificity. If our discussion of clock time and Sandrini explored how the rationalization of temporality attempted to mitigate the irruptive force of contingency while paradoxically systematizing and producing the conditions for the irruption of contingency, Georg Simmel identifies a similar paradoxical structure at the heart of money, attempting to make comparative and calculable while abstracting persons and objects in such a way that nothing has intrinsic value to compare or calculate. Simply put, in a money economy everything has a price, and everything risks becoming priceless. Contingency once again becomes the central concern of modernity, only understood as a matter of valuation and exchange rather than temporalization.

Of course, the money economy never quite amortizes contingency in the same way in Latin America. The late nineteenth and early twentieth centuries were exceptional moments in the Western history of monetary geography because monetary space was made to coincide with national space when governments claimed the right to monopolize control over the issue of money.[28] This process happened unevenly across Latin America, complicated by the legacy of colonialism and its de facto monopoly control over currency issue and management in the region. The consolidation of monetary space in Latin America is both old hat and new deal, both colonial legacy and modern apparatus.[29] Further, the process occurs relatively later in Latin America, coinciding, not insignificantly, with the emergence of technologies of mass reproducibility and the arrival of cinema in the region. In fact, the chanchada's popularity coincides with the implementation of the cruzeiro, the first postindependence national currency after over a century of continuing to use the colonial réis. Mock classicism must be understood within a (signifying) economy with longer histories of asymmetric exchange and greater aneconomical risk, where images have less purchase and where giving credit and collecting on debts is significantly more precarious.[30] If Flora Süssekind finds that the return to réis in the 1990s corresponds to a certain crisis of scale in cultural production related to the problematization of the concept of value, then I want to suggest the chanchada must be understood within an analogous historical moment in the 1940s. Drawing on Benjamin's analysis of hyperinflation in Weimar Germany, Süssekind argues that the change from one currency to another currency not only dematerializes money but also affects any sense of belonging based on standards of measurable value and undergirded by guarantees of future redemption. Süssekind argues that cultural production responds accordingly to this "situação de 'desmedida'"—*desmedida* meaning both "unmeasured" and "excessive"—by challenging questions of form through scalar relations.[31] The chanchada must be thought of alongside a change in monetary sign that augured a comparable crisis of value.

An early Cinédia comedy, *O jovem tataravô* (The young great-grandfather) (Luiz de Barros, 1936), released the same year as its *musicarnavalesco* smash *Alô, alô carnaval,* opens onto this question of desmedida. Although *Alô, alô* is often cited as the definitive precursor to the chanchada because it was a backstage musical that intercalated musical numbers and comedic skits in a theatrical revue, this second release from September 1936 compels us to look at the genre's origins beyond the its musical content and theatrical origins. Directed by Luiz de Barros, director of the first Brazilian sound film, *Acabaram-se os otários* (No more suckers) (1929), *O jovem tataravô* was an adaptation of the popular play *O tataravô* (1926), by Gilberto de Andrade. By way of synopsis, the film's title character is conjured back to life in 1936 through magical fiat after dying young at the age of 35 in 1832. The great-grandfather, Vitor Eulálio Gonçalves Imbiraçu de Almeida Costalá, enjoys the amenities and liberties of the modern capital city, from a haircut and a makeover to a tour by seaplane of the city to a night out at a cabaret. Vitor eventually falls for his great-grandson's daughter, Dora, and in order to avoid the incestuous genealogical loop this union would produce, his great-grandson Eduardo goes to a macumba to exorcise Vitor.

The film opens with an auction of historical relics, an auctioneer atop a table encouraging bidders to spend a few more réis to claim these nineteenth-century objects. The dialogue is barely audible and highly reverberant, the auctioneer's gavel nearly as loud as his cry. The sequence

FIGURE 12. The making of *O jovem tataravô* (1936). Image courtesy of Cinédia.

continues with a medium shot of the auctioneer asking for 100,000 réis for a crown that belonged to Dom João VI, acclaimed king of the Portuguese empire while residing in Brazil in 1818. The auctioneer is perfectly audible, so that the very first transition in the film exhibits this scale matching; the screen space edited in continuity is disrupted by a sound space of changing sound intensities. Eduardo appears in a medium shot debating the authenticity of the object. The auctioneer's cry is audible and reverberant with the qualities of a voice-off. A fellow bidder sits next to Eduardo and explains that he brought the object for sale and clarifies that the crown is not a royal crown but a dental crown. The homonymic slippage is a source of amusement, compounded by a currency itself referring to the crown: "100.000 Réis por uma coroa não é caro" (100,000 réis [sovereigns] for a crown is not expensive).[32] From a royal crown and *symbolon* of power to an object that covers the tooth to improve its appearance, the shift is one that speaks more broadly to a certain crisis of valuation in modernity expressed in relation to forms of symbolization. The crown's value inhered by virtue of its synecdochic relationship to the sovereign power and its qualitative properties that cannot be absorbed into exchange relationships; however, the auction marketplace stages an exercise in the assignation of value whereby "the qualitative itself becomes a special case of quantification."[33] Value becomes pegged to pricing and contingent on competition. That our auctioneer is equivocating between the king's crown and a dental crown adds to this question of value, for each symbolizes in a way that speaks to how sign and exchange are reconfigured in modernity. The former endows; the latter simulates. The crown granted the ability to wield sovereign power, a power New Economic Criticism reminds us is bound to its ability to purpose the crown as symbol for the act of monetary (and symbolic) transfer.[34] If the royal crown has a necessary relation to réis, the dental crown can only simulate the real—a shift from trafficking in nonfungible parcels *with* value to fungible tokens *of* value.[35]

After the lot with the dental crown is bought, the auctioneer holds up a small *caixa de segredos* (box of secrets) allegedly belonging to Estácio de Sá, the founder and former governor of Rio de Janeiro in the sixteenth century. The camera pans left to reframe the scene when Eduardo approaches the auctioneer to ask what is inside the box. The auctioneer remarks, "Se eu dissera o que tem dentro, deixará de ser uma caixa de segredos" (If I revealed what's inside, it would cease to be a box of secrets). The auctioneer has made the relic a commodity-as-fetish. Eduardo's response makes this explicit. He offers 200,000 réis for the box, closely scrutinizing the coffer in his hands. The auctioneer, now just off screen, begins his cry, asking whether anyone will top Eduardo's bid. Despite not having any competitors, Eduardo surprisingly doubles his bid. He explains to a confused friend that he upped his bid because "eu sou generoso . . . e eu quero valorizar a minha compra. 500.000 Réis!" (I am generous . . . and I want to increase the value of my purchase. 500,000 réis!). The scene then depicts "the mystification of the thing itself—and of the money form of which the commodity's simple form is the 'germ.'"[36] In other words, the sequence foregrounds the mystery or "spectral effect" of the commodity, its exchange value increasingly unrelated to use value, its valuation increasingly an alchemical operation founded on secrets without substance and a value form backed by nothing but the promise of future redemption.[37] That the box contains the secret for reincarnating spirits makes this spectrality textual.

Thinking the chanchada within a *situação de desmedida* means being attendant to how the film does not abide by the logic of the commodity in its money form in ways textual, discursive, and material. Cinédia's musicarnvalescos trafficked in *contos de réis*, whereas Atlântida circulated its chanchadas. I want to underscore the polysemy here: *conto* means both "count, number" and "tale, story"; the real—the Brazilian currency before (and after) the Vargas-era cruzeiro—is so called because of "its 'real' material and its 'royal' [inscription]."[38] The 1930s Cinédia films were made under the regime of *contos de réis,* or "tales of the real." The new currency untethered this relationship between sign and substance. In fact, the cruzeiro also introduced the *centavo,* or cent, to Brazil; value became partitive. The widespread use of the generic appellation *chanchada* coincided with the regime of the cruzeiro. An evaluation of the chanchada, either worthless in itself or trying to make the worthless seem valuable, seems incomplete without accounting for speculation, appreciation, and devaluation of currency—both are indices of a certain crisis of value. *Chanchada* is not simply a pejorative term; it also strikes at the heart of a period concerned with making the worthless seem valuable. I argue against appraising or valuating the genre—against claiming the chanchada is a bad object without value or lobbying for its redemption—and propose that these historiographic debates speak to and revolve around this *desmedida* and crisis of value.

PARALLEL MARKETS

Changing money lies at the heart of studio cinemas in Latin America and its mock classicism. Whether writing a history of media imperialism and Hollywood's global reach or recovering national histories derived from or in opposition to classical Hollywood, Latin America cinema in the period cannot be understood without accounting for currency and trade, without understanding the material conditions of transnational exchange. The currency regulations imposed during the period resulted in an official and a market exchange rate, that is, a *câmbio oficial* and a *câmbio livre.* These currency restrictions, whereby the government pegs the exchange rate and regulates the supply of foreign currency, often result in a parallel market with a higher exchange rate—you pay more for access to the foreign currency in short supply.[39] These different exchange rates create an incentive for using the official rate to pay fees or buy currency and using the market rate to collect fees or sell currency. Although protectionism is often mentioned as a cornerstone of statist developmentalist policy (and even a countermeasure to classical Hollywood), monetary policy features less prominently in film histories. And yet monetary policy complicates the nativist insistence on protectionism and domestic markets opposite a rampant and voracious mass media empire. Currency complicates regional and national film histories premised on national identity, periodized developmental narratives, or center-periphery models of (counter)hegemony.

For instance, the wartime decline of the Argentine film industry is often ascribed to the country's neutrality and the subsequent American trade restriction of film stock and equipment. Although accurate, this narrative fails to account for the preexisting currency and trade restrictions that made the film industry favor Europe over the United States during the interwar period. Before the Second World War, Kodak film stock was difficult to come by because importation of American materials was unofficially restricted due to trade difficulties between the United States and Argentina.[40] The trade difficulties were related to money exchange: "Latin American countries don't get enough American exchange to pay for all their American imports."[41] Additionally, American film studios and distributors were at a disadvantage relative to their European counterparts because the currency exchange for Hollywood films' revenue had to be bought at the market value while importers of German, Italian, and French films could buy currency at a fixed value directly from the Argentine Central Bank.[42] After the crisis situation during the Second World War, protectionism under Perón entailed not only taxation on American imports, government financing of national production (i.e., the Argentine Central Bank was financing some 70 percent of production by 1948), and a ban on American film advertisement, but more importantly centralizing monetary policy and freezing exchange remittances.[43] These currency restrictions began in August 1947 and created a fixed exchange value and a (black) market exchange value that made both domestic production and foreign importation increasingly cost prohibitive, despite the guarantees of support by the Argentine Central Bank.[44] American distributors negotiated with the Argentine Central Bank and the Economic Council for months, with Argentine producers turning to Europe for film stock and equipment.[45] Despite the announcement of the unfreezing of dollar holdings in June 1948 and the later pact signed in August 1948, distributors still found themselves subject to restrictions governing import permits and the release of funds.[46] Funds were technically available but the conditions necessary for their disbursement effectively perpetuated the freeze: "[The] Argentine peso has been bolstered by the Central Bank, prohibiting the sale of paper currency at prices exceeding 10% over and above the quotations ruling in the free market at the time the operation is effected."[47] This meant that American distributors could not exact their revenues at the more desirable market value.

The postwar case of Brazil is similar to the interwar Argentine example, except that without centralized monetary policy until 1960, support had to be secured through a patchwork of banking institutions.[48] During the second Vargas regime, the implemented protectionist measures had somewhat unintended consequences on domestic production. The regulations of the Superintendência da Moeda e do Crédito (SUMOC) (Bureau of Currency and Credit)—precursor to the centralized monetary agency, the Banco Central do Brasil—and the Diretoria do Imposta de Renda (Director of Income Tax) made the cost of importing a film print an average of 3,000 cruzeiros, "uma concorrência desleal com cinema brasileiro que, para fazer um filme, por pior que seja, gasta 3 milhões" (an unfair competition with Brazilian cinema that, in order to make a film, no matter how bad, spends 3 million [cruzeiros]).[49] Local producers claimed that the implementation of currency exchange policy and the collection of taxes, customs tariffs, and censorship fees provided few actual protections for domestic production.

Importing a print took place through a currency exchange policy where 70 percent was remitted at the official rate and the remaining 30 percent at the market rate; however, the film's earnings were disbursed entirely at the market rate because of the trade categories established in the Instrução (Directive) no. 118 of the SUMOC. In addition, the Director of Income Tax applied the same tax code to both domestic and foreign film, collecting taxes at a 20 percent rate on only 30 percent of the film's earnings because the remaining 70 percent was deducted as the cost of production. A measure intending to offset domestic production costs became a tax loophole for Hollywood: "Isso determina uma evasão anual de 11 milhões de dólares" (This results in the annual tax evasion of $11 million).[50] Finally, foreign films needed to pay only a minimal censorship fee of Cr$0,40 per meter on a single printed copy (despite importing multiple copies) and a customs fee of Cr$80 per kilogram.[51]

While Hollywood spent a paltry Cr$3,000 (roughly US$40 in 1957) to import a title, the Brazilian film industry spent significant amounts of money under unfavorable currency and trade conditions to import film stock and film and sound technologies from the United States. Film stock from the United States often had to be purchased at the higher market exchange rate, less because of the demands of American companies than because the national government could not sell foreign currency at more favorable rates to these producers. Printed copies and raw film stock were categorized differently by regulatory agencies like the SUMOC, so that the latter was subject to tighter restrictions and caps on foreign currency: "O filme impresso entra livremente no pais, mas a importação de filme virgem depende das disponibilidades cambiais. No ano passado, a SUMOC destinou apenas 692 mil dólares a importação do produto" (Printed film enters the country freely, but the importation of film stock depends on the availability of currency. Last year [1956], the SUMOC earmarked only US$692,000 toward the importation of the product).[52] Once foreign currency available at the official exchange rate had been spent or claimed, the film producer was left to secure the necessary material through the black-market exchange rate. This explains how producer Fernando de Barros spent Cr$10,000 to buy three hundred meters of film stock at the black-market rate for *Arara vermelha* (Red macaw) (Tom Payne, 1957); the same reel would normally cost Cr$3,400 at the official exchange rate.[53] This provides an unusual wrinkle to the narrative of uneven exchange that predominates center-periphery models of economic dependence and cultural diffusion. The trenchant defense of national industry in both the Vargas regimes and later Second Republic regimes was undone by loopholes in domestic monetary policy. This also provides some context for both the chanchada and the Cinema Novo's "às pressas" (on the fly) aesthetics. The poorly executed chanchada and the imperfect "reality effect" of the Cinema Novo are indices of similar material conditions of production—both had limited access to film stock at affordable rates of exchange.[54] National and regional film agencies, including the Comissão Federal de Cinema (Federal Commission of Cinema) and the Comissão Estadual de Cinema de São Paulo (State Commission of Cinema of São Paulo), lobbied to get film stock recategorized by the SUMOC and advocated for increased caps and more equitable access to and disbursement of foreign currency. The chanchada, in effect, was made with contraband raw material.[55]

AFTER CARNAVAL: TOWARD AN UNSEASONAL COMMODITY

The generic term of choice for producers and exhibitors, particularly in the prewar period, was the carnavalesco. The shift from carnavalesco to chanchada loosely maps onto the shift from Cinédia studios to Atlântida. Both the film narrative and the production schedule of the carnavalesco revolved around Carnaval: the events depicted often took place during Carnaval, providing the justification for the inclusion of popular marchas and sambas, and the production schedule was designed to ensure the premiere of the film during the summer release window. At the height of the carnavalesco, Cinédia coordinated its tight shooting schedule with a discographic production process. The original compositions featured in the musical numbers had to be recorded, reproduced, and distributed in 45 and 78 rpm vinyl records in conjunction with the brief summer release of the film. Unlike the vertically integrated Hollywood studio, Cinédia studios engaged in horizontal alliance across media producers, coordinating film production, music recording, and radio broadcasting. Shooting for Cinédia's first musical comedy, *Alô, alô, Brasil!* (Hello, hello Brazil!) (Wallace Downey, 1935), occurred in December 1934 in conjunction with the discographic release of its musical numbers through RCA Victor and Odeon. The film's most popular song, "Cidade Maravilhosa," composed by André Filho, was the first musical number released as a 78 rpm disc through Odeon in October 1934 and was featured in the theatrical review *Cidade maravilhosa* in January 1935. Another nine songs recorded for the film were released during the same window, culminating in the film's Carnaval premiere in February 1935.

Classicism is all about timing in ways both textual and material; we must think the steady construction of a diegetic (screen) temporality in relation to the rationalization of production *and* product release. To mock classicism means to be attendant to how the latter bears on the former. Films had to be made on the fly, "às pressas, pobres de técnica e arte, com o único fim de, sob qualquer titulo carnavalesco, atrair o público amigo de Momo" (made quickly, with poor technique and little artistic quality, with the sole objective, under any carnivalesque title, to attract the public friendly to King Momo).[56] Take the example of *Bonequinha de seda* (Little silk doll) (Oduvaldo Vianna, 1936), a Cinédia comedy produced and scheduled for release outside the Carnaval window. The film began production on May 28, 1936, and was scheduled for a premiere in the capital city on October 26, 1936. On the day of its premiere, a copy of the film was not finished. According to studio lore, each reel was dried in alcohol and delivered piecemeal by taxi from the Cinédia laboratories to the Cinema Palácio, even causing traffic problems in the city center. As studio production became more regular, musical production settled into a groove, particularly around the lucrative Carnaval holiday window. In October, producers began choosing and commissioning musical compositions intended for inclusion in the film *and* music recording and radio broadcasting. The scenario was drawn up and the script generated in November, and the filming took place in the early summer during December. Music recording roughly coincided with this process, and the discographic release sometimes preceded and sometimes followed the film's release, at first through RCA Victor and Odeon in the late 1930s and later Continental and Columbia in the early 1940s.[57] This well-oiled machine sputtered around the end of the Second World War. Cinédia's hit for Carnaval 1945, *Pif-paf* (Luiz de Barros, 1945) was released on February 5, 1945, although with fewer coincident music recordings, arguably a function of the scarcity of raw material for film and music recording.

Classical Hollywood cinema meant to make film a better commodity, and working through classicism elsewhere must first identify what a better commodity looks like in a particular market. In the case of Brazil, the Cinédia model represents a model for commodity production that required cooperation between different media industries and targeted its output for a period of increased leisure time and peak consumption. This industrial model perfected by Cinédia was emulated by the studio's contemporaries. Cinédia's early hits, *Alô, alô Brasil!* and *Alô, alô carnaval!*, were coproduced with Waldow Filme, the Wallace Downey and Alberto Byington venture later renamed Sonofilmes in 1937.[58] In 1939, Sonofilmes inaugurated a new space in northern Rio de Janeiro, which featured brand new sound equipment imported from the United States and an entire unit dedicated to disc recording and music production.[59] In fact, Wallace Downey and Alberto Byington came to cinema by way of sound: Downey, a Columbia Phonograph Company representative sent to São Paulo in 1928 to open an outpost in Brazil, contracted with Byington's electric company to open Columbia's factory.[60] Sonofilmes released the Carmen Miranda vehicle *Banana da terra* (Ruy Costa, 1939) the following month. The film sidestepped exhibitor monopolies by securing its distribution through Metro Goldwyn Mayer of Brasil, premiering in the studio's downtown Metro movie palace during Carnaval 1939.[61] Coinciding with the film's premiere, the film's well-known number, the Dorval Caymmi classic "O que é que a baiana tem," was released through the Odeon label.[62] The exchanges between cinema and popular music in Brazil are extensively documented in film histories, but these histories often depict a certain continuity (if not teleological trajectory) from Cinédia to Atlântida.[63] Earlier operations synchronized the production of original music and film content with the annual festivities in an early form of cross-platform promotion and transmedia convergence. After 1948, Atlântida wanted to release films year round in the Severiano Ribeiro theaters, abiding by protectionist legislation to foment domestic production without having to account for middlemen distributors and independent producers.

FIGURE 13. Eliana and Grande Otelo perform "No tabuleiro da baiana" in *Carnaval Atlântida* (1952). Image courtesy of Cinemateca Brasileira.

Atlântida had its origins in the good intentions of its founder Moacyr Fenelon, attempting to reconstruct what had been lost in the fire of the Sonofilmes studio. Atlântida secured its early capitalization by selling shares door to door and through advertisement in the periodical *A scena muda* and the newspaper *O journal do Brasil*. Fenelon's sales pitch came in the form of a manifesto of sorts, calling for a proper national film industry for a Brazil that "vive a fase definitiva de uma emancipação econômica" (lives in the definitive phase of its economic emancipation).[64] Atlântida quickly became a major producer between 1943 and 1947. The studio deliberately attempted to diversify its offerings; however, its struggles with capitalization made it return regularly to the musical-comedy well in order to stay afloat. The immense success of *Este mundo é um pandeiro* (This world is a tambourine) (Watson Macedo, 1946) compelled Luis Severiano Ribeiro, the carioca exhibition tycoon, to invest in and become the majority stakeholder of Atlântida by gradually buying out early investors.[65] After allegedly profiteering from the war and buying shares of the Distribuidora de Filmes Brasileiros and the Distribuidora Nacional in order to create the largest national distributor, União Cinematográfica Brasileira, Severiano Ribeiro consolidated his media empire by turning to production. In another ironic case of protectionist measures with unexpected consequences, the magnate used Atlântida to provide the content needed to abide by the 1946 Law 20.493, which forced exhibitors to screen three feature-length national films during the year.[66] Severiano Ribeiro redirected the efforts of the studio toward single-mindedly producing the popular genre, producing only enough films to meet the law's stipulations.[67] Even after this law was superseded by the *decreto-lei* 30.179 of November 19, 1951—also known as the 8 x 1 Law of 1951, because it stipulated that one national film had to be screened for every eight foreign films—the production of chanchadas only increased without complementary antitrust measures.[68]

The seasonal demand of the carnavalesco had resulted in idle capacity and high fixed costs and made film production a riskier enterprise requiring more forecasting and speculation because it was subject to seasonal fluctuations. The musicarnavalesco operated under a logic of commodity *not yet* money-form. The Cinédia film as seasonal commodity was not an item of universal exchange and commensurability because it was subject to a peculiar organization of time dependent on seasonal change and rhythmic activity, one which Stephen Kern characterizes as premodern.[69] The later Atlântida model, particularly after exhibitor Severiano Ribeiro's purchase of Atlântida that resulted in de facto vertical integration, loosened its collaboration with (if not dependence on) the recording industry. With exhibitors driving production, Atlântida attempted to make its commodities for year-round consumption. But all these films could not be released at the same time. The need for national cinema to become a year-round commodity meant undoing this concatenation of transmedia production and distribution. This process had effects both material—delinking the film studio from collaborating mass media producers—and narrative-aesthetic—films began departing from plots revolving around Carnaval and began borrowing from genres with unseasonal appeal. The schedule for Brazilian films had to be disarticulated from Carnaval.

When Alex Viany uses the term *chanchada* in his seminal film history *Introdução ao cinema brasileiro*, the term is not figured in relation to the nation but designates an industrial strategy whereby the musical comedy is disarticulated from the "compromissos com as músicas de sucesso do carnaval, os cartazes do rádio, ou mesmo os poucos nomes cinematográficos de bilheteria" (commitments to the musical hits of carnival, the song catalogs of radio stations, and even the few box-office names).[70] Making Brazilian cinema classical meant making film production unseasonal and nurturing the consumption habits of consumers to make demand unseasonal. Atlântida was faced with the dilemma of producing carnavalescos not meant for Carnaval. How to increase output while preserving the generic formula for commercial success? For starters, the Atlântida chanchada featured fewer original numbers. Much as Arthur Freed conceived his unit's productions as vehicles for older song catalogs from earlier MGM musicals, Atlântida preferred to recycle and reissue sambas and marchas from previous Cinédia and Atlântida films. Furthermore, the music was no longer exclusively the typical sambas and marchas of Carnaval, featuring a wider array of music types, such as the increasingly popular *baião* from the Brazilian Northeast and *sertanejo* country music.[71] The need for more content and lower production costs in a risk-averse scheme coupled with the declining value of cinema as a platform for music distribution in relation to radio (and eventually television) explains this change from the musicarnavelsco to the chanchada. The chanchada's unseasonal production meant to make the film a better commodity because its production was not subject to lived time but to modern atomistic time. Mock classicism must think the ways Latin American cinema became commodity at the intersection of temporal, cultural, and social factors, not simply operating in the abstract time and space of the money-form.[72]

In order to make the genre unseasonal, Atlântida moved away from the reluctant Carnaval-goer and toward more contrived gangster plots. João Luiz Vieira argues that the studio's *Carnaval no fogo* (Carnival on fire) (Watson Macedo, 1949) became the narrative blueprint for Atlântida under Severiano Ribeiro. Subsequent films would attempt to replicate its ten-week box-office run by cribbing its story elements: a triangulated romantic struggle between a hero (usually Anselmo Duarte) and a villain (usually José Lewgoy) for the affection of a *mocinha,* or young lady (usually Eliana), often with a schematic gangster plot interrupted by comedic bits with Oscarito and Grande Otelo.[73] The record-breaking success of this film cannot be argued; however, I turn to the earlier and less heralded *E o mundo se diverte* (And the world has fun) (Watson Macedo, 1948), only the second film released after Severiano Ribeiro's takeover. Made before the cementing of the Atlântida blueprint, the film provides a window onto the transition in Atlântida leadership and arguably the transition from the 1930s (Cinédia) model of film production to the later Atlântida model. *E o mundo se diverte* tells a backstage musical plot. In this cross between *The Producers* (Mel Brooks, 1967) and *The Bandwagon* (Vincente Minnelli, 1953), the film features a wealthy theater producer who wants to bring serious drama to Brazil but cannot find success staging European opera. What the producer does not realize is that his assistant producer conspires against him, laundering money by overvaluing his boss's investments, paying top dollar for "overseas" performers he actually finds in the neighboring city of Niterói. The assistant producer is engaged to the producer's daughter (Eliana), but the producer's secretary, Alberto (Alberto Ruschel in the Anselmo Duarte role), also pines for her. Alberto visits a doctor to quell his ardor at the suggestion of the theater's janitor (Oscarito), but his chest X-rays are swapped for those of an older gentleman with an aortic aneurysm. Oscarito decides to keep the two-week prognosis from his friend and persuades the producer to help Alberto realize his dream of staging a successful musical revue. The producer agrees, confident that Alberto will soon die, making his contract null and void, and the revue will never be staged. The assistant producer conspires to bring about Alberto's death, but Alberto survives and the show goes on. The film concludes on opening night, the opera a flop and the revue a massive success.

As a transitional film, *E o mundo se diverte* features both seasonal references to Carnaval and unseasonal narrative elements less tethered to the annual celebration. Eliana and Alberto begin their courtship when they go together to a Carnaval party overlooking a parade, or *bloco*. The sequence begins with a high-angle long shot of a crowded room with disguised partygoers singing and dancing a circle dance. Eliana and Alberto eventually enter the frame and the camera frames them in a medium shot, pushing back slightly before returning to the circle dance in long shot. The couple exits the frame and we see them steal away to a balcony. Alberto throws serpentine confetti before leaving Eliana to chat with Oscarito's love interest. This other woman reveals Alberto's tragic prognosis to Eliana, advising her not to let him get overly excited because he might drop dead. Eliana gazes out sullenly from the balcony; the sequence cuts to point-of-view shots of Carnaval floats from early 1948, silent footage recorded on location made continuous with Eliana's close-up through continuous music cues from the preceding dancing scene. Eventually, Alberto returns in a medium close-up asking her why she is sad and reminding her that "o mundo se diverte" (the world has fun). The music is lowered during this exchange, and Eliana wistfully repeats the refrain, now a fatalistic lament. Carnaval always seems haunted by its end as one final extreme long shot of a passing float punctuates the sequence. Setting the story events during Carnaval and including footage from the previous year's festivities was a common narrative gambit in Cinédia films, from the obvious *Alô, Alô* cycle to minor films such as

Tereré não resolve (Luiz de Barros, 1938) and the late Cinédia film *Caídos do céu* (Fallen from the sky) (Luiz de Barros, 1946). Although future Atlântida films featured landscape shots of Rio de Janeiro or characters in various recognizable sites in silent footage usually underscored for the sake of continuity, they would seldom return to footage from actual Carnaval festivities.

And yet, minutes before this extended sequence, we have one of Atlântida's first explicit attempts to delink the musicarnavalesco from Carnaval. An early scene between the two women is interrupted by a radio broadcast. Eliana shushes her interlocutor and the camera reveals the radio sound source on an end table nearby. The sequence cuts to an extreme long shot of a stage with a painted backdrop decorated with cacti and a giant sombrero. The (live?) audience applause provides a slight sound bridge as four performers come on stage and surround a central microphone. We return to the bedroom where the applause is audible and the music begins to play, far louder than the earlier announcer. Eliana curls up in bed and the camera shifts back to the depicted broadcast. A close-up of the lead singer as he intones the opening bars of Pepe Agüero's "Abandonado" is intercut with a close-up of a listening Eliana. The scene presents a remarkable example of radio listening, of hearing without seeing, what Michel Chion might call acousmatic listening.[74] Chion coins the acousmatic to move away from the diegetic/nondiegetic distinction and to discuss sounds in tension with their visualization rather than their diegiticization. For Chion, radio broadcasting encouraged the imagination of sonic sources, causes, and scenes; we listeners produce the radiophonic scene. Could we think the chanchada along similar lines, the narrative space less a discrete diegesis than a conjuring of sound sources, less an exercise in phonofixation than telephony? The on-the-air sound blurs the zones of on-screen, offscreen, and nondiegetic.[75]

Unlike conventional musicarnavelscos, this is not music associated with Carnaval. Although other music genres feature in earlier musical comedies, this bolero, written by a Cuban composer, is performed by the *gaúcho* quartet Quitadinha Serenaders wearing Mexican garb. The quartet featured the well-known guitarist Luis Bonfá, responsible for the musical effects on the soundtrack, and the romantic lead of the film, Alberto Ruschel. The quartet came to prominence because of their radio success in the previous year, releasing their records through Continental in 1948. The inclusion of the Serenaders responds to a certain change in the mediascape afforded by radio, one that began including music types outside the capital region both because of the growth of the radio industry beyond its early regional origins *and* because of a transition away from the seasonal programming of Carnaval hits. The film later includes a paulista comedic singing duo, Alvarenga and Ranchinho. Famous for its scathing parodies of Getúlio Vargas in the 1930s, the duo performs in Mexican costume at the Ali Baba night club. The duo works in a tight medium shot, a vaudeville-era back-and-forth that culminates with a song. "Vamos cantar uma coisinha" (Let's sing something), says one man. The other asks, "Mexicana ou estrangeira?" (Mexican or foreign?). They decide on a "foreign" song, yet they perform a *sertaneja,* a protocountry song with explicit references to the recently deposed Brazilian dictator and his militaristic brother (Getúlio and Benjamin Vargas, respectively). Not quite the foreign song we had expected.

The film relies on one additional collaborator who demonstrates how far removed we are from the sambas and marchas of Carnavals past. The penultimate musical number is a dress rehearsal for the revue featuring an accordion player (Luis Gonzaga) singing his "Que mentira que lorota boa" (What a lie, that's a good one!) on a fairgrounds set surrounded by dancing children on carnival rides. Gonzaga, of course, would later be dubbed a national icon and "Rei do Baião," but in 1948 he had only begun making a name for himself. The baião is a folk music genre associated with the Northeast, popularized in the radio by Gonzaga, especially his first success "Asa branca" (1947), later featured in the Atlântida film *É com êste que eu vou* (I'm going with this one) (José Carlos Burle, 1948).[76] Again, we see a departure from the Carnaval genres, both a function of the growing popularity and radio airplay of the baião and the unseasonal demands of increased film production. Additionally, the scene is an example of a restaged musical number; Gonzaga had appeared two years prior in *Este mundo é um pandeiro* singing the same song, "Que mentira que lorota boa."

Film criticism from the period disparaged this evacuation of the carnivalesque. The review of the Oscarito vehicle *É com este que eu vou* in the daily Carioca newspaper *A noite* explains: "O título é ilusório. Aproveitar a denominação de música carnavalesca—que não faz parte do celuloide—quando a finalidade é diferente, sendo mesmo raras e fracas as composições dessa festa. As únicas melodias e instantes aproveitáveis são os poucos do atos folclóricos, mas que não chegam para compensar os aspectos débeis" (The title is misleading. Taking advantage of the designation of carnivalesque music—which is not a part of the film—when its end goal is different, with the compositions for that festival being sporadic and poor. The only worthwhile moments and melodies are those few folkloric acts, but they cannot make up for the weaknesses).[77] The review lauds the performance of only a few numbers, particularly the Quitadinha Serenaders also featured in *E o mundo se diverte,* but disparages their narrative integration, made more difficult without the necessary Carnaval setting—"bastante fracos são os pretextos arranjados para os shows" (the pretexts for the shows are very weak).[78] The film was a chanchada not because of its carnivalesque themes but because it no longer indexed Carnaval.

FIDUCIARY FICTIONS

In lieu of plots revolving around Carnaval, Atlântida film narratives concern making (or stealing or inheriting or finding) money. From the machinations of the banker twin brother in the comedy of errors *É com este que eu vou* to the jewel heist in the paradigmatic *Carnaval no fogo;* from the Robin Hood parody *Os dois ladrões* (The two thieves) (Carlos Manga, 1960) and the trafficking and extortion plots in *Um caçula do barulho* (The topsy-turvy kid) (Ricardo Freda, 1949) or the later *Esse milhão é meu* (That million is mine) (Carlos Manga, 1958) to the inheritance plots in *Aí vem o barão* (There comes the baron) (Watson Macedo, 1951), where Oscarito impersonates an heir to a great fortune, *Treze cadeiras* (Thirteen chairs) (Carlos Manga, 1957), where he accidentally sells an heirloom containing hidden money, and *Os apavorados* (The scaredy-cats) (Ismar Porto, 1962), the final Atlântida production, its films were *ficciones del dinero* (fictions of money).[79] Even the musical comedies made in rival studios produced comedies as fictions of money. The 1950s dubbing studio Herbert Richers S.A., founded by the defecting Atlântida producer of the same name, produced original content in competition with Atlântida: the gambling intrigue in *E o bicho não deu* (And the gamble didn't pay off) (J. B. Tanko, 1958) and the patchwork financing of a theatrical production in *Mulheres à vista* (Women ahoy) (J. B. Tanko, 1959). The Atlântida director Watson Macedo would start his own Watson Macedo Produções Cinematográficas with titles such as the land speculation comedy *O petróleo é nosso* (The oil is ours) (1954) and yet another heiress impersonation film, *A baronesa transviada* (The misplaced baroness) (1957), which would make comedienne Dercy Gonçalves a star. Even Moacyr Fenelon's Cinedistri produced *De pernas pro ar* (Topsy-turvy) (Vitor Lima, 1957) and the aptly titled *Se men dólar falasse* (If my Dollar could talk) (Carlos Coimbra, 1970), both films where the protagonists find money stolen

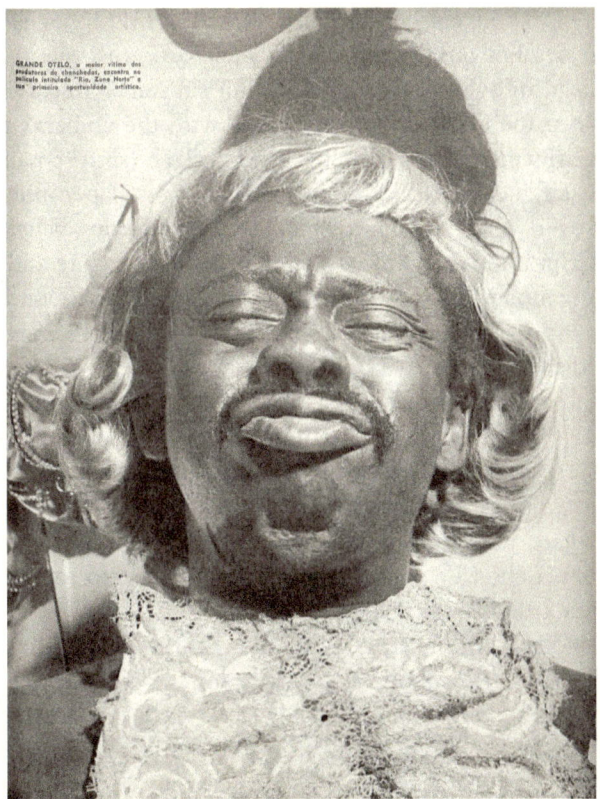

FIGURE 14. Grande Otelo mugs for the cameras of photomagazine O *cruzeiro* in 1957. Image courtesy of D.A. Press.

by criminals, the latter a remarkable vehicle for Grande Otelo, featuring a title card eulogizing the recently deceased Oscarito.

My argument is not that money is a theme in the chanchada or in Latin American film comedy. The question is only partly about the depiction of economic scenes (films about money) or the external economy of filmmaking (films cost and earn money). Echoing Süssekind's earlier observations about Brazilian cultural production during the change from the cruzeiro to the real under neoliberalism, I want to propose that the desmedida caused by the 1942 currency change in Brazil had effects beyond the thematic and material levels. Because money is an "internal participant in logical or semiological organization," I want to propose that money matters to classicism as a system of "tropic production and exchange" and participates actively in the rise of fictionality (and, inversely, the claim to the real).[80] Money is a form of economic symbolization; that is, money concerns the relationship between sign or symbol (inscription) and substance (metal/ingot/electrum). When the first coin was engraved with the numeral 2, the real was fiduciarily dissociated from the symbol.[81] The shift to paper money represents a fiduciary escalation in symbolization. Paper money augurs concerns over value, and Marc Shell relates conferring belief in fiduciary and scriptural money to conferring belief in literature and art.[82] For Shell, paper money does not simply become an aesthetic concern represented in artists' work. If economic form determines language and thought, then monetary symbolization finds aesthetic expression in literature and art. Credit or belief "involves the very ground of aesthetic experience."[83] Simply put, belief underwrites money and fiction, and twentieth-century Brazilian cultural production has a long tradition of considering money as fiction and fiction as money: from the work of conceptual artists Cildo Meirelles and Jac Leirner to the poetic seriality of Sebastian Uchoa Leite and Paulo Henriques Britto to the narrative play of Bernardo Carvalho.[84]

Paper money appears to be a symbol entirely dissociated from the commodity that it symbolizes. If paper money distorts our everyday understanding of the relationship between symbols and things, then a change in currency affects the relationship between symbols and symbols. A change of currency forces all participants to toggle between parallel forms of symbolization in a two-step conversion process that reduces things to symbols and relates those to other symbols. Paper money is never as obvious an arbitrary common denominator as during the implementation of such monetary policy. I want to suggest that the Brazilian chanchada must be understood under the aegis of such monetary policy—to mock classicism means to negotiate the relationship between the symbolic and the material and to understand fiction as economic form.

Alejandra Laera makes a similar claim about the late-nineteenth-century Argentine novel. In the context of a newly minted national currency and the boom years of industrial capitalism, the novel attempted to process this change in monetary symbolization and challenge this new monetary fiction through referentiality and realism.[85] Asked through Laera, if money changes, what happens to fiction? Money attempts to compel belief in its relation to material substance, and verisimilitude must be understood operating in a similar vein. Through these *ficciones del dinero,* money reveals its own fiction and inscribes itself as one of fiction's very origins.[86] In fact, the rise of fictionality, or what Derrida calls "the birth of the naturalization of literature," coincides with the emergence of money, "the age of value as monetary sign."[87] Derrida analogizes the money form of exchange with language, both systems structured on symbolic equivalence. As such, Derrida argues that currency shares the condition of fiction, not because it is false but because it relies on an ability to circulate and a capacity to provoke events. Perhaps we could think film language under a similar economic logic, more significant as a form of symbolization and medium of communicative exchange than as a representative of the real.

REFINANCING CLASSICAL HOLLYWOOD

Cinema would seem to share with money the faculty for "turning an image into reality and reality into a mere image."[88] This shift from a (numismatic) sign where signifier and referent are interdependent to an (alchemic) sign where the signifier has no necessary relation to its referent can perhaps shed light on cinema.[89] This shared faculty of money and cinema suggests we think about classical Hollywood cinema in relation to the rise of fictionality and the emergence of the money-form rather than realism and the novel form. Catherine Gallagher explains that the eighteenth-century novel is remarkable neither for its verisimilitude nor its realism but for its fictionality. She suggests readers "developed the ability to tell [fiction] from both fact and (this is the key) deception."[90] The eighteenth-century reader went from taking fiction as a lie to taking fiction as a suspension of normal referential truth claims. Rather than suppose that readers naively identified with characters or mistook fiction for reality, Gallagher points to early novels that "gave us numerous Quixotic characters to laugh at for confusing textual with actual people."[91] The modern reader, like Miriam Hansen's classical spectator, trains in acquiring disbelief as a sign of superior discernment.[92] Ironic credulity becomes the condition not only of the novel's reader but also of the classical spectator. Although screen theory would have us believe that this spectator was under "maximum delusion," to borrow from Paul De Man, the rise of fictionality suggests otherwise.[93] Much like the monetary sign, fiction requires giving credit on a sign without referent: "Modernity is fiction-friendly because it encourages disbelief, speculation and credit."[94]

Before the classic realist text, spectators had to learn that what happened on screen was credible while affirming nothing. As Philip Rosen has argued, constructing a cinema institution dominated by narrative had to first deal with a preexisting audience familiarity with actuality.[95] The rise of fictionality requires a monetary form of meaning where the symbol is dissociated from the thing, where the symbolic is separable from the indexical. The transition to classical cinema is still motivated by the demands of industrial rationalization, but Rosen's account foregrounds how classicism meant fiction first had to negotiate and compromise with "the desire to see actuality through the moving indexical image."[96] Read through early cinema, the transition to classical cinema refers less to a natural narrative configuration than it does to the fictionality of the moving picture in tension with the fascination derived from the photographic assertion of the past (i.e., its indexical referentiality). The transition to classical cinema that entailed a separation of screen space from theater space, a separation motivated by producers standardizing their commodity and wresting control from exhibition, required endowing the image with a type of nonreferentiality.

To characterize verisimilitude as the defining criterion for classical Hollywood cinema ignores the fact that it first required taking as fiction the information in analog storage and transmission media. To borrow Catherine Gallagher's turn of phrase, the diegesis had to be credible while affirming nothing. The canonical if overstated account of Gorky's "Kingdom of Shadows" suggests the continuity of screen and theater space is a function of an image that is (more than) referential. Fiction seems less aligned with absorption than with a certain *lack* of belief, a "kind of cognitive provisionality [and] a competence in investing contingent and temporary credit."[97] The image has purchase less because of what it depicts than because of its logic of representation as exchange. The film image is increasingly a symbol of credit or trust in the eventual redemption of physical reality; perhaps it should come as no surprise that the Portuguese *acreditar* is one common translation for the verb "to believe." Classicism understood through the emergence of fictionality means thinking about how film images became something in which we could invest credit because they could store time and make it available for future redemption. The codification of the proper relations among viewer, projector, and screen are no longer simply matters of spatial arrangement or coordinating viewer identification but also of orchestrating tempor(al)ization.[98] The tension between events transpired and actions unfolding through our engagement adds a new dimension to the relationship between screen space and theatrical space.[99] Classical Hollywood narrative is also the orchestration of a suspensive delay. The classical Hollywood logic of communicative and economic narration displays a certain capacity to organize sense impressions within the temporality of the récit, attempting to contain the possibility of meaningless contingency.[100] The classicism of Hollywood attempted to abate the "existential present," to register contingency by narrativizing change and yoking singularity to meaning: "the present—as the mark of contingency in time—is made tolerable, readable, archivable, and, not least, pleasurable."[101] Hollywood classical cinema attempted to separate the past-present-future regime of temporal chronology (i.e., screen time) from the pregnant moment of scenic display and the present tense of the spectator (i.e., theater time). The production of a closed diegesis, where fiction and reality are discrete worlds, is precisely the way money aspires to relate sign and substance. Fiction realizes time and space in a diegetic world cut to the measure of currency and its circulation.

THE *REAL* ON THE SCREEN

If the discourse of fictionality and its relation to the novel form developed differently outside the West, perhaps fictionality and its relation to Hollywood classicism also develops differently outside Hollywood.[102] Mock classicism, then, not only means a different coordination of spatial relations between screen space and theater space but also a different mode of organizing the "indexically imprinted profilmic . . . according to the hierarchies of a 'virtual' time, that of the fiction world."[103] Early sound experiments in Brazilian cinema bear out this different relation between actuality and fictionality. Cinédia purchased older sound-on-film cameras used mostly for nonfiction filmmaking and adapted these for filming its fiction films, starting with *Tataravô*.[104] Adhemar Gonzaga had imported an Akeley sound camera from the Akeley Camera Company, which was not the camera of choice for the American film industry, used instead in the late 1920s and early 1930s by newsreel companies such as Paramount News.[105] Because the Akeley camera had a sound-recording unit attached to its heavy camera, the sequences in *Tataravô* feature quite a bit of scale matching, a sound practice already phased out by the mid-1930s in classical Hollywood because it disrupted the production of a sonic vraisemblable. A fiction film made using newsreel technology: these are precisely the material conditions that determined how the mock classical diegesis would be constructed.

Both Cinédia and Atlântida films provide excellent examples of this diegetic world that can be neither a discrete symbolic realm nor cut to the measure of currency. Returning to *O jovem tataravô*, the diegesis does not abide by the time-bound. When Vitor proposes to Dora, Eduardo and his wife protest in a lengthy explanation of the ramifications of such a union: "Então meu tataravô quer casar-se com minha filha? ... O senhor não vê que não pode casar-se com a sua bitataraneta? Que casando com ela, eu seria o sogro do meu tataravô? E que minha mulher, sendo sogra do meu tataravô, sera tataraneta da própria filha? E minha filha será tataravó do seu próprio pai?" (So my great-grandfather wants to marry my daughter? But don't you see you can't marry your great-great-grandaughter. If you marry her, I would be my great-grandfather's father-in-law? And my wife, being my great-grandfather's mother-in-law, would be the [step-]great-granddaughter of her own daughter? And my daughter would be her own father's great-grandmother?). The threat the great-grandfather poses is one of incest, an excess of categories of kinship. Judith Butler reminds us that the symbolic gives us kinship as a function of language, so that when Vitor twists genealogical linearity into a knot, he risks making language (and the social) unintelligible.[106] Incest does to kinship what puns do to language, threatening with variable structures that do not allow us to place ourselves in the social or symbolic. Vitor does not return to the present to reveal something hidden or forgotten but to remind us how the present is not quite as self-sufficient as it claims.[107] Vitor then allows an insight into textuality as such, making established certainties vacillate at multiple levels, perhaps also a reminder that the diegesis is scarcely as self-sufficient as Hollywood would presume.

The way sound technologies otherwise shaped the diegetic world is particularly evident in the great-grandfather's appearance and later disappearance. The seance begins with a wipe to an overhead shot of the family sitting around a table. His wife and daughter mock this *brincadeira*, or joke. Eduardo brushes off the skeptics in a close-up, asking the party whom they should reincarnate. He consults the family tree and decides on his great-grandfather. The family continues to interject in the subsequent long shot, disbelief tinged with fear as Eduardo begins the incantation. A sound punctuates an abrupt cut to another space, and a body materializes in a trick partial dissolve shot. Vitor appears in an old-fashioned swimsuit in the long shot. The startled family bolts out of the reverse shot and scatters. Each member comments on the action in a close-up, the sound necessarily synced to the depicted sound source in successive shots. These separate shots ensure we cannot quite pinpoint where Vitor is in relation to the seance and cannot quite produce a continuous narrative space, compounded by the inability to edit sound separately from the image and the discontinuous space the voice-offs would produce. That narrative space fractures at the moment of temporal unfolding should not surprise, resolved eventually in a long shot that frames the great-grandfather in the foreground facing his family, each member gradually coming out of hiding in the mid- and backgrounds. The shot composed in depth does not allow the reincarnated man in the foreground to speak because the sound men would be unable to level the sounds issuing from different distances to the camera. Finally, the scene is framed from the side, panning with the great-grandfather as he approaches the family and restores the almost theatrical framing of the narrative space.

Returning the spirit from whence it came proves a challenge and occurs in the final minutes of the film. The great-grandfather sits in front of the family's radio. In a shot/reverse-shot, he asks his relatives about the wonders of the radio: "É com isso que se escutam todas as partes do mundo? . . . Assim, sim fio, sim nada" (Is this how we hear all the corners of the world? With no wires, with nothing?). The world arrives through electromagnetic waves. A close-up of the radio tuner coincides with a *noticiário* (newscast) detailing automobile-related deaths in New York. A twist of the knob, the same voice reports the deaths from a police standoff in Madrid. Vitor scours for something else on the radio but only finds the same voice reporting on the inevitability of another world war. The necessity to record sound with the image likely explains why the same voice broadcasts on different stations. Vitor sits back in his armchair in a medium shot and laments the fate of the world: "A humanidade não era assim tão mala" (Humanity was not this bad). An abrupt cut to a long shot comes with blaring music, framing Vitor next to the radio in this death scene. The music is ostensibly from the radio and yet Vitor begins to sing an aria before his death in an impressive tracking long take. A final cut features Vitor immobile in his chair, the continuity afforded by the final notes of the song, and a partial dissolve offers a final trick shot whereby the character vanishes and his clothing remains.

This evident instance of playback singing is particularly uncanny because of the tensions between ostensible diegetic sound sources. The only music in the film has either been performed in musical numbers or accompanies montages of location shooting in Rio de Janeiro. This final aria is unusual in the film because it sits at the threshold of the diegesis: perhaps issued from the radio, perhaps accompanying the singing character. This progression from diegetic track through diegetic music to nondiegetic orchestration became a convention of the classical Hollywood film musical, orchestrated mechanically in *Tataravô* rather than accomplished through an audio dissolve in postproduction.[108] Rick Altman argues these musical moments in classical Hollywood mediate the time-bound diegesis to the timeless transcendence of the supradiegetic in order to lend "order and regularity to diegetic time [and conform] the irregularities of diegetic space to a pattern."[109] What do we make of this function in the case of mock classicism, where the diegesis is never quite a discrete narrative space? This vanishing spirit accompanies (non) diegetic music not to avow narrative space. In fact, other musical numbers in the film also fail to mediate these narratological registers.

During the cabaret sequence when Vitor steals away from a stuffy party to enjoy the Carioca nightlife, a conventional musical stage number begins with a medium shot of the singer introducing the foxtrot "Night and Fog." The music begins over a panning shot of the party's defectors, which precedes another shot of three performers with megaphones. Suddenly, the scene changes to a long shot of a nighttime scene where a woman stops and speaks to a man on the street. In this meet cute, the film shows the pair in shot/reverse-shot before the man follows the woman. We return to the performers, this time three trumpeters. We go back to the man, now alone in a long shot and sitting on a public bench. The singer finally croons in his own medium shot. The relation of these exterior night scenes to the musical performance is completely unclear. The instrumental music continues uninterrupted over both spaces, ostensibly simultaneous but very much not contiguous. The song lyrics eventual provide a small clue, describing a brief encounter before cutting to a racy shot of the couple in a car framed through the rear window. The man gets closer to the women before lowering the shade of the rear window. We return to the performers in a series of shots featuring different instrumental arrangements in the image and on the soundtrack. Is the street scene a performance on the stage during the number? There are no editing or cinematography conventions that would suggest this possibility. Is this a scene happening in parallel with some effect on the narrative? None of the players are recognizable. If this is a scene simply depicting the events in the song, how do we explain what has happened to the diegesis? The staged musical number is the most conventional pretext used in the chanchada to include the requisite marchas and sambas. The chanchada is never quite an integrated musical, opting instead to include numerous scenes of theatrical spectatorship (and the occasional backstage plot). Unlike the Mexican and Argentine examples from chapters past, the chanchada remarkably never stages a self-reflexive scene of film spectatorship. Recalling Hansen's discussion of *Uncle Josh at the Moving Picture Show* (1902), these moments of errant spectatorship in the transition from early to classical Hollywood cinema trained spectators to recognize that the diegesis is distinct from the theater space.[110] That the Brazilian chanchada avoids such a conceit is peculiar, especially for a genre so unabashedly characterized by its debt to Hollywood conventions. Instead of staging the misrecognition of screen space, the chanchada offers scenes where the spectacle and the audience are ostensibly contiguous. Once the musical number begins, the camera abandons the coordinates of space and time, tracking backward and forward in impossible stage sets as countless performers crowd the frame. The impossible architecture of this narrative space is bookended by the spectating audience, a guarantor for the integrity of the diegesis.

METALEPSIS AND MOCK CLASSICISM

Appearing over a decade later, the final act of *E o mundo se diverte* uses successive musical numbers to provide distinct visions of the diegetic world. With Alberto not dead yet, the film's conclusion takes place on the opening night of the opera. After an extreme long shot of the theater at capacity with the orchestra tuning its instruments, we head backstage where Grande Otelo sneaks up to a turntable. The orchestra sounds provide a semblance of continuity between the backstage and the house, but the music slowly changes to underscored accompaniment to Grande Otelo's stealth actions. He motions an offscreen Oscarito to approach. Grande Otelo swaps a stack of vinyl discs for another set Oscarito carries. After a cutaway to the assistant producer and his boss squabbling in a loge box about the revue company also backstage, the camera returns backstage where a hapless stage manager sets a disc in the recorder as the unseen orchestra finishes its prologue. The camera turns to an extreme long shot of the stage with the beginning of the opera on the vinyl disc. A diva moves downstage and opens her mouth; however, she unexpectedly belts a bass voice. Another woman steps to her left, her voice a baritone. A final player to her left is a tenor. Cutaways to the perplexed and later amused audience are intercalated with the gender-swapped performance. A bespectacled man is a coloratura soprano. The camera pushes back and his female companion responds as a tenor.

They sing together, each synchronized to the wrong voice. A pair of male comprimario singers are soprano and mezzosoprano. The diva is a bass voice in her close-up when the camera pans to the first woman, still a tenor. The camera returns backstage where the frantic assistant producer stops the record and abruptly halts the music, both on the soundtrack and (ostensibly) from the stage. He reprimands the stage hand and breaks the disc over his head. Immediately, the camera returns to an audience, an abrupt transition because their audible boos and hisses were inaudible in the previous shot. The performers in early modern period garb are pelted with produce as they flee the stage.

The evening performance is saved when Alberto and Eliana appeal to the producer to let them stage the revue, its performers still waiting in the wings. Despite sharing the same stage, the staging of the revue performance is completely different from the opera. This is not a theatrical performance edited in continuity but an impossible architecture. The well-known performance of "Aves sem ninho" ("Birds without a Nest") is a remarkable sequence. The number begins with neither the proscenium-establishing shot nor a shot of the audience; instead, a close-up of tree limbs underscored by woodwinds pans slowly before some trick editing suggests a continuous whip pan to our performer, the gaúcha Horacina Correia, in the background. She begins singing and slowly approaches the camera, walking down a path flanked by the leafless trees. The camera slowly pushes into a medium close-up until she finishes the verse. A drumbeat changes the music's rhythm, and the camera tilts up with another bit of trick editing that reveals an extreme long shot of a line of Afro-Brazilian dancers in slave garb dancing in stage smoke. The dancers begin dancing to the beat and the editing cuts discontinuously between canted shots of the writhing dancers. The sequence culminates in a tracking long shot that reveals a staircase railing in the foreground with another slew of dancers in top hats descending the stairs in a single file. The men in top hats whistle as the music slowly fades from the percussion to a brassy samba. The camera reveals the grand staircase in a long shot from the position formerly occupied by the retreating black dancers, now vanished. The men in tuxedos exit frame left and the camera cuts to a line of women dancing in ball gowns. Horacina Correia returns in a medium shot, and the camera pushes back with the line of women dancing toward the staircase right to left and the top-hat-wearing men passing left to right just behind Correia in the foreground. Eventually, a high angle shot shows the women and the men in a circle dance, twirling together. After some canted close-up of

FIGURE 15. Oscarito as Helen of Troy mocks classicism in *Carnaval Atlântida* (1952). Image courtesy of Cinemateca Brasileira.

the spinning bodies, Correia appears in a final long shot as the dancers head upstage. As the background light is turned off, Correia is left alone in a single key light. The number ends with a cut to the audience and the abrupt eruption of applause.

Why present these successive musical numbers so differently? One immediate explanation: the final act celebrates forms of popular music and theater above the foreign tradition of opera and dramatic theater. This opposition between low and high culture returns in later films, most notably the self-reflexive *Carnaval Atlântida* (José Carlos Burle, 1952), where the head of a movie studio aspires to make an epic film set in antiquity but resolves to make a profitable popular comedy. That these forms of popular culture are deeply indebted to foreign influence suggests we take a closer look. The difference between the musical performances lies not only in their content but in the ways they coordinate space and time. At first glance, the opera performance presents successive narrative events causally related occurring in a space edited in continuity. From the opening establishing shot of the proscenium and the analytic editing that cuts into the stage to show us the mismatched performers in close-up, to the countershots of the audience and the bookended cutaways to the backstage area, we spectators are never disoriented in space.

We remain aware of the performers metonymically related to the larger performance, and every transition is motivated dramatically, whether to elaborate the lip-sync bit or to provide reactions (and explanations) to the events on stage. The humor derives from the bad ventriloquism, from the opera as bad sound cinema. The film's diegesis coheres even as it presents a spectacle of incoherence.

The subsequent sequence inverts this relationship of image and sound, using the continuity of the song to unfold the stage into a space that cannot cohere. Gone are the conventions of continuity editing. Without establishing shots of the proscenium or intercalated reaction shots of the onlookers, these successive pieces cannot be metonymically assembled into a spatial whole. There are suggestive spatial cues in the camera movement, but they are no help: the dozen Afro-Brazilian dancers cannot be continuous in time with Correia, much less contiguous in space, when the camera tilts upward to reveal them in a low angle. Time and again, the canted angles of the dancing bodies are narratively redundant, motivated not by dramatic causality but by rhythm. And yet this transformation from "a narratively organized space to a rhythmically organized image" cannot be characterized simply as a shift from classical continuity to modernist fragmentation.[111] Let us avoid claiming too quickly that this departure from continuity editing is an example of (vernacular) modernism, of resisting the codes of classical Hollywood. As Altman explains, the supradiegetic mediating function of musical numbers, particularly before the integrated musical, was a common feature of the American film musical. What Altman suggests is the possibility of a screen space organized under a "new mode of causality," one that he reads as a utopian space of unity foreclosed with the later dominance of the integrated musical governed by temporal, psychological causality.[112] The chanchada opens onto the possibility not of modernist subversion but of mock classicism, of a narrative space governed by a new mode of causality, but not quite the utopian space Altman imagines because nothing comes together. This freedom from the realistic and causal constraints of the diegesis does not occur exclusively in film musical numbers but also structures the narrative architecture of the chanchada, one that can never be entirely over there because it threatens to unfold and enfold.

Instead of simply moving the goalposts back and figuring a more expansive diegesis,[113] the chanchada works in a metaleptic mode, incorporating the world of the telling and the world of the told. The diegesis always entails a certain construction, a certain framing, a certain coordination of space and time. Metalepsis stages the collapse of the spatial and temporal protocols that normally hold the audience on one side of a line and the text on the other. In Gérard Genette's narratology, the metalepsis is a "transgression of the threshold of embedding" that often produces an effect of "humor."[114] Although this kind of transgression could be read in a modernist light, the chanchada does not abide the separation of narrative levels, instead involving "the beholder in an ontological transgression of universes and point[ing] toward a theory of fiction."[115] The modernist use of metalepsis would (critically) distance the spectators from narrative space, evicting them from the narrative world. Recalling the first chapter, classicism and modernism conceived as separation (of diegesis) and distance (from diegesis) depend on abstracting space. "The predominance of the abstraction in modern art," Henri Lefebvre reminds us, "accompanies the extension of the world of merchandise and merchandise as a world, along with the unlimited power of money and capital."[116] The source of abstraction lies in the structure of money and its forms of circulation, so that the construction of the diegesis indexes the social forms of experience of the money-form.[117] The separation of the diegesis from theatrical space in classical Hollywood and the estrangement of the spectator from the diegesis in European modernism are *both* processes of alienation, both cultural effects of the abstraction of the money form. To claim these transgressions of the diegesis in the chanchada are moments of (vernacular) modernism supposes a discrete story world, a certain coordination of space and time founded on the money form of value as the general equivalent of exchange. Instead, these metaleptic moments point to a certain inability to abstract space, indexing the experience of a money-form shaped by barter, scarcity, conversion, devaluation, and hyperinflation. When the chanchada collapses the distinctions and hierarchies between distinct narrative levels, it produces an uneasiness in the unchecked powers of fiction, indexing a money form not quite abstracted from older logics of perception (the coordination of space and time) and production (the order of personal relations).[118]

Thinking the chanchada through mock classicism and the orchestration of tempor(al)ization forces us to think about the debates about the merits of the chanchada differently. If film historian Paulo Emílio Salles Gomes claims that the chanchadas "traziam, como seu público, a marca do mais cruel subdesenvolvimento" (carried, much like their audience, the mark of the most cruel underdevelopment), Jean-Claude Bernardet argues that "a chanchada são filmes críticos, não tenha a menor dúvida quanto a isso" (the chanchada are critical films, make no mistake).[119] Both historiographical approaches understand the chanchada through the concept of parody. The former argues that the carnivalesque musical romps are symptoms of economic and cultural dependency whereas the latter claims these moments function as subversive hybrid cultural objects, locating the politics of parody in producing an awareness of marginality: an "*ironic* consciousness of simultaneously belonging to two cultures—one's own and that of the metropolitan centers of powers" (emphasis mine).[120] The chanchada is understood within a schema of cultural dependency where parody vacillates between upholding or subverting the cultural emitter at the center. Parody becomes productive in an anti-illusionistic ironic vein, "instead of customary realistic depiction."[121] This ironic posture, however, aligns fiction with deception and opposes truth and fiction.[122] The idea that *behind* language and actions there is a ground or subject to be expressed relies on the logic of the signifier in its money-form. In other words, for words to "mean otherwise," the signifier must be separate from its signified and belong to a noncommensurate and generalizable system that functions because what is said necessarily means and points to something other than the specific enunciation.[123] Sign and substance are dissociated in the institution of paper money much as word is dissociated from meaning in irony *(eironeia)*.[124] Faulting the genre as deceptive and privileging parodic moments is to prescribe a mode of demystification founded on the image as immediacy.[125] Thinking the chanchada earnestly ("it refers"), symptomatically ("it reveals"), or ironically ("it's never serious") all presume (anti)realism rather than fictionality. Figuring the genre in relation to realism is to desire the concealment of fictionality and a mode of spectatorship that disavows economic symbolization, that gives credit on a sign without referent.

Economic symbolization is never as effective as the nation-state and its desire for monetary uniformity would design.[126] These distinctions are particularly evident in the periphery where stability derives from another currency, where local currency is never the substance worth accumulating, where local currency never has the same purchase, where a standard of equivalence might be universal and also has a strong local component related to immediate material concerns.[127] Evaluating the genre by its verisimilitude fails to account for the widening divide between sign and substance that competing fiduciary fictions—the inflationary real and the nationalist cruzeiro—augured. Mock classicism refers to a discourse of fictionality less beholden to the law of the signifier. Its humor foregrounds the desmedida of the system of language. In lieu of irony *(eironeia)*, the chanchada gives this economic crisis aesthetic expression through humor as *eutrapelia*. Irony commits us to meaning and signification; humor commits us to (non)sense, the latter term understood as a nonsensical proposition.[128] To conceive fictionality's irony as *eutrapelia* avoids foreclosing the gap between saying and meaning—that is, to remain in a humorous position of not knowing, a "co-extensiveness of sense and non-sense."[129]

Humor entails the abandonment of a logic of time: "We laugh when the order of time and explanation no longer holds."[130] Its pleasure derives from a fictional disposition as suppositional speculation; we do not buy into *(acreditar)* the narrative world so much as we play along *(e o mundo se diverte*, indeed). We watch the chanchada not to believe its lie or expose its truth but to speculate and to traffic in suspensive delays. This is not the abatement of contingency through significant verisimilitude (i.e., classical Hollywood) or the delivery of contingency to radical unintelligibility (i.e., high modernism). The chanchada is an image trying to find purchase and a fiction in search of disbelief. To claim it deceives is to suppose an image we believe; to demand it reveal reality aspires to an image we can believe.

CHAPTER 5

Comedy Circulates Circuitously

Toward an Odographic Film History of
Latin America

Loosely adapted from the Jules Verne novel, *Around the World in 80 Days* (Michael Anderson, 1956) was Cantinflas's Hollywood crossover success. The film tells the story of Englishman Phileas Fogg, who raced around the world on a wager in 1872. For Mariano Siskind, the omnipotent characters and travel plots of Jules Verne's novels make them paradigmatic of the novelization of the global, providing "some of the most radical imaginaries of the transformation of the planet into a totality of modern culture and sociability."[1] For Siskind, *Around the World in 80 Days* is not simply a representation of the global but a reinforcement of the possibility of global expansion, of a world available to bourgeois subjectivity, where diegetic totalization is constitutive of the bourgeois subject. Verne imagines the world as a global space in which the novel will inscribe itself.[2] The film adaptation thematizes the global march of classical Hollywood *and* the ways it was subject to the friction of circumstance in ways both textual and material—a globe-trotting narrative both on and off screen that does not so much depict the world as index the conditions and the limits of such a planetary project.

The film opens with a prologue that makes such a project explicit: "Not even [Verne's] imagination could shrink the earth to the point it has now reached," remarks news anchor Edward R. Murrow. The television personality is sitting in his study, framed in the Academy aspect ratio. Murrow begins this brief survey of Verne with his 1865 novel *From the Earth to the Moon* and introduces the Méliès adaptation, shown practically in its entirety without colorization. Murrow serves as the silent film's voice-over narrator: "Since man began to walk upright, he has been interested in space and speed. . . . The stretching fingertips of science have moved him higher and faster than man has ever moved before." Within this ad hoc film history lesson—"this is the first photographic dissolve," Murrow adds—we also get a narrative of the planetary designs of modernity; perhaps they are both one and the same. The Méliès film concludes with a transition from the silent, black-and-white film in 35 mm to the color Todd-AO footage of a 1950s rocket launch, a transition punctuated by a graphic match between the vertical descent of the cardboard rocket and the vertical ascent of the present-day projectile. The edges of the frame slowly spread as the voice-over countdown of the launch seems to time the Academy ratio's transformation. The rocket takes off, and the film shows aerial photographs in a time lapse panorama of the surface below. Murrow explains, "This is how the Earth looks from a camera in the rocket," a perspective Murrow charges with Cold War anxieties. He continues, "Jules Verne wrote a book about going around the world in 80 days. . . . Today it can be done is less than [20 hours]. . . . Speed is good only when wisdom leads the way. The end of this journey, whether to the high horizons of hope or the depths of destruction, will be determined by the collective wisdom of the people who live on this shrinking planet." Murrow's voice accompanies a staccato panorama that dissolves to a spinning globe in his study. The prologue ends with one final dissolve to the film proper, set in the year 1872, when "the world was already shrinking." The unusual prologue inserts the cinema into a broader (re)scaling project of modernity. The world shrinks as it becomes traversable and imageable, and this film promises a circumnavigating trajectory in the widest possible screen.

The transition to the Victorian past comes with a series of remarkable long shots of London sites in Todd-AO widescreen. These images are composed along the horizontal axis, their narrative actions often centered because of the wrapping Cinerama screen. Cantinflas's introduction is perhaps the most impressive camera work from the London sequence. Astride a velocipede, he approaches the camera and dodges horse-drawn carriages. The camera begins to track backwards, keeping the comedian in frame as he ambles from left to right in movement that required spectators' heads to turn and scan the Cinerama screen. The following shot finds the camera mounted behind Cantinflas, Victorian London rushing past on either side, until he reaches the employment agency where he secures the valet job for Niven's Phileas Fogg. As

FIGURE 16. Monsieur Gasse (Charles Boyer) sells Passepartout (Mario Moreno) an itinerary in *Around the World in 80 Days* (1956).

Fogg's companion, the valet embarks on a globe-trotting adventure. A European leg features bullfighting in Spain and a Middle Eastern bazaar in Marseille. After their transoceanic voyage to Bombay and a derailed train to Calcutta, they rescue a young Indian widow from a funeral pyre before fleeing to Hong Kong and later Yokohama. Following the entr'acte, they find themselves in San Francisco on election eve before heading on another train to New York later attacked by Native Americans. A freighter to Venezuela is commandeered and rerouted to Liverpool in the hopes of meeting the eighty-day deadline.

Their departure, however, coincides with a bank robbery, and Fogg becomes the main suspect. A Scotland Yard inspector gives chase, so the travel narrative becomes a chase film. The spatial logic of the former, which concatenates points in a linear trajectory with a temporality of succession, becomes reinforced through the narrative structure of the latter, where parallel trajectories exist in simultaneity. Recall the role of the chase film in the transition to classical cinema, founded on the production of a synthetic (diegetic) space across separate shots.[3] As Tom

Gunning explains, the chase film provided a model for narrative causality and established the continuity of space and time that "created a new involvement for the spectator."[4] If Verne's novel and travel literature more broadly played an important role in the production of Europe's "planetary consciousness," with Europe as the organizing site for capitalist expansion in the nineteenth century, then the chase film extends this planetary project into the image and makes classical Hollywood the measure of narrative space.[5] Classical Hollywood narrative produces a synthetic space that would territorialize the world in ways textual and material.

If *Around the World*'s story concerns a gentlemen's wager, its production was also a significant gamble for its producer, Michael Todd. The showman-producer invested large amounts of (mostly other people's) money into this continent-spanning epic. Todd wanted to shoot his film on location, so the film quite literally journeys around the world in its production process. To that end, Todd secured talent, both on- and off-screen, in different sites. The film shot 112 locations in thirteen countries, employing 60,000 people from every country represented. The world became a Hollywood studio. The film not only included a gallery of Hollywood stars, including Charles Boyer, Ronald Colman, Marlene Dietrich, and Red Skelton, but also featured Noel Coward as a British employment agent, José Greco performing a flamenco dance, and French comedian Fernandel as a French coachman. The use of stars was meant to increase the profitability of the film in international markets. As Todd explained, "This picture will be as international as we can possibly make it, and therefore securing players from different countries, if they fit into the screenplay, will be the thing to do."[6] At the time, trade papers speculated that Cantinflas was the highest paid performer in the world, earning an estimated $1.2 million per year. Producer Todd secured Cantinflas for a reported $300,000, a hefty sum that was still below his annual income.[7] He also assembled (and reassembled) the talent behind the scenes: from swapping cinematographers for primary shooting (Lionel Lindon) and foreign locations (Kevin McCrory), to changing directors mid-picture and hiring writers for rewrites (S. J. Perelman, James Poe, and John Farrow all contributed to the script).[8] The circulation of laboring bodies made possible this narrative of circumnavigation.

Around the World aspired to make the world a diegesis. And yet the plot already suggests one way that this form of territorialization does not hold. The pair are detained upon arrival at the finish line and ostensibly lose the wager. The following day, however, they learn that by crossing the

International Date Line they have "gained" a day and rush to the Reform Club, winners. This temporality governed by succession cannot be emplotted linearly. Classical Hollywood's organization of time, which would concatenate real time into a series of before-and-afters, confronts the abstract standardization of global time—eighty-one days can also be eighty days. In this film, the coordination of time both allows and complicates worlding. In fact, the lauded sharpness of the image was a function of the frame rate of the Todd-AO process: 30-frames-per-second speed in both camera and projector.[9] Eliminating flicker and smoothing out action meant retemporalizing the film image, so that fitting the world onto the Cinerama screen would find classical Hollywood style at its limits. Bosley Crowther explains in his review for the *New York Times*, "Mr. Todd didn't think in terms of conventional motion-picture entertainment. He wasn't making a film that had a form. He was using the screen as a canvas on which to mount a giant variety show."[10] This "film without form" is a cinema of expanse, celebrated less for the dramatic organization of a narrative space than for "fill[ing] the screen with wondrous effects."[11] This film about circumnavigating the world was the epitome of the Todd-AO process, developed outside the industry in response to the demand for a new kind of special-attraction, road-show motion picture entertainment.[12] This was a film made to travel in the "expensive, multi-dimensional Todd-AO process at reserved-seating, carriage-trade prices."[13]

The Todd-AO process promised to deliver the world but only to theaters equipped with the right technologies, a particular challenge for nondomestic markets. Cantinflas was even involved in the plans for a 3,200-seat house equipped for Todd-AO designed in Mexico City to be completed in time for *Around the World*'s premiere.[14] For a film so much about circulation, the circulation of the film would be more difficult to secure. The American box-office success of the film would seem to vindicate Todd's foresight, and yet the critical reception abroad belies this story of Hollywood gone global. In Latin America, Cantinflas received top billing and distributors anticipated record-breaking returns. The Latin American premiere occurred in Venezuela in July 1957, a standing-room-only affair that garnered mixed to negative reviews.[15] Similarly, although it earned $80,000 in its first week in five first-run screens in 1960, Mexican critics dubbed the film a "super-duper churro," mourning the loss of a "'great national comic' who has been seduced by Hollywood gold and become 'just another more or less competent film comic.'"[16] *Around the World in 80 Days* provides an excellent point of departure to consider how the world is (un)made in its circulation. In a similar vein to Siskind's analysis of generic attempts at world creating in Latin American literature, I argue that world creating in the margins cannot simply study the symbolic representation or material configuration of a priori geographical entities but must also consider the possibility of circulation and the limits of exchange. Mock classicism attempts to capture a world that slips through its fingers. How to depict a world that we do not have the power to shape? The hegemonic totalization of the world in classical Hollywood is in productive tension with the region's particular geopolitical determinations. This is not to celebrate the particular over the universal. I want instead to suggest that the construction of a (mock classical) diegesis in the margins speaks to its relation to a hegemonic totalization of the world, an attempt to figure the world marked by the region's lateral geocultural position. The desire to totalize the world and the inability to produce it as a self-contained aesthetic totality illuminate the uneven conditions of material and symbolic exchange. This chapter invites us to study the (im)possibility of the world as aesthetic totality and global field of material exchange.

IN THEATERS: ITINERARIES OF LATIN AMERICAN FILM

In April 1948, an exhibitor catalog published in São Paulo celebrated the cosmopolitan taste of the Paulista public, remarking on the eclectic provenance of the previous week's releases: "tres filmes italianos, um mexicano, dois argentinos, um inglês e um português contra apenas um notre-americano!" (Three Italian films, one Mexican, two Argentine, one British and one Portuguese versus only one American!).[17] Katharine Hepburn's *Song of Love* (Clarence Brown, 1947) was the only American release that week opposite Latin American films such as the Argentine *La sangre fría* (Daniel Tinayre, 1947), produced by Interamericana and distributed in Brazil by Continental Filmes; the Delia Garcés vehicle *Rosa de América* (Alberto de Zavala, 1946), produced by Estudios San Miguel and distributed in Brazil by DIPA Filmes; and the Mexican *Jesús de Nazaret* (José Cibrián, 1942).

This is not to say that Hollywood exerted any less influence because of the diverse provenance of films in theaters. The coming of sound meant sharing Hollywood technology with multiple language versions of films concurrently produced around the world. Directors, producers, and performers traveled across national boundaries to work in North American and European studios, legitimating and diffusing a Hollywood filmmaking tradition, contributing to an emergent continental star system, and defining a niche for popular local genres. The material Americanization of film practice along with an emergent nationalism spearheaded by ascendant urban entrepreneurs contributed to several attempts to establish foreign production models in these dependent contexts. As Paulo Antonio Paranaguá explains, the period must be understood as a response from the periphery to an American cultural center;[18] however, the narrative of Hollywood market dominance and American cultural imperialism must be qualified in light of this distribution and reception material. If Paranaguá posits an outward-looking triangle between Latin America, the United States, and Europe, then I attempt to delineate an inward-looking triangle within Latin America's main cinema industries. Paranaguá's triangulation provides an excellent rejoinder to binary understandings of foreign-inauthentic/national-authentic forms of cultural representation but risks homogenizing the Latin American vertex and perhaps overstating the relationship to the United States: flattening the star systems, leveling the generic practices, and homogenizing the production, distribution, and exhibition mechanisms in the region.

This chapter attempts to avoid the homogenization of Latin American film production and reception through a comparative approach that engages with the concept of circulation in multiple ways, relating film as commodity, film as narrative, and film as spatial practice. Circulation by definition entails traversing, (re)organizing and (re)coordinating space and time, and this chapter takes advantage of the delimited and particularized circulation of popular genre cinema within and between diverse national contexts to telescope local, regional, national, and continental geographic frameworks. Circulation figures mostly at the level of the material circulation of popular cinema both within and outside national borders, a circulation that occurs differently from contemporaneous Hollywood and European examples. I propose that the unevenness and variability of intracontinental distribution mock classicism, arguing that popular cinema and its delimited circulation foreground the inward-looking dimensions of the reflective cinema experience situated in the periphery. As Susan Stanford Friedman elegantly proposes, "circulation is the archive of mobility."[19] To chart circulation is to ask how relationality was reflected upon and experienced, beckoning us to see linkages across space and time rather than discern intentional meaning, to conjunct rather than to construe.

My turn to circulation draws on anthropological models of cultural circulation that challenge the center-periphery narrative overdetermining most Latin American film histories about the industrial period.[20] Arjun

Appadurai and Anna Tsing provide frameworks for thinking through the circulation of ideas and tracing traveling cultures across intercultural networks.[21] Can these models of planetary cultural traffic equip film studies to think the discrete location *and* the networked imbrication of cultural production without situating cultural production in a pregiven geopolitical formation or a nativist insistence on difference? When he provocatively claims that "histories produce geographies," Appadurai encourages us to move away from essentialist area studies frameworks that write history atop a pregiven national or regional geography.[22] Appadurai moves away from models of hybridity of content and toward models that trace the reinforcing (or obstructing) conditions of connection of cultural forms. This would mean writing a film history that considers how the circulation of cultural forms and the forms of circulation produce the region.[23] Through this lens, the conventional study of hybrid cultural production becomes inflected with the questions of time, speed, and scale, less an index of "mixing" than of movement, less an ontogenetic method than a method of atelicity. Circulation invites us to ask why do certain things travel? How quickly? How far? How long? This chapter fully elaborates this question of circulation on multiple fronts: it looks at the "circulation of [cultural] forms" (i.e., the comedic films) and the "forms of circulation" (i.e., the shapes and flows of distribution and exhibition circuits that allowed for the films' intracontinental circulation). The study of cultural forms is not a function of cartography but of *odography*, of a writing of itineraries and traversals. My project argues alongside and at the limits of what I call this odographic turn.

While significant historical work has documented the penetration of the Latin American market by Hollywood studios and some European cinemas, significantly less attention has been paid to the way cinemas from Latin America circulated within the region. While Hollywood studios established outposts headquartered in metropolitan capitals and European cinemas took advantage of immigrant exhibitor networks, the popular cinemas from the region often circulated through haphazard intracontinental distribution networks. This inward-looking triangle takes shape by following the circulation of Argentine and Mexican film in Brazil and demonstrates how Brazilian exhibition monopolies functioned as a drag coefficient to the historical trajectories of cinema as vernacular modernism. Brazilian exhibitors were heavy power brokers in the region, particularly the rivals Francisco Serrador, with his controlling market share in São Paulo and the country's south, and Luis Severiano Ribeiro, with his control of Rio de Janeiro and the country's northeast cemented by the establishment of his distribution company, União Cinematográfica Brasileira, in 1948.[24] The march of classical Hollywood, not to mention the growth of national cinema and the circulation of other cinemas from the region, was subject to the friction of economic and cultural circumstances.

The identification of networks of film and media exchange prior to the 1960s challenges the diffusionist and center-periphery models that overdetermine understandings of cinema in the period. For Brazilian cultural critic Renato Ortiz, core-periphery models tend to privilege models of diffusion and acculturation. This one-way exchange, where the receiving nation opens outward, underwrites a long-standing understanding of Latin American cultural output as either derivative of foreign models or as defensive authentic cultural expression. In literary studies, the tension and conflict around the incorporation of foreign techniques determines the lines of development of cultural production: innovation and development (vanguardism/modernism) or resistance and autonomy (regionalism/tradition).[25] The odographic emphasis on the social trajectory of an art object allows us to refigure this process less as the adoption and adaptation of foreign modes of cultural production than as a vernacular mode of address bounded spatiotemporally by particular techniques of circulation and to finite audiences. This does not make these art objects and their circulation a necessarily resistant practice, but it does suggest a different form of territorialization dictated by the horizon of reception. This (de)territorialization occurs courtesy of techniques that control or reconfigure time and space—that is, techniques of circulation. Once the nation is no longer the telos but one form of organization among others, the routes of circulation can carve out spaces differently. If we need to think about culture through its extension rather than its origin, then circulation becomes as important an object of study as production: "Circulation is a structuring element of an emergent modernity" because it configures space and time and therefore (dis)embeds social relations.[26] Looking at circulation discloses the workings of power because it does not suppose the site of production as source of legitimacy and therefore does not suppose a pregiven territorial formation.

An odographic history asks us to think a culture less determined by place of origin than by its extension or reach, and that this extensivity should not be reduced to homogeneity. In his project that refigures the commodity form, Appadurai studies the social relations embedded in objects not by looking at determining relations of production but by looking at the context and type of exchange. The commodity form has the possibility of disclosing something about social relations when we are attendant to the materiality of the object in its circulation. An object has a certain social trajectory, and an ontogenetic or symptomatic analysis risks arresting it within this trajectory. The life of things is lived in the tension between being for someone and being for anyone. What can cinema as commodity disclose about social relations, particularly in light of a Hollywood classicism that sought to make it a better commodity? If classicism was a process of making the cinema a better commodity—that is, making it *for anyone*—then the conditions of exchange and circulation of comedy films suggest a commodity that is also *for someone*. As such, comedy marks a site where the cultural form acts as a possible obstacle or detour for its own circulation and bears on the social trajectory of the object.

Comedy not only designates a genre where a differentiated hermeneutic can yield varied social forms disarticulated from pregiven locations but compels us to reflect on the very conditions of possibility of signification within the semiotic and social field. The circulation of comedy makes the question of the location of culture not only a matter of where it was made but also where it circulates. In other words, locational thinking is complicated not simply by where the film circulates but also who can get the joke. What does it mean that comedy cannot be translated, and how might this align with the untranslative excess that Alberto Moreiras argues for the future of Latin Americanist reflection?[27] The untranslatability of comedy points to a hermeneutic circle that can never be foreclosed and where forces intrinsic and extrinsic to this circle are continually shaping the horizon of comedy's reception. Getting one joke but not the next is an inside and an outside that is constantly being made and unmade and where the effect is precisely in imagining oneself inside (by positing an outside). By thinking about the ways comedies succeed *and* fail on multiple fronts—as eliciting audience laughter, as generic text, as commodity, as enduring comic remanence, and as representative of the nation-state—comedy affords the possibility of a differently oriented transculturation, one less conciliatory and more disjunctive. Mexico (and Cantinflas) in Brazil provides a case in point. As each film remains in different theaters for different durations, we are following less a strategic tour governed by calendrical time than an asynchronous circuit.

CANTINFLAS "OUT OF ORDER"

With a few exceptions made available through American distribution networks such as RKO Radio and United Artists, Mexican cinema did not sustain a significant share of the Brazilian market until the end of World War II. The decline in production in Europe and Argentina during the final years of the war created a demand for new film content, a demand Mexican cinema was more than ready to meet.[28] The increased output from Mexico's film industry and the entrepreneurial formation of new distribution ventures in Brazil meant that Mexican cinema quickly outpaced Argentine and Brazilian cinema in the Brazilian market. By the end of the 1940s, the visibility of Mexican films in Brazil reached its peak with the opening of Cine Azteca in 1951 on Avenida Presidente Vargas, the modern thoroughfare inaugurated the previous year that had transformed the city's historic center. Based in Rio de Janeiro to promote and circulate Mexican films in the Brazilian market, the Distribuidora Pelmex planned to screen its Mexican films in a throwback "mexico-romano-renacentista" atmospheric movie palace designed by León Escoffier—a "Mexico" on- and offscreen.[29]

Before Pelmex and its Azteca theater, the largest distributor of Mexican films in Brazil in the immediate postwar period was the Distribuidora Importadora Nacional de Filmes (DiFilmes). Responsible for the first Brazilian successes of Pedro Armendáriz, Dolores del Rio, and Agustín Lara—*El Corsario negro (The Black Pirate)* (Chano Urueta, 1944), *María Candelaria* (Emilio Fernández, 1944), and *Amok* (Arturo Momplet, 1944), respectively—DiFilmes marketed Mexican cinema as the acme of filmmaking in Spanish America because "os costumes e as tradições do povo mexicano apresentam uma afinidade estreita, constante mesmo, com a maneira de pensar e de sentir de nossa gente" (the Mexican people's customs and traditions present a strong affinity [with] the ways of thinking and feeling of our people).[30] DiFilmes was established in late 1946 and, for a three-year period, was the exclusive representative in Brazil for several major Mexican film studios: CLASA / Films Mundiales, Grovas, Filmex, and Raúl de Anda.[31] In 1947, its first year of operations, DiFilmes distributed a staggering thirteen films and was largely responsible for the remarkable uptick in Mexican cinema releases in the country.[32]

The year 1947 also marked Cantinflas's introduction to Brazilian audiences, and yet his distribution in Brazil speaks to the tricky work of retracing film circulation. While we would like to presume an itinerary

FIGURE 17. *Ni sangre ni arena* (1941) premieres in Brazil as *Nem sangue nem areia* in 1947, as advertised in *A folha de São Paulo*.

that abides by either filmographic chronology—which would help us identify provenance—or a hub and spoke network model—which would delimit film practices in a center-periphery structure—the path traced by Cantinflas's film circulation never quite coordinates time and space, perhaps appropriate given the comedian's typical elusiveness. By 1947, Cantinflas had been starring in films in his native Mexico for nearly a decade and had already become popular in Spanish America. The arrival of the Mexican comedian to Brazilian screens happened mostly courtesy of the American distributor RKO Radio. Cantinflas's extensive back catalog meant every few months a new Cantinflas film would hit theaters before circulating in different paths across the country. The first Cantinflas film released by RKO Radio on January 1947 in Rio de Janeiro was *Los tres mosqueteros* (1943), the film that launched his career in other Hispanic countries, including Perú and Venezuela.[33] The film arrived in São Paulo one month later in late February 1947, followed in mid-March with a successful run in Curitiba, and late June in Recife.[34] Cantinflas's *Ni sangre ni arena* (1941) premiered two months later over the same weekend in São Paulo on April 9 and Rio de Janeiro on April 11.[35] By the end of 1947, *El circo* (1943) would slip into cinemas following an entirely different route, starting with a successful run in Curitiba on December 25, 1947, before making its way to Rio de Janeiro in May 1948 and São Paulo in June 1948.[36]

We can draw several preliminary conclusions based on this release schedule. First, these films loosely adapt material already available, if not familiar, to foreign audiences: Dumas's historical novel, the successful Hollywood adaptations of *Blood and Sand*, and Chaplin's silent comedy, respectively. Further, Cantinflas films are released "out of order," arguably a function of a distributor abiding less by chronology than by previous international box-office receipts and available copies of the print. If star studies histories are often organized around star-is-born narratives aligned with the performer's biography, then the construction of a star text outside its national context cannot quite follow the same schema. The case of Cantinflas is particularly fraught because the political currency of the pelado in much criticism is so tethered to this schema and the identification of some lapsarian moment. The question of chronology is further complicated by the fact that Cantinflas's first Mexican box-office hit, *Ahí está el detalle* (1940), was also released in 1947. The film was panned by local criticism, which called it "uma autêntica chanchada" (an authentic chanchada) as a way of designating it as his worst film, salvaged only by "seu típo . . . um palhaço com personalidade" (his type . . . a clown with personality).[37] This watershed film, however, was not released by RKO Radio. *Detalle* was not produced by Cantinflas's Posa Films, which had entered into a distribution agreement with RKO Radio. Instead, it was produced by Grovas-Oro Films, which had its own agreement with DiFilmes. Its DiFilmes distribution meant this earlier film was released in different theaters and followed yet another route. For instance, in São Paulo, the RKO Radio releases were in the Serrador chain's Cine Ópera, whereas the DiFilmes release premiered in Paulo Sá Pinto's Ritz theater.[38] One final kink in this network we are reconstructing: by 1949, Posa Films would no longer distribute its Cantinflas movies through RKO Radio but through Columbia Pictures, starting with the comedian's *¡A volar joven!* (1947).[39] Further, DiFilmes ceased operations in 1949, although Mexican cinema still arrived in Brazil courtesy of American studios and the newly launched distributor Pelmex.[40]

Hollywood enjoyed a more centralized distribution of films and could afford more prints and less delay across its distribution circuit, capitalizing on a certain continuity in market presence guaranteed by long-standing distribution outposts in the region and by studio agreements with exhibition trusts. The delimited circulation of comedy yields a different map of the distribution circuit. Each comedy film circulates along its own circuitous path, not always traveling from a centralized hub to peripheral sites, not always following a logic of presumptive geopolitical or demographic hierarchy, and not always staggered over time across its network. The release calendar becomes a release isochrone map.

AN ISOCHRONE MAP OF FILM NETWORKS

This isochrone map avoids opposing homogenous global structures to heterogeneous local reactions, instead telling the story of classical cinema worked out in particular times and places through what Anna Tsing calls friction, "the awkward, unequal, unstable, and creative qualities of interconnection across difference."[41] Tsing traces forms of global circulation because she finds in their specificity a site to study the work of the universal at the site of encounter across difference. Specificity is neither a site of anticapitalist resistance nor a type ranged under a universal but a function of "bringing capitalist universals into action through worldly encounters."[42] The unpredictable effects of these encounters belie the assumption that capitalism makes everything everywhere the same. I want to suggest that classical Hollywood cinema operates as such a universal in film studies, determining both a mode of spectatorship and a filmmaking style taken as totalizing standard. In the spirit of Miriam Hansen, I want to restore historical specificity to the concept of classical cinema.[43] Hansen's project provincializes classical Hollywood cinema by tracing both its mechanisms of standardization and the diversity of ways this cinema was reconfigured in particular contexts of reception.[44] She echoes Tsing when she calls for writing an international history of classical Hollywood that studies how the classical is shaped and transformed in global encounters across difference.

Rather than simply identify practices in production and reception that depart from Hollywood, we must explore the vicissitudes of the social trajectory of this commodity. To work with classicism in this odographic mode avoids naturalizing the exportable as universal, which makes the universal only a function of consumption rather than a movement for thought and action.[45] This means looking to the ways the classical mode of film practice and reception is inflected by heterogeneous and unequal encounters. How is the classical shaped by regional networks of meaning, power, and trade? Because classicism is effective within a particular historical conjuncture, classicism appears less a norm imposed from without than "a practical project accomplished in a heterogeneous world."[46] I engage the classical as a framework for the practice of power, but one that is never fully successful in being everywhere the same.[47] Classicism is a category worth recovering (and mocking) in Latin

American film studies because of the ways it indexes diverse forms of territorialization, from global Hollywood to cultural nationalism. Rather than simply relocating culture within ever more particular sites of reception or ever broader flows of transnationalism, mock classicism capitalizes on the limits of different forms of territorialization. Both former modes of film historiography naturalize the spatial logic of neoliberalism at the global scale. Moreover, they both suppose what Henri Lefebvre would call abstract space—space as an empty container that simply needs to be carved differently—which he explains is a hallmark of modernization.[48] Mock classicism capitalizes on the circumscribed circulation and intelligibility of comedy in order to write a history that does not suppose the abstract space of modernization. There is no right way to locate culture and, by extension, no (historicist) position of narrative control.[49] This is a classicism of peripeteia, showcasing displacements and recursions and emphasizing the failures of histories built atop linear or progressive temporality. Peripeteia is a hallmark of these films' material circulation and their episodic narratives.

Following the peripatetic circulation of Argentine cinema in Brazil provides such an isochrone map, riven by the final years of the Second World War. During the boom years in the early 1940s, film studios first ventured into the Brazilian market. The fact that Niní Marshall and Luis Sandrini worked for different film studios in the 1940s helps us parse the different parties and their evolving relationships over time. Marshall was an exclusive player for Argentina Sono Films, which claimed by 1939 that roughly half the theaters in Chile, Peru, Venezuela, Colombia, Mexico, and Cuba screened the studio's releases.[50] In fact, Argentina Sono Film pioneered the international distribution of industrial Argentine cinema, using a logic of exclusivity with distributors and exhibitors, an extension of the labor exclusivity it had required of its stars. The Mentastis made a pioneering entry into the Brazilian market when they established the Corporação Cinematographica Sul-Americana (Cinesul) as the exclusive representative for Argentina Sono Film in Brazil under the stewardship of Ramon Pesquera.[51] The Mentastis regularly traveled to Brazil to cultivate their relationships with the exhibition trusts, which often had the final word on whether a Cinesul release would ever make it on screen.[52] Cinesul began its operations in late 1938. Its only release in 1938 was the Pepe Arias comedy *El pobre Pérez* (Luis Cesar Amadori, 1938), dubbed *Um infeliz rapaz* upon release and renamed *O amigo Perez* later in its run.[53] The film's advertisement touted how the distributor brought "o primeiro film rio-platense, para iniciar o intercambio cinematographico sul-americano, interpretado pelo mais famoso comico argentino" (the first Argentine film, to begin a South American film exchange, featuring the performance of the most famous Argentine comedian).[54] Argentina Sono Film followed up the film comedy with the studio's brightest tango stars, Libertad Lamarque and Hugo del Carril, in *Puerta cerrada (Closed Door)* (Luis Saslavsky and John Alton, 1939) and *La vida de Carlos Gardel (The Life of Carlos Gardel)* (Alberto de Zavala, 1939), respectively. Libertad Lamarque had a five-picture deal with the studio for 1940 and 1941, and her films were Cinesul's biggest draws in its early years.[55] Following the circulation of Lamarque's film is a microcosm of the studio and distributor's prewar operations. In Rio de Janeiro, Cinesul showcased her most recent film (i.e., *Puerta cerrada*), then quickly made available her earlier hit *Madreselva (Honeysuckle)* (Luis Cesar Amadori, 1938), and renamed her third project *Caminito de gloria* (The little path of glory) (Luis César Amadori, 1939) as *Romance no Rio*. The latter film was developed by Argentina Sono Film with the Brazilian market in mind. Lamarque filmed a Carmen-Miranda-lite performance of "A jardineira," and the studio even reshot scenes in its San Isidro studios after its national run and added more outdoor sequences in Rio de Janeiro for its Brazilian audience.[56] Lamarque's circulation also reveals the endemic circulation of Argentine films in Brazil. Cinesul had more success breaking into the Paulista market and the southern states before gradually making inroads in Rio de Janeiro and the northern states, even launching tirades in the press about how "o exibidor carioca não programma o film argentino. Por que? [. . .] A maioria por não acreditarem no film argentino" (The Carioca exhibitor does not program Argentine film. Why? [. . .] Most of them do not believe in Argentine film).[57] Whereas São Paulo received Lamarque's films in the "correct order" with *Madreselva* before *Puerta cerrada*—Libertad Lamarque even traveled to São Paulo to perform *Madreselva*'s songs live in the Rosario theater before the screening of the film—Rio de Janeiro and most of the country received *Puerta cerrada* before *Madreselva*.[58] Further, Cinesul's relatively small scale meant only a few prints could circulate from city to city over time.[59]

The following year saw the announcement of Niní Marshall's impending Brazilian debut.[60] Marshall's introduction to Brazilian audiences had been a long time coming. She was a regular news item in releases and updates from Buenos Aires. Roundups of film production in Argentina touted her "record-breaking" successes for Lumiton in *Casamiento en*

FIGURE 18. Cinesul advertises its Argentina Sono Film pictures in *A scena muda*.

Buenos Aires (Marriage in Buenos Aires) (1939) and for EFA with *Cándida* (1939).[61] Neither Lumiton nor EFA, however, boasted of distribution in Brazil. Only after her contract with Argentina Sono Film was the possibility of a Brazilian debut feasible. In fact, the contract disputes discussed in chapter 2 trickled their way to Brazil, framed as breaking news that promised to bring her to the Brazilian public. News came that "Niní Marshall (Catita) deverá multiplicar-se" (will have to multiply herself) because she was currently filming *Cándida se divoricia* (later released as *Los celos de Cándida* (Cándida's jealousy) [1940]) and immediately thereafter would film for Argentina Sono Film "um typo comico inedito" (a brand-new comic type).[62] Cinesul geared up to introduce Marshall to Brazil as "Niní Marshall" without the foreknowledge of Catita or Cándida. But Cinesul never delivered on its promise. It tried to expand its operations in Brazil, planning to launch some seventeen films in 1940 and use Portuguese-language titles, subtitles, and *letreiros* in its releases.[63] Despite this push, Cinesul folded in 1941.

Marshall would have to wait until 1942 for her debut, when Lumiton, the rival studio that first hired Marshall as Catita and had been the

FIGURE 19. "Incomprehensible hostilities toward Argentine cinema": The failure of *Mujeres que trabajan* in Rio de Janeiro in the pages of *A scena muda*.

major loser in her October 1939 contract dispute, used a Marshall star vehicle to try its luck in the Brazilian market.⁶⁴ The 1939 Manuel Romero film *Mujeres que trabajan (Women Who Work)*, Marshall's first, was released in April 1942 in the Rio de Janeiro art-deco Pathé movie palace, managed by the Serrador Companhia Brasil Cinematographica (CBC).⁶⁵ *Mujeres que trabajan* was distributed through CINEAC, a Carioca film company dedicated to moral uplift with a couple of movie houses screening exclusively documentary and educational films aimed mostly at children and families. CINEAC released *Mujeres* as part of its Hispano America Filmes, a short-lived distribution initiative in 1942 and 1943.⁶⁶ Marshall was singled out in the ensemble comedy, celebrated in the press as "uma artista de muita verve, de ótimo desempenho em papéis humorísticos, sal de que tanto precisamos nestes dias de filmes de fusilamentos, de bombardeiros e despotismos hitlerianos" (an artist with plenty of verve, delivering excellent performances in humorous roles, something much needed in these days of films with shootings, bombings, and Hitlerian despotisms).⁶⁷ *Mujeres* failed to open doors for Lumiton, much less Argentine cinema, in the then-capital of Brazil.

It might be tempting to attribute the failures of Cinesul and Hispano America Filmes to linguistic, national, or cultural difference, but how do we reconcile the box-office "legs" of Lamarque's early films with the fact that her final two films for Argentina Sono Film, *La casa del recuerdo* (Luis Saslavsky, 1940) and *Cita en la frontera* (Mario Soffici, 1940), never made it to Brazil despite their promoted release in periodicals?[68] The story behind both Cinesul's last gasp in the Carioca market and the days-long theatrical run of *Mujeres* shows us that something else was also in play. Cinesul and Argentina Sono Film's last attempt to secure a theatrical release was the Enrique Muiño film *El viejo doctor* (The old doctor) (Mario Soffici, 1939). Cinesul had been unable to reach an agreement with the Carioca mogul Severiano Ribeiro, who owned and operated a majority share of theaters in Rio de Janeiro. In a market dominated by monopolies, Cinesul turned to the only other option, the CBC. The Serrador chain offered to release the film in its downtown Rex theater, even organizing a special press screening, a novel marketing ploy at the time, which yielded a "cine romance" treatment in the pages of *A scena muda*.[69] The distributor balked at the CBC's terms, and the film was never released to the Brazilian public.[70] The following year, Lumiton released its *Mujeres* in the CBC-owned Pathé. The Pathé, however, was sold to Ponce and Irmão before winding up in the hands of Severiano Ribeiro, who almost exclusively programmed Hollywood content. The CBC also lost its other major space in Rio de Janeiro—the Cine Teatro Broadway became the Capitólio in 1942—so that all the spaces open to Argentine films were gone.[71] The film critic Renato de Alencar remarked that the Argentine industry was left with few alternatives: either find another possible chain of theaters, such as those operated by Vital Ramos de Castro, or build its own movie theaters, which Metro-Goldwyn Mayer had done in 1940 in an attempt to circumvent Severiano Ribeiro.[72] The circulation of Argentine cinema in Brazil was only partly constrained by content. The turf war between exhibition trusts made Argentine films an unfortunate casualty in the early 1940s.

After this initial land grab, one Brazilian distribution company, Continental Films, emerged as the main pipeline for Argentine films, a function of its relationships to exhibition trusts and the crisis in industrial Argentine cinema under embargo in the final years of World War II. Its directors, João Ferraris and Constantino Basso, began working with Argentina Sono Film's competitors, particularly Estudios Filmadores Argentinos (EFA). EFA was the home of comedian Luis Sandrini, who would become the largest Argentine box office draw in Brazil after

Cinesul's demise.[73] By 1946, Continental Films was the source for films from all Argentine major studios, including Argentina Sono Film, Lumiton, and EFA. That same year found the firm distributing Mario Soffici's *Prisioneros de la tierra* (Prisoners of the earth) (1939), produced by Pampa Film and distributed domestically by Argentina Sono Film; Luis Sandrini's *La casa de los millones (The House of the Millions)* (Luis Bayón Herrera, 1942), produced by EFA; and Niní Marshall's more recent *Madame Sans-Gêne* (Luis César Amadori, 1945), produced by Argentina Sono Film. This hodgepodge of titles demonstrates how Continental Films distributed the back catalog of Argentine films produced earlier in the decade.

Unlike present-day worldwide release schedules where simultaneity is a prized limit, Continental Films crafted a release schedule that strategically capitalized on the glut of Argentine films that never made their way to Brazil. For instance, because Sandrini was working with EFA, a studio without a distribution agreement in Brazil in the early 1940s, his entire library reached the neighboring country only after EFA's 1946 agreement with Continental Films.[74] This explains why the first Sandrini film released in Brazil in late 1946 was *La casa de los millones*, a 1942 film for EFA costarring Olinda Bozán. Continental announced the upcoming release of his 1940 Pampa Film release, *Chingolo*, and the planned release of his 1946 Argentine box office smash *El diablo andaba en los choclos* (The devil was on the loose) (Manuel Romero), produced by Interamericana.[75] By mid-1947, Continental Films' distribution agreements expired and a new deal was struck with Paulo Sá Pinto, the owner of an exhibition company and chain of theaters in São Paulo. The Distribuidora Paulista de Filmes (DIPA Filmes) was formed when Sá Pinto traveled to Buenos Aires to negotiate an arrangement with Distribuidora Pan Americana to take over the lapsed agreements from Continental.[76] DIPA Filmes released films from Lumiton, EFA, Interamericana, and Artistas Argentinos Asociados over the next few years.[77]

Argentina's erratic circulation in Brazil was only partly a function of the industry's changeable levels of production. The carrousel of distribution agreements and the competition between exhibition companies played a significant role in shaping the Brazilian itineraries of Argentine cinema. Argentine films circulated on a delay, released years after their domestic premieres. They appeared in staggered bursts and only in regions where distributors had agreements with exhibitors. For example, Sá Pinto's ownership of DIPA Filmes meant films distributed under its seal had access to his chain of movie theaters in São Paulo and the country's southern states.[78] On the other hand, most Argentine films never made it to Rio de Janeiro. Continental Films occasionally managed to secure space in Serrador theaters—for example, releasing Marshall's film *Santa Cándida* in April 1949 in the downtown Império nearly three years after the film's 1946 premiere in Curitiba and São Paulo.[79] DIPA Filmes had even less luck in Rio de Janeiro, especially when the Severiano Ribeiro group purchased the majority ownership in Atlântida in 1947 from Moacyr Fenelon and José Carlos Burle and created the União Cinematográphica Brasileira (UCB). The UCB merged the exhibition monopoly of Severiano Ribeiro (and the output of their newly acquired Atlântida studio) to the already extant newsreel and feature-film distribution of the Distribuidora Nacional and Distribuidora de Filmes Brasileiros (DFB), respectively.[80]

PERIPATETIC TRAVELS WITH CATITA

Although her films never quite made it to Rio de Janeiro, Catita did celebrate her honeymoon in the Cidade Maravilhosa. Her *Luna de miel en Rio* (Honeymoon in Rio) (Manuel Romero, 1941) was the final entry in a trilogy that narrated the romantic travails of our *porteña* heroine in serialized form across Latin American urban spaces.[81] I read these narratives of circulation paratactically in order to identify unexpected lines of conjunction and highlight the networked, circulating aspects of classicism within a particular historical conjuncture. Unlike chapter 2's analysis of her films for Argentina Sono Film as screen actress Niní Marshall, this chapter looks to the screen iterations of her radio personae to identify how the spatial practice in her radio broadcasts bears on the narratives of circulation in her early films. Not only were Marshall's Catita and Cándida spoken into the air for radio receivers across the country, but Marshall developed her characters by circulating in the port city. She walked the streets armed with a tape recorder, capturing the many vernacular speech types in the city.

Mock classicism offers a certain manifestation of a social texture and a perceptual voyage where we are invited to absorb and connect spaces in a traversal athwart of classical Hollywood cinema. The presence of Catita as sidekick and scene stealer in these films suggests that we can trace a particular (comedic) mode of constituting the world. The etymological relation that Diana Niebylski identifies between *travesura* (prank, mischief) and *travesía* (crossing) or *atravesar* (to cross)—all related to the Latin *transversare,* which arrived in English through the

Germanic variant *thwart*—suggests that the comedic must be conceived as spatial practice, as constituting a transversal space produced athwart conceived spaces.[82] When Catita steals scenes, she thwarts the scene as both unit of classical narrative organization as well as the visual terrain of the conceived city.

After Catita's first appearance in the ensemble of *Mujeres que trabajan*—which had been inspired by *Stage Door* (Gregory La Cava, 1937)—she was offered a starring role in *Divorcio en Montevideo (Divorce in Montevideo)* (Manuel Romero, 1939). In *Divorcio*, Catita and her friend Adriana are manicurists in Buenos Aires. The women work together while listening to radio soap operas and sharing their thoughts on the latest serialized romance literature, *Romance de juventud,* a fictional narrative about a stenographer who magically finds love, wealth, and happiness. In the film narrative, a wealthy young man, Claudio, is in love with a self-proclaimed "modern woman," Dora, who takes advantage of his advances. His misogynistic friend Goyena recommends that he finally rid himself of Dora and her machinations to extort more affection and gifts. During a routine manicure, they devise a plan to have Claudio marry and quickly divorce another girl in order to make Dora jealous and collect his inheritance. Claudio proposes to Adriana, his manicurist, and the girl accepts in order to pay for an operation for her sick father. Despite Adriana's best efforts to win Claudio over, he abandons the poor girl and returns to Dora after their marriage of convenience. Adriana later refuses payment, noting that she has been compensated with some fleeting moments of fantasy more valuable than money. After Dora proves less than faithful, Claudio realizes his affection for Adriana and reunites with the girl. Goyena begrudgingly admits he has grown fond of her friend Catita, and the two also end the picture coupled. The film presents two features both related to spatial practice: first, the film is the first of a serialized trilogy and cinematic feuilleton; second, the construction of the visual terrain of the (foreign) city gets figured in the mobility of the comedic female characters. If *Around the World in 80 Days* reinforced the possibility of global expansion where diegetic totalization is constitutive of the bourgeois subject, Catita's displacements do not produce the same reconciled and available modern world.[83]

Divorcio's narrative begins in Buenos Aires, follows the honeymooning fake couple across the Atlantic to Paris, and ends in Montevideo. The film's climax is set in Montevideo, the land of the expedited divorce. The title card over the cityscape announces our (and our characters')

FIGURE 20. Catita (Niní Marshall) the globetrotter in *Divorcio en Montevideo* (1939). Image courtesy of Museo del Cine Pablo Ducrós Hicken.

arrival to the city, followed by a series of extreme long shots of landmarks of the city accompanied by nondiegetic music. The succession of representational spaces metonymically constitutes the city. The women characters arrive on a boat, framed in a medium long shot in front of a rear projected view of the port in Montevideo. The use of rear projection to insert the women characters into diverse locales is similarly deployed during the Parisian honeymoon. After an establishing montage full of dissolving views of the landmarks of Paris, Claudio abandons Adriana and goes to London. Catita accompanies the girl through the streets of the City of Light. After a stint at the Louvre, which Catita describes as a flea market full of "old things and broken statues," the two embark on a bus tour. Framed together in a long shot atop a two-story tour bus, the women marvel as the city passes by behind them, flattened in rear projection. Unable to understand French, Catita looks confused as Adriana translates their guide's observations. Passing La Madeleine, Adriana translates: "It's a very old church." Catita scoffs: "Qué va a ser antigua, mija. No estás viendo que se la copiaron de la catedral de nosotros" (How old can it be? Can't you see they copied our cathedral?). Recalling Lefebvre, who argues that space is not an abstract thing in itself but imbricated with the concept of production and inseparable from forces of labor that shape it, these monuments function as representational spaces formed by social activity. The monument makes space intelligible in an entirely different mode than both the planner's blueprint (i.e., conceived space) and practiced space.[84] The subject's situation, in its both temporal and spatial meanings, becomes a function of relating perceived, lived, and conceived space within their lived experience. Space is brought into conjunction through social practice, and the tourist cannot grasp the social relationships inhering in space because they conjunct these differently.[85] Catita as tourist in Paris is unable to situate herself in space. She does not fragment space, which would suppose space as a passive receptacle and reproduce embedded social relationships; instead, she playfully deciphers the space according to a different code.[86] Marshall produces a transversal Paris, shot through with an inversion of the relations of dependence. Later on during the bus tour, the obelisk is visible in rear projection. Catita glowers: "Pero no te dije. ¡Qué copiones son estos franceses! Hasta el obelisco se lo copiaron. . . . Las calles son iguales, las fortunas, las inteligencias. Eso sí, en Buenos Aires no cualquiera le sabe el francés. En vez aquí hasta las criaturas lo hablan a corrido" (Didn't I tell you? These French are copycats! They even copied our obelisk. . . . The streets are the same, the wealth, the intelligence. Except in Buenos Aires not everyone knows French, whereas here even the children can speak it fluently). The city of Paris is produced atop a map of Buenos Aires in *Divorcio*.

Of course, historically, the Haussmannization of Paris and modernization of the medieval city served as a model for the comparable modernization of Buenos Aires during the fin-de-siècle period preceding Argentina's centennial. The production of abstract space, particularly in the periphery, meant to perpetuate power and the cultural and socioeconomic structure this power guaranteed.[87] Catita's spatial practice is not a mere reversal, which would only reinstantiate the copy as derivative of the original. The landmarks do not mark this concrete space but rather another, so that perceived space is articulated to a different lived space. When Marshall jokes upon seeing the Arc de Triomphe that the goalkeepers in France must have terribly long arms to tend the goal, or *arco*, of the soccer club Triunfo, she restores the body in space over and against abstract space. She articulates the contradictions of space and therefore articulates the contradictions of uneven social relations. She uncovers embedded social relations of dependency in the production of space in the context of Argentine modernity (and perhaps less directly commenting on colonialist social relations undergirding the production of space in Paris given the Egyptian origins of the Luxor Obelisk). By locating Buenos Aires as origin and center, she underscores the inversion of the European urban narrative that determined the design of Latin American cities.

Buenos Aires gets produced differently than Paris in *Divorcio*. The women characters' arrival is presented similarly to the Montevideo sections through a series of extreme long shots of the dock and panoramic vistas of the cityscape. Noticeably absent in this Buenos Aires are the landmarks associated with the city, a code already accessible and a space already intelligible to its spectators, a function of textual address for someone. The concluding sequence of the film, where a repentant Claudio searches desperately for Adriana in Buenos Aires, presents a search in the city that forces our characters and us spectators to make sense of this space, articulating conceived, perceived, and lived space in different ways. The first strategy devised by the male characters finds them sending out a search party for the manicurist in every salon in the city. A series of canted exterior long shots of several barber shops and hair salons is alternated with the occasional interior shot of the men grabbing at random women and forcing them to reveal themselves for visual inspection. The diagonal wipes and frantic sound effects punctuate the search sequence. Unable to find Adriana, the men resort to the police, who methodically search for the girl. The investigation of the police colludes with the epistephilic tendencies of the camera, using a spatial practice that treats space as an abstract thing to be carved out, apportioned, and scrutinized in a search area. The final attempt to search for Adriana occurs after Claudio recalls Adriana's fascination with *radionovelas* and her distracted listening to the radio while working. Claudio buys advertising time in order to broadcast his search. The women are found when space is considered as lived. Much like our odographic historiography, the solution is not to localize in preexisting space but to spatialize a social activity and constitute a spatiotemporal unit.[88]

Divorcio was followed by two sequels, *Casamiento en Buenos Aires* and *Luna de miel en Rio*. Unlike other comedian comedies that situate the comedian's character in new but homologous generic scenarios, these early films are heavily serialized. The characters and intrigues from the first film carry over into the subsequent films. Catita and Goyena's marriage in the second film and their honeymoon in the third, provide the organizing narrative events; however, Dora, Adriana, and Claudio's love triangle also persists. These early Catita films not only use the radio as narrative device and borrow the radio persona of our female star but also organize the narrative in the tradition of the *radionovela* and feuilleton. This tradition of feminine serialized popular culture is textualized in the opening beats of *Divorcio* when Catita encourages Adriana to accept Claudio's proposition. She understands the situation through the lens of the feuilleton: "Qué coincidencia. Lo mismo, lo mismo que la novela que estoy leyendo. Resulta que el amigo bueno, que viene a ser él [Claudio] está enamorado, y entonces el amigo sinvergüenza, que viene a ser usted [Goyena]" (What a coincidence. The same thing is happening in the novel I'm reading. The good friend, that would be him [Claudio] is in love, and then the scoundrel friend, that would be you [Goyena]).

The serial film was a so-called low genre of early cinema often credited as an intermediate genre between the chase film and the feature. Halfway between early cinema and classical cinema in the American and European context, the serial film is a particularly useful genre through which to trace the lines of development of a mock classicism in Latin America. The pleasure from the serialized romance narrative derives not from hermeneutic closure or a return to order but from continuous disorder and the anticipation of an ending, what Tania Modleski calls "the drama of perepetia *[sic]* without anagnorisis."[89] *Peripecia* (peripeteia) in Latin American Spanish refers both to a reversal of fortune or dramatic turn as well as in more colloquial usage to the roundabout maneuvers used to arrive at a destination or resolution. The serial romantic fiction complicates the economic, restorative, progressive classical narrative. The revelation, recognition, and possession of truth that resolves dramatic action is always already deferred, and the pleasure derived from waiting entails a different experience of time and, by extension, a different production of space. The repetition generated by the technological form and its distribution colludes with its story, and this repetitiveness deemed alien to classical film narrative proves the recursive ground for mock classicism.[90] Marshall's early Catita films mock classicism by charting an itinerary without destination through a mode of watching resolutely *for someone*.

GOING POSTAL

Marshall's circulation was enshrined in December 2002, when the Correo Argentino (the Argentine Postal Service) and the Museo del Cine Pablo C. Ducrós Hicken issued a series of commemorative stamps

FIGURE 21. Luis Sandrini and Niní Marshall commemorative stamps issued in 2002.

showcasing the comedians Niní Marshall and Luis Sandrini.[91] The illustrator and humorist Luis Scafati drew the 75-cent postage stamps in his typical style: using delicate lines drawn in *tinta china* (india ink), heavy crosshatching, and touches of watercolor in a simple gradient to produce minimalist portraits that highlight Sandrini's expressive brow and Marshall's trademark Cándida scowl. The comedians' commemoration on a postage stamp makes overt the national representativity of the comedic star as icon. The ubiquity of these state-issued notes makes it a site for citizen education and a de facto *lieu de mémoire*. This picture of the nation enhances "a sense of 'us' by creating a cherished identity–political landscape that confirms the majority's feelings of belonging."[92]

And yet a postage stamp merits analyses that move beyond style and content. To ask what is depicted on the postage stamp ignores the complex ways stamps signify. We cannot treat the image as mere rhetoric. The stamp has a nominal value (its 75-cent denomination) and a practical value (its production cost). The little piece of paper becomes denomination by way of signifying alchemy. The stamp is not simply metaphoric symbol of the nation because it also functions as tender, an asset-backed note to be redeemed. Above and beyond paper money, stamps also provide evidence of past payment of postage. The stamp then is both receipt and promissory note, an image made present because it indexes past actions and remains open to future redemption. This is redemption less in the sense of Benjamin's *erlösen* and its religious connotations of deliverance than Kracauer's *einlösen,* meaning "to fulfill promises" or "to reclaim pawned objects."[93] The subtle distinction pertains to how (or when) an object has value: value is not a property but an attribute. Images are not significant because of the meanings that inhere but because of the meanings that accrue or erode. Kracauer does not so much posit images that deliver physical reality as he emphasizes the attribution of value and significance that the image indexes and we "cash" or redeem as beholders. Kracauer's redemption refers to the historicity of beholding. When we look at the photo image, we not only sight the photographed subject but also glimpse the shapings and colorings of perception over time and across space. The photo image is not just a picture of the photographed subject because it also offers a portrait of (the photograph's) appraisal. The potential of the cinema lies not simply in discovering what was once present in front of the lens but also in gleaning the appreciation and depreciation of the work.

This phila*telic* tangent opens onto the atelicity of the unmarked stamp, not (yet) referring to actions or events with distinct endpoints. The stamp exists in a temporality at the threshold of the realized and the contingent. Once affixed, the (a)telicity of the stamp bears on the letter. We send a message that necessarily may not arrive. As Derrida reminds us, the post is built atop the possibility of (non)arrival. When we drop a letter in a mailbox, it follows an accidented path to its destination (we hope). Geoffrey Bennington expands this "necessary possibly not" logic of the postcard in order to deconstruct the postal network as an institution that facilitates delivery and delivery's failure.[94] The postal institution attempts to bind space and time, usually as an index of the nation-state. The case of Argentina's postage is paradigmatic of how the issuance of the stamp was part of the staking of the nation. Argentina's first stamps were issued shortly after the secession of the Estado de Buenos Aires from the Confederación Argentina in 1852. By 1856, both the Confederación and the Estado de Buenos Aires began issuing competing postage stamps. The end of the Confederación in 1862 and the victory of the Estado de Buenos Aires was marked by the latter's issuance of a new postage stamp, the escudito, the first to bear the country's name and the image of its first president, Bernardino Rivadavia.[95] The nation was a function of where your letter could go and where the postage stamp could take it. If the letter failed to arrive, what does this say about this network and by extension the nation? The nation, like the postal service, is predicated on connecting spaces, where network paths bind despite (or perhaps because) their necessarily possible failures.

The national territory cannot be simply the pregiven basis of state formation because its formation is always already haunted by its possible failure. What Bennington suggests is that the nation is formed precisely through this iterative process that risks the nation's loss.[96] The possible (non)arrival of the letter means the nation is never quite constituted; instead, it is the effect of an opening or transmission that carries the possibility of a performative misfire. In a feedback loop of sorts, the nation is not the stable site of emission but an iterative process that keeps open a horizon. The continued legitimacy of the nation is determined by the extension of these postal circuits and the indefinite future they project. But even after the message is delivered, the horizon persists less as indefinite future than in its imperfective aspect. When we receive a letter in the mail, we also receive proof of the letter's journey. "Where has it been" and "where can it go" become as important to defining the nation as "where is it from."

What can film studies learn from the atelicity of the stamp or the geography of money? The postal service and the central bank were institutions intending to consolidate the nation, and yet the circulation they effected complicates (if not belies) the nation they were meant to consolidate. In a period of film practice discussed in film histories in terms of cultural nationalism or, more recently, in terms of the experience of modernity (as sometimes substitute for the nation), the cinema has also been understood as an apparatus for consolidating the nation. Given the historical coincidence and structural affinities between cinema, post, and mint, perhaps the cinema's circulation also belies the very nation it was supposed to consolidate. The traditional film history grounded on spaces of film production and the more recent empirical turn to sites of reception both locate culture similarly—a film history written along the lines of "where is it from." Looking to film circulation results in a film history attendant to "where has it been" and "where can it go." If melodrama was the genre of choice for histories framed along the former lines, comedy becomes a privileged genre in the odographic approach.[97] Its delimited circulation indexes the "necessary possible" failure of the nation. The nation need not be tossed to the scrap heap and substituted for hyperparticular case studies.

THE ANECONOMIC RISK OF MOCK CLASSICISM

This is what the odographic turn promises: an emphasis on circulation less as interstate exchange between pregiven territorial formations than as a structure of atelicity akin to currency or postage—film not meant to represent (or be representative of) but to be exchanged. As Alejandra Laera reminds us in her discussion of currency, the former model of circulation departs from a local phenomenon with a transnational horizon whereas the latter supposes an always already mundial logic of exchange shaped by frictional determinants.[98]

Let us traffic in the periphery one final time by returning to the figure of Luis Sandrini, a star text conventionally discussed entirely along national lines. And yet Sandrini was never quite as bounded by the nation as film histories would have us believe. His second film, *Los tres berretines*, received positive notices in Mexico in May 1934, only a few months after its domestic premiere. Sandrini would be positively compared to Hollywood comedians—"tan bueno como cualquiera de los ases del humorismo hollywoodense" (as good as any of the stars of Hollywood comedy)—and his film celebrated for a national character that was not imitative of Hollywood.[99] The reviewer celebrated the film as an important *esfuerzo* (effort) in Hispanic cinema, one worthy of applause "por dondequiera que haya gente nuestra e interesada en lo nuestro" (wherever our people or people interested in our matters might be).[100] *Los tres berretines* was for a "gente nuestra" imagined less as a function of national boundaries or place of origin. This gente nuestra even appeared in the United States. Sandrini's *Riachuelo* was the first Argentine-produced film imported into the United States, premiering in the Campoamor theater in East Harlem on December 7, 1934, and *Los tres berretines* made its debut at the Campoamor the following month.[101]

Sandrini is less a cartographic marker of Argentine expansion than he is an odographic relay akin to the commemorative postage stamp bearing his image. The odographic emphasis on Sandrini sees him as (de)territorializing force. Much like that postage stamp, he less represents a pregiven nation than he territorializes through his circulation. To find him at the Campoamor invites us not simply to tout Argentina's might—which would (a) conflate Sandrini with Argentina and (b) more significantly, operate under the same imperial logic that grants Hollywood its discursive force—but to consider how cinema, like the stamp, operates through a logic of exchange where redemption promises territorialization always haunted by its necessary possible failure.

Trying to follow Sandrini is both a matter of his films' reception *and* his films' production. Even before Sandrini would famously journey overseas to star in films produced outside Argentina, the comedian's feature *Don Quijote del altillo* was produced in Argentina and Brazil, the outcome of the agreement of SIDE's Alfredo Murúa to use Genaro Ciavarra's studio in Rio de Janeiro in order to make year-round production possible in the fair-weather capital.[102] Nearly a decade later, Sandrini began working in earnest outside Argentina immediately following the Second World War, making one picture in Chile in late 1945 before heading to Mexico for radio and film work.[103] While shooting his Mexican debut, *La vida íntima de Marco Antonio y Cleopatra* (Roberto Gavaldón, 1947), for Filmex,[104] Sandrini began radio programs for XEW, relayed through Radio El Mundo in Buenos Aires, which still had him under contract for Cocinero oil broadcasts.[105] Perhaps even more than film, radio provided the most opportunities for Argentine talent looking for work abroad.[106] From Pepe Arias in Cuba to Juan Carlos Thorry in Venezuela, Sandrini was simply one of several radio stars making their way abroad.[107] The comedian also staged four comedies during the summer season of 1946, most notably headlining *Cuando el diablo sopla* in the Abreu theater with his then-partner Tita Merello.[108] Although Sandrini did not remain in Mexico for the duration of his career, this marked the beginning of a period of frequent travel under different "exclusive" film and radio commitments. Sandrini returned briefly to Argentina in late 1946, under a two-picture contract with Argentina Sono Film.[109] After concluding his final picture for Argentina Sono Film, *Don Juan Tenorio* (Luis César Amadori, 1949), Sandrini signed another exclusive agreement through 1951 with Interamericana.[110] Sandrini was under contract not only in Mexico and Argentina; he also had a two-picture agreement with Spanish director Benito Perojo for Suevia Films.[111]

Unlike the 1939 case of Niní Marshall—whose "exclusivity" we discussed in chapter 2 in terms of property rights, radio advertising, and evolving labor practices in an industrial studio model—Sandrini's exclusive contracts with Filmex, Suevia Films, and Argentina Sono Film underscore how "exclusivity" was also determined by jurisdiction.[112] Radio only further complicates the star's exclusivity, as radio broadcasts could be transmitted and relayed. Sandrini's postwar career provides another wrinkle in the alignment of Latin America and classical Hollywood. The star's exclusivity is part monopoly strategy and part jurisdictional claim. To make a film is to execute a contract enforceable

FIGURE 22. Luis Sandrini becomes a contract player for Filmex in postwar Mexico, as seen in the pages of *Cinema Reporter*.

in a jurisdiction, so that classical Hollywood as industrial mode of production with contracted labor supposes monopoly capitalism and the national form of the state.[113] In a striking departure from most discussions of classical cinema, classical Hollywood and its organization of the labor force is necessarily dependent on the nation-state as jurisdiction. Latin America's mock classicism presents a jurisdictional challenge, a different organization of the labor force whereby Sandrini could sell his labor in multiple (Hispanic) jurisdictions. In a period so overdetermined by the nation in film histories, the circulation of labor between different centers of Hispanic film production is partly a testament to the cosmopolitan orientation of the region's cinema and partly a symptom of the limits of national jurisdiction as the basis for monopoly control.

This jurisdictional challenge becomes text in Sandrini's third film under this "exclusive" agreement with Filmex, the Julio Bracho–directed *El ladrón (The Thief)* (1947).[114] In the film, Sandrini is Plácido, a bank clerk responsible for taking bills out of circulation by incinerating them in the bank's subbasement. Plácido grew up an orphan and is a longtime employee in love with the elevator girl Rosa (Elsa Aguirre), a working-class femme fatale who tries to seduce the bank clerk to spare a few bills from incineration to spend on her. The film opens with a close-up tracking back from the bank's facade, an interior long shot of the bank lobby and a series of close-ups of machines at work: a close-up of a typewriter in profile, another of a mimeograph, a table of market rates. A long shot of the bowels of the bank, somewhat reminiscent of King Vidor's *The Crowd* (1928), dissolves to a close-up of an open furnace and Sandrini lighting a cigar stub with a flaming 10,000 peso bill. From recording to duplicating to exchanging to incinerating, the sequence provides a shorthand life cycle of the billfold (and obliquely the film material). The camera pushes out when Sandrini is reprimanded for his habit and later informed by his supervisor that the bank president wants to speak with him. A nervous Sandrini frets he will be reprimanded for stealing *(hurtar)* the boss's cigar butts and defends himself to his supervisor: "No las hurto del cenicero sino del cesto de la basura por lo que bien sé que en la gramática castellana habría que encontrar otro verbo que definiera exactamente esta acción" (I take them from the trash can and not the ashtray, so we'd need another verb in Spanish to define this action). His supervisor cuts him off—"No me venga con sus definiciones" (Don't start again with your definitions).

Sandrini later returns to this semantic dilemma twice more when he is inspected by the security guard and when Rosa propositions him. To the security guard he complains, "Esta inspección sí que es un hurto en el sentido figurativo de la palabra. Hurto a la dignidad y a la honradez de un empleado al quien sin derecho alguno se le supone capacidad de hurtar por distracción" (This inspection really is theft in the figurative sense of the word. A theft of the dignity and honor of an employee who without cause is thought capable of being a distracted thief). Immediately thereafter, when Rosa suggests he steal some money to buy her a fur coat, Sandrini adds, "A eso la gramática castellana le llama hurto" (That's what Spanish grammar calls theft). The opening minutes of the film find our comedian no longer struggling to communicate because he stutters but because he defines. He is at a loss for words not because they outpace him but because they are imprecise.

In this ultimate (literally) *ficción del dinero,* Sandrini is economic symbolization at its limits, an incinerator of paper money who makes money worthless concerned with making words significant. Sandrini is pleasantly surprised by his boss with a minor raise of 10 pesos per month—"es decir 120 pesos al año, 1,200 pesos cada diez años, una fortuna" (that is to say, 120 pesos per year, 1,200 pesos every ten years, a fortune), his boss adds. An underwhelmed Sandrini continues, "O sea, o pesos con 33 centavos y fracción por cada día de los 365 por diez de los 3,650 días de servicio constante" (In other words, 33⅓ cents for each day of the 365 [days] times ten [or] the 3,650 days of constant service). The meeting is cut short when the headmistress of an orphanage comes to ask for a 10,000-peso donation for Christmas presents for her three thousand orphans. The bank president refuses to meet her and excuses Plácido. Sandrini finds small comfort in this back-of-the-envelope math, repeating the absurd calculation to the guard when he returns from his meeting:

Sandrini: Me subieron el sueldo ... diez pesos.

Guard: ¿Diarios?

Sandrini: Casi diarios. Por mes ... no es tan poco dinero, no vaya creer. Son 1,200 pesos cada diez años, o sea, ¿usted cuántos años tiene?

Guard: 63.

Sandrini: 63. Calcule lo que se hubiera ahorrado usted en su vida si hubiera trabajado desde el primer día con mi aumento. A diez pesos son ... 7,560 pesos en toda su vida!

Sandrini: They raised my salary ... ten pesos.

Guard: Per day?

Sandrini: Almost. Per month ... it's not an insignificant amount of money, you better believe it. That's 1,200 pesos every ten tears, in other words ... How old are you?

Guard: 63.

Sandrini: 63. Imagine what you would have saved in your lifetime had you been working from day one with my raise. Ten pesos per month would be ... 7,560 pesos in your lifetime!

The conversation is ironically punctuated with Sandrini returning to his desk to toss three stacks of 10,000 pesos into the furnace. After a fade to black, we return to Sandrini in the same position, now at the end of the work day. He stands up to stretch and his coworker reprimands him, reminding him that he has 100,000 pesos to go. Sandrini reassures him, "Que me despacho en cinco minutos" (I'll get rid of them in five minutes).

His meddling coworker is unconvinced, "¿20,000 por minuto? Quién sabe?" (20,000 per minute? We'll see).

Sandrini remarks, "10,000 en 30 segundos. *(sotto voce)* La Navidad de 3,000 niños quemada en medio minuto" (10,000 [pesos] in 30 seconds. *(sotto voce)* The Christmas of 3,000 children up in smoke in half a minute). Of course, a similar calculation could be made of the film itself.

A 10,000 peso bill falls to the floor. A drawn-out sequence in real time finds Sandrini glancing at the bill, the furnace, the guard, and the clock, equivocating on whether to swipe the money. He decides to spit out his gum and use it to affix the bill to the sole of his shoe. After making it out past the guard, Sandrini briefly loses the money in an extended comedic sequence where the bill attaches itself to a woman in the elevator. The camera movement tracks with the bill and not the comedian. Sandrini eventually recovers the bill and with it the camera's sight. Plácido decides to donate the money to the orphanage but hasn't realized his coworker has spotted him in flagrante. Plácido refuses to be extorted and his coworker turns him in to the bank president. The president, surprised Plácido would be capable of such an act, defers judgement until the bill returns to the bank. We cut to the headmistress, in a tracking shot from right to left, arriving at a cash teller to deposit the money. A series of dissolving scenes follows the revaluated paper money back in circulation: a tilting shot at an accounts-received window, a close-up of a cash withdrawal, a close-up of jewelry in a display case with a $10,000 price tag, and finally another medium shot of a bank teller's window that tracks the bill being exchanged four times over partitions. Plácido is discovered, and the president demands he return whatever he has purchased to restore the value.

What value is there to be restored when the money was going to be incinerated? Sandrini has produced fiat money. Much like counterfeit money, this 10,000 peso bill is not backed and yet successfully circulates. The film makes explicit that paper money indexes a standard of exchange and transfer (and does not represent the value of the commodity). Sandrini's speculation makes explicit how paper money estranges in order to be available for exchange. This process renders paper money neither valuable substance nor token of value. Value does not inhere in things but in a certain capacity to become symbol—to be estranged or alienated from substance—in order to be exchanged. As

Marx explains in his dialectical method: "Gold circulates because it has value, paper has value because it circulates," so that paper money as a token of value no longer functions as a token of value.[115] The case of counterfeit money makes us reflect on money as such because counterfeit money can only be counterfeit "by being able to be, *perhaps,* what it is."[116] In other words, when both true and false money have no referent, how do we tell them apart? Both suppose credit or an act of faith, of taking the nominal as the real.[117] Fiat money shares the condition of fiction, not because it is false but because it relies on an ability to circulate and a capacity to provoke events. Derrida suggests that this tells us something about fiction and the place of belief from which we read; we are less receivers than debtors and creditors.[118] To suspend our disbelief means a willful extension of credit with the promise of a "payoff," of an intended meaning or an unveiled enigma. The interest of the text derives from the promise of a payoff, which is necessarily deferred because the text is hermeneutically inexhaustible.

Plácido, of course, cannot return the equivalent value—he cannot deliver a payoff. In this moralistic saccharine ending, he has purchased something "que no tiene precio" (that is priceless), he explains. What could be more valuable than money? The irritated bank president explains, "Todo tiene precio, hasta el amor" (Everything has a price, even love). The sentimental conclusion that rewards Sandrini and teaches the bank about the "priceless value" of orphans' happiness cannot resolve this economic circuit: it can neither restore the relation between sign and substance nor inhere value in the money-form. The accounts do not quite balance in this comedy of calculative errors, where an interruption of the continuum of a monetary (and narrative) exchange poses an aneconomic risk. The aneconomic risk is a less a refusal to circulate than it is a refusal to be in calculable time that threatens exchangist rationality. This aneconomic risk does not subvert the law of economy; it is the mitigation of aneconomic risk that lies at the heart of the economic and its forms of estrangement.[119] The comic is necessarily the expression of the limits of economic symbolization, of the failures of exchange grounded in (monetary and linguistic) symbolization, of the aneconomic as aesthetic form.

The aneconomic risk that subtends the law of economy returns us to the question of atelicity. As Derrida reminds us, the monetary sign is constantly reappropriated by a teleology, the payoff as the realization of a telos.[120] For Derrida, what is at stake in the economic (and aneconomic) is time—not what is *in* time, but time itself. A balance sheet accounts for not simply assets and liabilities but time given, time owed, and time expected. Perhaps it should come as no surprise that the implementation of standardized time and the consolidation of currency roughly coincide in the late nineteenth and early twentieth centuries. Both ostensibly give symbolic form to the nation as preexisting territorial formation; however, they arguably constitute the nation through (or perhaps despite) their circulation. The case of money makes this particularly clear as the conventional wisdom on currency is that "nations assert and express their sovereign authority by maintaining national money and protecting its use within their respective jurisdiction."[121] Money seems tethered to the nation because it signifies as national symbol or functions as fragment of its vast reserves, but in practice, currency use is never quite confined by states' territorial limits. This means supplementing the "topological presuppositions" of physical geography with a more functional notion of space, less tied to place of origin than to networks of transactions.[122] Put simply, what kind of space takes shape when we shift away from the question of who issued the money to who uses it, where can it be redeemed, and what can it purchase. The critique of "one nation, one money" can be refashioned into a critique of "one nation, one cinema." The logic of money is less a logic of tradition than a logic of circulation, less a local custom that expands outward than a standard of value that aspires to be universal although determined by its local conditions of enunciation. The isochrone map becomes a fiduciary odography, a map of where trust in redemption extends. This trust is a function of legitimacy and power. Although deterritorialized currency spaces are freed from strict dependence of physical location, their fiduciary reach is determined by competition and hierarchical relationships. This gives us language to move away from national film history frameworks without the rupture or homogeneity implicit in modernity because accounting for the ways power determines "the reciprocal faith of a critical mass of like-minded transactors" and shapes this transactional domain.[123]

CONVERTING SANDRINI

And so we come full circle, or rather we can never really come full circle. Thomas Elsaesser argues that "the history of Hollywood could be written as the successive moves to install and define the commodity 'film,' while at the same time extending and refining the service 'cinema' . . . turning an experience into a commodity."[124] For Elsaesser, studying Hollywood requires tracing how "everything connects"—that is, articulating external profit-oriented connections across industry, technology, and finance to internal pleasure-oriented connections related to narrative structure, aesthetic form, and film spectatorship.[125] Elsaesser's historiographic model explains the shift away from classicism as an escalation at the macro level—from growing market share through geographic expansion to controlling experience through service development and concentric diversification—and the micro level—from diegetic discreteness to "the destruction of the diegetic unity through a [modular] reconfiguration of the film's narrative in media."[126] Latin American film comedy forces us to reckon with the ways everything does not connect. Its atelicity indexes the tensions between the uneven formation of Latin American national modernities and the dynamics of transnational market forces, or how, recalling Sandrini, "[el mundo] se nos escapa de las manos" ([the world] slips through our fingers).[127]

Sandrini's first film under his agreement with Filmex was *La vida íntima de Marco Antonio y Cleopatra* (Roberto Gavaldón, 1947), a mashup of the sword-and-sandals epic and the Mexican musical comedy. One of the first Alfredo Ripstein Jr. productions, the film features a gullible Sandrini as Marco Antonio, who falls for his boss's conniving wife, Cleo (Maria Antonieta Pons).[128] Sandrini's boss is a fortune-telling grifter, Julio, who swindles folks hoping to communicate with the dead. Unfortunately, Cleo is having an affair with Julio's partner, and the film narrative is organized around their plot to cheat Marco Antonio and Julio. While under the spell of the fortune-teller, Sandrini becomes a medium who successfully calls forth a Praetorian Guard and astral projects to ancient Rome, so that the present-day heist becomes a framing narrative for a loose adaptation of the historical plot. Sandrini comes armed with an Espasa encyclopedia to warn Julius Caesar of his impending assassination, take Mark Antony's place in Egypt, and foil Cleopatra's murder-suicide.

After telling Mark Antony of his grim fate in Egypt, Sandrini agrees to take the Roman's place as envoy to Cleopatra. He arrives in Egypt with his "dogs of war," amusingly not with the ancient army's signature Great Danes but with two rascally (anatopistic) Chihuahuas. The Egyptian queen flirts with the man, her machinations to vanquish Rome dependent on her signature looks, and Sandrini retorts with the anachronistic quip, "Hagamos la política de la buena vecindad" (Let's play the Good Neighbor Policy). Eventually, a council of elders interrupts this courtship to inform the ersatz Mark Antony the treasury is empty and they are unable to pay their debts. Sandrini asks the men how many animals there are in Egypt: "¿Cuántos elefantes, cuántos camellos, cuántos burros hay, sin despreciar los presentes?" (How many elephants, how many camels, how many donkeys, present company excluded?). He is assured there are millions, and Sandrini promises to deliver the necessary revenue. The medium shot of Sandrini and Pons dissolves to a tracking long shot of an Egyptian street and a horse-drawn cart, the latter emblazoned with a license plate: Alejandria C 20. The cart passes and the camera frames a policeman directing traffic and eyeing carefully every moving "vehicle." A horse enters the frame and heads away from the camera and toward the palace. The policeman whistles and halts the rider: "¿Su licencia para guiar?" (Your rider's license?).

The rider, Cleopatra's brother and coconspirator, Ptolomeo, is aghast. "40 monedas de multa por no tenerla. Ahora debe llevarla todo el mundo. ¿Y la placa?" (That's a 40-coin fine for not having it. Everyone has to carry it now. And your plate?). Ptolomeo asks what plate he's speaking about.

The traffic cop explains, "Es un nuevo impuesto de Marco Antonio. ¡200 monedas más!" (It's a new decree by Mark Antony. 200 more coins!). The cop hangs a license plate on Ptolomeo's saddle, who complains about this extortion.

The guard explains, "Gracias a esto, la administración anda al día" (This is keeping our government in the black). The medium long shot confrontation ends with another dissolve to a close-up of a coin purse emptied on a table with the council of elders looking in amazement. The camera pushes out to a long shot with Sandrini explaining, "la vaca da leche según cómo se la ordeñe . . . y eso que todavía no hay income tax" (a cow gives milk depending on how you milk it . . . and we haven't even started collecting income tax). The film imagines antiquity as a monetary space, and Sandrini introduces a modern bureaucratic state apparatus to levy taxes.[129]

The emperor becoming modern bureaucrat is perhaps partly a commentary on the postrevolutionary shift from traditional caciquismo to bureaucratic authoritarianism.[130] Gareth Williams credits this period with a transition from traditional forms of patronage and subjectification to modern, rational, and bureaucratic forms of patronage that normalized extraordinary powers as an instrument of governmentally.[131] And yet this film seems to be more than a national allegory of the bureaucratization of the state. The anatopistic and anachronistic parodic elements in the narrative suggest a lack of spatiotemporal hierarchy that bears on the construction of the diegesis, particularly in the scene of astral projection.

The fortune-telling ruse and the scene of Sandrini's becoming a medium, aside from featuring some remarkable visual effects orchestrated by the Machado brothers, offers an almost self-reflexive staging of the cinema. Julio, *espiritista*/spiritualist and *simulador*/simulator, is missing his partner and medium, and he coaxes Sandrini into being a medium for a grieving widow. The widow Hernandez pleads with Julio to communicate with her husband, Septimio, with whom she has a standing appointment at 6 P.M. Julio explains that the spirits wander through space and that time is nothing to them. Julio assures a scared Sandrini that nothing will happen to him: "Te desdoblo y te doblo enseguida" (I'll unfold you and fold you right back).

Sandrini bites back, "¿Pero usted que se piensa que soy, un periódico para que me doble y me desdoble otra vez? (But what do you take me for, a newspaper you can fold and unfold over and over?).

Julio assures him he'll direct him—"With radar?" Sandrini quips—because he has mastery over the great beyond.

Sandrini pleads he'd rather stay in the great nearby, but the fortune-teller induces his trance by force. Sandrini backs away from Julio before we cut to his unusual point-of-view close-up of Julio gesturing with his arms, the lens shifting so that his face comes in and out of focus. Sandrini sits in a medium long shot, and Julio demands, "Libera tu espíritu para que puedas captar los mensajes astrales. ¡Desdóblate! ¡Desintégrate! Vaga por el espacio. ¡Conviértete!" (Free your spirit so that you can receive astral messages. Unfold yourself! Come undone! Wander through space. Become!).

Sandrini chimes in with a numismatic play on words—"¿A cómo está el dólar?" (What's the exchange rate for the dollar?)—a pun on the verb *convertir*, meaning both "to exchange money" and "to become."

Julio clarifies, "Conviértete en plasma sensible y trata de comunicarte con el otro mundo" (Become sensible plasma and try to communicate with the great beyond).

Sandrini seems to speak in tongues and then explains, "Estoy tratando de comunicarme con larga distancia. Parece que las líneas están ocupados. Pido por Edison" (I'm trying to make a long-distance call. Seems like the line is busy. Hello, Edison?).

Julio looms back-lit in a medium shot in an ostensible point-of-view shot, but the spiritualist backs up and pivots to the side as the camera tracks back into a long shot of the pair. Sandrini's body jerks and squirms to the strumming harp: "Comienza a desdoblarse" (He's beginning to unfold), Julio reassures. A medium close-up of an entranced Sandrini pushes out as Julio steps in and pricks the medium to demonstrate he is under his spell. Julio commands, "Despréndete de la materia" (Detach yourself from matter). A trick shot of Sandrini uses double exposure to show the comedian doubling on screen, his spectral projection rising from his body on command. His spirit moves forward before turning back to pickpocket his body. Sandrini's spirit begins calling for Septimio in a remarkable tracking shot where the spirit seems to be floating in the fortune-teller's room. The shot is unusual, however, because the camera's framing is determined by the spirit and not the room. In other words, rather than having the edges of the frame coincide with the dimensions of the room, they coincide with Sandrini's body.

This scene of unfolding recalls Deleuze's concept of the fold, particularly in its more baroque incarnation where the fold refers to a mystical venture or an individual's account of their voyage to and from an induced trance. Deleuze uses the fold to describe the nature of the human subject not through the structural and psychoanalytic frameworks that posit a subject effected by an external lost object but as an outside folded in. The lost object is not an external unit awaiting reincorporation; instead, the outside is a "temporal modulation," neither separate nor static because a function of our orientation.[132] The changing status of the object also changes the status of the subject. The subject is open-ended, inexhaustive, and nonexclusive. Figured in relation to Sandrini's unfolding, this is not simply a scene of a subject's interiority made external. When Septimio, the Praetorian Guard and not the widow's husband, appears in an extreme long shot atop the stairs, he complains in Latin about being awoken. Sandrini approaches the guard. Sandrini moves from the first floor to the second floor without using the set's actual stairs; instead, he climbs some unseen steps so that he appears to ascend in the middle of the frame. His is a manufactured ghostliness that makes the comedian's body an actual medium between actual and astral as well as diegetic and pictorial space. Sandrini's spirit is not so much expressing his interiority; when he manifests, he strains the diegesis as architectural and topological form.

Sandrini's voice becomes reverberant as he heads up and away from the camera; in lieu of intelligible close-miked sound, the sound design offers an uncanny (and uncharacteristic) use of scale matching. The sound envelope that binds sound space and narrative space is unbound as camera distance (and framing) and microphone distance change from one shot to the next. Sandrini explains to the spiritualist that he must have dialed a wrong number as he descends with the guard toward the grieving widow. Sandrini remains double-exposed, "disfrazado de radiografía" (in an X-ray costume) and "vestido de celofán" (dressed in cellophane). The comedian's body and not the built environment is the measure of the diegesis in this sequence that unfolds narrative space. His is not simply an astral plane in the diegesis because the diegesis ceases to become a spatial and temporal frame of reference. There is a long history of astral or celestial plane intervening in the narrative space, often in continuity with (if overseeing) the narrative space, but this is less a case of celestial suture than astral dispersion, less oversight than undersight.[133] It is no longer easy to determine what is the great beyond (or the great nearby). The session is interrupted by a police raid, and Julio cannot manage to fold Sandrini back into his body. The comedian must wait to be incarnated and follows the guard back to Rome, when the latter explains, "En los espacios astrales, todas las épocas perduran" (In astral planes, all the epochs survive). Mistaken invocation, off-center framing, delayed incarnation: this is a comedy of spatiotemporal errors. The diegesis is not quite governed by the temporality of the récit, a point underscored when Sandrini becomes a fortune-teller to Caesar, or as he explains, "un historiador con efecto de retruque, adivino en marcha atrás o en reversa" (a historian in verso, a soothsayer in reverse). All spaces and all times are available to this historian in verso.

If the diegesis relies on interiority and exteriority defined as areas within the narrative, then what happens when the discrete diegeses become indiscrete?[134] The spectator of mock classicism is not quite a subject yearning for a lost object. Without spatiotemporal hierarchy at the formal and narrative level, the narrative space is not quite a separable diegesis but a fold. Deleuze analogizes the fold-as-(de)subjectivization to the perception of/in background—that is, peripheral vision. The background is not quite perceived as an object but rather it is the condition of the emergence of the object.[135] Similarly, the subject intends or orients from a relative position with shadows, obscurities, and edges. Peripheral vision is precisely the condition of emergence of the subject: how we decide the beyond and the nearby within (and without) the narrative, how the salient emerges in relation to what we relegate. Mock classicism *convierte* its spectators; it does not so much represent the world as it provides our expression (or folding in) of the world.

Notes

Unless otherwise noted, all translations are my own.

INTRODUCTION

1. Jeffrey Pilcher, *Cantinflas and the Chaos of Mexican Modernity* (Wilmington, DE: Scholarly Resources, 2001), 165.
2. Walter Armbrust, "The Golden Age before the Golden Age: Commercial Egyptian Cinema before the 1960s," in *Mass Mediations: New Approaches to Popular Culture in the Middle East and Beyond*, ed. Walter Armbrust (Berkeley: University of California Press, 2000), 293.
3. David Bordwell, Janet Staiger, and Kristin Thompson, *The Classical Hollywood Cinema: Film Style and Mode of Production to 1960* (New York: Routledge, 1985), 17.
4. Thomas Elsaesser, "What Might We Mean by Media History?" *Geschiedenis, Beeld en Geluid* 28 (1994): 22.
5. Wai Chee Dimock, "Pre-National Time: Novel, Epic, Henry James," *Henry James Review* 24, no. 3 (2003): 219.
6. Esther Gabara, *Errant Modernism: The Ethos of Photography in Mexico and Brazil* (Durham, NC: Duke University Press, 2008), 14.
7. Daryle Williams, *Culture Wars in Brazil: The First Vargas Regime, 1930–1945* (Durham, NC: Duke University Press, 2001), 98.
8. Gabara, *Errant Modernism*, 30.
9. Miriam Hansen, "The Mass Production of the Senses: Classical Cinema as Vernacular Modernism," *Modernism/Modernity* 6, no. 2 (1999): 71.
10. Miriam Hansen, "Vernacular Modernism: Tracking Cinema on a Global Scale," in *World Cinemas, Transnational Perspectives*, ed. Natasha Durovicova and Kathleen Newman (New York: Routledge, 2009), 295.

11. Hansen, "Mass Production of the Senses," 71.
12. William Solomon, "Slapstick Modernism: Charley Bowers and Industrial Modernity," *Modernist Cultures* 2, no. 2 (2006): 171; Siegfried Kracauer, *Theory of Film: The Redemption of Physical Reality* (Chicago: University of Chicago Press, 1997), 62, 108–9. Malcolm Turvey recently coined the more expansive "comedic modernism" to include a broader range of comedic practices from the comedian comedy before the 1920s and beyond slapstick. Malcolm Turvey, "Comedic Modernism," *October* 160 (2017): 5.
13. Hansen, "Vernacular Modernism," 298.
14. Neepa Majumdar, *Wanted Cultured Ladies Only!: Female Stardom and Cinema in India, 1930s–1950s* (Champaign, IL: University of Illinois Press, 2009), 4.
15. Ibid., 9.
16. Franco Moretti, "Planet Hollywood," *New Left Review* 9 (2001): 94.
17. Ana López, "Early Cinema and Modernity in Latin America," *Cinema Journal* 40, no. 1 (2000): 50.
18. Rielle Navitski, *Public Spectacles of Violence: Sensational Cinema and Journalism in Early Twentieth-Century Mexico and Brazil* (Durham, NC: Duke University Press, 2017), 12–13.
19. Hansen, "Mass Production of the Senses," 67.
20. Matthew Karush, *Culture of Class: Radio and Cinema in the Making of a Divided Argentina, 1920–1946* (Durham, NC: Duke University Press, 2012); Charles Ramírez Berg, *Classical Mexican Cinema: The Poetics of the Exceptional Golden Age Films* (Austin: University of Texas Press, 2015).
21. Alberto Moreiras, *The Exhaustion of Difference* (Durham, NC: Duke University Press, 2001), 14.
22. Ibid., 15.
23. Ibid., 188.
24. For a thorough discussion of the modernity thesis debates, see Ben Singer, *Melodrama and Modernity: Early Cinema and Its Sensational Contexts* (New York: Columbia University Press, 2001), 104.
25. Moreiras, *Exhaustion of Difference*, 3.
26. Ibid., 4.
27. Ibid., 16.
28. Ibid.
29. Mariano Siskind, *Cosmopolitan Desires: Global Modernity and World Literatures in Latin America* (Evanston, IL: Northwestern University Press, 2014), 21.
30. Ibid., 19.
31. Ibid., 23.
32. Michel Foucault, *Power/Knowledge* (New York: Pantheon Books, 1980), 134–45.
33. Siskind, *Cosmopolitan Desires*, 43.
34. Ibid., 45.
35. Eric Hayot, *On Literary Worlds* (New York: Oxford University Press, 2012), 45.
36. Siskind, *Cosmopolitan Desires*, 32.

37. Michael Hardt, "Affective Labor," *Boundary 2* 26, no. 2 (1999): 89–100; Laura Podalsky, *The Politics of Affect and Emotion in Contemporary Latin American Cinema* (New York: Palgrave Macmillan, 2011), 14.
38. Podalsky, *Politics of Affect and Emotion*, 8, 12. See also Gilles Deleuze, *Cinema 1: The Movement-Image* (Minneapolis: University of Minnesota Press, 1986), 99–100.
39. Laura Marks, *The Skin of the Film: Intercultural Cinema, Embodiment, and the Senses* (Durham, NC: Duke University Press, 2000).
40. Gilles Deleuze, *Cinema 2: The Time-Image* (Minneapolis: University of Minnesota Press, 1989), 99–105, 133.
41. Moreiras, *Exhaustion of Difference*, 5.
42. John Ellis, "Made in Ealing." *Screen* 16, no. 1 (1975): 113.
43. Frank Krutnik, "The Clown-Prints of Comedy," *Screen* 25, no. 4–5 (1984): 51.
44. Steve Seidman, *Comedian Comedy: A Tradition in Hollywood Film* (Ann Arbor, MI: UMI Research Press, 1981), 64.
45. Mick Eaton, "Laughter in the Dark," *Screen* 22, no. 2 (1981): 22.
46. Henri Bergson, *Laughter: An Essay on the Meaning of the Comic*, trans. Cloudesley Brereton and Fred Rothwell (New York: Macmillan, 1914), 102.
47. Henri Bergson, *Matter and Memory*, trans. Nancy Margaret Paul and W. Scott Palmer (New York: Macmillan, 1913); Henri Bergson, *Creative Evolution*, trans. Arthur Mitchell (New York: Henry Holt, 1911).
48. Bergson, *Laughter*, 5.
49. Krutnik, "Clown-Prints of Comedy," 58.
50. Ibid., 52.
51. Miriam Hansen, *Babel and Babylon: Spectatorship in American Silent Film* (Cambridge, MA: Harvard University Press, 1991), 281.
52. Linda Williams, "Melodrama Revised," in *Refiguring American Film Genres: History and Theory*, ed. Nick Browne (Berkeley: University of California Press, 1998), 42.
53. Agustín Zarzosa, "Melodrama and the Modes of the World," *Discourse* 32, no. 2 (2010): 236.
54. See Julianne Burton-Carvajal, "Mexican Melodramas of Patriarchy: Specificity of a Transcultural Form," in *Framing Latin American Cinema: Contemporary Critical Perspectives*, ed. Anne Marie Stock (Minneapolis: University of Minnesota Press, 1997), 191; Silvia Oroz, *Melodrama: O cinema de lágrimas da América Latina* (Rio de Janeiro: Funarte, 1999); and Elena Lahr-Vivaz, *Mexican Melodrama: Film and Nation from the Golden Age to the New Wave*, (Tucson: University of Arizona Press, 2016), 11.
55. Oroz, *Melodrama*, 32.
56. Zarzosa, "Melodrama," 237.
57. Thomas Elsaesser, "Tales of Sound and Fury: Observations on the Family Melodrama," in *Home Is Where the Heart Is: Studies in Melodrama and the Woman's Film*, ed. Christine Gledhill (London: BFI, 1987), 50.
58. Peter Brooks, *The Melodramatic Imagination: Balzac, Henry James, Melodrama and the Mode of Excess* (New Haven, CT: Yale University Press, 1976), 42.
59. Ibid., 57.

60. Linda Williams, *Playing the Race Card: Melodramas of Black and White from Uncle Tom to O.J. Simpson* (Princeton, NJ: Princeton University Press, 2001), 17.

61. López, "Early Cinema," 50.

62. Ibid., 72.

63. Dimock, "Pre-National Time," 217.

64. Ibid., 219.

65. Homi Bhabha, "DissemiNation: Time, Narrative, and the Margins of the Modern Nation," in *Nation and Narration,* ed. Homi Bhabha (New York: Routledge, 1990), 301.

66. Ibid., 302.

CHAPTER 1. *CANTINFLISMO* AND *RELAJO*'S PERIPHERAL VISION

1. Mario Moreno, interview by Jacobo Zabludovsky, *Efemérides,* 1967, Museo Cantinflas, https://youtu.be/HEVQk8ccLMo.

2. Jeffrey Pilcher, *Cantinflas and the Chaos of Mexican Modernity* (Wilmington, DE: Scholarly Resources, 2001), xvi.

3. Samuel Ramos, *Profile of Man and Culture in Mexico,* trans. Peter G. Earle (Austin: University of Texas Press, 1962), 59–60.

4. See Natalia Bieletto-Bueno, "Peladito (Pelado)," in *Celebrating Latino Folklore: An Encyclopedia of Cultural Traditions,* ed. María Herrera-Sobek (Santa Barbara, CA: ABC-CLIO, 2012), 896; Carlos Monsiváis, "Cantinflas and Tin Tan: Mexico's Greatest Comedians," in *Mexico's Cinema: A Century of Film and Filmmakers,* ed. Joanne Hershfield and David R. Maciel (Wilmington, DE: Scholarly Resources, 1999), 51.

5. Carlos Monsiváis, "Cantinflas: That's the Point!" in *Mexican Postcards,* trans. John Kraniauskas (New York: Verso, 1997), 99.

6. Gareth Williams, *The Mexican Exception: Sovereignty, Police, and Democracy* (New York: Palgrave Macmillan, 2011), 70.

7. Ibid., 73.

8. Miriam Hansen, *Babel and Babylon: Spectatorship in American Silent Film* (Cambridge, MA: Harvard University Press), 1991, 24.

9. Emilio García Riera, *Breve historia del cine mexicano. Primer siglo: 1897–1997* (Mexico, DF: Ediciones Mapa, 1998),107.

10. Carmelo Esterrich and Angel M. Santiago-Reyes, "From the Carpa to the Screen: The Masks of Cantinflas," *Studies in Latin American Popular Culture* 17 (1998): 45.

11. The pronoun *su* refers to the formal second-person *usted* as opposed to the informal second-person *tú.*

12. Esterrich and Santiago-Reyes, "From the Carpa to the Screen," 44.

13. The particular connection between the name (the sign) and the individual (its referent) occurs by virtue of an established convention. See Charles Sanders Peirce, *The Essential Peirce,* ed. Nathan Houser and Christian Kloesel, vol. 1, *Selected Philosophical Writings (1867–1893)* (Bloomington: Indiana University Press, 1992), 260.

14. If the signature functions as a rhematic indexical legisign, then the fingerprint functions as a dicent indexical sinsign. Both signature and fingerprint draw attention to an object, but the former functions as a degenerate index, factually connected to the object even if not bearing the marks of the object's actual existence, whereas the latter functions as a genuine index, calling attention to its object as having a real being independent of the representation and carrying the marks of the history of its object. See Peirce, *Essential Peirce,* vol. 1, 260.

15. J. L. Austin, *How to Do Things with Words* (London: Oxford University Press, 1962), 13.

16. John Mraz, *Looking for Mexico: Modern Visual Culture and National Identity* (Durham, NC: Duke University Press, 2009), 126.

17. Carlos Monsiváis, *Antología personal* (San Juan: Universidad de Puerto Rico, 2009), 73.

18. Daniel Chávez, "The Eagle and the Serpent on the Screen: The State as Spectacle in Mexican Cinema," *Latin American Research Review* 45, no. 3 (2010): 125.

19. Gareth Williams, "Comrades, There Are Moments in Life That Are Truly Momentary": Cantinflas and the Administration of Public Matters," in *Humor in Latin American Cinema,* ed. Juan Poblete and Juana Suárez (New York: Palgrave Macmillan, 2016), 62.

20. Ibid., 58.

21. Ana López, "Tears and Desires: Women and Melodrama in the 'Old' Mexican Cinema," in *Mediating Two Worlds: Cinematic Encounters in the Americas,* ed. John King and Ana López (London: BFI Publishing, 1993), 153.

22. Carl Mora, *Mexican Cinema: Reflections of a Society, 1896–1988* (Berkeley: University of California Press, 1989), 59.

23. Andrea Noble, *Mexican National Cinema* (New York: Routledge, 2005), 15.

24. Monsiváis, *Antología personal,* 81.

25. Jorge Ayala Blanco, *Búsqueda del cine mexicano* (Mexico, DF: Editorial Posada, 1986), 69.

26. Rafael Medina de la Serna, "Sorrows and Glories of Comedy," in *Mexican Cinema,* ed. Paulo Antonio Paranaguá, trans. Ana M. López (London: BFI Publishing, 1995), 167.

27. Mraz, *Looking for Mexico,* 127.

28. Monsiváis, *Antología personal,* 80.

29. Ilan Stavans, "The Riddle of Cantinflas: On Laughter and Revolution," *Transition* 67 (1995): 41.

30. Carlos Monsiváis, "Mexican Cinema: Of Myths and Mystifications," in *Mediating Two Worlds: Cinematic Encounters in the Americas,* ed. John King and Ana López (London: BFI Publishing, 1993), 146.

31. Ibid.

32. Maricruz Castro Ricalde and Robert McKee Irwin, *El cine mexicano "se impone": Mercados internacionales y penetración cultural en la época dorada* (Mexico, DF: Universidad Nacional Autónoma de México, 2011), 9.

33. Ibid., 83.

34. Ibid., 9.

35. Ibid., 45–48.
36. Ibid., 19.
37. Ibid., 62.
38. Ibid., 36.
39. Ibid., 84.
40. Ibid.
41. Ibid., 9.
42. Alberto Moreiras, *The Exhaustion of Difference* (Durham, NC: Duke University Press, 2001), 15.
43. Edmundo Baez, "El extranjerismo, un peligro del cine nacional," *Cinema Reporter*, 30 October 1943, 17.
In a similar vein, Alberto Roca comments on the adaptation of foreign narratives in Argentina, lamenting the fact that national literature, with an autochthonous profile more attuned to the needs of the Argentine screen, remains both underused as source material and understudied as a model for national cultural production. See Alberto Roca, "Balzac, Ibsen y Daudet en el cine argentino," *Cinema Reporter*, 18 December 1943, 4.
44. V. S, "Comentarios del cine mexicano en Argentina," *Cinema Reporter*, 6 November 1943, 5. The author even notes that Argentine cinema would suffer a similar decline were it to produce exclusively gaucho films.
45. Ibid.
46. Monsiváis, *Antología personal*, 73.
47. Monsiváis, "Cantinflas: That's the Point," 102.
48. Charles Ramirez Berg, *The Classical Mexican Cinema: The Poetics of the Exceptional Mexican Films* (Austin: University of Texas Press, 2015).
49. David Bordwell, *Narration in the Fiction Film* (New York: Routledge, 1985), 166.
50. David Bordwell, Kristen Thompson, and Janet Staiger, *The Classical Hollywood Cinema: Film Style and Mode of Production to 1960* (New York: Routledge, 1985).
51. Ramirez Berg, *Classical Mexican Cinema*, 35.
52. Stephen Heath, "Narrative Space," *Screen* 17, no. 3 (1976): 99.
53. Hansen, *Babel and Babylon*, 85.
54. Ibid., 24.
55. Ibid., 57.
56. Ibid., 246.
57. Ibid., 281.
58. Carlos Monsiváis, "All the People Came and Did Not Fit onto the Screen: Notes on the Cinema Audience in Mexico," in *Mexican Cinema*, ed. Paulo Antonio Paranaguá, trans. Ana M. López (London: BFI Publishing, 1995), 150.
59. Ibid., 151.
60. Ibid., 149.
61. Monsiváis, "Mexican Cinema," 146.
62. Austin, *How to Do Things with Words*, 25.
63. Jason Borge, *Latin American Writers and the Rise of Hollywood Cinema* (New York: Routledge, 2008), 32.
64. Heath, "Narrative Space," 393.

65. Miriam Hansen, "The Mass Production of the Senses: Classical Cinema as Vernacular Modernism," *Modernism/Modernity* 6, no. 2 (1999): 59.

66. Ibid., 60.

67. Ibid., 72.

68. Ibid., 71.

69. Weihong Bao, "'A Vibrating Art in the Air': Cinema, Ether, and Propaganda Film Theory in Wartime Chongqing," *New German Critique* 41, no. 2, 122 (2014): 172.

70. This form of reflexivity that does not turn on medium ontological questions is also found in other forms of cultural production from the period. Notably, Esther Gabara argues that modernist photography from the early twentieth century gestures toward the frame and what lies beyond the frame, foregrounding the context sublimated by and in formalism in centers of high modernism. For Gabara, these photographs are not mere abstraction but paradoxically abstraction with a reference. See Esther Gabara, *Errant Modernism: The Ethos of Photography in Mexico and Brazil* (Durham, NC: Duke University Press, 2008), 56.

71. Zhang Zhen, *An Amorous Screen of the Silver Screen: Shanghai Cinema, 1896–1937* (Chicago: University of Chicago Press, 2005), xxvi.

72. The declining international box office returns of Hollywood comedies, Moretti argues, are due in part to the way humor arises out of tacit assumptions with particular cultural associations. See Franco Moretti, "Planet Hollywood," *New Left Review* 9 (2001): 94.

73. Zhen, *An Amorous Screen*, xviii.

74. In Mexico, John Mraz credits the American invasion of Mexico and the arrival of photography in 1847 with the beginnings of a modern visual culture; however, the urbanization, nationalization, and breakdown of traditional values that characterized the experience of modernity in the Mexican context become particularly marked after the Mexican Revolution in the late interwar period. See Mraz, *Looking for Mexico*, 13.

75. Moreiras, *Exhaustion of Difference*, 13.

76. Jorge Portilla, *Fenomenología del relajo, y otros ensayos.* (Mexico, DF: Fondo de Cultura Económica, 1966), 13.

77. Ibid., 19.

78. Ibid., 18.

79. Sara Ahmed, *Queer Phenomenology* (Durham, NC: Duke University Press, 2006), 27.

80. Lauren Berlant, *Cruel Optimism* (Durham, NC: Duke University Press, 2011), 25.

81. Ahmed, *Queer Phenomenology*, 27.

82. Monsiváis, *Antología personal*, 80.

83. Portilla, *Fenomenología del relajo*, 19.

84. Ibid., 20.

85. Ibid., 25.

86. Ahmed, *Queer Phenomenology*, 38.

87. Lauren Berlant and Jordan Greenwald, "Affect in the End Times: A Conversation with Lauren Berlant," *Qui Parle: Critical Humanities and Social Sciences* 20, no. 2 (2012): 87.

88. Ibid.
89. Portilla, *Fenomenología del relajo*, 24.
90. D. N. Rodowick, "Subjects without Skin," *New German Critique* 41, no. 2 (2014): 14.
91. Alexander Fiske-Harrison, *Into the Arena: The World of the Spanish Bullfight* (London: Profile Books, 2011), 155.

CHAPTER 2. THE CALL OF THE SCREEN

1. This problematic still persists in popular media. See Linda Mizejewski, *Pretty/Funny: Women Comedians and Body Politics* (Austin: University of Texas Press, 2014), 5.
2. Niní Marshall and Salvador D'Anna, *Mis memorias* (Buenos Aires: Editorial Moreno, 1985), 6.
3. Octavio Getino, *Cine argentino: Entre lo posible y lo deseable* (Buenos Aires: Ediciones Ciccus, 1998), 20.
4. Tamara L. Falicov, "Argentine Cinema and the Construction of National Popular Identity, 1930–1942," *Studies in Latin American Popular Culture* 17 (1998): 68.
5. Matthew Karush, *Culture of Class: Radio and Cinema in the Making of a Divided Argentina, 1920–1946* (Durham, NC: Duke University Press, 2012), 15.
6. Neepa Majumdar, *Wanted Cultured Ladies Only!: Female Stardom and Cinema in India, 1930s–1950s* (Champaign: University of Illinois Press, 2009), 3.
7. Ibid., 6.
8. Falicov, "Argentine Cinema," 66.
9. Ricardo Gallo, *La radio: Ese mundo tan sonoro* (Buenos Aires: Corregidor, 1991), 67.
10. Karush, *Culture of Class*, 24–25.
11. Ana López, "The Radiophonic Imaginary in Latin American Transitional Cinema and Transmedial Relations" (conference presentation, Universidad Carlos III de Madrid, Madrid, Spain, 9 November 2012).
12. Jane Gaines, *Contested Culture: The Image, the Voice, and the Law* (Chapel Hill: University of North Carolina Press, 2000), 37.
13. Richard DeCordova, *Picture Personalities: The Emergence of the Star System in America* (Champaign: University of Illinois Press, 2001), 98.
14. The Galician stereotype still persists in Latin America, often highlighting the Spanish region's rural and classed characteristic and its emigrants' presumed unsophistication and stubbornness.
15. In lieu of direct advertising—such as an interrupting "word from our sponsor"—indirect advertising commonly names an advertiser as program sponsor—for example, "Llauró Soaps brings you Cándida." See Susan Murray, *Hitch Your Antenna to the Stars: Early Television and Broadcast Stardom* (New York: Routledge, 2013), 4.
16. Marshall quoted in Karush, *Culture of Class*, 125.
17. David Tannenbaum, "Enforcement of Personal Service Contracts in the Entertainment Industry," *California Law Review* 42, no .1 (1954): 18–27.

18. "'Cándida' ira el miércoles en el Monumental," *La nación,* 2 October 1939, 18.
19. Por los estudios locales, *La nación,* 8 October 1939, 16.
20. "En 1940, Niní Marshall actuará como Cándida en otro film de la EFA," *La nación,* 10 October 1939, 12.
21. Ibid.
22. "Niní Marshall actuará como Catita en 1940 en una obra de ASF," *La nación,* 11 October 1939, 12.
23. Por los estudios locales, *La nación,* 15 October 1939, 14.
24. "A propósito del contrato de una intérprete," *La nación,* 17 October 1939, 11.
25. Ibid.
26. Marshall's 45,000 Argentine pesos represented almost $192,000 in 1940 U.S. dollars, or over $3,200,000 adjusted for inflation in 2015.
27. "Más en torno al contrato de una intérprete," *La nación,* 18 October 1939, 11.
28. "Un comunicado sobre el contrato de una intérprete," *La nación,* 19 October 1939, 12.
29. Murray, *Hitch Your Antenna,* 22.
30. Marshall began her career writing under a pseudonym (Ivonne D'Arcy) for the journal *Sintonía.*
31. By the 1940s, film criticism was not allowed to publicize the private lives of its screen stars in "noticiarios," an ostensible nationalist move toward making film stars appear as laborers in a Peronist initiative: "Se prohibe la irradiación de cuestiones baladíes referentes a la vida, costumbres, etc. del artista" (The diffusion of trivial concerns related to the life or habits of the artist is prohibited). "La crítica y la difusión radial de cine," *Cinema Reporter,* 16 October 1943, 32.
32. Murray, *Hitch Your Antenna,* 14.
33. Maggie Hennefeld, "Slapstick Comediennes in Transitional Cinema: Between Body and Medium," *Camera Obscura: Feminism, Culture, and Media Studies* 29, no. 2 (2014): 86.
34. Ibid., 98.
35. Ibid., 86.
36. Ibid., 88.
37. Michael Slowik, *After the Silents: Hollywood Film Music in the Early Sound Era, 1926–1934* (New York: Columbia University Press, 2014), 11.
38. Ibid., 22.
39. Ibid., 25.
40. This might help explain why Catita in her Lumiton films, despite receiving top billing, always remains the sidekick to a central romantic drama.
41. Quoted in Gallo, *La radio,* 186.
42. Claudio España, "A modo de prólogo," in Marshall and D'Anna, *Mis memorias,* 2.
43. Kaja Silverman, *The Acoustic Mirror: The Female Voice in Psychoanalysis and Cinema* (Bloomington: Indiana University Press, 1988), 69.
44. Rick Altman, "Moving Lips: Cinema as Ventriloquism," *Yale French Studies* 60 (1980): 74.

45. Ibid.
46. Quoted in Gallo, *La radio,*186.
47. Mary Ann Doane, "The Voice in the Cinema: The Articulation of Body and Space," *Yale French Studies* 60 (1980): 39.
48. Silverman, *Acoustic Mirror,* 44.
49. Doane, "Voice in the Cinema." 38.
50. Silverman, *Acoustic Mirror,* 12.
51. Altman, "Moving Lips," 67.
52. Steve Connor, *Dumbstruck: A Cultural History of Ventriloquism* (New York: Oxford University Press, 2000), 18.
53. Ibid., 13.
54. Ibid., 34.
55. Miriam Hansen, *Babel and Babylon: Spectatorship in American Silent Film* (Cambridge, MA: Harvard University Press), 1991, 85.
56. For commedia dell'arte stock character types, see John Rudlin, *Commedia dell'arte: An Actor's Handbook* (New York: Routledge, 1994), 84, 127.
57. Silverman, *Acoustic Mirror,* 39.
58. Ibid., 14.
59. Pascual Quinziano, "La comedia: Un género impuro," in *Cine argentino: La otra historia,* ed. Sergio Wolfe (Buenos Aires: Letra Buena, 1994), 143.
60. Ibid.
61. Mary Ann Doane, "Film and the Masquerade: Theorising the Female Spectator," *Screen* 23, no. 3–4 (1982): 78.
62. Ibid., 79.
63. For instance, literary critic Lucía Guerra uses Mikhail Bakhtin to argue that the Latin American woman is "an efficient ventriloquist" and woman writers in the region juggle multiple codes. Sara Castro-Klarén suggests women writers play with the ventriloquial structure, speaking both a Western phallocentric discourse and an imperialist foreign discourse (and quite possibly more). See Lucía Guerra, "Las sombras de la escritura: Hacia una teoría de la producción literaria de la mujer latinoamericana," in *Cultural and Historical Grounding for Hispanic and Luso-Brazilian Feminist Literary Criticism* (Minneapolis, MN: Institute for the Study of Ideologies and Literature, 1989), 136–37; and Sara Castro-Klarén, "La crítica literaria feminista y la escritora en América Latina," in *La sartén por el mango,* ed. Patricia Elena González and Eliana Ortega (Río Piedras, Puerto Rico: Huracán, 1985), 39.
64. Gayatri Chakravorty Spivak, "Echo," *New Literary History* 24, no. 1 (1993): 38.
65. Ibid., 23.
66. Ibid., 25.
67. Ibid., 26.
68. Lucía Guerra, "Silencios, disidencias y claudicaciones: Los problemas teóricos de la nueva crítica feminista," in *Escribir en los bordes: Congreso Internacional de Literatura Femenina Latinoamericana,* ed. Carmen Berenguer et al. (Santiago, Chile: Editorial Cuarto Propio, 1990), 77.
69. Rey Chow, *Woman and Chinese Modernity: The Politics of Reading between West and East* (Minneapolis: University of Minnesota Press, 1991), 42.

CHAPTER 3. TIMING IS EVERYTHING

1. Matthew Karush, *Culture of Class: Radio and Cinema in the Making of a Divided Argentina, 1920–1946* (Durham, NC: Duke University Press, 2012), 118; and Jason Borge, "Replaying Carlitos: Chaplin, Latin American Film Comedy and the Paradigm of Imitation," *Journal of Latin American Cultural Studies* 22, no. 3 (2013): 272.

2. Stephen Kern, *The Culture of Time and Space, 1880–1918: With a New Preface* (Cambridge, MA: Harvard University Press, 2003), 4.

3. Peter Osborne, *The Politics of Time: Modernity and the Avant-Garde* (New York: Verso, 1995), 28.

4. Although 1920 marks Argentina's official time zone standardization, Lila Caimari's recent work on transoceanic cables teaches us that the use of such cables, operated by private British and American companies for diplomatic, commercial, and journalistic purposes, required consenting to Greenwich Mean Time shortly after the International Meridian Conference of 1884. See Ian Bartky, *One Time Fits All: The Campaigns for Global Uniformity,* (Palo Alto, CA: Stanford University Press, 2007); and Lila Caimari, "News from Around the World: South American Newspapers in the Era of Submarine Cables" (Arthur Aiton Lecture in Latin American History, University of Michigan, Ann Arbor, MI, 12 April 2017).

5. Venezuela and Uruguay used half-hour deviations from standard time. *Time Zone Chart of the World* (Washington, DC: Hydrographic Office, January 1927).

6. Henri Lefebvre, *Introduction to Modernity: Twelve Preludes, September 1959–May 1961* (New York: Verso, 1995), 187.

7. Osborne, *Politics of Time*, 25, 36.

8. There is a certain homology between this play on words and the conditions of the actor's appearance in the film itself. Sandrini was not originally meant to be such an important character in the film. Fellow comedian Pepe Arias was supposed to have a larger role as the comedic foil to the melodramatic narrative; however, the comedian had several scheduling conflicts. The better-known comedian still appears in the film with top billing but in significantly fewer scenes than Sandrini. Sandrini was repeatedly called back for additional scenes, filling in gaps, providing bridges, and offering commentary to the side of the action.

9. Henri Bergson, *Laughter: An Essay on the Meaning of the Comic,* trans. Cloudesley Brereton and Fred Rothwell (New York: Macmillan, 1914), 102.

10. Garret Stewart, "Modern Hard Times: Chaplin and the Cinema of Self-Reflection," *Critical Inquiry* 3, no. 2 (1976): 299.

11. See Paula Amad, *Counter-Archive: Film, the Everyday, and Albert Khan's Archives de la Planète* (New York: Columbia University Press, 2010); and Scott Curtis, *The Shape of Spectatorship: Art, Science, and Early Cinema in Germany* (New York: Columbia University Press, 2015).

12. Julio Navarro Monzó, "El individuo y la experiencia colectiva," *La nación* (22 October 1939): sec 2, 1. For additional examples of Bergson in Latin American periodicals, see also "Bergson" *Fon-Fon* 46 (16 November 1912); and Fortunat Strowski, "O pensamento de Bergson," *Movimento Brasileiro* 1, no. 1 (1928): 6.

13. Monzó, "El individuo y la experiencia colectiva," sec 2, 1.

14. Sandrini quoted in *Ciclo retrospectivo: Luis Sandrini*, handout (Buenos Aires: Museo del Cine, August 1977). See also "Felipe 'Cachuso' Sandrini," in Mariano Calistro et al., *Reportaje al cine argentino: Los pioneros del sonoro* (Buenos Aires: America Norildis, 1978), 152.

15. The sainete was a popular genre that drew on the traditions of the *género chico*, the zarzuela, and the grotesque. See Domingo Di Núbila, *Historia del cine argentino* (Buenos Aires: Editorial Schapire, 1959), 95.

16. In the major Romance languages, the fixed do system uses *si* for the seventh syllable and musical note (i.e., Sancte Iohannes). In Germanic and Anglophone countries, the musical scale system uses the English variant of the basic syllables *(ti* instead of *si)*.

17. James Berger, *The Disarticulate: Language, Disability, and the Narratives of Modernity* (New York: NYU Press, 2014), 62.

18. Barbara Johnson, *The Critical Difference: Essays in the Contemporary Rhetoric of Reading* (Baltimore, MD: Johns Hopkins University, 1980), 94.

19. D.N. Rodowick, *The Virtual Life of Film* (Cambridge, MA: Harvard University Press, 2007), 42–45.

20. Experiments with Vitaphone and native sound-on-disc technologies began a few years earlier, with "una veintena de títulos nacionales" (a score of national titles), most notably José Agustín Ferreyra's *Muñequitas Porteñas* (1931). See Claudio España, "El cine sonoro y su expansión," in *Historia del cine argentino*, ed. Jorge Miguel Couselo (Buenos Aires: Centro Editor de América Latina, 1984), 48.

21. Karush, *Culture of Class*, 144.

22. Ibid., 92.

23. There is some uncertainty whether *movietone* in this instance corresponded to the use of the Fox Movietone recording system or the general industry term for the composite sound and action print. Later scholars have taken *movietone* to designate the use of the Fox Movietone system despite its industry-wide use in the period. In Latin America, evidence suggests *movietone* was used contra *vitaphone* to designate sound on film rather than the Fox Movietone recording system. See Charles Felstead, "Types of Sound Records," *Projection Engineering*, February 1932, 23; and "Preguntas y Respuestas," *Cine Mundial*, January 1931, 6.

24. Rodowick, *Virtual Life*, 69.

25. Charles Felstead, "Motion Picture Sound Recording: Chapter VII," *International Photographer*, March 1934, 24–25.

26. See Charles Felstead, "Motion Picture Sound Recording, Chapter IV," *International Photographer*, December 1933, 11; and Michel Chion, *Audio-Vision*, ed. and trans. Claudia Gorbmann (New York: Columbia University Press, 1994), 17.

27. Charles Felstead, "Motion Picture Sound Recording," *International Photographer*, September 1933, 6.

28. Louis Loeffler, "Cutting Movietone Pictures," *American Cinematographer*, June 1929, 19.

29. Claudio España, "El cine sonoro y su expansión," in *Historia del cine argentino,* ed. Jorge Miguel Couselo (Buenos Aires: Centro Editor de América Latina, 1984), 48.

30. Later, major studio director Francisco Mujica was a sound engineer in Sandrini's first film for the studio. See España, "El cine sonoro," 74.

31. José Martínez Suárez recalls that at the time the peso was pegged at just over three pesos to the dollar and the president earned eight hundred pesos monthly. See Domingo Di Núbila, *La época de oro del cine argentino* (Buenos Aires: Ediciones del Jilguero, 1998), 78.

32. España, "El cine sonoro," 47.

33. American John Alton came to Argentina under a six-month contract with Susini in June 1932 and stayed through the late 1930s. His reports to professional organizations to the United States provide one small window onto the technical state of affairs in the film industry. See John Alton, "Motion Picture Production in South America," *International Photographer,* May 1934, 27.

34. Nicolas Poppe, "Sounding Out Temporality in the Argentine Film Musical of the 1930s," *Arizona Journal of Hispanic Cultural Studies* 16, no. 16 (2012): 215.

35. Christian Metz, "Aural Objects," *Yale French Studies* 60 (1980): 24–32; and Michel Chion, *Audio-Vision,* ed. and trans. Claudia Gorbmann (New York: Columbia University Press, 1994), 97.

36. Rick Altman, McGraw Jones, and Sonia Tatroe, "Inventing the Cinema Soundtrack: Hollywood's Multiplane Sound System," in *Music and Cinema,* ed. James Buhler, Caryl Flinn, and David Neumeyer (Hanover, NH: Wesleyan University Press, 2000), 343.

37. Ibid., 347.

38. Ibid., 341.

39. Rick Altman, "Deep-Focus Sound: Citizen Kane and the Radio Aesthetic," *Quarterly Review of Film and Video* 15, no. 3 (1994): 17.

40. Poppe, "Sounding Out Temporality," 216.

41. The tango lyrics caution the approach of a policeman and a pair of eyes that has him under arrest.

42. *Lunfardo* is an Argentine dialect originating at the turn of the twentieth century in the lower classes of Buenos Aires.

43. Pablo Alabarces, *Fútbol y patria: El fútbol y las narrativas de la nación en la Argentina* (Buenos Aires: Prometeo Libros, 2002), 60.

44. Mary Ann Doane, "The Voice in the Cinema: The Articulation of Body and Space," *Yale French Studies* 60 (1980): 38.

45. Di Núbila, *Historia del cine argentino,* 44.

46. John Alton. "News Letter from South America," *International Photographer,* May 1936, 16.

47. For instance, RCA's Photophone variable-area, constant-density system would decline in favor of the Western Electric recording system (and to a lesser degree Fox Movietone system) and its variable-density, constant-area system. Similarly, the need to accommodate for a physical soundtrack on the print led to variations in the size of the image eventually standardized to the Academy ratio

by 1932. See Felstead, "Motion Picture Sound Recording," 7; and "Progress in the Motion Picture Industry," *Journal of the Society of Motion Picture Engineers,* August 1932, 118.

48. H. F. Olson and F. Massa, "On the Realistic Reproduction of Sound with Particular Reference to Sound Motion Pictures," *Journal of the Society of Motion Picture Engineers,* August 1934, 65; and H. G. Tanker. "Multiple-Channel Recording," *Journal of the Society of Motion Picture Engineers,* October 1938, 381.

49. Carl Frederick Nelson, "South America Makes Movies," *American Cinematographer,* January 1941, 14.

50. Soifer's score is an early example of film scoring in a film industry where music was usually reserved for musical numbers and had some loose diegetic connection. See Jorge Finkielman, *The Film Industry in Argentina: An Illustrated Cultural History* (Jefferson, NC: McFarland, 2004), 208.

51. Altman, Jones, and Tatroe, "Inventing the Cinema Soundtrack," 351.

52. Rick Altman, "Moving Lips: Cinema as Ventriloquism." *Yale French Studies* 60 (1980): 74.

53. Ibid., 69.

54. Noel Carroll, "Notes on the Sight Gag," in *Theorizing the Moving Image* (New York: Cambridge University Press, 1996), 150.

55. Celuloide, "El cine: No seamos tontos," *El hogar,* 5 March 1948, 73.

56. Ibid.

57. "Luis Sandrini y el cine nacional: Una alianza que cumple 35 años," *La nación,* 2 April 1968.

58. Carlos Ulanovsky, "Luis Sandrini: Cosquillitas en los dedos, garrotazos en la cabeza," *Satiricon,* 19 July 1973, 25–27.

59. César Tiempo, "Adiós a un ídolo," *Clarín,* 6 July 1980, 30–31.

60. Ulanovsky, "Luis Sandrini, 25–27.

61. Osborne, *Politics of Time,* 10, 30.

62. Ibid., 163, 197.

63. Ibid., 156.

64. Susan Buck-Morss, *The Dialectics of Seeing: Walter Benjamin and the Arcades Project* (Cambridge, MA: MIT Press, 1991), 97.

65. Osborne, *Politics of Time,* 156.

66. "Sandrini: El Quijote del altillo," *Primera plana,* 19 July 1966, 73.

67. Caroline Caffin, *Vaudeville: The Book* (New York: Mitchell Kennerley, 1914; repr., Charleston, SC: Nabu Press, 2012), 135.

68. Ibid., 44.

69. Ibid., 147.

70. Béla Balázs, *Béla Balázs: Early Film Theory: Visible Man and the Spirit of Film,* vol. 10 (New York: Berghahn Books, 2010), 96.

71. Rubén Benitez, "Luis Sandrini," *La nueva provincia,* suplemento fin de semana, 30 December 1979, 3.

72. See Meyerhold's biomechanical acting technique, behaviorist analysis, Taylorist labor management, vitalistic theories, and typage in Lukacsean realism as part of a broader scientific discourse concerning the perils and pleasures

of contingency. This discourse is perhaps best captured by the rise of statistics in opposition to mathematics, a turn from a logic of certainty to a logic of probability.

73. Leo Bersani, "Realism and the Fear of Desire," in *A Future for Asyntax: Character and Desire in Literature* (Boston: Little Brown, 1976), 56.

74. C.A.J., "Reportajes Insolentes: Luis Sandrini: Toco un solo instrumento," *Confirmado*, 28 March 1968.

75. André Bazin, "Charlie Chaplin," in *What Is cinema?*, vol. 1 (Berkeley: University of California Press, 1974), 148.

76. Ibid., 144.

77. Giorgio Agamben, *The Signature of Things*, trans. Luca D'Isanto and Kevin Attell (London: Zone Books, 2009), 20.

78. The clarifying example Agamben uses is the grammatical paradigm. Indeed, for Agamben grammar is built on paradigms. A word used as an example of conjugation or declination is necessarily suspended from its denotative character when it operates as example, constituting instead a more general set. See Agamben, *Signature of Things*, 19.

79. Osvaldo Pellettieri, *De Totó a Sandrini: Del cómico italiano al 'actor nacional' argentino* (Buenos Aires: Galerna, 2001), 18.

80. Karush, *Culture of Class*, 80.

81. Ibid., 119.

82. *Revista semanario, Tal cual*, October 1984, 41.

83. Caffin, *Vaudeville*, 135.

84. György Lukács. "Art and Society," *Mediations* 29, no. 2 (2016): 15.

85. György Lukács, "Art as Misunderstanding," *Mediations* 29, no. 2 (2016): 30.

86. Justus Nieland, *Feeling Modern: The Eccentricities of Modern Life* (Urbana: University of Illinois Press, 2008), 38.

87. Bergson, *Laughter*, 14.

88. Siegfried Kracauer, *Theory of Film: the Redemption of Physical Reality* (Oxford, UK: Oxford University Press, 1997), 95.

89. Miriam Hansen, "Benjamin and Cinema: Not a One-Way Street," *Critical Inquiry* 25, no. 2 (1999): 329.

90. Walter Benjamin, "On the Mimetic Faculty," in *Selected Writings, 1926–1934*, ed. Michael W. Jennings, Howard Eiland, and Gary Smith; trans. Rodney Livingstone et al. (Cambridge, MA: Belknap Press, 1999), 722.

91. Miriam Hansen, "Benjamin, Cinema and Experience: 'The Blue Flower in the Land of Technology,'" *New German Critique* 40 (1987): 195.

92. Georg Lukács, "On Walter Benjamin," *New Left Review* 110 (1978): 86.

93. Ibid., 87.

94. Hansen, "Benjamin and Cinema: Not a One-Way Street," 332.

95. Miriam Hansen, "Room-for-Play: Benjamin's Gamble with Cinema," *October* 109 (2004): 26.

96. Hansen, "Benjamin, Cinema, and Experience: Blue Flower," 217.

97. Giorgio Agamben, "What is a Paradigm?" (presentation, European Graduate School, Saas-Fee, Switzerland, August 2002).

98. Ibid. Agamben evocatively posits that philosophy and poetry both contemplate phenomena in the medium of their seeming; that is, they use examples to discern what is knowable.
99. Lauren Berlant, *Cruel Optimism* (Durham, NC: Duke University Press, 2011), 73.
100. Di Núbila, *Historia del cine argentino*, 252.
101. Berlant, *Cruel Optimism*, 23.
102. Dagmar Barnouw, *Critical Realism: History, Photography, and the Work of Siegfried Kracauer* (Baltimore, MD: Johns Hopkins University Press, 1994), 105.
103. Sandrini quoted in "La importancia de reir," *La careta*, 9 August 1978.
104. Berlant, *Cruel Optimism*, 263.
105. Karush, *Culture of Class*, 80.

CHAPTER 4. FICTIONS OF THE REAL

1. Carlos Ortiz, "De 'Alô, alô carnaval' a 'Tudo azul'," *Folha da manhã*, 24 February 1952, 4.
2. Ibid.
3. Ibid.
4. Carlos Ortiz, "Barnabé, tu és meu," *Folha da manhã*, 4 March 1952, 6.
5. Ibid.
6. Ibid.
7. Paulo Emílio Salles Gomes, *Cinema: Trajetória no subdesenvolvimento* (Rio de Janeiro: Paz e Terra, 1980), 91; Pedro Lima, "Cinelândia: Cinema, indústria real," *O cruzeiro*, 19 May 1962, 76; and Pedro Lima, "Não condenemos a chanchada," *O cruzeiro*, 25 August 1962, 91.
8. Rafael de Luna Freire, "Descascando o abacaxi carnavalesco da chanchada: A invenção de um gênero cinematográfico nacional," *Contracampo* 23 (2001): 70.
9. The marcha is a festive "Afro-Brazilian form with strong accent on the downbeat, influenced in the 1920s by one-step and ragtime." The samba is a song and dance "musically characterized by a 2/4 meter and interlocking syncopated lines in melody." The samba emerged alongside the marcha and soon eclipsed it in popularity by the mid-twentieth century. Chris McGowan and Ricardo Pessanha, *The Brazilian Sound: Samba, Bossa Nova, and the Popular Music of Brazil* (Philadelphia: Temple University Press: 1998), 210–11.
10. Freire, "Descascando," 74.
11. Raymond Williams, *Marxism and Literature* (New York: Oxford University Press, 1977), 162.
12. Lisa Shaw, "The Chanchada and Celluloid Visions: Brazilian Identity in the Vargas Era," *Journal of Iberian and Latin American Studies* 6, no.1 (2000): 70; and Lisa Shaw, "The Brazilian Chanchada of the 1950s and Notions of Popular Identity," *Luso-Brazilian Review* 30, no.1 (2001): 17.
13. Freire, "Descascando," 71.
14. "'Hollywood Party,'" *O cruzeiro*, 25 August 1934, 26.
15. Ibid.

16. Jean Claude Bernardet's generous periodization. See Stephanie Dennison and Lisa Shaw, *Popular Cinema in Brazil: 1930–2001* (Manchester, UK: Manchester University Press, 2004), 26.

17. João Luiz Vieira, "A chanchada e o cinema carioca," in *História do cinema brasileiro*, ed. Fernando Ramos (Sao Paulo: Arte Editora, 1987), 180.

18. Robert Stam, *Tropical Multiculturalism*, (Durham, NC: Duke University Press, 1997), 83.

19. M. Filho, "Contra," *A scena muda*, 5 May 1943, 7.

20. "Filmes em parada: 'Orgulho,'" *A scena muda*, 29 July 1941, 10.

21. "As cotações da semana," *A scena muda*, 6 July 1943, 22.

22. "Revista das estréias," *Cine-Reporter*, 2 November 1946, 2.

23. "As cotações da semana: Ai é que está a coisa," *A scena muda*, 13 May 1947, 33.

24. Sérgio Augusto, *Este mundo é um pandeiro: A chanchada de Getúlio a JK* (São Paulo: Editora Companhia das Letras, 1989), 17.

25. Ismail Xavier, "Chanchada," in *Encyclopedia of American and Caribbean Cultures*, ed. Daniel Balderston, Mike González, and Ana M. López (New York: Routledge, 2000), 325.

26. Cynthia Tompkins, *Experimental Latin American Cinema: History and Aesthetics* (Austin, TX: University of Texas Press, 2013), 5.

27. Georg Simmel, "Money in Modern Culture," in *Simmel on Culture: Selected Writings*, ed. David Frisby and Mike Featherstone (London: SAGE, 1997), 247.

28. Benjamin Cohen, *The Geography of Money* (Ithaca, NY: Cornell University Press, 1998), 28.

29. See the complicated history of the Mexican mint and its relations to Europe and later postindependence United States and the creation of a central bank only after the bellicose phase of the Mexican Revolution, or the continued use of colonial currency in Brazil until the transition to the cruzeiro under the Estado Novo regime of Getúlio Vargas, or the more conventional consolidation of local coins under the aegis of the Argentine peso that coincided with the unification of the country and the rise of the Generación del 80.

30. I borrow the term *aneconomy* from Derrida's account of the gift, where the aneconomical gift is not part of the exchange cycle. Economy risks ungrounding by aneconomy and yet the true gift cannot be considered separately from economy. See Jacques Derrida, *Given Time: I. Counterfeit Money* (Chicago: University of Chicago Press, 1992), 18; Jacques Derrida, "How to Avoid Speaking: Denials," in *Psyche: Inventions of the Other, Volume II*, ed. Peggy Kamuf and Elizabeth Rottenberg (Palo Alto, CA: Stanford University Press, 2008), 308; and Jacques Derrida, *The Gift of Death* (Chicago: University of Chicago Press, 1995), 112.

31. Flora Süssekind, "Escalas e ventríloquos," *Folha de S. Paulo* (2000): 8–23.

32. The João VI crown was actually made in Brazil by the royal jeweler and is the only extant crown among the Portuguese crown jewels.

33. Theodor Adorno, *Minima Moralia*, trans. E.F.N. Jephcott (London: Verso, 2005), 120.

34. Recall *sovereign* also refers to a gold coin minted in England in the early modern period with the (nominal) value of one pound. OED Online, s.v. "sovereign, n. and adj.," accessed December 2016, http://www.oed.com.proxy.lib.umich.edu/view/Entry/185332.

35. Marc Shell, *Money, Language, and Thought: Literary and Philosophic Economies from the Medieval to the Modern Era* (Baltimore, MD: Johns Hopkins University Press, 1993), 35–36.

36. Jacques Derrida, *Specters of Marx*, trans. Peggy Kamuf (New York: Routledge, 1994), 186.

37. Ibid., 193.

38. Marc Shell, *Art and Money* (Chicago: University of Chicago Press, 1995), 10.

39. By the late 1950s, the market rate was nearly three times the official rate. See Jorge Lyra and E. Pacote, "Cinema Nacional: Marco Zero," *O cruzeiro*, 25 May 1957, 11.

40. Carl Fredrick Nelson, "South America Makes Movies," *American Cinematographer*, January 1941, 14.

41. "Permanent Equipment Market," *Motion Picture Herald*, 15 April 1939, 15. Whereas a company like Western Electric had to obtain a separate license for each shipment of American products, equipment companies from Italy, Germany, and France were willing to barter and enter into trade agreements that would circumvent foreign currency restrictions.

42. Fred Marey, "Argentina Pushes U.S. Trade Pact," *Variety*, 20 September 1939, 17.

43. "Arg. Pix Takeover Seen Closer in Bank's 70% Coin Move," *Variety*, 12 May 1948, 15.

44. "Arg. Pix Activity Stepped Up as Coin Situation Stymies Foreign Distribs," *Variety*, 26 May 1948, 15.

45. "Foreign Distribs Await Arg. Thaw," *Variety*, 28 January 1948.

46. "Ease on Argentine Exchange Rules Seen Boon to Foreign Pix Distribs," *Variety*, 30 June 1948, 16; and "Argent. Bans Quotas, Holds Coin," *Variety*, 11 August 1948, 15.

47. "Argentina Still Holds Pix Funds," *Variety*, 21 July 1948, 17.

48. For instance, Paulista studios like Vera Cruz garnered support from the Banco do Estado (State Bank) and the Comissão Estadual de Cinema (State Commission of Cinema). After 1955, São Paulo's mayor Lino de Matos created a Fundo de Auxílio ao Cinema Paulista (Auxiliary Fund for Paulista Cinema) funded through minor fees added to ticket prices (Cr$0,50 for regular films, Cr$1,00 for Cinemascope films. See Jorge Lyra and E. Pacote, "Cinema nacional: Marco zero," *O cruzeiro*, 25 May 1957, 12.

49. Lyra and Pacote, "Cinema nacional," 9.

50. Ibid.

51. As a frame of reference, the exchange rate in May 1957 was roughly Cr$74 cruzeiros per US$1, so the censorship fee was less than 1 ¢ per meter and the customs fee was roughly $1 per kilogram. Compare this to the Mexican example, which charged $2.54 per kilogram of print copies and another $11.56

for every three hundred meters of a feature-length film. See Lyra and Pacote, "Cinema nacional," 10.

52. Lyra and Pacote, "Cinema nacional," 11.

53. Ibid.

54. However, the literature suggests that the more powerful players in the domestic film market often had easier access to foreign currency at the official exchange rate and curried favor with different regulatory agencies, particularly with regard to censorship. See Lyra and Pacote, "Cinema nacional," 12.

55. "Ibanez Filho (entre as beldades) 'Vamos ter filmes de classe em breve,'" *O cruzeiro*, 6 May 1961, 61.

56. J. Arnaldo, "Será que agora vai mesmo?," *A scena muda*, 24 February 1948, 2.

57. Cinédia also produced comedies for mid-year release outside the Carnaval holiday window. These films (e.g., *Bonequinha de seda* and *O jovem tataravô*) were often adaptations of popular theater and featured fewer musical numbers, produced with less coordination across media.

58. Dennison and Shaw, *Popular Cinema in Brazil*, 48.

59. "O estudio de Sonofilms," *A noite*, 27 January 1939, 5.

60. Rafael de Luna Freire, "Da geração de eletricidade aos divertimentos elétricos: A trajetória empresarial de Alberto Byington Jr. antes da produção de filmes," *Estúdios históricos* 26, no.51 (2013): 121.

61. Premiering at the Metro meant accepting the Hollywood studio's terms, so that the film was barred from circulating elsewhere until two months after its debut at the Metro. After a February premiere in Metro theaters in Rio de Janeiro and São Paulo, the film did not screen elsewhere until May 1939.

62. The Caymmi number was chosen because the rights to the studio's original choice, the Ary Barroso samba "Na baixa do sapateiro," were too expensive.

63. See João Luiz Vieira, "Industrialização e cinema de estúdio no Brasil: A 'Fábrica' Atlântida," Centro de Pesquisadores do Cinema Brasileiro, www.cpcb.org.br/artigos/industrializacao-e-cinema-de-estudio-no-brasil-a-fabrica-atlantida.

64. In Máximo Barro, *Moacyr Fenelon e a criação de Atlântida* (São Paulo: SESC São Paulo, 2006), 46.

65. José Inácio de Melo Souza, *Imagens do passado: São Paulo e Rio de Janeiro nos primórdios do cinema* (São Paulo: SENAC, 2004), 86; and Bernadette Lyra, "A emergência de gênero no cinema brasileiro: Do primeiro cinema às chanchadas e pornochanchadas," *Capa* 6, no. 11 (2007): 156.

66. Afrânio Mendes Catani and José Inácio de Melo, *A chanchada no cinema brasileiro* (São Paulo: Brasiliense, 1983), 50–52.

67. Vieira, "A chanchada e o cinema carioca," 160.

68. This principle of proportionality was unlike the more widespread measures implemented in other Latin American and European countries that required exhibition of domestic films for a certain number of days per year. Coupled with caps on the importation of foreign films, these protectionist measures ultimately undermined their own attempts to grow the national film industry. Moreover,

these laws came with little oversight and enforcement. When a representative of the Sindicato dos Produtores (Producers' Guild) in Porto Alegre sought the enforcement of the law and the closure of a local cinema, its owner allegedly said, "Moço, essa lei existe mesmo? Veja se não me vai fazer passar vexame!" (Young man, does that law really exist? You best not make me look bad!). See Lyra and Pacote, "Cinema Nacional," 12.

69. Stephen Kern, *The Culture of Time and Space, 1880–1918: With a New Preface*. (Cambridge, MA: Harvard University Press, 2003), 19.

70. Alex Viany, *Introdução ao cinema brasileiro* (Rio de Janeiro: Ministério da Educação e Cultura, Instituto Nacional do Livro, 1959), 165.

71. The success and availability of other music trends was partly a function of the development of national radio during and after the Estado Novo regime in a country of historical regionalism. For instance, Luis Gonzaga, the King of Baião, was the musical director for the Atlântida chanchadas of 1948, two years after his hit song "Baião" was released in 1946. See Dennison and Shaw, *Popular Cinema in Brazil*, 121n23.

72. Arjun Appadurai, "Commodities and the Politics of Value," in *The Social Life of Things* (Cambridge, UK: Cambridge University Press, 1988), 15, 25.

73. Vieira, "A chanchada e o cinema carioca," 161.

74. Michel Chion, *An Acoulogical Treatise* (Durham, NC: Duke University Press, 2015), 113.

75. Michel Chion, *Audio-vision: Sound on Screen* (New York: Columbia University Press, 1994), 77.

76. Gonzaga was the musical director for the film.

77. "É com este que eu vou," *A noite*, 4 February 1948, 5.

78. Ibid.

79. I borrow this term from Alejandra Laera's study of Argentine literature produced before and during the Argentine depression of the late 1990s. Laera compares Argentine literature from the late twentieth century to the realist novels from the late nineteenth and early twentieth centuries to argue that both cycles of Argentine literature negotiate the circulation of money and process economic crises and their effects on everyday life. See Alejandra Laera, *Ficciones del dinero: Argentina, 1890–2001* (Buenos Aires: Fondo de Cultura Económica, 2014), 72.

80. Shell, *Art and Money*, 4.

81. Ibid., 10.

82. Shell, *Money, Language, and Thought*, 7; and Shell, *Art and Money*, 73.

83. Shell, *Money, Language, and Thought*, 7.

84. See Shell, *Art and Money*, 10, 18, 85; Süssekind, "Escalas e ventríloquos"; and Bernardo Carvalho, "Fiction as Exception," *Luso-Brazilian Review* 47, no. 1 (2010): 1–10.

85. Laera, *Ficciones del dinero*, 20.

86. Ibid., 21.

87. Jacques Derrida, *Given Time: I. Counterfeit Money* (Chicago: University of Chicago Press, 1992), 124, 161.

88. Karl Marx, *The Economic and Philosophic Manuscripts of 1844*, ed. Dirk J. Struik, trans. Martin Milligan (New York: International Publishers, 1964), 169.

89. It should come as no surprise that the classical Hollywood cinema was in fact a metallurgic image with its silver nitrate films—a literal silver screen—which gave way to cellulose acetate film stock after 1948.

90. Catherine Gallagher, "The Rise of Fictionality," *The Novel* 1 (2006): 338.

91. Ibid., 350.

92. Miriam Hansen, *Babel and Babylon: Spectatorship in American Silent Film* (Cambridge, MA: Harvard University Press, 1991), 59.

93. Paul De Man, "The Crisis of Contemporary Criticism," *Arion: A Journal of Humanities and the Classics* 6, no. 1 (1967): 50.

94. Gallagher, "Rise of Fictionality," 345.

95. Philip Rosen, *Change Mummified: Cinema, Historicity, Theory* (Minneapolis: University of Minnesota Press, 2001), 165.

96. Ibid., 166.

97. Gallagher, "Rise of Fictionality," 347.

98. Hansen, *Babel and Babylon,* 57.

99. If the spatial arrangement of classical cinema is a key insight of Hansen's early work, this temporal conflict is also implicit in her later work on the Frankfurt School and its ambivalence toward mass culture. The interpenetration of subject and object meant subjectivity could be manufactured through the capture (commodification) of objects, and yet the very contingency undergirding these techniques of capture as well as the open temporal horizon of reception suggest the (im)possibility of fixing subject-object relations.

100. Friedrich Kittler, *Gramophone, Film, Typewriter* (Palo Alto, CA: Stanford University Press, 1999), 162; and Frederic Jameson, *The Antinomies of Realism* (New York: Verso, 2013).

101. Mary Ann Doane, *The Emergence of Cinematic Time: Modernity, Contingency, the Archive* (Cambridge, MA: Harvard University Press, 2002), 107.

102. The novel form in India in the late nineteenth century developed in distinct ways: novelists in regional languages embraced fictionality while English-language writers turned toward known subjects. See Priya Joshi, *In Another Country: Colonialism, Culture, and the English Novel in India* (New York: Columbia University Press, 2002), 32.

103. Rosen, *Change Mummified,* 179.

104. *Tataravô* was the first Brazilian film with outdoor scenes with sound on location, years after the first sound-on-film feature *In Old Arizona* (Raoul Walsh, 1928) had also featured moments of location sound. See Fernando Morais da Costa, *O som no cinema brasileiro* (Rio de Janeiro: Sete Letras, 2008), 131.

105. Akeley was a minor company that had launched an early hand-crank 35 mm "pancake" camera most notably used in Robert Flaherty's *Tabu* (1931). The original Akeley camera had a revolutionary shutter mechanism that allowed longer shutter speeds and more light into the camera, hence its ideal use for "newsreel and wildlife cinematography." See H. Mario Raimondo-Souto,

Motion Picture Photography: A History, 1891–1960, trans. Herbert Grierson (Jefferson, NC: McFarland, 2007), 30, 150.

106. Judith Butler, *Antigone's Claim: Kinship between Life and Death* (New York: Columbia University Press, 2000), 15.

107. Frederic Jameson, "Marx's Purloined Letter," in *Ghostly Demarcations: A Symposium on Jacques Derrida's 'Spectres de Marx,'* ed. Michael Sprinker (London: Verso, 1999), 39.

108. Rick Altman, *The American Film Musical* (Bloomington: Indiana University Press, 1985), 66–67.

109. Ibid., 70.

110. Hansen, *Babel and Babylon,* 59.

111. Altman, *American Film Musical,* 68.

112. Ibid., 69.

113. We must bear in mind that the film studies and narratological use of diegesis (*diégèse*) is in tension with the original Platonic meaning of diegesis (*diégèsis*) as the other of mimesis. Its latter use refers to a point of view or the construction of a distance from which the reception of the work may take place. See Gérard Genette, *Narrative Discourse Revisited,* trans. Jane E. Lewin (Ithaca, NY: Cornell University Press, 1988), 17–18.

114. Ibid., 88.

115. John Pier, "Metalepsis," in *Handbook of Narratology,* ed. Peter Hühn et al. (Berlin: De Gruyter: 2009), 190.

116. Henri Lefebvre, "The End of Modernity?" in *Key Writings* (New York: Bloomsbury, 2003), 94.

117. Frederic Jameson reminds us that "the fundamental source of abstraction" lies in the money-form, and he raises formal questions about the relationship between the money-form's abstractions and those to be found in cultural texts. See Frederic Jameson, "The Brick and the Balloon: Architecture, Idealism and Land Speculation," *New Left Review,* 228 (1998): 25–26; and David Cunningham, "The Architecture of Money: Jameson, Abstraction and Form," in *The Political Unconscious of Architecture* (New York: Routledge, 2011), 48.

118. Gérard Genette, *Narrative Discourse,* trans. Jane E. Lewin (Ithaca, NY: Cornell University Press, 1980), 236.

119. Paulo Emílio Salles Gomes, *Cinema: Trajetória no subdesenvolvimento* (Rio de Janeiro: Paz e Terra, 1980), 91; and Lúcia de Oliveira Almeida, "Do povo ao público: A crítica de Jean-Claude Bernardet ao cinema de Amácio Mazzaropi," *Boletim de Pesquisa NELIC* 5, no. 6 (2003): 52.

120. João Luiz Vieira and Robert Stam, "Parody and Marginality: The Case of Brazilian Cinema," *Framework* 28 (1985): 22.

121. Ibid., 43.

122. Claire Colebrook, *Irony* (New York: Routledge, 2004), 20.

123. Gilles Deleuze, *The Logic of Sense,* trans. Constantin V. Boundas (London: Continuum, 2004), 141.

124. Comedic tropes would seem particularly well suited to economic form; the homophonic and homonymic are also based on the equivocation of sign and substance. See Shell, *Money, Language, and Thought,* 22.

125. Gallagher, Rise of Fictionality," 359.

126. Laera, *Ficciones del dinero*, 293.
127. Ibid., 345.
128. Deleuze, *Logic of Sense*, 31.
129. Ibid., 141.
130. Colebrook, *Irony*, 134.

CHAPTER 5. COMEDY CIRCULATES CIRCUITOUSLY

1. Mariano Siskind, *Cosmopolitan Desires: Global Modernity and World Literatures in Latin America* (Evanston, IL: Northwestern University Press, 2014), 53.
2. Ibid., 57.
3. Tom Gunning, *D. W. Griffith and the Origins of the American Narrative Film: The Early Years at Biograph* (Urbana: University of Illinois Press, 1991), 67.
4. Ibid.
5. Mary Louise Pratt, *Imperial Eyes: Travel Writing and Transculturation* (Routledge: New York, 1992), 29.
6. Todd quoted in Edwin Schallert, "Hollywood Finally Captures Mexico's Beloved Cantinflas," *Los Angeles Times*, 10 July 1955, D3.
7. Ibid., D1.
8. Hift, "Around the World in 80 Days," review, *Variety*, 24 October 1956, 6.
9. John Belton, *Widescreen Cinema* (Cambridge, MA: Harvard University Press, 1992), 160.
10. Bosley Crowther, "A Bravura Show," review of *Around the World in 80 Days*, *New York Times*, 28 October 1957, 117.
11. Hift, "Around the World," 6.
12. Belton, *Widescreen Cinema*, 162.
13. Cecil Smith, "Mike Todd—Bright Young Man in a Rush," *Los Angeles Times*, 12 May 1957, E1.
14. "Cantinflas's Realty Venture" *Variety*, 20 April 1955, 10.
15. "Caracas," Chatter, *Variety*, 17 July 1957, 62.
16. "Cantinflas Too Classy for Mexican Fans But '80 Days' Prospects Big" *Variety*, 21 September 1960, 15.
17. "O gosto do público paulistano," *Cine-Reporter*, 3 April 1948, 1.
18. Paulo Antonio Paranaguá, *Tradición y modernidad en el cine de América latina* (Mexico, DF: Fondo de Cultura Económica, 2003), 246–47.
19. Susan Stanford Friedman, *Planetary Modernisms: Provocations on Modernity across Time* (New York: Columbia University Press, 2015), 77.
20. Jeff Himpele has similarly invoked anthropological models of cultural circulation in his analysis of indigenization and the performance of circulation to reconstruct the Bolivian mediascape. See Jeff D. Himpele, *Circuits of Culture: Media, Politics, and Indigenous Identity in the Andes* (Minneapolis: University of Minnesota Press, 2007).
21. Friedman, *Planetary Modernisms*, 62.
22. Arjun Appadurai, "How Histories Make Geographies: Circulation and Context in a Global Perspective," *Transcultural Studies* 1, no. 1 (2010): 9.

23. Ibid., 7.
24. Randal Johnson, *The Film Industry in Brazil: Culture and the State* (Pittsburgh, PA: University of Pittsburgh Press, 1987), 70.
25. Angel Rama, "La tecnificación narrativa," *Hispamérica* 10, no. 30 (1981): 30.
26. Renato Ortiz, *Mundialización y cultura*, trans. Elsa Noya (Bogotá: Cultural Libre, 2004), 56.
27. Alberto Moreiras, *The Exhaustion of Difference* (Durham, NC: Duke University Press, 2001), 23.
28. "O proximo lançamento dos filmes mexicanos no Brasil," *Cine-Reporter*, 28 June 1947, 3.
29. "Un gran cine en Rio de Janeiro para películas mexicanas," *Cinema Reporter*, 10 March 1945.
30. Ibid.
31. *A manhã*, movie showtimes, 22 December 1946, 2.
32. Brazil had received a total of fourteen Mexican films in the previous five years. In 1947, the combined distribution of Mexican films across distributors was twenty-one. See "Relação dos filmes lançados em São Paulo de 1 de janeiro a 31 de dezembro de 1947, *Cine-Reporter*, 26 June 1947, 38, 41.
33. *A noite*, movie showtimes, 24 January 1947, 5.
34. *Cine-Reporter*, movie showtimes, 28 June 1948, 40; *O dia*, movie showtimes, 12 March 1947; and *Diario de Pernambuco*, movie showtimes, 28 June 1947.
35. *Cine-Reporter*, movie showtimes, 28 June 1948, 40; and *A noite*, movie showtimes, 11 April 1947, 8.
36. *O dia*, movie showtimes, 25 December 1947, 6; *A noite*, movie showtimes, 25 May 1948, 6; and *Cine-Reporter*, movie showtimes, 24 July 1948, 2.
37. "As cotações da semana," *A scena muda*, 13 May 1947, 33.
38. *Detalle* was released in mid-May 1947 in Rio de Janeiro by DiFilmes before making its way around the country, first to Curitiba in early June and only later to São Paulo in mid-August. Ibid.; *O dia*, 7 June 1947, 6; and *Cine-Reporter*, 18 August 1947, 4.
39. "Relação dos filmes lançados em São Paulo," *Cine-Reporter*, 24 June 1950, 81.
40. The latter released twenty-six pictures in 1950, its first full year of operations. "Quadro comparativo de um trezeno," *Cine-Reporter*, 30 June 1951, 5.
41. Anna Tsing, *Friction: An Ethnography of Global Connection* (Princeton, NJ: Princeton University Press, 2011), 3.
42. Ibid., 4.
43. Miriam Hansen, "The Mass Production of the Senses: Classical Cinema as Vernacular Modernism," *Modernism/Modernity* 6, no. 2 (1999): 66.
44. Ibid., 69.
45. Ortiz, *Mundialización y cultura*, 205.
46. Tsing, *Friction*, 8.
47. Ibid., 10.
48. Henri Lefebvre, *The Production of Space*, vol. 142 (Oxford, UK: Blackwell, 1991), 38.

49. Homi Bhabha, "DissemiNation: Time, Narrative, and the Margins of the Modern Nation," in *Nation and Narration,* ed. Homi Bhabha (New York: Routledge, 1990), 302.

50. "O cinema é uma arte e tambem uma indústria," *A scena muda,* 24 October 1939, 23.

51. Ibid.

52. See José Atilio Mentasti's three-week trip to Rio de Janeiro in August 1940 or Angel Mentasti's trip in January 1940. "O cinema argentino através da palavra de um industrial," *Correio do Paraná,* 26 August 1940, 6; and Oriam, Cinema argentino, *A scena muda,* 23 January 1940, 23.

53. *Correio da manhã,* movie showtimes, 12 November 1938, 8; and Lavrador, "Producção argentina," *O imparcial,* 30 December 1939, 1.

54. *Correio da manhã,* movie showtimes, 13 November 1938, 8.

55. Oriam, Cinema argentino, *Cinearte,* 1 January 1940, 42; and "O cinema é uma arte," *Cinearte,* 24 October 1939, 23.

56. Oriam, Cinema argentino, *Cinearte,* 15 September 1939, 12.

57. Oriam, Cinema argentino, *A scena muda,* 26 March 1940, 27.

58. *Correio paulistano,* 2 July 1939, 6.

59. Her *Puerta cerrada* was released in Rio de Janeiro on August 9, 1939, and in Recife on August 27, but it premiered later in São Paulo on January 1940, in Curitiba on October 12, 1940, and even as late as October 14, 1941, in the rural town of Uberaba, Minas Gerais.

60. Lavrador, "Producção argentina," 1.

61. Oriam, Cinema argentino, *A scena muda,* 23 January 1940, 23.

62. "Notícias diversas," *A scena muda,* 7 May 1940, 28.

63. Oriam, Cinema argentino, *A scena muda,* 26 March 1940, 27.

64. Lumiton had tried its luck before, releasing *Tres anclados en París* (1938) in São Paulo in May 1940 through I.C.I. Ltda. and *Embrujo* (1941) in Rio de Janeiro in late 1941 through Columbia Pictures. See "Tres ilhados em Paris," *A scena muda,* 21 May 1940; and *A scena muda,* 2 September 1941, 30.

65. *A noite,* movie showtimes, 23 April 1942, 4–5.

66. "Filme argentino da Lumiton dirigido por Manuel Romero, distribuido no Rio pela organização CINEAC," *A scena muda,* 5 May 1942, 8.

67. Renato de Alencar, "Hostilidades incompreensíveis contra o cinema argentino," *A scena muda,* 9 June 1942, 3.

68. "Cinema argentino: Por que não podemos fazer o mesmo?" *Fon-Fon,* 6 April 1940, 20–21.

69. Renato de Alencar, "O velho doutor," *A scena muda,* 19 March 1940, 13–20.

70. Alencar, "Hostilidades incompreensíveis," 3.

71. Ibid.

72. Ibid.

73. "A Continental Films fala dos seus programas através das palavras dos srs. João Ferraris e Constantino Basso," *Cine-Reporter,* 28 June 1947, 1.

74. Although Sandrini worked for Argentina Sono Film's first sound film success, he departed in breach of contract after a publicized spat with Mentasti.

75. "A Continental Films fala dos seus programas," 1, 10.

Actual theater listings show a slightly different story with the December 1946 release of his film with Hugo del Carril, *Los dos rivales* (Luis Bayón Herrera, 1944) and the March 1947 release of his second pairing with Olinda Bozán, *La danza de la fortuna* (Luis Bayón Herrera, 1944), both EFA productions. See *Folha da manhã*, movie showtimes, 31 October 1946, 5; *Cine-Reporter*, movie showtimes, 7 December 1946, 2; and *Folha da manhã*, movie showtimes, 8 March 1947, 7

76. "Lançamento no Brasil dos melhores filmes argentinos," *Cine-Reporter*, 26 July 1947, 1.

77. See *Safo, historia de una pasión* (Carlos Hugo Christensen, 1943), *Una mujer sin importancia* (Luis Bayón Herrera, 1945), *A sangre fría* (Daniel Tinayre, 1947), and *Donde mueren las palabras* (Hugo Fregonese, 1946), respectively.

78. The regional constraints on distribution even affected national cinema. Tapuia Filmes' 1948 releases *Folias cariocas* and *O homem que chutou a consciencia* were distributed by the Programa Barone in São Paulo and the Triângulo Mineiro but the Cia. Cinematogáfica Tapuia for the rest of Brazil. See *Cine-Reporter*, 28 August 1948, 5.

79. *A noite*, movie showtimes, 18 April 1949, 5; *O dia*, movie showtimes, 31 July 1946, 6; *Jornal do noticias*, movie showtimes, 1 August 1946, 5.

80. *Cine-Reporter*, UCB advertisement, 3 April 1948, 5.

81. The other entries were *Divorcio de Montevideo* (Manuel Romero, 1939) and *Casamiento en Buenos Aires* (Marriage in Buenos Aires) (Manuel Romero, 1940).

82. Diana Niebylski, *Humoring Resistance: Laughter and the Excessive Body in Latin American Women's Fiction* (Albany, NY: SUNY Press, 2004), 9.

83. Mariano Siskind, *Cosmopolitan Desires*, 62.

84. Lefebvre, *Production of Space*, 38.

85. Ibid., 137.

86. Ibid., 89.

87. Angel Rama, *The Lettered City*, trans. John Charles Chasteen (Durham, NC: Duke University Press, 1996), 16.

88. Henri Lefebvre, *Writings on Cities* 63, no. 2 (Oxford, UK: Blackwell, 1996), 237.

89. Tania Modleski, "The Search for Tomorrow in Today's Soap Operas: Notes on a Feminine Narrative Form," *Film Quarterly* 33, no. 1 (1979): 17.

90. Miriam Hansen, *Babel and Babylon: Spectatorship in American Silent Film* (Cambridge, MA: Harvard University Press, 1991); and Jean Mitry, "Time and Space of the Drama," in *The Aesthetics and Psychology of the Cinema*, trans. Christopher King (Bloomington: Indiana University Press, 1997), 288.

91. "Un homenaje postal a las letras y las tablas," *Pagina 12*, 5 December 2002, http://www.pagina12.com.ar/diario/sociedad/3-13801-2002-12-05.html.

92. Paulina Rento and Stanley Brunn, "Picturing a Nation: Finland on Postage Stamps, 1917–2000," *National Identities* 10, no. 1 (2008): 49–75.

93. In the German translation of his *Theory of Film: The Redemption of Physical Reality*, Kracauer opts for the latter term. See Dagmar Barnouw, *Critical Realism: History, Photography, and Work of Siegfried Kracauer* (Baltimore, MD: Johns Hopkins University, 1994), 54.

94. Geoffrey Bennington, "Postal Politics and the Institution of the Nation," in *Nation and Narration* (New York: Routledge, 1990), 129.

95. "Historia del sello postal," Correo Argentino, www.correoargentino.com.ar/historia-del-sello-postal.

96. Bennington, "Postal Politics," 125.

97. Ana López, "Tears and Desires: Women and Melodrama in the 'Old' Mexican Cinema," in *Mediating Two Worlds: Cinematic Encounters in the Americas*, ed. John King and Ana López (London: BFI Publishing, 1993), 149.

98. Alejandra Laera, *Ficciones del dinero: Argentina, 1890–2001* (Buenos Aires: Fondo de Cultura Económica, 2014), 71.

99. Ariza, "Los estrenos: Los tres berretines," *Cine-Mundial* 19, no 5 (May 1934).

100. Ibid.

101. *Riachuelo* was booked through J.H. Hoffberg Company. See "Argentine Film Booked," *Film Daily*, 27 November 1934, 8; and "Reviews of the New Feature Films: Foreign," *Film Daily*, 8 January 1935, 8.

102. N. Bruski, "Argentine and Brazil Close Studio Deals," *Motion Picture Daily* 40, no. 55 (3 September 1936): 8.

103. Chile Films produced a few films with Argentine talent in the mid-1940s, most notably *Amarga Verdad* (Carlos Borcosque, 1945). "Buenos Aires," *Variety*, 14 November 1945, 55.

104. "Cleo Film in Mexico," *Variety*, 21 August 1946, 24.

105. "Argentina's Film, Radio Stars Look to Mexico, Cuba for Big Salaries," *Variety*, 21 August 1946, 24.

106. Like cinema, postwar radio was shaped by greater capitalization abroad and the government intervention of domestic broadcasters, notably the détente between the national Broadcasters Association and the Peronist regime. For instance, the dispute over taxation of commercial outlets to finance a government-operated network climaxed with Radio Belgrano's government intervention. "Arg. Broadcasters Gird vs. Peron Plans for Govt.-Operated Web," *Variety*, 27 August 1947, 12.

107. "B.A. Talent's Lush Fields Abroad," *Variety*, 10 July 1946, 39.

108. "De plateros a la Quinta Avenida," *Cine-Mundial*, August 1946, 374.

109. "Star Exodus to Mexico, Cuba Forces Argent. Producers to Seek New Faces," *Variety*, 6 November 1946, 22.

110. Sandrini would earn $75,000 per picture for Interamericana. See "Peron Promises Spur Argentine Film Production; Studios Outline Plans," *Variety*, 3 March 1948, 16; and "Argentine Pix Star Pay Soars," *Variety*, 30 June 1948, 16.

111. Sandrini traveled to Madrid in early 1948 for primary shooting for ¡Olé, torero! (1948). See "Arg. Pix Production Active, With Foreign Star Influx Quite Marked," *Variety*, 10 December 1947, 20; and " Buenos Aires," Chatter, *Variety*, 26 May 1948, 55.

112. In the postwar period, Marshall was also working in Argentina and Spain, earning $22,500 per film with Argentina Sono Film and $52,500 per film in Spain. See "Argentine Pix Star Pay Soars," 30 *Variety*, June 1948, 16.

113. Rosa Luxemburg, *The National Question* (New York: Monthly Review, 1976), 162.

114. *El ladrón* was produced in the Azteca Film studios by Alfredo Ripstein Jr. nearly the final film the producer made for Filmex before founding his own Alameda Films in late 1947.

115. Karl Marx, *A Contribution to the Critique of Political Economy*, trans. N. I. Stone (Chicago: Charles Kerr, 1904), 160.

116. Jacques Derrida, *Given Time: I. Counterfeit Money* (Chicago: University of Chicago Press, 1992), 87.

117. Ibid., 97.

118. Ibid., 151.

119. Ibid., 7.

120. Ibid., 133.

121. Benjamin Cohen, *Geography of Money* (Ithaca, NY: Cornell University Press, 1998), 1.

122. Ibid., 21–22.

123. Ibid., 13.

124. Thomas Elsaesser, "The Blockbuster: Everything Connects but Not Anything Goes," in *The End of Cinema As We Know It: American Film in the Nineties*, ed. Jon Lewis (New York: NYU Press, 2002), 14.

125. Ibid.

126. Justin Wyatt, *High Concept: Movies and Marketing in Hollywood* (Austin: University of Texas Press, 2010), 46.

127. "La importancia de reir," *La careta*, 9 August 1978.

128. Alfredo Ripstein Jr. worked for over sixty years as a key figure in postwar Mexican cinema, from Filmex to his own Alameda Film to his son's films and later canonic films such as *Midaq Alley* (Jorge Fons, 1995) and *El crimen del Padre Amaro* (Carlos Carrera, 2002). Additionally, the film's editor and cinematographer, Carlos Savage and Juan Ortiz Ramos, were later Buñuel collaborators in the early 1950s.

129. Minted coins were not known in Egypt until after the conquest of Alexander some three hundred years prior to Cleopatra's reign. In reality, Egypt had long levied taxes on harvest and property and some historians credit the empire's collapse to its burdensome levies. See Mahmoud Ezzamel, *Accounting and Order* (New York: Routledge, 2012), 144.

130. Gareth Williams, *The Mexican Exception: Sovereignty, Police, and Democracy* (New York: Palgrave Macmillan, 2011), 28.

131. Ibid., 73.

132. Gilles Deleuze, *The Fold: Leibniz and the Baroque*, trans. Tom Conley (London: Continuum, 2006), 19.

133. Kaja Silverman, *Male Subjectivity at the Margins* (New York: Routledge, 1992), 93.

134. Kaja Silverman, *The Acoustic Mirror: The Female Voice in Psychoanalysis and Cinema* (Bloomington: Indiana University Press, 1988), 54.

135. Sara Ahmed, *Queer Phenomenology* (Durham, NC: Duke University Press, 2006), 38.

Selected Bibliography

Adorno, Theodor. *Minima Moralia*. Translated by E. F. N. Jephcott. London: Verso, 2005.
Agamben, Giorgio. *The Signature of Things*. Translated by Luca D'Isanto and Kevin Attell. London: Zone Books, 2009.
———. "What Is a Paradigm?" Presentation at the European Graduate School, Saas-Fee, Switzerland, August 2002.
Ahmed, Sara. *Queer Phenomenology*. Durham, NC: Duke University Press, 2006.
Alabarces, Pablo. *Fútbol y patria: El fútbol y las narrativas de la nación en la Argentina*. Buenos Aires: Prometeo Libros, 2002.
Altman, Rick. *The American Film Musical*. Bloomington: Indiana University Press, 1985.
———. "Deep-Focus Sound: Citizen Kane and the Radio Aesthetic." *Quarterly Review of Film and Video* 15, no. 3 (1994): 1–33.
———. "Moving Lips: Cinema as Ventriloquism." *Yale French Studies* 60 (1980): 67–79.
Altman, Rick, McGraw Jones, and Sonia Tatroe. "Inventing the Cinema. Soundtrack: Hollywood's Multiplane Sound System." In *Music and Cinema*, edited by James Buhler, Caryl Flinn, and David Neumeyer, 339–59. Hanover, NH: Wesleyan University Press, 2000.
Amad, Paula. *Counter-Archive: Film, the Everyday, and Albert Khan's Archives de la Planète*. New York: Columbia University Press, 2010.
Appadurai, Arjun. "Commodities and the Politics of Value." In *The Social Life of Things*, edited by Arjun Appadurai, 3–63. Cambridge, UK: Cambridge University Press, 1988.
———. "How Histories Make Geographies: Circulation and Context in a Global Perspective." *Transcultural Studies* 1, no. 1 (2010): 4–13.

Armbrust, Walter. "The Golden Age before the Golden Age: Commercial Egyptian Cinema before the 1960s." In *Mass Mediations: New Approaches to Popular Culture in the Middle East and Beyond,* edited by Walter Armbrust, 292–328. Berkeley, CA: University of California Press, 2000.
Augusto, Sérgio. *Este mundo é um pandeiro: a chanchada de Getúlio a JK.* São Paulo: Editora Companhia das Letras, 1989.
Austin, J. L. *How to Do Things with Words.* London: Oxford University Press, 1962.
Ayala Blanco, Jorge. *Búsqueda del cine mexicano.* Mexico, DF: Editorial Posada, 1986.
Balázs, Béla. *Béla Balázs: Early Film Theory: Visible Man and the Spirit of Film,* vol. 10. New York: Berghahn Books, 2010.
Bao, Weihong. "'A Vibrating Art in the Air': Cinema, Ether, and Propaganda Film Theory in Wartime Chongqing." *New German Critique* 41, no. 2, 122 (2014): 171–88.
Barnouw, Dagmar. *Critical Realism: History, Photography, and the Work of Siegfried Kracauer.* Baltimore, MD: Johns Hopkins University Press, 1994.
Barro, Máximo. *Moacyr Fenelon e a criação de Atlântida.* São Paulo: SESC São Paulo, 2006.
Bartky, Ian. *One Time Fits All: The Campaigns for Global Uniformity.* Palo Alto, CA: Stanford University Press, 2007.
Bazin, André. "Charlie Chaplin." In *What Is Cinema?,* vol. 1, 144–53. Berkeley: University of California Press 1974.
Belton, John. *Widescreen Cinema.* Cambridge, MA: Harvard University Press, 1992.
Benjamin, Walter. "On the Mimetic Faculty." In *Selected Writings, 1926–1934,* edited by Michael W. Jennings, Howard Eiland, and Gary Smith, translated by Rodney Livingstone et al., 720–22. Cambridge, MA: Belknap Press, 1999.
Bennington, Geoffrey. "Postal Politics and the Institution of the Nation." In *Nation and Narration,* edited by Homi Bhabha, 121–37. New York: Routledge, 1990.
Berger, James. *The Disarticulate: Language, Disability, and the Narratives of Modernity.* New York: New York Press, 2014.
Bergson, Henri. *Laughter: An Essay on the Meaning of the Comic.* Translated by Cloudesley Brereton and Fred Rothwell. New York: Macmillan, 1914.
Berlant, Lauren. *Cruel Optimism.* Durham, NC: Duke University Press, 2011.
Berlant, Lauren, and Jordan Greenwald. "Affect in the End Times: A Conversation with Lauren Berlant." *Qui Parle: Critical Humanities and Social Sciences* 20, no. 2 (2012): 71–89.
Bersani, Leo. *A Future for Asyntax: Character and Desire in Literature.* Boston: Little, Brown, 1976.
Bhabha, Homi. "DissemiNation: Time, Narrative, and the Margins of the Modern Nation." In *Nation and Narration,* edited by Homi Bhabha, 291–322. New York: Routledge, 1990.

Bieletto-Bueno, Natalia. "Peladito (Pelado)." In *Celebrating Latino Folklore: An Encyclopedia of Cultural Traditions*, edited by María Herrera-Sobek, 895–98. Santa Barbara, CA: ABC-CLIO, 2012.

Bordwell, David. *Narration in the Fiction Film*. New York: Routledge, 1985.

Bordwell, David, Janet Staiger, and Kristin Thompson. *The Classical Hollywood Cinema: Film Style and Mode of Production to 1960*. New York: Routledge, 1985.

Borge, Jason. *Latin American Writers and the Rise of Hollywood Cinema*. New York: Routledge, 2008.

———. "Replaying Carlitos: Chaplin, Latin American Film Comedy and the Paradigm of Imitation." *Journal of Latin American Cultural Studies* 22, no. 3 (2013): 271–86.

Brooks, Peter. *The Melodramatic Imagination: Balzac, Henry James, Melodrama and the Mode of Excess*. New Haven, CT: Yale University Press, 1976.

Buck-Morss, Susan. *The Dialectics of Seeing: Walter Benjamin and the Arcades Project*. Cambridge, MA: MIT Press, 1991.

Burton-Carvajal, Julianne. "Mexican Melodramas of Patriarchy: Specificity of a Transcultural Form." In *Framing Latin American Cinema: Contemporary Critical Perspectives*, edited by Anne Marie Stock, 186–234. Minneapolis: University of Minnesota Press, 1997.

Butler, Judith. *Antigone's Claim: Kinship Between Life & Death*. New York: Columbia University Press, 2000.

Caffin, Caroline. *Vaudeville: The Book*. New York: Mitchell Kennerley, 1914.

Caimari, Lila. "News from around the World: South American Newspapers in the Era of Submarine Cables." Arthur Aiton Lecture in Latin American History, University of Michigan, Ann Arbor, MI, 12 April 2017.

Carroll, Noel. "Notes on the Sight Gag." In *Theorizing the Moving Image*, 146–58. New York: Cambridge University Press, 1996.

Carvalho, Bernardo. "Fiction as Exception." *Luso-Brazilian Review* 47, no. 1 (2010): 1–10.

Castro-Klarén, Sara. "La crítica literaria feminista y la escritora en América Latina." In *La sartén por el mango*, edited by Patricia Elena González and Eliana Ortega, 27–44. Río Piedras: Puerto Rico: Huracán, 1985.

Castro Ricalde, Maricruz, and Robert McKee Irwin. *El cine mexicano "se impone": Mercados internacionales y penetración cultural en la época dorada*. Mexico, DF: UNAM, 2011.

Chávez, Daniel. "The Eagle and the Serpent on the Screen: The State as Spectacle in Mexican Cinema." *Latin American Research Review* 45, no. 3 (2010): 115–41.

Chion, Michel. *An Acoulogical Treatise*. Durham, NC: Duke University Press, 2015.

———. *Audio-Vision*. Edited and translated by Claudia Gorbmann. New York: Columbia University Press, 1994.

Chow, Rey. *Woman and Chinese Modernity: The Politics of Reading between West and East*. Minneapolis: University of Minnesota Press, 1991.

Cohen, Benjamin. *The Geography of Money*. Ithaca, NY: Cornell University Press, 1998.
Colebrook, Claire. *Irony*. New York: Routledge, 2004.
Connor, Steve. *Dumbstruck: A Cultural History of Ventriloquism*. New York: Oxford University Press, 2000.
Cunningham, David. "The Architecture of Money: Jameson, Abstraction and Form." In *The Political Unconscious of Architecture*, edited by Nadir Lahiji, 37–56. New York: Routledge, 2011.
Curtis, Scott. *The Shape of Spectatorship: Art, Science, and Early Cinema in Germany*. New York: Columbia University Press, 2015.
DeCordova, Richard. *Picture Personalities: The Emergence of the Star System in America*. Champaign: University of Illinois Press, 2001.
Deleuze, Gilles. *The Fold: Leibniz and the Baroque*. Translated by Tom Conley. London: Continuum, 2006.
———. *The Logic of Sense*. Translated by Constantin V. Boundas. London: Continuum, 2004.
Dennison, Stephanie, and Lisa Shaw. *Popular Cinema in Brazil: 1930–2001*. Manchester, UK: Manchester University Press, 2004.
Derrida, Jacques. *Given Time: I. Counterfeit Money*. Chicago: University of Chicago Press, 1992.
———. *Specters of Marx*. Translated by Peggy Kamuf. New York: Routledge, 1994.
De Man, Paul. "The Crisis of Contemporary Criticism." *Arion: A Journal of Humanities and the Classics* 6, no. 1 (1967): 38–57.
Di Núbila, Domingo. *Historia del cine argentine*. Buenos Aires: Editorial Schapire, 1959.
Dimock, Wai-Chee. "Pre-National Time: Novel, Epic, Henry James." *Henry James Review* 24, no. 3 (2003): 215–24.
Doane, Mary Ann. *The Emergence of Cinematic Time: Modernity, Contingency, Archive*. Cambridge, MA: Harvard University Press, 2002.
———. "Film and the Masquerade: Theorising the Female Spectator." *Screen* 23, no. 3–4 (1982): 74–88.
———. "The Voice in the Cinema: The Articulation of Body and Space." *Yale French Studies* 60 (1980): 33–50.
Eaton, Mick. "Laughter in the Dark." *Screen* 22, no. 2 (1981): 21–28.
Ellis, John. "Made in Ealing." *Screen* 16, no. 1 (1975): 78–127.
Elsaesser, Thomas. "The Blockbuster: Everything Connects but Not Anything Goes." In *The End of Cinema as We Know It: American Film in the Nineties*, edited by Jon Lewis, 11–22. New York: NYU Press, 2002.
———. "Tales of Sound and Fury: Observations on the Family Melodrama." In *Home Is Where the Heart Is: Studies in Melodrama and the Woman's Film*, edited by Christine Gledhill, 43–69. London: BFI, 1987.
———. "What Might We Mean by Media History?" *Geschiedenis, Beeld en Geluid* 28 (1994): 19–25.
España, Claudio. "El cine sonoro y su expansion." In *Historia del cine argentino*, edited by Jorge Miguel Couselo, 47–88. Buenos Aires: Centro Editor de América Latina, 1984.

Esterrich, Carmelo, and Angel M. Santiago-Reyes. "From the Carpa to the Screen: The Masks of Cantinflas." *Studies in Latin American Popular Culture* 17 (1998): 33–50.

Falicov, Tamara L. "Argentine Cinema and the Construction of National Popular Identity, 1930–1942." *Studies in Latin American Popular Culture* 17 (1998): 61–78.

Finkielman, Jorge. *The Film Industry in Argentina: An Illustrated Cultural History*. Jefferson, NC: McFarland, 2004.

Fiske-Harrison, Alexander. *Into the Arena: The World of the Spanish Bullfight*. London: Profile Books, 2011.

Foucault, Michel. *Power/Knowledge*. New York: Pantheon Books, 1980.

Gabara, Esther. *Errant Modernism: The Ethos of Photography in Mexico and Brazil*. Durham, NC: Duke University Press, 2008.

Gaines, Jane. *Contested Culture: The Image, the Voice, and the Law*. Chapel Hill: University of North Carolina Press, 2000.

Gallagher, Catherine, "The Rise of Fictionality." *The Novel* 1 (2006): 336–63.

Gallo, Ricardo. *La radio: Ese mundo tan sonoro*. Buenos Aires: Corregidor, 1991.

García Riera, Emilio. *Breve historia del cine mexicano. Primer siglo: 1897–1997*. Mexico, DF: Ediciones Mapa, 1998.

Genette, Gérard. *Narrative Discourse*. Translated by Jane E. Lewin. Ithaca, NY: Cornell University Press, 1980.

———. *Narrative Discourse Revisited*. Translated by Jane E. Lewin. Ithaca, NY: Cornell University Press, 1988.

Gerow, Aaron. *Visions of Japanese Modernity: Articulations of Cinema, Nation, and Spectatorship, 1895–1925*. Berkeley: University of California Press 2010.

Getino, Octavio. *Cine argentino: Entre lo posible y lo deseable*. Buenos Aires: Ediciones Ciccus, 1998.

Guerra, Lucía. "Las sombras de la escritura: Hacia una teoría de la producción literaria de la mujer latinoamericana." In *Cultural and Historical Grounding for Hispanic and Luso-Brazilian Feminist Literary Criticism*, 127–64. Minneapolis, MN: Institute for the Study of Ideologies and Literature, 1989.

Gunning, Tom. *D. W. Griffith and the Origins of the American Narrative Film: The Early Years at Biograph*. Urbana: University of Illinois Press, 1991.

Hansen, Miriam. *Babel and Babylon: Spectatorship in American Silent Film*. Cambridge, MA: Harvard University Press, 1991.

———. "Benjamin and Cinema: Not a One-Way Street." *Critical Inquiry* 25, no. 2 (1999): 306–43.

———. "Benjamin, Cinema and Experience: 'The Blue Flower in the Land of Technology.'" *New German Critique* 40 (1987): 179–224.

———. "The Mass Production of the Senses: Classical Cinema as Vernacular Modernism." *Modernism/Modernity* 6, no. 2 (1999): 59–77.

———. "Room-for-Play: Benjamin's Gamble with Cinema," *October* 109 (2004): 3–45.

———. "Vernacular Modernism: Tracking Cinema on a Global Scale." In *World Cinemas, Transnational Perspectives*, edited by Natasha Durovicova and Kathleen Newman, 287–314. New York: Routledge, 2009.

Hayot, Eric. *On Literary Worlds.* New York: Oxford University Press, 2012.
Heath, Stephen. "Narrative Space." *Screen* 17, no. 3 (1976): 68–112.
Hennefeld, Maggie. "Slapstick Comediennes in Transitional Cinema: Between Body and Medium," *Camera Obscura: Feminism, Culture, and Media Studies* 29, no. 2, 86 (2014): 85–117.
Himpele, Jeff D. *Circuits of Culture: Media, Politics, and Indigenous Identity in the Andes.* Minneapolis: University of Minnesota Press, 2007.
Jameson, Frederic, *The Antinomies of Realism.* New York: Verso, 2013.
———. "The Brick and the Balloon: Architecture, Idealism and Land Speculation," *New Left Review* 228 (1998): 25–46
———. "Marx's Purloined Letter." In *Ghostly Demarcations: A Symposium on Jacques Derrida's 'Spectres de Marx,'* edited by Michael Sprinker, 26–67. London: Verso, 1999.
Johnson, Barbara. *The Critical Difference: Essays in the Contemporary Rhetoric of Reading.* Baltimore, MD: Johns Hopkins University Press, 1980.
Johnson, Randal. *The Film Industry in Brazil: Culture and the State.* Pittsburgh, PA: University of Pittsburgh Press, 1987.
Joshi, Priya. *In Another Country: Colonialism, Culture, and the English Novel in India.* New York: Columbia University Press, 2002.
Karush, Matthew. *Culture of Class: Radio and Cinema in the Making of a Divided Argentina, 1920–1946.* Durham, NC: Duke University Press, 2012.
Kern, Stephen. *The Culture of Time and Space, 1880–1918: With a New Preface.* Cambridge, MA: Harvard University Press, 2003.
Kittler, Friedrich. *Gramophone, Film, Typewriter.* Palo Alto, CA: Stanford University Press, 1999.
Kracauer, Siegfried. *Theory of Film: The Redemption of Physical Reality.* Oxford, UK: Oxford University Press, 1997.
Krutnik, Frank. "The Clown-Prints of Comedy." *Screen* 25, no. 4–5 (1984): 50–59.
Laera, Alejandra. *Ficciones del dinero: Argentina, 1890–2001.* Buenos Aires: Fondo de Cultura Económica, 2014.
Lahr-Vivaz, Elena. *Mexican Melodrama: Film and Nation from the Golden Age to the New Wave.* Tucson: University of Arizona Press, 2016.
Lefebvre, Henri. "The End of Modernity?" In *Key Writings*, 93–95. New York: Bloomsbury, 2003.
———. *Introduction to Modernity: Twelve Preludes, September 1959–May 1961.* New York: Verso, 1995.
———. *The Production of Space,* vol. 142. Oxford, UK: Blackwell, 1991.
———. *Writings on Cities,* vol. 63, no. 2. Oxford, UK: Blackwell, 1996.
López, Ana. "Early Cinema and Modernity in Latin America." *Cinema Journal* 40, no. 1 (2000): 48–78.
———. "The Radiophonic Imaginary in Latin American Transitional Cinema and Transmedial Relations." Conference presentation at Universidad Carlos III de Madrid, Madrid, Spain, 9 November 2012.
———. "Tears and Desires: Women and Melodrama in the 'Old' Mexican Cinema." In *Mediating Two Worlds: Cinematic Encounters in the Americas,* edited by John King and Ana López, 147–63. London: BFI Publishing, 1993.

Lukács. György. "Art and Society." *Mediations* 29, no. 2 (2016): 7–17.
———. "Art as Misunderstanding." *Mediations* 29, no. 2 (2016): 19–45.
———. "On Walter Benjamin," *New Left Review* 110 (1978): 83–92.
Luna Freire, Rafael de. "Da geração de eletricidade aos divertimentos elétricos: A trajetória empresarial de Alberto Byington Jr. antes da produção de filmes." *Estúdios Históricos* 26, no. 51 (2013): 113–31.
———. "Descascando o abacaxi carnavalesco da chanchada: A invenção de um gênero cinematográfico nacional." *Contracampo* 23 (2011): 66–85.
Luxemburg, Rosa. *The National Question*. New York: Monthly Review, 1976.
Lyra, Bernadette. "A emergência de gêneros no cinema brasileiro: Do primeiro cinema às chanchadas e pornochanchadas." *Capa* 6, no.11 (2007): 141–59.
Majumdar, Neepa. *Wanted Cultured Ladies Only!: Female Stardom and Cinema in India, 1930–1950s*. Champaign: University of Illinois Press 2009.
Marshall, Niní, and Salvador D'Anna. *Mis Memorias*. Buenos Aires: Editorial Moreno, 1985.
Marx, Karl. *A Contribution to the Critique of Political Economy*. Translated by N.I. Stone. Chicago: Charles Kerr, 1904.
———. *The Economic and Philosophic Manuscripts of 1844*. Edited by Dirk J. Struik. Translated by Martin Milligan. New York: International Publishers, 1969.
Medina de la Serna, Rafael. "Sorrows and Glories of Comedy." In *Mexican Cinema*, edited by Paulo Antonio Paranaguá, translated by Ana M. López, 163–70. London: BFI Books, 1995.
Melo Souza, José Inácio de. *Imagens do passado: São Paulo e Rio de Janeiro nos primórdios do cinema*. São Paulo: SENAC, 2004.
Mendes Catani, Afrânio, and José Inácio de Melo Souza. *A chanchada no cinema brasileiro*. São Paulo: Brasiliense, 1983.
Metz, Christian. "Aural Objects." *Yale French Studies* 60 (1980): 24–32.
Mitry, Jean. *The Aesthetics and Psychology of the Cinema*. Translated by Christopher King. Bloomington: Indiana University Press, 1997.
Mizejewski, Linda. *Pretty/Funny: Women Comedians and Body Politics*. Austin: University of Texas Press, 2014.
Modleski, Tania. "The Search for Tomorrow in Today's Soap Operas: Notes on a Feminine Narrative Form." *Film Quarterly* 33, no. 1 (1979): 12–21.
Monsiváis, Carlos. "All the People Came and Did Not Fit onto the Screen: Notes on the Cinema Audience in Mexico," In *Mexican Cinema*, edited by Paulo Antonio Paranaguá, translated by Ana M. López, 145–51. London: BFI Books, 1995.
———. *Antología personal*. San Juan: Universidad de Puerto Rico, 2009.
———. "Cantinflas and Tin Tan: Mexico's Greatest Comedians." In *Mexico's Cinema: A Century of Film and Filmmakers*, edited by Joanne Hershfield and David R. Maciel, 49–80. Wilmington, DE: Scholarly Resources, 1999.
———. "Cantinflas: That's the Point!" In *Mexican Postcards*, translated by John Kraniauskas, 88–105. New York: Verso, 1997.
———. "Mexican Cinema: Of Myths and Mystifications." In *Mediating Two Worlds: Cinematic Encounters in the Americas*, edited by John King and Ana López, 139–46. London: BFI Publishing, 1993.

Mora, Carl. *Mexican Cinema: Reflections of a Society, 1896–1988*. Berkeley: University of California Press 1989.
Morais da Costa, Fernando. *O som no cinema brasileiro*. Rio de Janeiro: Sete Letras, 2008.
Moreiras, Alberto. *The Exhaustion of Difference*. Durham, NC: Duke University Press, 2001.
Moretti, Franco. "Planet Hollywood." *New Left Review* 9 (2001): 90–101.
Mraz, John. *Looking for Mexico: Modern Visual Culture and National Identity*. Durham, NC: Duke University Press, 2009.
Murray, Susan. *Hitch Your Antenna to the Stars: Early Television and Broadcast Stardom*. New York: Routledge, 2013.
Navitskli, Rielle. *Public Spectacles of Violence: Sensational Cinema and Journalism in Early Twentieth-Century Mexico and Brazil*. Durham, NC: Duke University Press, 2017.
Niebylski, Diana. *Humoring Resistance: Laughter and the Excessive Body in Latin American Women's Fiction*. Albany, NY: SUNY Press, 2004.
Nieland, Justus. *Feeling Modern: The Eccentricities of Modern Life*. Urbana: University of Illinois Press, 2008.
Noble, Andrea. *Mexican National Cinema*. New York: Routledge, 2005.
Oliveira Almeida, Lúcia de. "Do povo ao público: A crítica de Jean-Claude Bernardet ao cinema de Amácio Mazzaropi." *Boletim de Pesquisa NELIC* 5, no. 6 (2003): 45–57.
Osborne, Peter. *The Politics of Time: Modernity and the Avant-Garde*. New York: Verso, 1995.
Oroz, Silvia. *Melodrama: O cinema de lágrimas da América Latina*. Rio de Janeiro: Funarte, 1999.
Ortiz, Renato. *Mundialización y cultura*. Translated by Elsa Noya. Bogotá: Cultural Libre, 2004.
Paranaguá, Paulo Antonio. *Tradición y modernidad en el cine de América Latina*. Mexico, DF: Fondo de Cultura Económica, 2003.
Peirce, Charles Sanders. *The Essential Peirce*, vol. 1, edited by Nathan Houser and Christian Kloesel. Bloomington: Indiana University Press, 1992.
Pellettieri, Osvaldo. *De Totó a Sandrini: Del cómico italiano al 'actor nacional' argentino*. Buenos Aires: Galerna, 2001.
Pilcher, Jeffrey. *Cantinflas and the Chaos of Mexican Modernity*. Wilmington, DE: Scholarly Resources, 2001.
Podalsky, Laura. *The Politics of Affect and Emotion in Contemporary Latin American Cinema*. New York: Palgrave Macmillan, 2011.
Poppe, Nicolas. "Sounding Out Temporality in the Argentine Film Musical of the 1930s." *Arizona Journal of Hispanic Cultural Studies* 16, no. 16 (2012): 211–26.
Portilla, Jorge. *Fenomenología del relajo, y otros ensayos*. Mexico, DF: Fondo de Cultura Económica, 1966.
Pratt, Mary Louise. *Imperial Eyes: Travel Writing and Transculturation*. Routledge: New York, 1992.
Quinziano, Pascual. "La comedia: Un género impuro." In *Cine argentino: La otra historia*, edited by Sergio Wolfe. Buenos Aires: Letra Buena, 1994.

Raimondo-Souto, H. Mario. *Motion Picture Photography: A History, 1891–1960*. Translated by Herbert Grierson. Jefferson, NC: McFarland, 2007.
Rama, Angel. *The Lettered City*. Translated by John Charles Chasteen. Durham, NC: Duke University Press, 1996.
———. "La tecnificación narrativa." *Hispamérica* 10, no. 30 (1981): 29–82.
Ramirez Berg, Charles. *The Classical Mexican Cinema: The Poetics of the Exceptional Mexican Films*. Austin: University of Texas Press, 2015.
Ramos, Samuel. *Profile of Man and Culture in Mexico*. Translated by Peter G. Earle. Austin: University of Texas Press, 1962.
Rodowick, D.N. "Subjects without Skin." *New German Critique* 41, no. 2 (2014): 14–16.
———. *The Virtual Life of Film*. Cambridge, MA: Harvard University Press, 2007.
Rosen, Philip. *Change Mummified: Cinema, Historicity, Theory*. Minneapolis: University of Minnesota Press, 2001.
Rudlin, John. *Commedia dell'Arte: An Actor's Handbook*. New York: Routledge, 1994.
Salles Gomes, Paulo Emílio. *Cinema: Trajetória no subdesenvolvimento*. Rio de Janeiro: Paz e Terra, 1980.
Seidman, Steve. *Comedian Comedy: A Tradition in Hollywood Film*. Ann Arbor, MI: UMI Research Press, 1981.
Shaw, Lisa. "The Brazilian Chanchada of the 1950s and Notions of Popular Identity." *Luso-Brazilian Review* 30, no.1 (2001): 17–30.
———. "The Chanchada and Celluloid Visions Brazilian Identity in the Vargas Era." *Journal of Iberian and Latin American Studies* 6, no.1 (2000): 63–74.
Shell, Marc. *Art and Money*. Chicago: University of Chicago Press, 1995.
———. *Money, Language, and Thought: Literary and Philosophic Economies from the Medieval to the Modern Era*. Baltimore, MD: Johns Hopkins University Press, 1993.
Silverman, Kaja. *The Acoustic Mirror: The Female Voice in Psychoanalysis and Cinema*. Bloomington: Indiana University Press, 1988.
———. *Male Subjectivity at the Margins*. New York: Routledge, 1992.
Simmel, Georg. "Money in Modern Culture." In *Simmel on Culture: Selected Writings*, edited by David Frisby and Mike Featherstone, 243–54. London: SAGE, 1997.
Singer, Ben. *Melodrama and Modernity: Early Cinema and its Sensational Contexts*. New York: Columbia University Press, 2001.
Siskind, Mariano. *Cosmopolitan Desires: Global Modernity and World Literatures in Latin America*. Evanston, IL: Northwestern University Press, 2014.
Slowik, Michael. *After the Silents: Hollywood Film Music in the Early Sound Era, 1926–1934*. New York: Columbia University Press, 2014.
Spivak, Gayatri Chakravorty. "Echo." *New Literary History* 24, no. 1 (1993): 17–43.
Stam, Robert. *Tropical Multiculturalism*. Durham, NC: Duke University Press, 1997.
Stanford Friedman, Susan. *Planetary Modernisms: Provocations on Modernity across Time*. New York: Columbia University Press, 2015.

Stavans, Ilan. "The Riddle of Cantinflas: On Laughter and Revolution." *Transition* 67 (1995): 22–46.
Stewart, Garret. "Modern Hard Times: Chaplin and the Cinema of Self-Reflection." *Critical Inquiry* 3, no. 2 (1976): 295–314.
Süssekind, Flora. "Escalas e ventríloquos." *Folha de São Paulo* (2000): 8–23.
Tompkins, Cynthia. *Experimental Latin American Cinema: History and Aesthetics*. Austin: University of Texas Press, 2013.
Tsing, Anna. *Friction: An Ethnography of Global Connection*. Princeton, NJ: Princeton University Press, 2011.
Turvey, Malcolm. "Comedic Modernism." *October* 160 (2017): 5–29.
Viany, Alex. *Introdução ao cinema brasileiro*. Rio de Janeiro: Ministério da Educação e Cultura, Instituto Nacional do Livro, 1959.
Vieira, João Luiz. "A chanchada e o cinema carioca." In *História do cinema brasileiro*, edited by Fernão Ramos, 131–87. São Paulo: Arte Editora, 1987.
———. "Industrialização e cinema de estúdio no Brasil: A 'Fábrica' Atlântida." Centro de Pesquisadores do Cinema Brasileiro. n.d. www.cpcb.org.br/artigos/industrializacao-e-cinema-de-estudio-no-brasil-a-fabrica-atlantida.
Vieira, João Luiz, and Robert Stam. "Parody and Marginality: The Case of Brazilian Cinema." *Framework* 28 (1985): 20–49.
Williams, Daryle. *Culture Wars in Brazil: The First Vargas Regime, 1930–1945*. Durham, NC: Duke University Press, 2001.
Williams, Gareth. "Comrades, There Are Moments in Life That Are Truly Momentary": Cantinflas and the Administration of Public Matters." In *Humor in Latin American Cinema*, edited by Juan Poblete and Juana Suárez, 47–66. New York: Palgrave Macmillan, 2016.
———. *The Mexican Exception: Sovereignty, Police, and Democracy*. New York: Palgrave Macmillan, 2011.
Williams, Linda. "Melodrama Revised." In *Refiguring American Film Genres: History and Theory*, edited by Nick Browne, 42–88. Berkeley: University of California Press 1998.
———. *Playing the Race Card : Melodramas of Black and White from Uncle Tom to O.J. Simpson*. Princeton, NJ: Princeton University Press, 2001.
Williams, Raymond. *Marxism and Literature*. New York: Oxford University Press, 1977.
Wyatt, Justin. *High Concept: Movies and Marketing in Hollywood*. Austin: University of Texas Press, 2010.
Xavier, Ismail. "Chanchada." In *Encyclopedia of American and Caribbean Cultures*, edited by Daniel Balderston, Mike González, and Ana M. López, 325. New York: Routledge, 2000.
Zarzosa, Agustín. "Melodrama and the Modes of the World." *Discourse* 32, no. 2 (2010): 236–55.
Zhen, Zhang. *An Amorous Screen of the Silver Screen: Shanghai Cinema, 1896–1937*. Chicago: University of Chicago Press, 2005.

Index

Note: Page numbers followed by *f* indicate a figure.

¡A volar joven! (Delgado), 50–52, 53f, 204
Agamben, Giorgio, 148, 249n78, 250n98
Ahí está el detalle (Bustillo Oro), 19, 25–34, 37, 51, 57, 159, 204
alemanismo, 23, 36
Alô, alô Brasil! (Downey), 168–69, 173
Alô, alô carnival (Macedo), 153, 161–63, 196, 173
Altman, Rick, 90, 126, 154, 184, 188
Amadori, Luis César, 77–78, 80
analytic editing, 122, 187
Appadurai, Arjun, 198–200
Argentina, 19, 137, 160, 165, 247n33; centennial of, 215; early sound film production in, 71, 121, 123, 131, 207; film market in, 74; film practices in, 76; film stardom in, 73, 81; foreign narratives in, 240n43; industrial filmmaking in, 72, 82; infrastructure of, 17; popularity of Cantinflas in, 37; postage stamps in, 219–20; radio personality in, 82; reception of Mexican cinema in, 40; standardized time in, 113, 245n4; transition cinema in, 83. *See also* Argentine cinema
Argentina Sono Film, 69, 75, 77, 80–82, 85, 87, 94, 99, 108, 124–25, 131, 206–208, 210–12, 222, 259n74, 261n112

Argentine cinema, 19, 70, 83–84, 117, 240n44; in Brazil, 209–11; circulation of, 206; golden age of, 68–69, 73, 120; wartime decline of, 165, 202. *See also* Estudios Filmadores Argentinos (EFA)
Arias, Pepe, 18, 206, 222, 245n8
Around the World in 80 Days (Anderson), 36, 192–96, 213
atelicity, 199, 219–21, 227, 229
Atlântida studios, 20, 154, 160, 163, 167, 169–72, 174–76, 178, 212, 254n71. *See also carnavalescos; chanchadas*
audition, 88, 92, 104, 110, 127–29. *See also* sound; vision
Ávila Camacho, Manuel, 23, 35–36

baiao, 172, 175
Banana da terra (Costa), 158, 169
Barnabé tu és meu (Burle), 154
Bartolo tenía una flauta (Botta), 111–14, 116, 149–50
Bayón Herrera, Luis, 75–76
Bennington, Geoffrey, 219–20
Bergson, Henri, 15–16, 115–16, 145, 245n12. *See also* laughter
Bernardet, Jean-Claude, 189, 251n16
Bonequinha de seda (Vianna), 168, 253n57
Bordwell, David, 44–45
brasilidade, 155–56

273

274 | Index

Brazil, 17, 162, 222, 260n78; Argentine cinema in, 197, 199, 206–11; early cinema of, 8, 113, 156, 158, 169–70 (*see also* Brazilian cinema); film criticism in, 154; foreign films in, 156, 158–59; Mexican cinema in, 199, 201–204, 258n32; *modernismo* in, 5; monetary policy in, 20, 159–61, 163–67, 177–80, 190 (*see also* monetary sign)

Brazilian cinema, 20, 153–54, 156, 166, 171, 181, 202. See also *Alô, alô Brasil!; Alô, alô carnival;* Atlântida studios; *Carnaval Atlântida; Carnaval no fogo; carnavalescos; chanchada*

Caffin, Caroline, 140, 144

Cándida (Bayón Herrera), 69, 75, 208

Cantinflas (Mario Moreno), 1–2, 18–19, 22–38, 40–43, 46–52, 53f, 55–57, 60–67, 96, 118, 139–40, 159, 192–93, 195–96; circulation of, 37–38, 41, 203–204; as lumpen figure, 23, 36; Mexicanness of, 38; reception of, 41, 48, 201. See also *¡A volar joven!; Ahí está el detalle; Around the World in 80 Days; cantinflismo; El gendarme desconocido; Gran Hotel; Ni sangre ni arena; peladito; pelado; Pepe; Los tres mosqueteroscantinfleo,* 34, 43

cantinflismo, 19, 25–26, 32, 34, 43, 51, 54, 56–57, 59, 65–66

capitalism, 10–11, 24, 34, 59, 115, 178, 205, 223

Carnaval, 153, 167–69, 171–79, 253n57. See also marchas; samba

Carnaval Atlântida (Burle), 170f, 187

Carnaval no fogo (Macedo), 172, 176

carnavalescos, 20, 153–54, 161, 167, 171–72, 174

carpas, 23, 30, 32

La casa de Quirós (Moglia Barth), 117–19

Casamiento en Buenos Aires (Romero), 69, 76, 216, 260n81

Castro Ricalde, Maricruz, 37–39, 44

Caymmi, Dorval, 169, 253n62

chanchada (Brazilian musical comedy), 20, 153–64, 167, 171–72, 174, 176–78, 184–85, 188–91, 204, 254n71; as pejorative term, 156, 164. See also Brazil: monetary policy in

Chaplin, Charles, 22–23, 115, 139, 143, 147–48, 204

character comedian, 140–41

Cinédia studios, 153, 158, 161, 163–64, 167–69, 171–74, 181, 253n57

circulation, 5, 7, 13–14, 18, 20–21, 40, 58, 196–201, 205, 221; of Argentine film in Brazil, 199–200, 206–207, 210–11; of comedy, 201, 204, 206; cultural, 257n20; of currency, 181, 228, 254n79; film, 202, 220; of film technology, 147; forms of, 189, 199; of labor, 195, 223; logic of, 228; of Mexican film in Brazil, 199; narratives of, 212; of popular culture, 70, 198

classical Hollywood cinema, 4, 9, 11–12, 52–53, 58, 100, 169, 179–80, 185, 212, 255n89; critique of, 48; provincializing of, 6, 8, 19, 58, 205; space in, 66, 92

classicism, 4, 8, 11–13, 21, 25, 44–46, 54, 84, 131, 169, 177, 180–81, 189, 205–206, 212, 229; Hollywood, 98, 110, 181, 201; mocking of, 9, 12, 21, 67, 110, 152, 168, 178, 187f, 198, 217. See also mock classicism

Columbia Pictures, 1, 23, 38, 169, 204, 259n64

comedic practices, 3, 236n12

comedy, 2–3, 8, 11, 14–18, 34, 55, 105, 112, 152, 220; ability to travel, 7, 58; Bergsonian, 115; bodily effects of, 14, 16; of Cantinflas, 36; circulation of, 21, 201, 204, 206; comedian, 143; ensemble, 209; of errors, 26, 32, 51, 95, 176, 227, 233; female voices and, 84; as film genre, 83; as limit case of classical Hollywood, 7, 14, 45–46, 159, 221, 241n72; land speculation, 176; in Latin America, 115; marginalization of, 9; Mexican, 18, 44, 159; of mistaken identity, 31; physical, 62; popular, 187; silent, 204; slapstick, 6; studies of, 14; untranslatability of, 11, 201. See also *chanchada;* film comedy; musical comedy

comic spirit, 16, 114–15

commodity form, 43, 83, 139, 200–201

Companhia Brasil Cinematographica (CBC), 209–210

Continental Films, 169, 174, 197, 210–12

contingency, 131, 160, 181, 191, 248–49n72, 255n99; of exhibition, 83; modernist aesthetics of, 7; of reception, 66–67, 108

continuity editing, 5, 8, 31, 45, 53, 58, 67, 83, 96, 98, 103, 122, 130, 132, 188

Corporação Cinematographica Sul-
  Americana (Cinesul), 206–208, 210–11
Corporación Cinematográfica Argentina,
  78, 111, 124
cosmopolitanism, 12, 21, 58. *See also*
  modernity: cosmopolitan
credit, 180, 190, 227
critical reason, 6, 14, 60
cultural forms, 21, 105, 199, 201
culture industry, 24, 49, 120, 138
currency, 20, 159–67, 177–79, 182, 190,
  221, 228, 251n29, 252n41, 253n54;
  circulation of, 181. *See also* money
cutaways, 31, 94, 185, 187

de Barros, Luiz, 159, 161, 167. *See also* O
  jovem tataravô
deconstruction, 15, 107
Deleuze, Gilles, 14, 115, 232–33
Delgado, Miguel M., 35–36
dependency, 2, 190, 215
Derrida, Jacques, 179, 219, 227, 251n30
desmedida, 161, 163–64, 177, 190
de-solidarity, 63–64
diegesis, 15, 20, 48, 92, 98, 101–102, 108,
  110, 129–30, 134, 182, 188–89, 230,
  232–33, 256n113; classical Hollywood
  and, 5, 13, 52, 180, 184–85; closed,
  181; hermetic, 49–50, 105; masquerade
  and, 106; mock classical, 197;sound
  and, 84, 90, 136
diegetic boundaries, 92, 99
diegeticization, 91, 98–99, 101–102, 110;
  double, 89
discontinuity, 9, 54, 84, 102, 151
Distribuidora de Filmes Brasileiros (DFB),
  170, 212
Distribuidora Nacional, 170, 212
Distribuidora Paulista de Filmes (DIPA),
  197, 211–12
Divorcio en Montevideo (Romero), 75,
  213–17, 260n81
Don Quijote del altillo (Romero), 124,
  131–36, 222
Downey, Wallace, 169
ductilidad, 87–88, 91–92

É com êste que eu vou (Burle), 175–76
E o mundo se diverte (Macedo), 172–76,
  185–88
economic symbolization, 1720, 178, 190,
  225, 227
Elsaesser, Thomas, 4, 17, 228–29
epistemology, 14, 142–43

Estado Novo, 20, 159, 251n29, 254n71.
  See also Brazil: monetary policy in;
  Vargas, Getúlio
Este mundo é um pandeiro (Macedo), 170,
  175
Estudios Filmadores Argentinos (EFA), 69,
  72, 75–78, 80, 85, 208, 210–11,
  260n75

farce, 19, 33, 49, 51, 95–97
female body, 83, 92, 100, 106
female voice, 84, 91–92, 100–101, 106. *See
  also* male voice; voice
Fenelon, Moacyr, 170, 176, 212
fiction, 178–81, 189–91; of money, 176,
  178, 190, 227
fictionality, 20, 178–81, 190–91, 255n102
film: as commodity, 4, 20–21, 45, 49, 83,
  131, 169, 171–72, 180, 198, 201,
  205, 228; as narrative, 21, 198; as
  spatial practice, 11, 21, 25, 66, 198,
  212–13
film comedy, 4, 21, 27, 58, 65, 105,
  113–14, 139, 143, 207; Latin American,
  7, 11, 54, 66, 98, 127, 177, 229; sound,
  82, 85
film criticism, 39, 53, 175, 243n31;
  Argentine, 138
film distribution, 23, 73, 125, 165, 169,
  171, 199, 204, 209–12, 258n32,
  260n78; of Argentine cinema, 206, 208;
  Hollywood, 17, 197–98; interconti-
  nental, 21; Mexican, 37–38; networks,
  20, 41, 199, 202
film history, 9, 18, 21, 150, 193, 199, 220;
  Argentine, 105, 120; Brazilian, 171;
  international, 3; Latin American, 9;
  national, 105, 228; new, 4, 108
film image, 120, 180, 196
film industry, 247n33; American, 181;
  Argentine, 69, 72, 165, 248n50;
  Brazilian, 166, 170, 253–54n68;
  Mexican, 23, 35–38, 202
film music, 91–92; early, 84
film studies, 3–4, 39, 59, 71, 115, 199, 205,
  220; classicism in, 12; comedy and, 14;
  diegesis and, 256n113; empirical turn
  in, 4–5, 17, 37–39, 220; Latin
  American, 10, 13, 16, 21, 54, 72;
  posthegemony and, 10; regional, 9
film theory, 5; classical, 141; Deleuze and,
  14; feminist, 106–107, 110
filmes cantantes, 154, 156
formalism, 4, 45, 123, 241n70

Frankfurt School, 60, 255n99
Freire, Rafael de Luna, 154–55

Gabara, Esther, 5, 241n70
gendarme desconocido, El (Delgado), 41–43
gender, 7, 83, 88, 100, 106, 185
genre, 3, 17–18, 155–56; national, 154, 156
Gothic horror, 102–103
Gran Hotel (Delgado), 61–63
Grande Otelo, 170f, 172, 177, 185

Hansen, Miriam, 6–9, 16, 45–46, 48, 50, 54, 58, 60, 98, 147, 179, 185, 205, 255n99
Hay que educar a Niní (Amadori), 82, 85–91, 108
Hennefeld, Maggie, 83, 91
Hollywood cinema, 2, 4, 8–9, 11–12, 44, 48, 52–53, 66–67, 70, 84, 92, 100, 169, 179–80, 185, 205, 212, 255n89; provincialization of, 6, 8, 19, 58, 205
Hollywood Party, 156, 157f
humor, 4, 7, 68, 121 188–89, 241n72; of Cantinflas, 19, 30–32, 36, 38, 57; *chanchada* and, 191; of Marshall, 105; of mock classicism, 190; proper names and, 118; slapstick, 146
hybridity, 10, 117, 199

identification, 15–16, 38–39, 45–46, 48–50, 52–53, 55, 67, 94, 106–107, 145
igualado, 30, 57
imitation, 31, 140, 145, 147, 156
irony, 190–91
Irwin, Robert McKee, 37–39, 44
isochrone map, 205–206, 228

jovem tataravô, O (de Barros), 161–63, 181–84, 253n57, 255n104

Karush, Matthew, 9, 73, 120, 144
Kern, Stephen, 113, 171
Kracauer, Siegfried, 6, 147, 150, 219, 260n93

ladrón, El (Bracho), 224–27, 262n114
Laera, Alejandra, 178, 221, 254n79
Lamarque, Libertad, 131, 207, 210
Latin American cinema, 3–5, 9, 13–14, 17, 45–46, 50, 54–55, 73, 172
Latin Americanism, 9, 11, 24, 59–60, 201
laughter, 11. See also Bergson, Henri
Lefebvre, Henri, 113, 189, 206, 214
locational thinking, 10, 201

López, Ana, 8, 17, 34, 73
Lumiton, 69, 72, 75–78, 80–82, 85, 99, 124–25, 131, 207–11, 243n40, 259n64
Luna de miel en Rio (Romero), 212, 216

Macedo, Watson, 176. See also *Alô, alô carnival; Carnaval no fogo; E o mundo se diverte; Este mundo é um pandeiro*
Majumdar, Neepa, 7, 71
male voice, 100–101
marchas, 155, 167, 172, 175, 184, 250n9. See also Carnaval; samba
Marshall, Niní (Marina Esther Traverso), 19, 67–69, 72–78, 80–110, 127, 206–209, 211–12, 214f, 215, 217–18, 222, 243n26, 243n30, 261n112; body of, 98; Brazilian debut of, 207; Cándida character, 74–76, 78, 80–81, 85, 208, 212, 218; Catita character, 69, 74–75, 77–78, 80–82, 85, 99, 208, 212–17, 243n40; circulation of, 217; as comedic star, 87, 109, 218; stardom of, 68–69; throat of, 88–89, 91. See also *Cándida; Casamiento en Buenos Aires; Hay que educar a Niní; La mentirosa; Mujeres que trabajan; Orquesta de señoritas*
mass culture, 6, 9, 19, 24, 54–55, 60, 70–73, 120, 124, 129, 255n99
medium ontology, 120, 155–56, 241n70
medium specificity, 105, 155–56, 158
melodrama, 7, 16–17, 34, 55, 71, 220, 245n8; urban, 89, 108
Mentasti, Angel Luis, 77–78, 206, 259n52, 259n74
Mentasti, José Atilio, 206, 259n52
mentirosa, La (Amadori), 99–105, 108
metalepsis, 16, 185, 188–89. See also *chanchada*
Mexican cinema, 25, 40, 44, 160; in Argentina, 40–41; in Brazil, 201–202; golden age of, 18, 23, 35, 44, 50; success abroad of, 37–38, 202, 204
Mexican Revolution, 18, 241n74, 251n29
Mexico, 17, 23, 36, 241n74; Argentine cinema in, 206, 221; early cinema of, 8 (*see also* Mexican cinema); Eisenstein in, 37; illiteracy in, 33–34, 43, 48; *relajo* and, 60; Sandrini in, 222, 223f
mimesis, 147, 256n113
mimicry, 31, 148
Miranda, Carmen, 158, 169
mise-en-bande analysis, 126–27, 131
misrecognition, 26, 30, 51, 89–90, 98, 108, 185

mock classicism, 21, 25, 72, 98, 110, 127, 136, 152, 184, 206, 217; *chanchada* as, 160, 188–89; Latin American, 67, 164, 223; Sandrini and, 134; spectator of, 233
modernism, 5–6, 13, 54–55, 57, 189, 200; comedic, 236n12; cosmopolitan, 8; European, 5, 21, 189; high, 9, 54–55, 57, 67, 108, 114–15, 191, 241n70; political, 9; slapstick, 6; vernacular, 6–9, 54, 58–59, 64, 188–89, 199
modernismo, 5, 12
modernity, 4, 6–7, 9–12, 19–20, 113–14, 119, 139, 144, 147, 160, 162–63, 179, 193, 200, 228; Argentine, 215; experience of, 6, 9, 12, 54, 58–59, 220; thesis, 235n24
modernization, 3–6, 9–10, 19, 48, 54, 58, 206, 215
Moglia Barth, Luis, 114, 118. See also *La casa de Quirós*; *Riachuelo*; *¡Tango!*
monetary sign (Derrida), 161, 179, 227
money, 20, 160–61, 163–65, 171–72, 177, 179, 181, 189–90, 227–28, 256n117; circulation of, 254n79; fiat, 226–27; geography of, 220; narratives about, 176–77; paper, 159, 178, 190, 219, 225–27. *See also* currency; monetary sign; valuation; value
Monsiváis, Carlos, 36–37, 39, 48, 50
Moreiras, Alberto, 10–11, 14, 39, 59, 201
Moretti, Franco, 7, 241n72
Mujeres que trabajan (Romero), 75, 209, 213
Murúa, Alfredo and Fernando, 72, 131, 222
musical comedy, 14, 20, 153–54, 168, 170–71, 174, 176; Mexican, 229. See also *chanchada*
musical film, 120–21, 126, 153, 161, 172; integrated, 184, 188; national, 158. See also *chanchada*

nación, La (newspaper), 69, 77, 79f, 80, 116
narrative strategies, 25, 54, 158
nation-state, 10–11, 14, 37–39, 59, 105, 190, 201, 219, 223
national film histories, 38, 105, 164, 228
national ontology, 45, 155–56. *See also* medium ontology
nationalism, 3, 5, 19, 23, 37, 41, 105, 120, 155, 159, 191, 198, 243n31 (*see also* Estado Novo); corporative, 70; critical, 54; cultural, 6, 9, 11–12, 18, 21, 206, 220; Indian, 71
nationness, 8, 17, 37, 39–41, 155–56
nativism, 12, 164, 199
New Latin American Cinema,
Ni sangre ni arena (Galindo), 46–50, 52, 64, 66, 203

odographic turn, 199–200, 205, 216, 220–21
odography, 199–200; fiduciary, 228
officialism, 5, 34, 43
Orquesta de señoritas (Amadori), 94–99
Oscarito, 172–73, 175–77, 185, 187f

parody, 46, 48, 55, 99, 190
peladito, 23–24, 34, 36, 46
pelado, 22–27, 30, 35–36, 41, 44, 46–47, 49–52, 55, 61, 66, 204. *See also* Moreno, Mario "Cantinflas"
Pelmex, 202, 204
Pepe (Sidney), 1, 36
Perón, Juan, 19, 70, 165
Peronism, 19, 70–71, 243n31, 261n106
photography, 140, 150, 153; arrival in Mexico of, 241n74; deep-focus, 129, modernist, 241n70
Podalsky, Laura, 13–14
popular culture, 6, 8, 23, 43, 54, 70, 120, 150, 187, 217
Portilla, Jorge, 60, 63
posthegemony, 9–11
proper name, 25, 32–34, 51, 61–63, 99, 115, 117–18
protectionism, 164–66, 169, 171, 253n68
psychoanalysis, 100, 104–105

Radio Belgrano, 72, 261n106
Radio El Mundo, 72, 74, 222
radionovelas, 72–73, 216
Ramírez Berg, Charles, 9, 44
RCA Victor, 126, 168–69
realism, 9, 12, 24, 31, 139, 141–44, 148, 178–79; anti-, 190; Lukacsean, 247n72; progressive, 71; sound, 126–27, 131, 133–34, 136
reception studies, 11, 37–38, 123
referentiality, 25, 30, 32–33, 52, 56–57, 178, 180
reflexivity, 241n70; immersive, 53–54; modernist, 6, 55, 134; self-, 55, 57–58, 60–61, 64, 85, 109
relajo, 19, 34–35, 60–61, 63–64, 67, 143. *See also* de-solidarity

278 | Index

Riachuelo (Moglia Barth), 143–46, 151, 221, 261n101
Ripstein Jr., Alfredo, 229, 262n114, 262n128
Romero, Manuel, 74, 76, 209. See also *Casamiento en Buenos Aires; Divorcio en Montevideo; Don Quijote del altillo; Luna de miel en Rio; Mujeres que trabajan*
Rosen, Philip, 179–80

samba, 155, 167, 172, 175, 184, 186, 250n9
Sandrini, Luis, 19–20, 111–25, 127–48, 150–52, 206, 210–11, 218, 221–33, 245n8, 247n30, 259n74, 261nn110–11; circulation of, 221; clock time and, 160; death of, 138; performance style of, 140, 144; stutter step of, 118, 147; typicality of, 148. See also *Bartolo tenía una flauta; La casa de Quirós; stutter; ¡Tango!; Los tres berretines*
Serrador, Francisco, 199, 204. See also Companhia Brasil Cinematographica (CBC)
sertanejo, 172, 175
Severiano Ribeiro, Luis, 169–72, 199, 210, 212
shot transitions, 122, 128, 130
Silverman, Kaja, 88, 98, 100
Siskind, Mariano, 12–13, 192, 197
slapstick comedy, 6, 14, 20, 41–42, 83, 146, 236n12
Slowik, Michael, 84, 91
Sociedad Impresora de Discos Argentinos (SIDE), 72, 124, 131, 222
Soifer, Alberto, 132, 248n50
sound: design, 100, 126, 129, 132, 136, 232; direct, 122, 128–31; discursive manipulation of, 127, 135; realism, 126–27, 131, 133–34, 136; transition to, 7, 20–21, 58, 70–72, 83–85, 93, 112, 123, 125, 159 (*see also* sound cinema)
sound aesthetics, 73; radio, 19, 89
sound cinema, 59, 83, 88, 90, 93, 112, 136, 188; Argentine, 82, 121, 151; Brazilian, 153, 161; early, 69, 73, 85, 94, 121–23, 133
sound engineers, 123, 247n30
sound hermeneutic, 88, 90, 98, 102, 125, 134
sound practices, 123–24, 126–27, 133, 147, 181

sound space, 94, 98, 108, 122, 126–31, 134, 162, 232
sound studies, 83, 92–93, 126
sound technologies, 19, 50, 58, 72–73, 83, 88, 95, 101, 120, 123, 128, 131, 148, 166, 182
soundtrack, 94, 98, 126–27, 131, 133, 247n47
spectatorship, 5, 9, 25, 27, 46–48, 50, 52–53, 88, 106, 108, 130, 145, 185, 229; errant, 46, 185; female, 16, 48; film comedy, 11, 21, 65; modes of, 21, 44, 48, 190, 205
standardized time, 20, 113, 147, 228
star: as commodity, 24, 81, 139; as symptom, 71, 137; as visible social icon, 70, 136, 218
star contract, 78, 81
star studies, 19, 41, 69–71, 136, 204
star system, 7, 19, 48–49, 69, 73–74, 197–98
stardom, 11, 19, 70–71, 73–75, 81–82; aural, 19, 69; Indian, 7; Niní Marshall's, 68–69, 93
stutter, 19, 111–19, 122–24, 127, 132–33, 139, 145, 147–49, 150–52, 225. *See also* Sandrini, Luis
Superintendência da Moeda e do Crédito (SUMOC), 166–67
Susini, Enrique, 72, 124–25, 247n33. See also *Los tres berretines*
Süssekind, Flora, 161, 177

tango (music), 70, 95, 104–105, 120–21, 124–25, 128–29, 131, 144, 207, 247n41
¡Tango! (Moglia Barth), 111–16, 120–22, 124–25
Thompson, Kristen, 44–45
Thorry, Juan Carlos, 74, 222
Todd, Michael, 195–96
Todd-AO process, 193, 196
transculturation, 9–10, 201
tres berretines, Los (Susini), 124–29, 127–31, 221
tres mosqueteros, Los (Delgado), 38, 55–57, 203
Tsing, Anna, 199, 205
Tudo azul (Fenelon), 153–54
typage, 141–43, 147, 248n72
type, the, 140–43, 148–51
typicality, 141, 143–45; Sandrini's, 148

União Cinematográfica Brasileira (UCB), 170, 200, 212

uniform public time, 112–13, 116. *See also* standardized time

valuation, 160, 163; crisis of, 20, 159, 162. *See also* Brazil: monetary policy in; money
value, 160–65, 172, 178–79, 218–19. *See also* Brazil: monetary policy in; money
Vargas, Getúlio, 175, 251n29; regimes of, 159, 166–67. *See also* Estado Novo
ventriloquism, 19, 69, 85, 87–88, 92–93, 96, 99, 102, 105–108, 110, 188, 244n63

verisimilitude, 178–80, 190–91
vernacular, 6–8, 43, 55, 58, 144, 200, 212. See also modernism: vernacular
vida íntima de Marco Antonio y Cleopatra, La (Gavaldón), 229–33
vision, 54, 76, 92, 104, 106–107, 110; central, 63; peripheral, 19, 53, 63–64, 233. *See also* audition

Williams, Gareth, 24, 34, 230
Williams, Linda, 16–17

Zabludovsky, Jacobo, 22, 64

www.ingramcontent.com/pod-product-compliance
Lightning Source LLC
Chambersburg PA
CBHW030527230426
43665CB00010B/791